# PAUL
## AND POLITICS

D1202535

*Krister Stendahl — professor, dean, bishop — was instrumental in opening up a field of study focused narrowly on individual salvation. Virtually from the beginning of his scholarly career Stendahl took important initiatives in bringing greater sensitivity to concrete human relations into the academic study of Paul's epistles. The contributors of these first essays from the Paul and Politics Group in the Society of Biblical Literature would like to dedicate their publication to Krister Stendahl in deep appreciation of those initiatives which in so many ways prepared the way for current concerns in Pauline studies.*

# PAUL
## AND POLITICS

### EKKLESIA, ISRAEL, IMPERIUM, INTERPRETATION

ESSAYS IN HONOR OF
## KRISTER STENDAHL

EDITED BY
RICHARD A. HORSLEY

TRINITY PRESS INTERNATIONAL
Harrisburg, Pennsylvania

BS
2655
.P64
H67
2000

Copyright © 2000 Trinity Press International

All rights reserved. No part of this book may be reproduced, stored in a retrieval system, or transmitted, in any form or by any means, electronic, mechanical, photocopying, recording, or otherwise, without the written permission of the publisher, Trinity Press International.

Trinity Press International, P.O. Box 1321, Harrisburg, PA 17105
Trinity Press International is a division of the Morehouse Group.

Cover Image: *Saint Paul Preaching at Athens.* Raphael. Tapestry. Palazzo Ducale, Mantua, Italy. Scala/Art Resource, NY.

Cover design: Laurie Westhafer

**Library of Congress Cataloging-in-Publication Data**

Paul and politics : Ekklesia, Israel, imperium, interpretation / edited by Richard A. Horsley.
    p.  cm.
    Includes bibliographical references and index.
    ISBN 1-56338-323-3 (pbk. : alk. paper)
    1. Bible. N.T. Epistles of Paul – Criticism, interpretation, etc. 2. Paul, the Apostle, Saint – Political and social views. 3. Christianity and politics. I. Horsley, Richard A.

BS2655.P64 H67 2000
225.9′2 – dc21

                         00-041790

*Printed in the United States of America*

00   01   02   03   04   05        10   9   8   7   6   5   4   3   2   1

JESUIT - KRAUSS - McCORMICK - LIBRARY
1100 EAST 55th STREET
CHICAGO, ILLINOIS 60615

# CONTENTS

Abbreviations                                                                vii

INTRODUCTION: KRISTER STENDAHL'S CHALLENGE              1
TO PAULINE STUDIES
*Richard A. Horsley*

1. PAUL AND THE POLITICS OF EMPIRE:                              17
Problems and Prospects
*Neil Elliott*

2. PAUL AND THE POLITICS OF INTERPRETATION               40
*Elisabeth Schüssler Fiorenza*

3. RESPONSE: Exegetical Support from Romans and Other Letters   58
*Robert Jewett*

4. RHETORIC AND EMPIRE — AND 1 CORINTHIANS               72
*Richard A. Horsley*

5. CORINTHIAN WOMEN PROPHETS AND PAUL'S              103
ARGUMENTATION IN 1 CORINTHIANS
*Cynthia Briggs Kittredge*

6. PAUL ON BONDAGE AND FREEDOM IN IMPERIAL           110
ROMAN SOCIETY
*Sheila Briggs*

7. RESPONSE: The Politics of the Assembly in Corinth            124
*Antoinette Clark Wire*

8. PAUL AS THE NEW ABRAHAM                                      130
*Pamela Eisenbaum*

9. THE INTER- AND INTRA-JEWISH POLITICAL CONTEXT    146
OF PAUL'S LETTER TO THE GALATIANS
*Mark D. Nanos*

10. PAUL'S GOSPEL AND CAESAR'S EMPIRE                          160
    *N. T. Wright*

11. RESPONSE: Some Aspects of Conversion and Identity          184
    Formation in the Christian Community of Paul's Time
    *Alan F. Segal*

12. COLLECTION FOR THE SAINTS AS ANTICOLONIAL ACT:  191
    Implications of Paul's Ethnic Reconstruction
    *Sze-kar Wan*

13. PAUL, *EKKLĒSIA*, AND EMANCIPATION IN CORINTH:   216
    A Coda on Liberation Theology
    *Allen Dwight Callahan*

14. RESPONSE: Paul and Those Outside Power                     224
    *Antoinette Clark Wire*

15. RESPONSE: How Anti-Imperial Was the Collection and         227
    How Emancipatory Was Paul's Project?
    *Calvin J. Roetzel*

    Contributors                                               231

    Scripture Index                                            233

    General Index                                              241

# Abbreviations

| | |
|---|---|
| AB | Anchor Bible |
| *ABR* | *Australian Biblical Review* |
| *ANRW* | *Aufstieg und Niedergang der römischen Welt.* Ed. W. Haase and H. Temporini. Berlin and New York, 1972– |
| BAGD | W. Bauer, W. F. Arndt, F. W. Gingrich, and F. W. Danker. *Greek English Lexicon of the New Testament.* Chicago, 1979 |
| BDF | F. Blass, A. Debrunner, and R. W. Funk. *A Greek Grammar of the New Testament.* Chicago, 1961 |
| BGU | *Ägyptische Urkunden aus den Königlichen Staatlichen Museen zu Berlin, Griechische Urkunden.* 15 vols. Berlin, 1895–1983 |
| *BibRev* | *Bible Review* |
| *BJRL* | Bulletin of the John Rylands University Library of Manchester |
| CBNTS | Coniectanea biblica. New Testament series |
| *CBQ* | *Catholic Biblical Quarterly* |
| *CP* | *Classical Philology* |
| *CQ* | *Classical Quarterly* |
| EKKNT | Evangelisch-Katholischer Kommentar zum Neuen Testament |
| *HeyJ* | *Heythrop Journal* |
| HThKNT | Herders theologischer Kommentar zum Neuen Testament |
| *HTR* | *Harvard Theological Review* |
| HTS | Harvard Theological Studies |
| HUT | Hermeneutische Untersuchungen zur Theologie |
| ICC | International Critical Commentary |
| *IGRom* | *Inscriptiones Graecae ad res Romanas pertinentes* |
| *JAAR* | *Journal of the American Academy of Religion* |
| *JBL* | *Journal of Biblical Literature* |

| | |
|---|---|
| *JSJ* | *Journal of the Study of Judaism in the Persian, Hellenistic, and Roman Period* |
| *JSNT* | *Journal for the Study of the New Testament* |
| JSNTSup | Journal for the Study of the New Testament Supplement Series |
| *JSP* | *Journal for the Study of the Pseudepigrapha* |
| JSPSS | Journal for the Study of the Pseudepigrapha Supplement Series |
| *JTS* | Journal of Theological Studies |
| *JTSA* | *Journal of Theology for South Africa* |
| LCL | Loeb Classical Library |
| MeyerK | H. A. W. Meyer. *Kritischexegetischer Kommentar über das Neue Testament* |
| *NovT* | *Novum Testamentum* |
| NTR | New Testament Readings |
| *NTS* | *New Testament Studies* |
| PW | Pauly-Wissowa. *Real-Encyclopädie der classischen Altertumswissenschaft* |
| SBT | Studies in Biblical Theology |
| SBLDS | Society of Biblical Literature Dissertation Series |
| SBLMS | Society of Biblical Literature Monograph Series |
| *SJT* | *Scottish Journal of Theology* |
| SNTSMS | Society for New Testament Studies Monograph Series |
| SUNT | Studien zur Umwelt des Neuen Testaments |
| *TDNT* | *Theological Dictionary of the New Testament.* Ed. G. Kittel. Trans. G. W. Bromiley. 10 vols. Grand Rapids, 1964–76 |
| TNTC | Tyndale New Testament Commentaries |
| *TToday* | *Theology Today* |
| *TWAT* | *Theologisches Wörterbuch zum Alten Testament.* Ed. G. J. Botterweck and H. Ringgren |
| WUNT | Wissenschaftliche Untersuchungen zum Neuen Testament |
| *ZNW* | *Zeitschrift für die neutestamentliche Wissenschaft und die Kunde der älteren Kirche* |
| *ZThK* | *Zeitschrift für Theologie und Kirche* |

— Introduction —

# KRISTER STENDAHL'S CHALLENGE TO PAULINE STUDIES

*Richard A. Horsley*

᠊᠊᠊᠊᠊᠊᠊᠊᠊᠊

K RISTER STENDAHL'S bold initiatives in making Pauline studies more re-
sponsive to contemporary human relations began early in his career,
shortly after he had taken up his position at Harvard Divinity School. In
1958, as the debate on the ordination of women in the Church of Sweden
reached its climax, Stendahl set forth a landmark essay in biblical hermeneutics, later published in English as "The Bible and the Role of Women"
(1966).[1] Several years earlier (1951) all of the faculty holding academic positions in New Testament studies in Swedish universities, with one exception,
declared "as our definite opinion, based on careful investigation, that the
ordination of women would be incompatible with New Testament thought
and would constitute disobedience to the Holy Scriptures." In preparation
for the Church Assembly in 1958 that would discuss the issue, Stendahl
boldly and carefully set forward the concise and compelling examination
that opened up serious and critical examination of "the role of women" in
the New Testament and laid out hermeneutical principles for critical appropriation of biblical materials highly problematic for the relations of women
and men in church and society.

Two years later Stendahl issued a fundamental challenge to the established understanding of Paul that stood at the center of Protestant theology
and biblical studies in the now-famous essay, "The Apostle Paul and the
Introspective Conscience of the West."[2] The importance of Stendahl's chal-

---

1. Krister Stendahl, "The Bible and the Role of Women," originally published as "Bibel-
synen och kvinnan," in *Kvinnan — Samhaellet — Kyrkan* (Stockholm: Svenska Kyrkans
Diakonistyrelses Bokfoerlag, 1958), 138–67.
2. Stendahl, "Paulus och Samvetet," *Svensk Exegetisk Årsbok* 25 (1960): 62–77; published
in English as "The Apostle Paul and the Introspective Conscience of the West," *HTR* 56 (1963):
199–215; reprinted and most accessible in *Paul among Jews and Gentiles, and Other Essays*
(Philadelphia: Fortress Press, 1976), 78–96, pages of which are followed below. Stendahl further
developed some of the same themes in *Paul among Jews and Gentiles*.

1

lenge to the standard theological interpretation of Paul can be measured by the scholarly reaction to his argument. It is not difficult to see why Stendahl's probings appeared to prominent Pauline scholars and theologians as a threat to the very foundations of Protestant theology and, indeed, as fraught with "fateful significance for the whole of Christianity."[3]

First of all, Stendahl drove a wedge between what are evidently the broader concerns of Paul's letters and the narrowly "introspective" Augustinian and Lutheran interpretation of Paul as focused on individual salvation and justification by faith, ideas that had dominated the Western scholarly interpretation of Paul. In effect, Stendahl thus demonstrated that the Protestant obsession with justification by faith as a solution to the quest for individual salvation had a questionable scriptural basis. Paul's statements taken out of their epistolary context "are now read as answers to the quest for assurance about man's salvation out of a common human predicament," whereas Paul himself was focusing on the possibility of Gentiles being "included in the messianic community."[4] What was in Paul's argument in Romans 7, for example, an argument about the goodness of the Law and "the acquittal of the ego, not one of utter contrition," is taken as a witness to "a deep and introspective conscience."[5] Stendahl was thus challenging in the bluntest terms the understanding of Paul as the great hero of faith over against the supposed Jewish obsession with the Law that stood at the center of Protestant theology.

Simultaneously, Stendahl also exposed the anti-Judaism at the core of modern Christian interpretation of Paul in particular and the New Testament in general. Against the standard Lutheran/Protestant understanding of Paul as an anti-Jewish Christian theologian focused on individual sin and salvation, Stendahl detected Paul as a Jew concerned far more broadly about salvation history and, in the letter to the Romans, about the eventual salvation of his own people, Israel. It is significant testimony to the strength of this deeply ingrained aspect of Christian theological interpretation of Paul that those who articulated the "new perspective on Paul," partly under the influence of Stendahl's challenge to the entrenched introspective Western understanding of Paul, continued to view Paul as struggling to become free of "Judaism" and its "Law." Stendahl himself, in close connection with his challenge to the anti-Judaism of the established theological understanding of Paul, became one of the leaders of Jewish-Christian dialogue, and throughout his roles as professor, dean, and bishop continued to play a significant role in interreligious discussions.

Included in Stendahl's challenge to the entrenched Western understanding of Paul were several other critical facets that have received less recognition

---

3. See the significant *theological* response to Stendahl's *historical* inquiry by Ernst Käsemann, "Justification by Faith and Salvation History in the Epistle to the Romans," in *Perspectives on Paul* (Philadelphia: Fortress Press, 1971), 60–78.

4. Stendahl, "Apostle Paul and the Introspective Conscience," 86.

5. Ibid., 92–93.

and discussion, some because the field of Pauline studies as a whole was moving in the same direction and others because the field was steadfastly entrenched in the distinctively Western ideology that Stendahl was trying to expose.

Implicitly in the "Introspective Conscience" article and explicitly in *Paul among Jews and Gentiles*, he summoned readers to recognize the "great difference of setting, thought, and argument between the various epistles of Paul." The letters were originally ad hoc communications to local communities. However, "[o]nce the individual letters were acknowledged as Scripture they quickly suffered homogenization." And "once the human predicament — timeless and exercised in a *corpus christianum* — became the setting of the church's interpretation of Paul's thought," Paul's theology was homogenized, with its "common denominator found in generalized theological issues."[6] The subfield of Pauline studies has until recently exercised only a curious half-recognition of Stendahl's point in this regard. For example, the Pauline Theology group in the Society of Biblical Literature did proceed, letter by letter supposedly, to avoid homogenization but continued to focus on and abstract from Paul's letters those "generalized theological issues."[7]

Stendahl, however, had also indicated clearly that Paul was concerned primarily with people and life, not so much with religion and thought. Paul's "theology" has secondary significance, as reflection on historical social/ human relations. Stendahl understands Paul's letter to the Romans, for example, in the wider context not simply of "salvation history," but of international affairs and history more generally: "To me the climax of Romans is actually chapters 9–11, i.e., his reflections on the relation between ... the church and the Jewish *people* — not 'Christianity' and 'Judaism.' "[8] That is, Paul's concerns were much broader than individual salvation and far more concrete than religious ideas. He was convinced that God was implementing a plan for the fulfillment of history, that he himself had a significant role therein to catalyze communities among the Gentiles, and that those communities were the beachheads of the new age, which was in the process of dawning in the Christ events.[9]

In the "Introspective Conscience" article and his subsequent work, Stendahl was also practicing and calling for a clear recognition of the difference between Paul's letters in their historical situation and concrete context on the one hand, and their subsequent interpretation in other contexts on the other — and for the importance of allowing the former to challenge the latter. "We note how the biblical original functions as a critique of inherited

---

6. Stendahl, *Paul among Jews and Gentiles*, 5–6.

7. See the collection of articles in Jouette M. Bassler, ed., *Pauline Theology*, vol. 1 (Minneapolis: Fortress Press, 1991); and David M. Hay, *Pauline Theology*, vol. 2 (Minneapolis: Fortress Press, 1995).

8. Stendahl, *Paul among Jews and Gentiles*, 4, 28.

9. Ibid., e.g., 2–3, 27.

presuppositions and incentive to new thought. Few things are more liberating and creative in modern theology than a clear distinction between the
'original' and the 'translation' in any age, our own included."[10]

In all of these aspects Stendahl was loosening up the previously obsessive
and imperial relationship between scripture and its appropriation by modern theology and the churches. In the important article "Biblical Theology,
Contemporary" in *Interpreter's Dictionary of the Bible* (1962) he laid out
a whole hermeneutical program of distinguishing between "what it meant"
and "what it means." As he subsequently pointed out, the latter included
the important specification "to whom."[11] Stendahl was already taking into
consideration that interpretation involved particular people in specific historical social locations, which has come prominently to the fore in recent
years. Although he is sometimes accused of simply perpetuating "scientific"
biblical studies in the distinction between "meant" and "means," he was
also working toward overcoming the constructed divorce of "objective" and
"engaged" scholarship, as illustrated in his earlier "Bible and the Rome of
Women." As part of his broader hermeneutical program he pressed diverse
interpreters in the contemporary world to come to grips with the diversity
embodied in the New Testament. Moreover, he cautioned against any compulsion to find answers in Paul's letters for modern problems. "We must
ask whether the issues to which Paul speaks apply to our situations, our
predicaments. The answer could at times be negative — for it is reasonable
to expect that our questions could be different ones. After all, he seems to
speak quite differently to different churches."[12] The implication is clear. Just
as Paul attended to the particular situations he confronted, so we have the
responsibility to attend to our own particular situations.

Furthermore, in striking contrast to most biblical scholars from the mid-
twentieth century to the present, Stendahl was remarkably undefensive
about the Bible, ready to acknowledge frankly how problematic the Bible
and its interpretation have been for certain groups of people. In articles
such as "The Bible and the Role of Women" and "Ancient Scripture and the
Modern World" he pointed out that both the Christian tradition and biblical
texts had clearly had a "detrimental and dangerous effect" on the lives of
women and African American slaves and that the New Testament "contains
within itself the seeds of much anti-Judaism."[13] "We need not defend God
or the Bible."[14] The implication seems obvious: we need to recognize and
explore critically the possible "detrimental and dangerous effect."

---

10. Stendahl, "Apostle Paul and the Introspective Conscience," 96.

11. Stendahl, *Paul among Jews and Gentiles*, 125.

12. Ibid., 75.

13. Krister Stendahl, "Ancient Scripture in the Modern World," in *Scripture in the Jewish and Christian Traditions: Authority, Interpretation, Relevance*, ed. Frederick E. Greenspahn (Nashville: Abingdon Press, 1982).

14. Stendahl, *Paul among Jews and Gentiles*, 74.

In keeping with his openness to contemporary contingencies, finally, Stendahl was from the beginning of his academic career open to other academic disciplines, while always being fiercely insistent on rigorous standards of historical-critical scholarly examination of biblical texts. Significantly the occasion for delivery of the "Introspective Conscience" essay that was instrumental in cracking open scholarly interpretation of Paul was an invited address to the annual meeting of the American Psychological Association in 1961. As an academic mentor, Stendahl consistently encouraged interested doctoral students to seriously appropriate the approaches of other academic disciplines for biblical interpretation, and not simply throw around some pilfered terminology.[15]

In all of these interrelated aspects Krister Stendahl, in key lectures and articles published nearly forty years ago, thus challenged an entrenched Western Christian understanding of Paul and opened the way toward a liberative criticism of Paul and his letters and their subsequent appropriation in Western culture. Most crucial was to crack open the introspective individualism and the focus on theological doctrines. Stendahl himself recognized that the "introspective conscience" was not only a distinctively Western development but a "Western plague" that had dominated historical understanding generally, far beyond its ostensible function in the evolution of Christian piety.[16] Whether directly or indirectly, in both his "objective" scholarship and his "engaged" hermeneutics, Krister Stendahl was perhaps the key precursor of the liberationist voices that emerged in the 1970s — African American, feminist, Latin American, and, more recently, a wider range of "Two-thirds World" voices — to broaden and deepen the criticism of Paul in significant ways that biblical studies must come to grips with.

## Broadening Criticism of Paul and Pauline Interpretation

Others followed Stendahl in challenging entrenched interpretation of Paul and questioning the effects of Paul's statements on people's lives. Other academics also questioned the received orthodoxies on Paul. More significantly, representatives of precisely those groups of people who had experienced the dangerous effects of Paul voiced their own challenges to Pauline interpretation and to Paul's statements. Given the hegemony of established academic interpretation of Paul, however, those voices were effectively marginalized or simply went unheard by the circles dominant in Pauline interpretation. The hegemony of Western Christian theological interpretation of Paul's letters is evident, for example, in the volumes of published papers from the Pauline

---

15. When I presented an idea for some modest adaptations of psychological theory and the sociology of knowledge as part of my dissertation, he scolded me for being too timid and encouraged me to go "whole-hog."

16. Stendahl, *Paul among Jews and Gentiles*, 17.

Theology Group of the Society of Biblical Literature, in which one looks in vain for voices that vary from the European-American, predominantly male Protestant viewpoint. In professional circles, deviant criticism of Paul has been confined largely to units on the margins such as "African American Theology and Biblical Hermeneutics," "Feminist Theological Hermeneutics of the Bible," and "Ideological Criticism."

Speaking out of centuries of their people's suffering under the lash of chattel slavery for which the slave masters claimed divine approval by quoting Pauline texts, African American theologians such as James Cone and Albert Cleage virtually wrote Paul off as a potential resource for Black liberation.[17] In illustration of the detrimental and dangerous effects of Paul, the great mystic theologian and preacher Howard Thurman told a now often-cited story of his grandmother's reaction when he read the Bible aloud to her.

> She would not let me read any of the Pauline letters. What she told me I shall never forget. "During the days of slavery," she said, "the master's minister . . . always used as his text something from Paul. At least three or four times a year he used as a text: 'Slaves, be obedient to them that are your master . . . , as unto Christ.' Then he would go on to show how it was God's will that we were slaves and how, if we were good and happy slaves, God would bless us. I promised my Maker that if I ever learned to read and if freedom ever came, I would not read that part of the Bible."[18]

Thurman himself noted that although Paul had a vision of society that "transcended all barriers of race and class and condition" there is still "this other side" in Paul, "always available to those who wish to oppress and humiliate their fellows."[19] White preachers and slaveholders had heavily exploited key (deutero-)Pauline texts in their efforts to sanction slavery.[20]

---

17. James H. Cone, *Black Theology and Black Power* (New York: Seabury, 1969), and Cone, *A Black Theology of Liberation* (Philadelphia: Lippincott, 1970), e.g., 68; and Albert B. Cleage Jr., *The Black Messiah* (New York: Sheed and Ward, 1968). While sharply maligning Paul for his contribution to slavery in America, Cone does make selective use of Pauline texts in his theology.

18. Howard Thurman, *Jesus and the Disinherited* (Nashville: Abingdon Press, 1949), 30–31. Renita J. Weems, "Reading *Her Way* through the Struggle: African American Woman and the Bible," in *Stony the Road We Trod: African American Biblical Interpretation*, ed. Cain Hope Felder (Minneapolis: Fortress Press, 1991), 62–72 (reprinted in *Bible and Liberation*, ed. Norman K. Gottwald and Richard A. Horsley [Maryknoll, N.Y.: Orbis, 1993], 31–50) explores the implications of Thurman's grandmother's statement.

19. Thurman, *Jesus and the Disinherited*, 33. It is interesting, given the dominating Western spiritualizing interpretation of Paul, to note how spiritualized is Thurman's own belief, apparently informed by that dominant interpretation: "It is my belief that in the Presence of God there is neither male nor female, white or black, Gentile or Jew, Protestant nor Catholic, Hindu, Buddhist, nor Muslim, but a human spirit stripped to the literal substance of itself before God." *The Creative Encounter* (New York: Harper and Row, 1954), 152.

20. Thurman, *Jesus and the Disinherited*, 30–31.

Other African American theologians and biblical scholars attempt rather to drive a wedge between Paul's genuine letters in which they find arguments for liberation on the one hand, and both deutero-Pauline letters and the dominant white interpretation of Paul on the other. Amos Jones Jr. argued that not only white clergy and slaveholders but, more recently, the most influential European (and European American) biblical scholars are responsible for the conservative, apolitical interpretation of Paul's letters that continues to view Paul as urging slaves to "stay in their place," even taking the Lutheran view of "calling" as a basis for such a reading.[21] Jones also suggests that black theologians and churches did not "investigate Paul's theology for themselves to see whether or not he was soft on slavery or had things to say on the question more revolutionary than they knew."[22] Allen Callahan offered a closely critical examination of the key passage, 1 Cor. 7:21–22. Its (mis)translation has been the basis for European and American views of Paul as a social conservative on such issues as slavery. Contrary to the standard interpretation, based on the Lutheran concept of "calling" and entrenched defense of the established social order, Paul was urging former slaves who had become freed persons by "ecclesial manumission" to "behave accordingly."[23] Noting how prominent women were in the early church, Jones also suggests that African Americans should make common cause with other subordinated groups to explore how "Paul's understanding of freedom in the context of the *ekklēsia* [can] assist in liberating those who are bound — black people, Indians, Mexican American, women, homosexuals, and the white middle class."[24] Sheila Briggs asked the hard question, "Can an Enslaved God Liberate?" and suggested that those committed to a liberationist biblical interpretation distinguish those texts in which the voice of the oppressed can still be heard under the processes of overwriting and canonization from those that merely articulate the values of the socially dominant and those that are mixed.[25]

Like African American criticism of Paul, feminist challenges to Paul's influence came initially not from within Pauline scholarship but from social movements for liberation from traditional subordination of women. Only gradually did biblical scholarship respond. This was partly because, as Elisabeth Schüssler Fiorenza points out, the mainstream of biblical studies

21. Amos Jones Jr., *Paul's Message of Freedom: What Does It Mean to the Black Church?* (Valley Forge, Pa.: Judson, 1984), chaps. 1 and 2, mentioning such leading Pauline scholars as C. K. Barrett, Gunther Bornkamm, Rudolf Bultmann, and Hans Conzelmann. For a New Testament scholar trained in standard graduate schools to write a book on an important social-political issue — such as C. Freeman Sleeper, *Black Power and Christian Responsibility: Some Biblical Foundations for Social Ethics* (Nashville: Abingdon Press, 1968) — was rare.

22. Jones, *Paul's Message of Freedom*, 38.

23. Allen D. Callahan, "A Note on 1 Corinthians 7:21," *Journal of the Interdenominational Theological Center* 17 (1989–90): 111.

24. Jones, *Paul's Message of Freedom*, 64–66.

25. Sheila Briggs, "Can an Enslaved God Liberate? Hermeneutical Reflections on Philippians 2:6–11," *Semeia* 47 (1989): 137–53.

was an almost exclusive "malestream." As she pointed out in her presiden-
tial address to the Society of Biblical Literature in 1987, whereas women's
membership of the SBL had been around 10 percent in 1920, by 1970 it
had shrunk to a mere 3.5 percent.[26] Like African Americans or other mi-
norities, women were allowed into the biblical studies academy only if they
carefully suppressed the distinctive characteristics of their humanity in deference to those established by the dominant "malestream" and its enforced
"objectivity."

In theological circles, the sharpest challenge came from outside biblical
studies. The eventually "postchristian" feminist Mary Daly, for example,
utterly rejected Paul (and the Bible generally) as hopelessly patriarchal and
misogynist. There was no point in distinguishing between genuine and
secondary Pauline texts, since the latter had for millennia exercised their
oppressive authority as from Paul himself. Although she initially imagined
that the principle of "There is no longer 'male and female' in Christ" of Gal.
3:28 might have some possibilities, she quickly came to recognize that being "in Christ" meant absorption of Christian women into an "exclusively
male symbol."[27] In more "moderate" approaches, early feminist criticism
found Paul's letters useful as historical sources indicating that women such as
Prisca and Phoebe took prominent leadership roles in the earliest "Pauline"
communities. But Paul's own statements about women's roles in those communities were problematic, countering whatever glimpse he may have had
of a more egalitarian possibility in Gal. 3:28 with an almost ontological
subordination and blunt silencing in 1 Cor. 11:2–16 and 14:34–35.[28] The
pioneering major work by Elisabeth Schüssler Fiorenza, *In Memory of Her*,
of course, became the groundbreaking and grounding feminist reconstruction of Christian origins, including its incisive examination of Paul and
the "Pauline" churches and writings. Antoinette Clark Wire then demonstrated how we can discern the voices and concerns of women through Paul's
oppositional rhetoric in *Corinthian Women Prophets*.[29]

African American and other women have also recognized that it is not
just Pauline texts that function authoritatively. "Rather it is reading strategies, and more precisely, *particular* readings that turn out, in fact, to be

---

26. Elisabeth Schüssler Fiorenza, "The Ethics of Biblical Interpretation: Decentering Biblical
Scholarship," *JBL* 107 (1988), 3–17; reprinted in Schüssler Fiorenza, *Rhetoric and Ethic: The
Politics of Biblical Studies* (Minneapolis: Fortress Press, 1999), 17–30.

27. See the earliest books: Mary Daly, *The Church and the Second Sex* (New York: Harper
and Row, 1968; cf. the "Feminist Postchristian Introduction" in the 1975 edition, esp. p. 22;
and *Beyond God the Father* (Boston: Beacon, 1973), 5, 80, 151.

28. See, e.g., Constance F. Parvey, "The Theology and Leadership of Women in the New
Testament," in *Religion and Sexism*, ed. Rosemary Radford Ruether (New York: Simon and
Schuster, 1974), 117–49.

29. Elisabeth Schüssler Fiorenza, *In Memory of Her: A Feminist Theological Reconstruction
of Christian Origins* (New York: Crossroad, 1983), which she followed with many important
hermeneutical articles and books. Antoinette Clark Wire, *The Corinthian Women Prophets: A
Reconstruction through Paul's Rhetoric* (Minneapolis: Fortress Press, 1990).

authoritative.... The dominant reading conventions and the dominant class interests in many instances reinforce one another. In other words, readers and reading strategies have far more power than isolated ancient texts in themselves."[30] Confronted by both problematic texts and problematic dominant reading conventions, as well as a malestream scholarly guild that has stoutly resisted their exegetical insights and hermeneutical innovations, feminist interpreters of Pauline and other texts have developed what has become arguably the most sophisticated theological interpretation of the New Testament currently on the scene.

In recent years voices from the "Two-thirds World" are finally being heard in Western biblical studies. Non-Western biblical interpreters are making it clear just how much biblical studies in general and Pauline studies in particular are implicated in Western colonialism. The great European powers used an expanding Christian missionary enterprise as a civilizing project of their colonialism, to "civilize the savages" and supposedly to ameliorate the dehumanizing effects of imperialism. In a developing "interfaith" or "multi-faith" hermeneutics, Asian scholars such as R. S. Sugirtharajah, Khiok-khng Yeo, and Kwok Pui-lan offer blunt critiques of how standard Western interpretations of Paul's mission constitute an imperial stance toward other peoples and religions and explore intriguing possibilities of ways in which Paul models dialogical encounters between cultures and faiths.[31] A number of non-Western biblical scholars are now cautiously and critically adapting postcolonial criticism, developed thus far mainly among literary critics, for application in biblical studies.[32] And, in related ways, African, Latin American, Hispanic American, and Asian American voices are contributing to the broad challenges to and the broad rethinking of Pauline studies.

The traditional "other" against which Western Christian theologians interpreted Paul as the hero of individual salvation by faith has been the Jewish people or "Judaism," as Stendahl recognized and attempted to counteract. No group of people has suffered more from the "detrimental and dangerous effect" of Pauline writings and their effective history. Jewish scholars such as Alan Segal and Daniel Boyarin have produced some important contributions to recent reexamination of Paul.[33] The most recent of these significant

---

30. Weems, "Reading *Her Way* through the Struggle," 64–65.

31. R. S. Sugirtharajah, "Inter-Faith Hermeneutics: An Example and Some Implications," in *Voices from the Margins: Interpreting the Bible in the Third World*, ed. Sugirtharajah (Maryknoll, N.Y.: Orbis, 1991), 352–63; Khiok-khng Yeo, "The Rhetorical Hermeneutic of 1 Corinthians 8 and Chinese Ancestor Worship," *Biblical Interpretation* 2 (1994): 294–311; Kwok Pui-lan, *Discovering the Bible in the Non-Biblical World* (Maryknoll, N.Y.: Orbis, 1995), esp. chap. 5.

32. E.g., Kwok, *Discovering the Bible*, chaps. 6 and 7; and the essays collected in R. S. Sugirtharajah, ed., *The Postcolonial Bible* (Sheffield: Sheffield Academic Press, 1998), and in *Postcolonialism and Scriptural Reading, Semeia* 75 (1996).

33. Alan Segal, *Paul the Convert: The Apostolate and Apostasy of Saul the Pharisee* (New Haven: Yale University Press, 1990); Daniel Boyarin, *A Radical Jew: Paul and the Politics of Identity* (Berkeley: University of California Press, 1994).

Jewish scholarly examinations of Paul indirectly provides a telling critique of the established Christian interpretation of Paul. Boyarin discerns a Paul who closely resembles the near-contemporary Jewish philosopher Philo of Alexandria in his "platonic hermeneutic." Philo clearly set forth the kind of "Hellenistic desire for the One" that Boyarin sees in Paul, and thus appears far closer to the modern Western universal human essence and male *homo religiosus* that Western Christian interpreters find in Paul. Thus when Boyarin criticizes Paul's universal human essence, in which every individual, regardless of social-cultural origins and background, becomes One (in contrast with the rabbinic emphasis on particular embodied identity), the effect is a critique of the sort of Western individualizing and universalizing interpretation of Paul that Stendahl had challenged.

Among the revisionist critics of Paul, finally, are scholars schooled in the standard Western individualistic apolitical interpretation but who were concerned about the dangerous effect of Paul and Pauline interpretation and discerned a Paul with a political agenda. Dieter Georgi pointed in this direction with his suggestion that Paul borrowed some of his principal symbolism, such as Christ as *Kyrios* or *Sotēr*, and even the term *pistis*, as political loyalty, from the Roman emperor cult. In *Liberating Paul: The Justice of God and the Politics of the Apostle*, Neil Elliott laid out a more complete reexamination of Paul as being potentially liberative in important respects rather than hopelessly dangerous.[34]

## Paul and Politics: Exploring Interrelated Concerns

Like African American scholars, both feminist scholars and recent postcolonial interpreters also see the need to communicate and cooperate with other groups that have the same or similar concerns. "[F]eminism...cannot just be concerned with gender inequities and gender marginalization but must also address other forms of domination, such as racism, poverty, religious exclusion, heterosexism, and colonialism, all of which are inflected by gender and inflect gender."[35] Pioneers of postcolonial criticism are from the outset also seeking to make alliances with those subjected to and seeking liberation from sexual, racial, colonial, and class domination. In the emerging structure of a more diversified biblical studies, however, there was no forum in which all of these groups of marginalized scholars could explore

---

34. Dieter Georgi, *Theocracy in Paul's Praxis and Theology*, trans. David E. Green (Minneapolis: Fortress Press, 1991). Neil Elliott, *Liberating Paul: The Justice of God and the Politics of the Apostle* (Maryknoll, N.Y.: Orbis, 1994).

35. Schüssler Fiorenza, *Rhetoric and Ethic*, 5. She further explains that her neologism and analytical category kyriarchy does not restrict itself to gender analysis but seeks to comprehend the complex multiplicative interstructuring of gender, race, class, and colonial dominations and their imbrication with each other.

their common interests amid their respective criticism of Paul and Pauline interpretation.

The Paul and Politics Group was formed precisely to provide such a forum for what were separate but often overlapping lines of criticism of Paul's mission, letters, and longer-range impact that challenged standard views: that is, both African Americans who dismiss Paul because Pauline letters figured so prominently in support of slavery and African Americans interpreters who argue that a critically reinterpreted Paul can still be a resource for liberation; a spectrum of feminist interpreters with varying degrees of criticism of Paul's subordination of women; Jewish and other critics of Paul's role in the separation of "Christianity" from "Judaism" and the Pauline contribution to anti-Judaism; interpreters from previously colonized peoples concerned about Pauline contribution to continuing "colonial" attitudes; and those ready to contest the standard interpretation of Paul as a social-political conservative strictly obedient to the empire of which he was supposedly a citizen. The common overarching rubric under which all of these constituencies and perspectives could convene for cooperative investigations and discussions was "Paul and Politics." Investigation and dialogue focused on the four overlapping areas, broadly conceived, of "Paul and the politics of the churches," "Paul and the politics of Israel," "Paul and the politics of the Roman Empire," and "Paul and the politics of interpretation." Virtually any investigation of an issue or text from Paul's mission, letters, and effects — such as Paul's stance on slavery or women's position — almost inevitably engages two or more of those overlapping areas.

A sense of the current situation in biblical studies generally and the principles and purposes of our interrelated concerns is gradually becoming clear in the course of our discussions, as illustrated in the following paragraphs.

A number of factors in the increasingly complicated contemporary interaction of peoples and cultures have resulted in the broadening and deepening of Stendahl's recognition of just how problematic Western privatized and depoliticized interpretations of biblical texts have become. In their claim of universalism, established biblical studies generally, but perhaps especially Pauline studies, have been imperialistic.[36] In claiming universal applicability, Western biblical studies unreflectively disguised its own distinctive identity. In assuming that all interpreters are the same whatever their concrete location, Western biblical scholars expected and trained others to read like male Western Europeans. The whole enterprise proceeded according to

---

36. See further the more extensive reflections about biblical studies in general by Schüssler Fiorenza, *Rhetoric and Ethic;* and by Fernando F. Segovia, "And They Began to Speak in Other Tongues: Competing Modes of Discourse in Contemporary Biblical Criticism," which is the introduction to *Reading from This Place*, vol. 1, *Social Location and Biblical Interpretation in the United States*, ed. Segovia and Mary Ann Tolbert (Minneapolis: Fortress Press, 1995), 29–30, on whom I am dependent in part for the following sketch of the current situation and agenda in Pauline studies.

their concerns, perspectives, and interests — disguised, of course, as those of "every man" or *homo religiosus*. Thus women and non-Europeans and less-educated people, in order to achieve the requisite "objectivity," were required in their interpretation to ignore or eliminate the very factors of gender, race or ethnicity, and class that constituted their identity, indeed their humanity. That is closely analogous to what happened in European colonization of the rest of the world: the experience and interests of other peoples were sacrificed to that of Europeans, particularly the elite males.

Needed is a process of decolonization, allowing a voice for the identity and interests of others. The old European colonial powers and the United States, their imperial successor, have lost their political grip. The rise of global capitalism has, if anything, tightened economic control and manipulation of peoples everywhere and imposes Western cultural forms in highly effective ways even while it purports to sponsor and thrive on multiculturalism. This makes it all the more important for academic disciplines such as biblical studies simultaneously to become critically aware of their own politics and to broaden their base in cultural diversity.

As some of the new voices in biblical studies insist, Pauline letters and Pauline interpretation have played a fundamental political role in support of slavery and the subordination of women. Those functions, however, are only the beginning of the politics of Paul and Pauline studies. The highly political process of canonization of the New Testament was clearly a victory for the deutero-Pauline understanding of Paul that was thus established as authoritative. The inclusion of Ephesians solidified Christian supersessionism over "Judaism" and assimilation into the Roman imperial order. The inclusion of Colossians, Ephesians, and the Pastoral letters also determined that thereafter the "genuine" letters of Paul would be read through the deutero-Paulines. As seen increasingly in recent analysis, the ad hoc, argumentative, and in some cases highly polemical character of Paul's "genuine" letters indicates that the letters themselves are sites of a struggle between Paul and others in the process of early community formation. The flimsy textual basis in passages of unstable translation such as 1 Cor. 7:21 (where the RSV and NRSV prefer opposite translations) betrays just how "ideological" the standard reconstruction of Paul as a social conservative on slavery and related issues is. And Bible interpreters from the margins who are only too aware of the effects of Pauline letters on their own lives and those of their ancestors as slaves, women, and people who were colonized, insist on critical analysis of the politics of Pauline interpretation. Concerned about keenly debated social and political issues, Bible readers outside of biblical studies are clamoring for intelligent and intelligible response from professional interpreters of the Bible. Indeed, the opportunity has been there for some time, as illustrated in the dispute over the ordination of women in the Church of Sweden, in which Stendahl's "The Bible and the Role of Women" became a significant intervention.

But biblical studies, along with religious studies generally, has remained in its private apolitical self-marginalization. Indeed, throughout the post-Holocaust debates, McCarthyism, the civil rights struggles, Vietnam war protests, the women's movement, anti-colonial struggles, and Third World cries for relief, biblical studies offered precious little response. That is surely largely because individualistic and depoliticized biblical and religious studies are unequipped to discern and address political-economic issues such as the globalization of inequality. The continuing focus on the question of religious salvation and the treatment of Paul's letters as purely spiritual texts to be appropriated by individual faith — challenged by Stendahl — leaves Pauline studies at a loss to address issues of political-economic domination and racial and gender inequality and injustice.

In the widespread dissatisfaction with the historical-critical method of standard biblical studies during the last generation, innovative approaches have proliferated. But most of them have not enabled the political competence of Pauline studies. Within Pauline studies itself, the "new perspective" on Paul picked up contemporary multicultural concerns. Ignoring the Roman imperial context of Paul's mission, however, homogenization by empire, then and now, purveyors of the "new perspective" continued to focus on Paul's opposition to "Judaism" under the guise of "nationalistic presuppositions" or "ethnic restrictions" or even ancient *Jewish* (rather than Roman) "cultural imperialism." "Hermeneutics" was sharply criticized for its conservative bias and blindness to the power relations involved in both the production and interpretation of texts. Social scientific approaches adopt sociological or anthropological models without discerning their problematic underlying theory and political implications — or their abandonment by social scientists themselves. Postmodernist interpretation seldom results in more than a playful proliferation of textual readings. And the recent "cultural studies" approach tends to avoid analysis of political-economic power relations.

Since Paul and Pauline letters have long played important roles in shaping political and cultural affairs, study of the Bible must be understood as an activity with political implications and responsibilities. As we struggle to develop a more politically aware and capable alternative to standard Pauline studies, certain principles have emerged that guide our discussions.

Both texts and interpretations are sites of struggle. Paul is arguing with or against or even attempting to silence other voices in his letters, and some of those voices are evident in or underneath the text. The oppressive as well as liberative possibilities in Paul's texts can be critically assessed from diverse perspectives and interpretative positions. But interpretations of Paul involve values and visions of their own, which can be examined and evaluated from other perspectives.

Both the production and interpretation of texts involve power relations, and interests, values, and visions. Paul used language not simply for transmission of ideas but as a form of action that affected people through power relations. Rhetorical criticism of Paul's letters has already shown how useful it can be in discerning some of the power relations involved in the production of the letters. Paul's arguments in 1 Corinthians, for example, may not have affected the Corinthian community all that much (considering the shaky relations between them evident in 2 Corinthians 10–13). But once his letters addressed to the Corinthians were collected, widely read, and revered — eventually becoming recognized as scripture — they surely affected subsequent situations and people. Previously marginalized interpreters who have been affected by some of the power relations inscribed in the text can help others toward more suspicious reading. Interpreters themselves cannot avoid particular locations, interests, perspectives, and interpretative constructs. Cooperative interpretation thus involves critical dialogue among interpreters with different but overlapping perspectives and interpretative constructs. Rather than seek a master narrative, cooperative interpreters can benefit from competing discourses.

Both texts and interpreters occupy particular social locations and contexts. Analysis of contexts (both of text and interpreter) is therefore as important as analysis of texts. To approach more adequate understanding of Paul's politics in its several relations to empire, Israel, and the assemblies he helped establish requires systematic analysis of wider political-economic-religious structures and power relations as well as the more local networks of power relations in Jerusalem, Galatia, Macedonia, Achaia, and Asia. In contrast to established Pauline studies that claim "objectivity" but depoliticize and domesticate Paul's letters, it is important to recognize from the outset the political and cultural remoteness of the text as conditioned by its historical context. The old "historical-critical" approach focused somewhat narrowly on the meaning of words and texts. A far more complex new critical historical approach strives to interpret the text amid the complex structures and contingencies of the historical context with which it was engaged.

Interpreters' identity and social location are hybrid and complex. With race, class, and gender now seen as more complex structures of relations, we can recognize that, far from possessing an essential identity, we move through several positions and attitudes vis-à-vis the dominant social order and hegemonic culture. For most this means various marginal and subordinate positions, although some do move through dominant positions at times. In any case, most have or move through multiple positions and perspectives. This suggests the desirability and likelihood of varying and shifting coalitions of interpreters in cooperative approaches to texts, issues, and interpretations that would mirror the interrelationships between class, gender, race, and ethnicity. It is hardly possible that issues and interests will not overlap and interconnect or for an interpreter to be totally absorbed in one issue to the exclusion of others. Because of common predicaments, common sensibilities, and overlapping agendas, interpreters will welcome mutually critical interaction in pursuit of overlapping interests and purposes.

The aims and agenda of the Paul and Politics group are, broadly, to problematize, interrogate, and re-vision Pauline texts and interpretations, to identify oppressive formulations as well as potentially liberative visions and values in order to recover their unfulfilled historical possibilities, all in critical mutual engagement among diverse participants. A diversity of participants as well as diversity in theory and approach, including "readings from below," may further the demystification of problematic practices in contemporary biblical interpretation. Interpretation as well as texts are sites of struggle. All interpretation has an agenda. Critical awareness means making a choice to exercise criticism on the side of the marginalized and oppressed and with demystification and liberation in mind. Diversity in interests, insights, and approach will generate a certain level of conflict among interrelated liberationist readings, which is to be valued rather than avoided.

## This Collection of Essays

This collection of essays, dedicated to Krister Stendahl in gratitude for the ways in which he opened the field of Pauline studies to broader concerns, includes most of the papers from the first four years of the Paul and Politics Group's annual deliberations. As we anticipated, papers that focus on a particular issue or text unavoidably engage discussion of two or more of the interrelated facets of "Paul and the politics of interpretation," "Paul and empire," "Paul and the politics of Israel," and "Paul and the politics of the assemblies."

In the inaugural session, devoted to exploration of issues and perspectives, Elisabeth Schüssler Fiorenza spoke on "Paul and the Politics of Interpretation" and Neil Elliott on "Paul and the Politics of Empire." Having already published a further developed version of her paper, Schüssler Fiorenza presents a new but parallel essay for this volume in which she engages other participants' work pertinent to the agenda of the group published since the original session. The result is to bring feminist concerns sharply to the fore in discussions of "Paul and empire" and "Paul and the politics of interpretation." In his response, Robert Jewett grounds these discussions more firmly in exegesis of Paul's letters, particularly Romans.

The second year's session focused on a particular letter, 1 Corinthians, as a key text for exploration of issues central to our broader agenda. In attempting to locate Paul's rhetoric in the broader context of the function of rhetoric in the Roman Empire, Richard Horsley discusses the other voices in the Corinthian assembly evident through Paul's rhetoric as well as Paul's indebtedness to the opposition to empire evident in Judean apocalyptic literature. In examining the subordination of women in 1 Corinthians, Cynthia Briggs Kittredge emphasizes the importance of Paul's reinscription of the very imperial language he ostensibly opposed in his rhetorical attempts to restore discipline in the Corinthian community. Sheila Briggs argues that Paul employs a rhetoric of evasion in discussion of slavery as a social institution, and then moves into a rhetoric of power when deploying slavery as a metaphor for the believer's relation to Christ. Antoinette Clark Wire, whose pioneering rhetorical and feminist analysis is utilized by all three papers, critically explores the interrelationships of these issues in her "Response: The Politics of the Assembly in Corinth."

The third year's session featured two papers mainly exploring "Paul and the politics of Israel" and one focused on "Paul and the politics of empire." Pamela Eisenbaum's argument that Paul understands himself as an Abrahamic figure who establishes a new kind of family made up of Jews and Gentiles has implications for the politics of interpretation as well as for Paul's role in the politics of ancient Israel. Distinguishing critically between Peter and James in Jerusalem, on the one hand, and those active in directly influencing the Galatians, Mark Nanos insists that the conflict Paul addresses in Galatia is an intra- and inter-Jewish dispute and cannot be understood as a conflict between some new religion about to be called Christianity and the old religion of Judaism. N. T. Wright's discussion of how Philippians 3 must be understood as Paul's opposition to the Roman imperial order also reveals how closely Paul's opposition to the empire was interrelated with his relationship with Israel. Alan Segal, who has dealt in depth with the relationship of the nascent Christian movement to Judaism, further reflects on this relationship in his "Response: Some Aspects of Conversion and Identity Formation in the Christian Community of Paul's Time."

For the fourth year's session we asked some relatively new voices in Pauline studies to present their perspectives and special concerns. In an essay that involves all of the interrelated facets of our agenda, Sze-kar Wan reexamines Paul's collection for the poor among the saints in Jerusalem as anti-imperial in its implications, utilizing recent discussion of "ethnicity" from a postcolonial perspective. Focusing again on 1 Corinthians Allen Callahan presents a boldly articulated emancipationist agenda for Pauline studies that has wide implications for the diverse constituencies we aim to involve and address. How these revisionist perspectives and agenda relate to previous understandings of Paul are discussed in responses by Calvin Roetzel and Antoinette Clark Wire, two well established and highly regarded interpreters of Paul.

We present these essays in hopes of further broadening the concerns of Pauline studies. And we present them in honor of Krister Stendahl, who pioneered the scholarly recognition that Paul was engaged in public, political processes, then and now.

— 1 —

# PAUL AND THE POLITICS OF EMPIRE

## PROBLEMS AND PROSPECTS

### *Neil Elliott*

🅂🅂🅂🅂🅂🅂🅂🅂🅂🅂

## The Relevance of Empire

"WE ARE AT A POINT in our work when we can no longer ignore empires and the imperial context in our studies." In his postcolonial manifesto, *Culture and Imperialism*, Edward Said has called interpreters to recognize, within the cultural texts they study, the importance of the attitudes and concepts by which empire finds legitimacy, the "notions that certain territories and people require and beseech domination." A prominent critic of U.S. policy in the Middle East, Said insists the interpreter's task be nothing less than an "intervention" in the production and transmission of imperialist culture. There can be no position of neutrality: "The world today does not exist as a spectacle about which we can be either pessimistic or optimistic, about which our 'texts' can be either ingenious or boring. All such attitudes involve the deployment of power and interests." We must choose between "the projection, or the refusal, of the wish to dominate, the capacity to damn, or the energy to comprehend and engage with other societies, traditions, histories." In contrast to what he calls the "astonishing sense of weightlessness" in Western academia "with regard to the gravity of history," Said notes that for interpreters in postcolonial nations, it has proven "impossible to write of liberation and nationalism...without also declaring oneself for or against them"; given the totalizing tendency of imperialism, "one either was on the side of empire or against it."[1]

Taking empire seriously has revolutionized recent study of the historical Jesus. In "a serious departure from much previous biblical scholarship,"

---

1. Edward Said, *Culture and Imperialism* (New York: Vintage Books, 1993), xx, 6, 279, 303; see also *Orientalism* (New York: Pantheon, 1978) and *Covering Islam: How the Media and the Experts Determine How We See the Rest of the World* (New York: Pantheon, 1981).

17

Richard Horsley began his book *Jesus and the Spiral of Violence* (1987) with chapters discussing "The Imperial Situation" and forms of popular Jewish resistance in Roman Palestine. He went on to argue that Jesus "directly and sharply opposed the oppression of the ruling groups" in Judea, and even "engaged more fundamentally in a revolt against the powers controlling the imperial situation in Palestine." Similarly, John Dominic Crossan began his study of *The Historical Jesus* (1991) with four chapters on "Brokered Empire"; anthropological studies of imperialist societies, by Gerhard Lenski and John Kautsky, played an important part in his method. Crossan concluded at length that Jesus' practice of "free healing and common eating" expressed "a religious and economic egalitarianism that negated alike and at once the hierarchical and patronal normalcies of Jewish religion and Roman power."[2] Debate will continue over Crossan's characterization of "Jewish religion,"[3] but it is clear that Roman imperialism is now firmly established as a relevant context for historical Jesus study.

The question of empire has begun to touch on our interpretation of the apostle Paul as well. New Testament interpreters are responding, in part, to recent advances in classical studies, which have moved beyond traditional themes of dynastic politics, military conquest, and law as seen from the perspective of the Roman aristocracy. Simon R. F. Price and Paul Zanker have described the production and dissemination of imperial ideology through images and ritual, a production of culture in which provincial elites were only too happy to participate.[4] G. E. M. de Ste. Croix, P. D. A. Garnsey, and Richard Saller, among others, have analyzed perceptively the fundamentally

---

2. Richard A. Horsley, *Jesus and the Spiral of Violence: Popular Jewish Resistance in Roman Palestine* (San Francisco: Harper & Row, 1987), 156; John Dominic Crossan, *The Historical Jesus: The Life of a Mediterranean Jewish Peasant* (San Francisco: Harper San Francisco, 1991), 422. Both scholars make good use of sociological and anthropological studies of imperial and colonial societies, for example, Gerhard Lenski, *Power and Privilege: A Theory of Social Stratification* (New York: McGraw-Hill, 1966), and John H. Kautsky, *The Politics of Aristocratic Empires* (Chapel Hill: University of North Carolina Press, 1982).

3. In an important critique of one aspect of recent Jesus scholarship, including Crossan's, Paula Fredriksen remarks that "E. P. Sanders' 1977 book *Paul and Palestinian Judaism* finally removed the Pharisees from the cross-hairs of Christian historical fantasy. But the replacement target of choice now seems to be the Temple and the biblically mandated laws of purity." Thus "the old polemical opposition 'law versus grace' has simply been replaced by an even more self-congratulatory antithesis, purity versus compassion." See Fredriksen, "What You See Is What You Get: Context and Content in Current Research on the Historical Jesus," *Theology Today* 52 (1995): 75–97; Fredriksen, "Did Jesus Oppose the Purity Laws?" *Bible Review* (June 1995): 19–47.

4. Simon R. F. Price, *Rituals and Power: The Roman Imperial Cult in Asia Minor* (Cambridge: Cambridge University Press, 1984); Paul Zanker, *The Power of Images in the Age of Augustus* (Ann Arbor: University of Michigan Press, 1988); see also Richard Gordon, "The Veil of Power: Emperors, Sacrificers and Benefactors," in *Pagan Priests: Religion and Power in the Ancient World*, ed. Mary Beard and John North (Ithaca, N.Y.: Cornell University Press, 1990). The preceding are helpfully excerpted in Richard A. Horsley, ed., *Paul and Empire: Religion and Power in Roman Imperial Society* (Philadelphia: Trinity Press International, 1997). See also Karl Galinsky, *Augustan Culture: An Interpretive Introduction* (Princeton: Princeton University Press, 1996).

exploitive, "parasitic" nature of economic globalization under the Roman "world system."[5] As a consequence, Justin Meggitt has been able to cast considerable doubt on the now-conventional wisdom that the Pauline churches were populated by lower-middle-class artisans and entrepreneurs, suffering perhaps from "status inconsistency," but not from real poverty. Given the nature of the Roman economy, Meggitt demonstrates that "poverty was an absolute and not relative phenomenon."[6]

It may not be obvious, however, what specific implications current studies of Roman imperial culture and ideology have for the interpretation of Paul and his letters. One may well ask what Rome has to do with Jerusalem, or Tarsus.

## Gaps in the "New Perspective"

Pauline studies have seen undeniable progress — some scholars speak, with good reason, of a "paradigm shift" — as an older interpretive agenda, driven by Christian dogmatics, opposing Paul's doctrine of justification by faith to a spurious scheme of Jewish "works-righteousness," has collapsed beneath the weight of historical improbability. Krister Stendahl's significant contribution to that development is widely recognized, and justly honored, along with roughly contemporary work by Rosemary Radford Ruether and E. P. Sanders.[7] One can argue, nevertheless, that the so-called "new perspective on Paul," now in the ascendancy, has not yet gone beyond the fundamental assumption that Paul must be interpreted over against Judaism.

Scholarship remains preoccupied with the contrast between "particularistic" or "ethnocentric" Judaism and the "universalism" of Paul's theology. Those categories remain problematic, however, for several reasons. First, they derive from the nineteenth-century idealist historiography of Ferdinand Christian Baur, and as Calvin Roetzel has shown, their use in current studies

---

5. G. E. M. de Ste. Croix, *The Class Struggle in the Ancient Greek World, from the Archaic Age to the Arab Conquests* (Ithaca, N.Y.: Cornell University Press, 1981); P. D. A. Garnsey and Richard Saller, *The Roman Empire: Society, Economics, Culture* (Berkeley: University of California Press, 1987); on the colonization of Greece, Susan E. Alcock, *Graecia Capta: The Landscapes of Roman Greece* (Cambridge: Cambridge University Press, 1993); on world-systems theory and Romanization, Greg Woolf, "World-Systems Analysis and the Roman Empire," *Journal of Roman Archaeology* 2 (1990): 44–58; Woolf, "Becoming Roman, Staying Greek: Culture, Identity, and the Civilizing Process in the Roman East," *Proceedings of the Cambridge Philological Society* 40 (1994): 116–43; Woolf, "Beyond Romans and Natives," *World Archaeology* 28:3 (1995): 339–50.

6. Justin Meggitt, *Paul, Poverty and Survival* (Edinburgh: T. & T. Clark, 1998). On "status inconsistency" see Wayne A. Meeks, *The First Urban Christians: The Social World of the Apostle Paul* (New Haven: Yale University Press, 1983), 51–73.

7. Krister Stendahl, *Paul among Jews and Gentiles, and Other Essays* (Philadelphia: Fortress Press, 1976); Rosemary Radford Ruether, *Faith and Fratricide* (New York: Seabury, 1974); E. P. Sanders, *Paul and Palestinian Judaism: A Comparison of Patterns of Religion* (Philadelphia: Fortress Press, 1977).

is all too often contaminated by now-defunct racial theory.[8] Furthermore, despite its initial promise to reverse centuries of theological anti-Judaism, the "new perspective" offers a Pauline "universalism" that leaves little room for the Torah-observant Jew. Jewish scholar Daniel Boyarin draws the ultimate conclusion from this reading of the apostle: Paul's "is a bitter gospel not a sweet one, because it is conditioned precisely on abandoning that to which we hold so dearly, our separate cultural, religious identity, our own fleshy and historical practice, our existence according to the flesh, our Law, our difference. Paul has simply allegorized our difference quite out of existence."[9] Finally, what is taken in this common reading for Paul's "universalism" is usually informed by, even identified with, the "universalism" of gentile Christianity as expressed in Ephesians. But there are good reasons to doubt that this is the theology of Romans, or of Paul himself.[10]

A preoccupation with Paul's supposed critique of Judaism, or Jewish ethnocentrism, prejudices the weight we give to social and ethical aspects of Paul's theology. Elaine Pagels perceives a "double standard" in conventional treatments of Paul's social thought:

> To continue observing kosher laws is to deny "the freedom for which Christ died," but to continue observing social, political and marital laws and conventions remains acceptable, even commendable. Although the "new humanity" has transformed the entire relationship between Jews and Gentiles, Paul does not allow it to challenge the whole structure of the believers' social, sexual, and political relationships.[11]

Halvor Moxnes perceives a similar "double standard" in the language of honor and shame in Romans. While Paul "broke down the barriers between Jews and non-Jews" in Rom. 1–4, in such a way as to establish for Paul's communities "a separate identity vis-à-vis the synagogue," the exhortation in Rom. 13:1–7 served rather to "strengthen an integration of Christians into the Hellenistic symbolic universe," reinforcing the social stratification

8. Ferdinand Christian Baur, *Paul: His Life and Works*, vol. 1, 2d ed., trans. E. Zeller (London: Williams & Norgate, 1873), chap. 3. On the "new perspective," see Sanders, *Paul and Palestinian Judaism;* James D. G. Dunn, "The New Perspective on Paul," *BJRL* 65 (1983): 95–122. For critiques, see Thomas Deidun, "James Dunn and John Ziesler on Romans in New Perspective," *HeyJ* 33 (1992): 79–84; and Calvin Roetzel, "No 'Race of Israel' in Paul's Letters," in *Putting Body and Soul Together: Essays in Honor of Robin Scroggs*, ed. Virginia Wiles, Alexandra Brown, and Graydon F. Snyder (Valley Forge: Trinity Press International, 1997).

9. Daniel Boyarin, *A Radical Jew: Paul and the Politics of Identity* (Berkeley: University of California Press, 1994), 203, 152.

10. For a response to Boyarin see Neil Elliott, "Figure and Ground in the Interpretation of Romans 9–11," in *The Theological Interpretation of Scripture: Classic and Contemporary Readings*, ed. Stephen Fowl (Cambridge, Mass.: Blackwell, 1996). On the theology of Israel in Romans, see William S. Campbell, *Paul's Gospel in an Intercultural Context* (Frankfurt: Peter Lang, 1992), and Mark Nanos, *The Mystery of Romans* (Minneapolis: Fortress, 1995).

11. Elaine Pagels, "Paul and Women: A Response to Recent Discussion," *JAAR* 42 (1974): 187–96; see also my *Liberating Paul: The Justice of God and the Politics of the Apostle* (Maryknoll, N.Y.: Orbis, 1994), chap. 6.

experienced in public life. Thus Paul seems to have "accepted the system of honor operating on the public world of Greco-Roman society," encouraging Christians "to live within the given power structures and to conform to the civic virtues of honor and praise."[12]

It is fair to say that much of the debate over Paul's social and ethical thought revolves around the question of this apparent "double standard." Is Paul more concerned in his letters to maintain a social and symbolic boundary against the public world of Hellenistic virtues and imperial ideology, or against the values of a more intimate social space, the diaspora synagogue? Moxnes shows that this question coheres with the interpretation of Romans, for there we find, almost side by side, the exhortation to "be subject to the governing authorities" (13:1–7), which appears to encourage civic conformity, and the exhortation "not to be conformed to this world" (12:2). Moxnes concludes that Paul "accepted the system of honor operating on the public world of Graeco-Roman society but rejected this society as shameful in the area of 'private life,' gender roles and sexuality." Paul's greater concern was to "ease the transition from the synagogue to the Christian groups and strengthen their independence"; thus "it is the particular boasting of the Jew" which Paul attacks.[13]

The same "double standard" regarding Paul reappears in John M. G. Barclay's sweeping study, *Jews in the Mediterranean Diaspora*. The question of culture and imperialism is central here, as Barclay seeks to explore "the varied modes of accommodation or resistance" which diaspora Jews like Philo, Josephus, or the author of 4 Maccabees adopted with regard to their Graeco-Roman environment. Barclay appeals to modern studies of colonialism showing that colonized people make "variant uses of the colonizers' culture — in some cases to modify or even obliterate their native cultural traditions, in others to equip them to resist the colonizers' cultural imperialism." Barclay finds the same range of responses among Jews of the Roman diaspora. Sensitive to "contemporary concerns in multicultural politics," he also hears in recent debate over Paul "echoes of the contemporary rejection of colonialism and the current concern with 'the politics of difference.' "[14]

Ironically, however, given that Hellenistic and Roman imperialism is in view through the rest of Barclay's work, it is primarily against Jewish "nationalistic presuppositions" or "ethnic restrictions" that he sees Paul to be struggling. True, Paul's apocalyptic perspective still regards the non-Jewish

---

12. Halvor Moxnes, "Honor, Shame, and the Outside World in Romans," in *The Social World of Formative Christianity and Judaism: Essays in Tribute to Howard Clark Kee,* ed. Jacob Neusner et al. (Philadelphia: Fortress Press, 1988), 207–19; Moxnes, "Honor and Righteousness in Romans," *JSNT* 32 (1988): 61–77.

13. Moxnes, "Honor and Righteousness in Romans," 71.

14. John M. G. Barclay, *Jews in the Mediterranean Diaspora: From Alexander to Trajan (323 B.C.E.–117 C.E.* (Edinburgh: T. & T. Clark, 1996), 9–10, 97–98; Barclay, " 'Neither Jew nor Greek': Multiculturalism and the New Perspective on Paul," in *Ethnicity and the Bible,* ed. M. G. Brett (Leiden: Brill, 1996), 205.

world as "a cess-pit of godlessness and vice (Rom. 1:18–32; Phil. 2:15)."
But in Barclay's view, although Paul did "try to lay down some limits to [his
converts'] assimilation to Graeco-Roman society," his "tactical abandonment of key Jewish practices... made him dangerously assimilated in the
eyes of many" of his Jewish contemporaries. Barclay has gone so far as to
refer to "*Jewish* 'cultural imperialism' " as the horizon against which Paul's
letters must be read.[15]

These examples suffice to show that even when questions of culture and
imperialism have been raised in Pauline studies, it is more often Judaism,
construed as an "imposition" on others, rather than Roman imperialism,
that continues to occupy center stage.[16] Even within a so-called "new
perspective," the abiding preoccupation with Paul's supposed debate with
Judaism continues to eclipse any critical interaction on his part with the
ideology of empire. Richard Horsley's summary of our predicament is apt:
"In the theologically determined metanarrative of the field, the replacement
of the overly political and particularistic religion 'Judaism' by the purely
spiritual and universal religion 'Christianity'... rendered virtually irrelevant
the overall imperial situation and particular colonial relations in response
to which those movements and writings emerged."[17] The consequence, as
Robert Jewett declares, is that Pauline interpretation in the United States remains "a cultural colony of Europe" in its preoccupation with a theological
agenda inherited from the Reformation.[18]

## Elements of a Paradigm Shift

Some recent studies nevertheless point us toward areas of investigation
where the question of Paul and empire is being addressed.

### The Politics of Paul's "Conversion"

Reconstructions of the social and political context in which Jesus moved
have relied heavily on our knowledge of the character of Pontius Pilate's

---

15. Barclay, *Jews in the Mediterranean Diaspora*, 104; "Neither Jew nor Greek," 205–6,
emphasis added. Barclay cites J. D. G. Dunn, *The Theology of Paul's Letter to the Galatians*
(Cambridge: Cambridge University Press, 1993), and his own *Obeying the Truth: A Study of
Paul's Ethics in Galatians* (Edinburgh: T. & T. Clark, 1988), 250–51.

16. Even as he argues in *The Mystery of Romans* that Romans is "not directed toward Jews,
or Jewish exclusivism, except paradigmatically," i.e., to correct misguided views "among the
*gentile* believers in Rome" (10), Mark Nanos occasionally refers (without argument) to "ethnocentric insistence [among *Jews*] that gentiles must become Jews" (9–10, 37–39). Similarly,
though recognizing that in Galatians "Paul's opponents are not actually Jewish Christians,"
Daniel Boyarin refers to "Jewish-Christian opponents" in Galatia (*A Radical Jew*, 116–17); he
declares, though without argument, that Romans 2 is an "attack" on Jews (87).

17. Richard Horsley, "Submerged Biblical Histories and Imperial Biblical Studies," in *The
Postcolonial Bible*, ed. R. S. Sugirtharajah (Sheffield: Sheffield Academic Press, 1998), 154.

18. Robert Jewett, *Paul the Apostle to America: Cultural Trends and Pauline Scholarship*
(Louisville: Westminster/John Knox Press, 1994), 19.

years as procurator. Strangely, although the Pharisee Paul's persecution of the Judean churches almost certainly began during these same years, similar attention to possible political motives for his activity has been absent until recently. Paula Fredriksen has explained that activity in terms of the imperial situation. She writes,

> News of an impending Messianic kingdom, originating from Palestine, might trickle out via the ekklesia's Gentiles to the larger urban population. It was this (by far) larger, unaffiliated group that posed a real and serious threat. Armed with such a report, they might readily seek to alienate the local Roman colonial government, upon which Jewish urban populations often depended for support and protection against hostile Gentile neighbors. The open dissemination of a Messianic message, in other words, put the entire Jewish community at risk.[19]

Along similar lines, Richard Horsley and Neil Silberman have contended that the *Iudaismos* in which Paul says he had advanced (Gal 1:14) was "not merely a matter of religious observance but a movement of political activism and autonomy by diaspora Jews." Thus Saul's "zeal" was directed toward "the end of ensuring community solidarity and security in Damascus" against "the specific political threat" posed to the larger Jewish community by the Jesus movement.[20]

A political explanation of Saul's persecuting activity suggests a political interpretation of Paul's "conversion" as well. In *Liberating Paul,* I argued that the sort of visionary experiences Alan Segal discussed so helpfully in *Paul the Convert* would have functioned, in first-century Judea, to provide self-authorizing scripts for differing policies of accommodation or resistance to Rome. It must suffice here to observe that on his own account, Josephus's surrender to Vespasian after the siege of Jotapata was motivated by his own expert knowledge of apocalyptic traditions, which revealed to him that "fortune has passed over to the Romans" (*War* 3.336–408). He speaks condescendingly of the common people of Jerusalem who failed to grasp the same import of heavenly prodigies just before that city was destroyed (*War* 6.312–13). Surely another apocalyptically minded Jew, also identifying himself as a Pharisee well versed in the ancestral traditions of his people, could have recognized direct political implications in the *Apokalypsis* that the crucified Jesus now stood vindicated at the right hand of God in heaven.[21]

19. Paula Fredriksen, "Judaism, The Circumcision of Gentiles, and Apocalyptic Hope: Another Look at Galatians 1 and 2," *JTS* 42:2 (1991): 556; Fredriksen, *From Jesus to Christ* (New Haven: Yale University Press, 1988), 154.

20. Horsley and Silberman, *The Message and the Kingdom* (New York: Putnam, 1997), 121; see also Elliott, *Liberating Paul,* 143–49.

21. Alan Segal, *Paul the Convert: The Apostolate and Apostasy of Saul the Pharisee* (New Haven: Yale University Press, 1990), chap. 2; Elliott, *Liberating Paul,* 149–67. Similarly Horsley and Silberman argue that ancient Jewish apocalypticism best informs our understanding of

## Political Aspects of Paul's Theology and Praxis

But what of Paul's activity as an apostle of Christ? Although we are repeatedly told that Paul's gospel was fundamentally apolitical,[22] social and
expressly political explanations have surfaced recently for various aspects
of Paul's work and thought.

Years ago Frederick Danker argued that "public documents" like Paul's
letters were best interpreted in the light of the public language of inscriptions;
in particular, he showed that Paul's conception of God had been shaped
by the ubiquitous Greco-Roman symbolization of the *Benefactor*.[23] More
recently, important studies of social stratification, depending on the pioneering work of Gerd Theissen, and of the steep social "pyramid of power and
patronage" in the empire have reshaped our understanding of 1 and 2 Corinthians, where "Gnosticism" was once the explanatory category of choice.[24]
Anthony Saldarini's work on the social location of Pharisees compares Paul
with the class of "retainers" within the imperial system;[25] similarly, Antoinette Clark Wire provides a compelling profile of Paul's situation as a
freeborn Jewish male who, like many of his compatriots, had watched "their
independence disintegrate under Roman rule," and had learned to "seek dignity in Stoic self-denial."[26] The ritualization of patronage in the imperial cult
has also informed Holland Hendrix's study of 1 Thessalonians.[27]

Aspects of Paul's theology echo the poetry and propaganda of the Augustan and Neronian eras. Paul calls his message *to euangelion*, borrowing "a
technical term for 'news of victory'" from the Hellenistic and Roman vocabulary of international diplomacy.[28] By specifying that he proclaims Jesus

Paul's reversal, not so much a "conversion" as a personal, visionary confirmation of ancient
promises to Israel (*Message and the Kingdom*, 121–24).

22. Paul's theology "denationalizes Christ," "praises a reality that is utterly spiritual," and
thus "shrinks the significance of contemporary politics" (Fredriksen, *From Jesus to Christ*,
173). "Apocalyptic turns his gaze continually to the future and it no longer matters to Paul
if his churches are vindicated in the historical and political realm" (Barclay, *Jews in the
Mediterranean Diaspora*, 393).

23. Frederick Danker, *Benefactor: Epigraphic Study of a Greco-Roman and New Testament
Semantic Field* (St. Louis: Clayton, 1982).

24. Gerd Theissen, *The Social Setting of Pauline Christianity: Essays on Corinth*, trans. John
Schutz (Philadelphia: Fortress, 1988); L. Michael White, ed., *Social Networks in the Early
Christian Environment: Issues and Methods for Social History*, Semeia 56 (Atlanta: Scholars
Press, 1992); G. E. M. de Ste. Croix, *Class Struggle in the Ancient Greek World* (Ithaca,
N.Y.: Cornell University Press, 1981), 364–72; John K. Chow, *Patronage and Power: A Study
of Social Networks in Corinth*, JSNTSup 75 (Sheffield: JSOT Press, 1992); Peter Marshall,
*Enmity in Corinth: Social Conventions in Paul's Relations with the Corinthians* (Tübingen:
J. C. B. Mohr [Paul Siebeck], 1987).

25. Anthony Saldarini, *Pharisees, Scribes, and Sadducees in Palestinian Society: A Sociological Approach* (Wilmington: Michael Glazier, 1988), 139.

26. Antoinette Clark Wire, *The Corinthian Women Prophets: A Reconstruction through
Paul's Rhetoric* (Minneapolis: Fortress, 1990), 66–67.

27. Holland Hendrix, "Thessalonicans Honor Romans," Th.D. thesis, Harvard Divinity
School, Cambridge, 1984.

28. Dieter Georgi, *Theocracy in Paul's Praxis and Theology*, trans. David E. Green
(Minneapolis: Fortress, 1991), 83; G. Friedrich, "εὐαγγελίζουαι, κτλ," *TDNT* 2:722–25.

as the "son of God," Dieter Georgi suggests, Paul implicitly parodies the theological claims made on behalf of the Julio-Claudian dynasty; such language must have been calculated to be politically provocative.[29] Similarly, Paul's references to the *parousia* of Christ (1 Thess. 2:19; 3:13) played on diplomatic language for the arrival of a king or general at the gates of a city, with all the potential for threat or promise that such an advent implied.[30] His warning of doom when others proclaim "peace and security" (1 Thess. 5:3) is widely regarded as a not-so-cryptic critique of imperial propaganda, for "peace and security" was the motto of the Roman world after the establishment of the Principate.[31]

Indeed, Paul's proclamation of Jesus as *kyrios,* the "lord of God's empire," relied heavily on Roman political concepts,[32] and "could easily be understood as violating the 'decrees of Caesar' in the most blatant manner."[33] As Calvin Roetzel and John L. White have shown, the very breadth of his eschatological vision — of an *oikoumené* of nations, united in faithful obedience to a single lord — relies upon Hellenistic, and most especially Roman, political ideology.[34]

The imperial context provides more than a conceptual background for Paul's theology, however. The ritual medium for the dissemination of imperial values, so thoroughly described by Simon Price, allows us to recognize the performative character of Paul's apostolic presence and proclamation.[35] Just as members of the provincial elites "drew on religious symbols to negotiate various power relationships in the Roman Empire,"[36] so Paul understood his apostolic praxis as the manifestation of divine power on the public landscape. Indeed, his repeated play on metaphor and imagery drawn from imperial ceremonial — being "led in triumph" by God (2 Cor. 2:14–16;

---

29. Georgi, *Theocracy,* 52–58; compare N. T. Wright, "Gospel and Theology in Galatians," in *Gospel in Paul: Studies on Corinthians, Galatians, and Romans for Richard N. Longenecker,* ed. L. Ann Jervis and Peter Richardson, JSNTSup 108 (Sheffield: Sheffield Academic Press, 1994), 228.

30. Georgi, *Theocracy,* 16–17; compare Karl P. Donfried, "The Cults of Thessalonica and the Thessalonian Correspondence," *NTS* 31 (1985), excerpted in Horsley, ed., *Paul and Empire,* 217.

31. Georgi, *Theocracy,* 28–29; Helmut Koester, "Imperial Ideology and Paul's Eschatology in 1 Thessalonians," in Horsley, ed., *Paul and Empire,* 158.

32. John L. White, *The Apostle of God: Paul and the Promise of Abraham* (Peabody, Mass.: Hendrickson, 1999), 173–205.

33. Donfried's suggestion ("Cults of Thessalonica," 217), referring to oaths of allegiance offered to the emperor in various provinces.

34. Calvin J. Roetzel, "*Oikoumene* and the Limits of Pluralism in Alexandrian Judaism and Paul," in *Diaspora Jews and Judaism,* ed. J. Andrew Overman and Robert S. MacLennon (Atlanta: Scholars Press, 1992); *Paul: The Man and the Myth* (Columbia: University of South Carolina Press, 1998), 16–19; White, *The Apostle of God,* 93–138.

35. On what might be called the "apodeictic" character of Paul's rhetoric (compare 1 Cor. 2:2, 4) see Raymond Pickett, *The Cross in Corinth: The Social Significance of the Death of Jesus,* JSNTSup 143 (Sheffield: Sheffield Academic Press, 1997), 9–36.

36. Douglas R. Edwards, *Religion and Power: Pagans, Jews, and Christians in the Greek East* (New York: Oxford University Press, 1996), 7; see also Price, *Rituals and Power,* passim.

5:14); being made a spectacle in the arena (1 Cor. 4:9–13); "carrying about" the dying of Jesus in the persecution he shared with his coworkers (2 Cor. 4:10; 6:4–10) — is more than irony. Paul opposes the apostolic manifestation of God's power to its inevitable rival in the city square, the imperial ritualization of power.[37]

## Re-examination of the "Pauline Legacy" of Social Conservatism

Over the last thirty years, significant challenges have been raised to the conventional view of Paul's "social conservatism," i.e., his perceived acceptance of social inequities and unjust social structures while proclaiming an "inner" or "spiritual" equality "in Christ." Close readings by S. Scott Bartchy and Norman Peterson of Paul's references to slavery overturned older interpretations that assimilated Paul's message to the pseudo-Pauline *Haustafeln*. Feminist readers highlighted the differences between references to women, especially in leadership positions, in the unquestioned letters of Paul and in the Pauline pseudepigrapha, including the suspected interpolation at 1 Cor. 14:33–35.[38]

These studies lead inevitably to the suspicion that the historical effect, and probable purpose, of the pseudo-Pauline writings has been to misdirect our interpretation of "the Pauline legacy." Indeed, I argued in *Liberating Paul* that interpretive strategies that assimilate Paul to the pseudo-Paulines, under the guise of describing a "Pauline school" or "Pauline churches," misconstrue literary resemblances, an effect of pseudepigraphy, as historical continuity. Given the pseudepigraphic intention to manage, or hijack, the authority of Paul's legacy, I suggested applying to the Pauline literature a "criterion of dissimilarity" similar to that used in historical Jesus research. That is, unless clearly required by evidence from the genuine letters of Paul, we should practice a healthy skepticism toward any interpretation that serves to assimilate Paul's thought and praxis to the recognized purposes of the pseudo-Paulines.[39] At the same time, due weight must be given to the functional resemblances of subordinationist language in Paul's genuine letters to codes of subordination in the wider Roman culture. Here critical essays by Elisabeth Schüssler Fiorenza, Cynthia Briggs Kittredge, and Elizabeth Castelli have proven invaluable.[40]

---

37. I have explored this theme at length in an unpublished paper, "Paul's Apostolic Presence as Anti-Imperial Performance," presented to the Birmingham Colloquium on Ideology and Interpretation in August 1997.

38. S. Scott Bartchy, *Mallon Chresai: First-Century Slavery and 1 Corinthians 7:21*, SBLDS 11 (Missoula, Mont.: Scholars Press, 1973); Norman Peterson, *Rediscovering Paul: Philemon and the Sociology of Paul's Narrative World* (Philadelphia: Fortress, 1985); Robin Scroggs, "Paul and the Eschatological Woman," *JAAR* 40 (1972), 283–303; Elaine Pagels, "Paul and Women: A Response to Recent Discussion," *JAAR* 42 (1974); Elliott, *Liberating Paul*, 32–48.

39. Elliott, *Liberating Paul*, 25–86.

40. Elisabeth Schüssler Fiorenza, "Rhetorical Situation and Historical Reconstruction in 1 Corinthians," *NTS* 33 (1987), 386–403; Elizabeth Castelli, *Imitating Paul: A Discourse*

While all of these studies suggest the contours and context of a dramatically new picture of the apostle Paul, several other areas in which that picture could have equally dramatic implications remain largely unexplored. I turn next to these challenges.

## Prospects for Further Research

### *Contextualizing Paul's Rhetoric within Empire*

Since Hans Dieter Betz's landmark 1973 essay and subsequent commentary on *Galatians*, rhetorical criticism has found a secure home in Pauline studies.[41] With some notable exceptions, most of the explosion of recent rhetorical-critical studies have sought to align tracts of Paul's argument, and especially whole letters, with the categories of genre and partition used in ancient Greek and Roman rhetorical handbooks. While such studies have brought occasional insights into Paul's argumentation, sometimes they have also simply "repackaged" standard historical and theological interpretations by means of a new technical vocabulary.[42] We have not yet seen a full-length exploration of Paul's rhetoric in the wider contexts of imperial or colonial *rhetorics*, that is, the discourses shaped by the social dynamics of imperialism and colonialism, what James C. Scott has called the "great" and "little" traditions," or "public" and "hidden transcripts."[43]

This is surprising and dismaying, for several reasons. Roman authors themselves offer ample evidence that the traditional categories of rhetoric reflected the privileged view of a narrow, but vastly powerful social elite. Judicial rhetoric was exercised by Roman lawyers serving "the interests of

---

*of Power* (Louisville: Westminster/John Knox, 1992); Cynthia Briggs Kittredge, *Community and Authority: The Rhetoric of Obedience in the Pauline Tradition,* HTS 45 (Harrisburg, Pa.: Trinity Press International, 1998).

41. Hans Dieter Betz, "The Literary Composition and Function of Paul's Letter to the Galatians," *NTS* 21 (1975): 353–80; Betz, *Galatians,* Hermeneia (Philadelphia: Fortress, 1979).

42. For discussions of the problem see C. J. Classen, "St. Paul's Epistles and Ancient Greek and Roman Rhetoric," in *Rhetoric and the New Testament: Essays from the 1992 Heidelberg Conference,* ed. Stanley E. Porter and Thomas H. Olbricht (Sheffield: Sheffield Academic Press, 1993): 265–91; Jeffrey Reed, "Using Ancient Rhetorical Categories to Interpret Paul's Letters: A Question of Genre," in ibid., 292–324; Stanley Porter, "The Theoretical Justification for Application of Rhetorical Categories to Pauline Epistolary Literature," in ibid., 100–22; Porter, "Ancient Rhetorical Analysis and Discourse Analysis of the Pauline Corpus," in *The Rhetorical Analysis of Scripture: Essays from the London Conference,* ed. Stanley E. Porter and Thomas H. Olbricht (Sheffield: Sheffield Academic Press, 1995), 249ff.

43. James C. Scott, "Protest and Profanation: Agrarian Revolt and the Little Tradition," *Theory and Society* 4:1 (1977): 1–38; 4:2 (1977): 211–46; Scott, *Domination and the Arts of Resistance: Hidden Transcripts* (New Haven: Yale University Press, 1990). Important beginnings at applying Scott's work to Pauline studies have been made by Richard Horsley, "Rhetoric and Empire — and 1 Corinthians," in the present volume; and Gerald O. West, *The Academy of the Poor: Towards a Dialogical Reading of the Bible* (Sheffield: Sheffield Academic Press, 1990); West, "Disguising Defiance in Ritualisms of Subordination," paper presented to the Biblical Criticism and Literary Criticism Section, SBL annual meeting, 1999.

the class to which they themselves and their clients belonged"; in practice, "there was one law for the rich and another for the poor."[44] The public assembly, the proper domain of deliberative rhetoric, was also the political arena of the aristocratic classes, well insulated from the peasantry;[45] thoroughly anti-democratic sentiments were quite at home there.[46]

The third classical genre, ceremonial or epideictic rhetoric, concerned the values of "praise and glory and disgrace and dishonor." But Cicero made it very clear in his *De re publica* that the "best men" in society may hope to promote such values through rhetoric only among their peers, who are motivated by the real possibility of winning honor from one another. Others, however — slaves, most notably — are more naturally motivated by terror, and for them, force is more effective than rhetoric (3:41). Thus shame and fear operate as twin mechanisms of public control (5:6).[47] Closer to Paul's day, the historian Velleius Paterculus and the philosopher Plutarch similarly contrasted rhetorical persuasion with coercive force.[48] Modern rhetoricians Chaim Perelman and L. Olbrechts-Tyteca confirm that epideictic rhetoric will be practiced "by those who, in a society, defend the traditional and

---

44. G. E. M. de Ste. Croix, *The Class Struggle in the Ancient Greek World, from the Archaic Age to the Arab Conquests* (Ithaca, N.Y.: Cornell University Press, 1981), 330; A. H. M. Jones, *The Later Roman Empire 284–602*, vol. 1 (Oxford: Norman, 1964), 517. Aristotle himself had regarded the "art of rhetoric" to apply when more customary means of arriving at the truth, such as the torture of slaves, was not available (*Rhetoric* 1:1376). Centuries later, the handbook *Ad Herennium* discussed a variety of reasons to doubt testimony given under torture, yet considers such testimony reliable in most cases because "men are compelled by violent pain to tell all they know" (2:6:10). Clearly more was at stake in judicial torture than the dubious enterprise of arriving at truth; see the illuminating study by Page DuBois, *Torture and Truth* (New York: Routledge, 1991).

45. Aristocrats "could never dream of permitting peasants as peasants to vote or participate in their councils." Kautsky, *The Politics of Aristocratic Empires*, 274.

46. In Xenophon's *Memorabilia*, Pericles is challenged by Socrates' student to admit that "whatever the assembled majority, through using its power over the owners of property, enacts without persuasion is not law but force" (*Memorabilia* 1:2:40–46). De Ste. Croix declares this passage "one of the best anti-democratic arguments produced in antiquity" (*Class Struggle*, 414–15).

47. Cicero, whose political speeches are "of prime value" for purposes of the study of Roman propaganda (P. A. Brunt, "*Laus Imperii,*" in P. D. A. Garnsey and C. R. Whittaker, eds., *Imperialism in the Ancient World* [Cambridge: Cambridge University Press, 1978],160), repeatedly expressed his contempt for the limited democracy practiced in the Greek assemblies, whose dominant feature was "irresponsibility" (*pro Flacco* 14–16). Indeed, as one of the dialogue partners in Cicero's *De re publica* puts it, "there can be nothing more horrible than that monster which falsely assumes the name and appearance of a people"; in contrast, "nothing could be more advantageous for a state than to be ruled by a select number of good men" (3:45). Dictatorship was clearly preferable.

48. Under Tiberius, "justice, equity, and industry, long buried in oblivion, have been restored to the state.... Rioting in the theater has been suppressed; all citizens have either been impressed with the wish to do right, or have been forced to do so by necessity" (Velleius Paterculus, *History of Rome*, 2:126). Later, Plutarch considers it significant that the Romans have numerous altars to Fortune, the god who has delivered countless military triumphs into their hands, but "they have no shrine of Wisdom or Prudence," or Mind or Reason, as do peoples who place value on persuasion (*The Fortune of the Romans*, 318).

accepted values," and will be encouraged, even as a matter of compulsion, by the powerful.[49]

I conclude from these brief examples that to continue seeking analogues to Paul's letters in the classical rhetorical handbooks, without giving sustained attention to the publicly acknowledged relationship between rhetorical patterns of persuasion and the coercive force inhering in slavery and empire, would be profoundly inattentive to the sources themselves.

Indeed, members of the Roman aristocracy spoke candidly enough among themselves regarding the clear, absolute, and necessary difference between those destined to rule and to be ruled.[50] In his discussion of "class struggle" in the Greco-Roman world "on the ideological plane," classical historian G. E. M. de Ste. Croix refers to

> the simplest form of psychological propaganda, which merely teaches the governed that they have no real option anyway but to submit; this tends to be intellectually uninteresting, however effective it may have been in practice, and consists merely of the threat of force. It was particularly common, of course, in its application to slaves.

Far more interesting to the historian was "the attempt of the dominant classes to persuade those they exploited to accept their oppressed condition without protest, if possible even to rejoice in it."[51] "In some cases," writes John H. Kautsky, "the exploitative relationship between aristocrat and peasant may be a brutally frank one.... However, that relationship can also be ideologically concealed by some concept of reciprocity," which functions to make the exploitation more acceptable to the peasantry and "to justify the aristocracy's rule in its own eyes."[52]

De Ste. Croix has shown that "the most common form" of imperialist propaganda was already well established in the ancient Greek world, namely, "that which seeks to persuade the poor that they are not really fitted to rule and that this is much better left to their 'betters.' " Plato had argued in the

---

49. Chaim Perelman and L. Olbrechts-Tyteca, *The New Rhetoric: A Treatise on Argumentation*, trans. John Wilkinson and Purcell Weaver (Notre Dame: University of Notre Dame Press, 1969), 55 (on "Argumentation and Violence").

50. Already Aristotle had found in the intimate coercion of slavery an apt metaphor for the political domination of empire: "Authority and subordination are conditions not only inevitable but also expedient; in some cases things are marked out from the moment of birth to rule or to be ruled" (*to archein kai archesthai, Politics* 1254a 22–24). Said observes that imperialism and colonialism "are supported and perhaps even impelled by impressive ideological formations that include notions that certain territories and people require and beseech domination": "notions about bringing civilization to primitive or barbaric peoples, the disturbingly familiar ideas about flogging or death or extended punishment being required when 'they' misbehaved or became rebellious, because 'they' mainly understood force or violence best; 'they' were not like 'us,' and for that reason deserved to be ruled" (Said, *Culture and Imperialism*, 8–9; xi). Noam Chomsky finds such sentiments regarding other peoples to be "the common coin of modern political and intellectual discourse" in the U.S. (*Deterring Democracy* [New York: Verso, 1994], 361).

51. De Ste. Croix, *Class Struggle*, 409.

52. Kautzky, *The Politics of Aristocratic Empires*, 110–11.

*Republic* that "ruling should be the prerogative of those who have the right kind of intellectual equipment and have received a proper philosophical education. In practice, needless to say, virtually all such men would be members of the propertied class."[53] A Roman imperialist like Cicero merely inherited the theme: "Do we not observe that dominion has been granted by Nature to everything that is best, to the great advantage of what is weak?" (*De re publica* 3:37). Romans like Cicero "did not concede that their subjects or dependents had any right to be free of Roman rule. Liberty was the privilege of the imperial people," and Jews and Syrians could be dismissed as "peoples born for slavery." During the Principate Virgil could similarly divide humanity "into two categories, those too insolent to accept [Rome's] god-given dominion, and those who submitted to it."[54] That applied to the Roman plebs as well, regarded by Nero's chief advisor as "this vast throng — discordant, factious, and unruly, ready to run riot alike for the destruction of itself and others" if it should break the yoke of empire (Seneca, *De Clementia* 1:1).

"The rhetoric of power all too easily produces an illusion of benevolence when deployed in an imperial setting," Said remarks.[55] The symbolism of benefaction in particular can function as an ideological concealment for the true exploitative nature prevailing between the aristocracy and the peasantry.[56] Cicero, for example, could declare that Roman taxation was primarily directed toward the benefit of the provincial population. To the frankly acknowledged combination of force and fortune that had brought Rome to the status of an imperial power, the Romans were eager to add a third factor, their own virtue. It was one of Cicero's favorite themes that Roman hegemony "was ordained by the gods, whose favor Rome had deserved by piety and justice"; the gods had implanted in the Roman people "a love of peace and tranquility which enable justice and good faith most easily to flourish." "Fortune and Virtue" had brought world hegemony to Rome, so that "it was by our scrupulous attention to religion and by our wise grasp of a single truth, that all things are ruled and directed by the will of the gods, that we have overcome all peoples and nations."[57]

Of course, successful colonization includes cultivating the acceptance of

---

53. De Ste. Croix, *Class Struggle*, 411.

54. Cicero, *De Provinciis consularibus* 10; see also Book 3 of *De re publica*; Brunt, "*Laus Imperii*," 183–84. See the full discussion of this *topos* in David Balch, *Let Wives Be Submissive: The Domestic Code in 1 Peter*, SBLMS 26 (Chico, Calif.: Scholars, 1981).

55. Said, *Culture and Imperialism*, xvii.

56. "The aristocrat's claim to provide benefits to the peasant probably serves the function of making the peasant's exploitation more acceptable to him so that he will pay his dues and perform his labor services more willingly and cause less trouble for his lord." But the relationship is not really reciprocal: "Even if the peasant does benefit from it, the provision of protection in return for his labor or taxes does not really involve a reciprocal relationship. Whereas the aristocrat is free to take or not to take the peasant's taxes, the peasant is not free to accept or reject the aristocrat's protection" (Kautsky, *The Politics of Aristocratic Empires*, 111–14).

57. Brunt, "*Laus Imperii*," 187; 165.

the colonial relationship among the colonized. De Ste. Croix observes that "Rome made sure that Greece was kept 'quiet' and friendly to her by ensuring that the cities were controlled by the wealthy class, which now had mainly given up any idea of resistance to Roman rule and in fact seems to have welcomed it for the most part, as an insurance against popular movements from below."[58] In essays in *Imperialism in the Ancient World* (1976), M. H. Crawford described the common interest shared by Greek and Roman aristocracies; he was hardly surprised to find the intellectual class in the provinces waxing eloquent on the inevitability of Roman rule.[59] And V. Nutton described a widespread "Beneficial Ideology," perpetuated by intellectuals in the provinces, hailing the "peace" and "security" Rome had established through military force. Provincials like Plutarch could revel in "the true freedom of the inhabitants of the Roman Empire, for an essential difference between it and other ancient empires is that the Romans govern free men, not slaves" (*Moralia* 814F). In another place Plutarch pretended to debate whether Virtue or Fortune had been more responsible for the Romans' sovereignty; the right answer, of course, was "both." Despite the evidence of Roman brutality ("the multitude of corpses and spoils"), Plutarch saw in Rome's dominion the sublime work of the gods: "For such a welding together of dominion and power," evidently Virtue and Fortune had "joined forces" and thus "cooperated in completing this most beautiful of human works" (*The Fortune of the Romans,* 316, 323).

As Nutton points out, through civic ritual and rhetoric, subject cities directed their energies "to preventing local disorder or at least restraining it lest the Romans be led to intervene"; the "concord" (*harmonia*) celebrated in the city square served "apotropaically to announce to the governor and the emperor that police action [was] unnecessary."[60]

The Romans secured their interests through an aristocracy in Judea as well, as Martin Goodman and Peter Richardson have recently made clear.[61] We should hardly be surprised, then, to find Roman benefaction echoing in some Jewish sources from the period, as in the aphorism attributed to the first-century Rabbi Hanina, "Pray for the welfare of the state, for were it not for the fear of it, we should have swallowed each other up alive" (*Avot* 3:2).

Josephus's *War* is merely the best example of the pattern, "the most

---

58. De Ste. Croix, *Class Struggle,* 344.

59. M. H. Crawford, "Greek Intellectuals and the Roman Aristocracy," in Garnsey and Whittaker, eds., *Imperialism in the Ancient World,* 193–207.

60. V. Nutton, "The Beneficial Ideology," in Garnsey and Whittaker, eds., *Imperialism in the Ancient World,* 212. On "harmony," or *homonôia,* speeches as background for 1 Corinthians see Margaret M. Mitchell, *Paul and the Rhetoric of Reconciliation: An Exegetical Investigation of the Language and Composition of 1 Corinthians* (Tübingen: Mohr [Siebeck], 1991), and Dale B. Martin, *The Corinthian Body* (New Haven: Yale University Press, 1995).

61. Martin Goodman, *The Ruling Class in Judaea: The Origins of the Jewish Revolt against Rome A.D. 66–70* (Cambridge: Cambridge University Press, 1987); Peter Richardson, *Herod the Great* (Columbia: University of South Carolina Press, 1996).

forthright expression of Jewish-Roman political accommodation known to us."[62] He is at pains at once to exonerate the Romans for the destruction of Judea and to describe Jerusalem as a hotbed of misguided insurrection on the part of Jews inadequately educated in their own traditions. The more authentic expression of Judaism, according to Josephus, involved recognizing that God had given the sovereignty of the world over to Rome, as the climactic speech from Herod Agrippa makes clear (*War* 2.345–404). Josephus even allows Agrippa to call his fellow Jews "those to whom thraldom is hereditary" (2.357). Echoing themes from Roman aristocrats and other provincial enthusiasts, Josephus could frankly declare that "the might of the Romans was irresistible," yet preferred to couch his counsel of submission in terms of "an established law" in the cosmos: " 'Yield to the stronger,' and 'The mastery is for those pre-eminent in arms.' " God was manifestly on the side of the Romans. But more, the Romans had proved, by their "reverence for the holy places of their enemies," to be more deserving of God's approval than the Jewish rebels occupying the Temple (*War* 5.363–68).

The Talmud preserves from the time of the Second Jewish Revolt a debate over the "benefits" of the Romans:

> "How splendid are the works of this people," declared Rabbi Judah; "they have built marketplaces, baths and bridges." . . . But Rabbi Simeon bar Yohai answered, "Everything they have made they have made only for themselves — marketplaces, for whores; baths, to wallow in; bridges, to levy tolls." (b. Shabbat 33b)

To be sure, as N. R. M. de Lange observes, the picture of empire in Jewish sources "is a complex one." But "between the two extremes of militant zealotry and fawning appeasement we must imagine a whole gamut of attitudes to Roman rule. Probably the majority of Jews grumblingly accepted the status quo. Belief in messianic redemption was not inherently incompatible with acceptance of Roman rule and even appreciation of its benefits."[63]

Such nuanced, "strategic" discourse is perhaps best illustrated in Philo, whose *Embassy to Gaius* both hails the benefits at first felt by the whole world after the emperor's accession (8–13), then goes on to detail the depredations of the "iron-hearted and utterly ruthless" tyrant. According to E. R. Goodenough, Philo provides, in his treatise *On Dreams*, "one of the most vital passages from ancient literature," one of the finest examples of what James C. Scott would later call a "hidden transcript." There Philo describes the caution and circumspection normally accorded the rulers who in other ways, Philo implies, appear as brutish as pack animals.[64]

---

62. Barclay, *Jews in the Mediterranean Diaspora*, 356.

63. N. R. M. de Lange, "Jewish Attitudes to the Roman Empire," in Garnsey and Whittaker, eds., *Imperialism in the Ancient World*, 262.

64. E. R. Goodenough, *An Introduction to Philo Judaeus*, 2d ed. (Oxford: Basil Blackwell,

Goodenough's work suggests we may find more evidence of "hidden transcripts" in Philo's work than previously imagined.[65] The point of this extended discussion, of course, is that achieving a thicker description of Jewish thought under Roman colonial pressures will allow us to appreciate similar nuances, either of accommodation or resistance, to those pressures in Paul's rhetoric as well. De Lange's remarks, quoted above, and Goodenough's observations regarding Philo of Alexandria suggest that we need not expect to find in Paul, or any other first-century Jew, a clear, consistent, univocal "pro-Roman" or "anti-Roman" posture,[66] but should look for more tenuous, situationally determined traces of his response to the pressures of Romanization. When we compare Paul with his contemporaries on these terms, we may find striking examples of antagonism not only to Hellenistic culture[67] but also to the propaganda and pretense of the Roman Empire itself.

## Which "Imperialism": Roman or Jewish?

Once we recognize the relevance of empire for reading Paul, how do these political aspects of his thought relate to the themes that have predominated in scholarship for so many centuries, Paul's theology of the Torah and of Israel?

In different ways, N. T. Wright and Robert Jewett have argued that Paul's theology addressed the covenant understanding of Israel's destiny under Roman imperialism. According to Wright, at the heart of Paul's theology is the apocalyptic question, "How shall God's justice be realized in a world dominated by evil powers?"[68] Paul's answer had everything to do with Israel's survival despite the hegemony of Rome. Jewett argues that, although Paul's hope for Israel's redemption (Rom. 11:26) was "not precisely fulfilled," nevertheless "some of the features of his program in Romans" — an "ethic of individual responsibility for the transformation of the secular world," for example — were embodied in the Jewish restoration after the catastrophic war of 66–70.[69]

In most Paul scholarship, however, the theological convention of reading Paul's theology as a critique of Jewish identity and practice remains almost

---

1962), 55–57. See my essay, "Romans 13:1–7 in the Context of Imperial Propaganda," in Horsley, ed., *Paul and Empire*, 184–204.

65. Goodenough's assessment is by no means universal; Frank H. Colson regarded *De Somniis* 2 as characterized by "a poverty of thought which makes it the weakest of the whole series" (*Philo* V, LCC [Cambridge: Harvard University Press, 1988], 433).

66. Literary traces of outright anti-Roman sedition may be few indeed; Josephus only allows faint echoes of "pompous panegyrics on liberty" as his pro-Roman protagonists set about to offer rebuttals (*War* 2.348, passim). We are most confident we are dealing with anti-Roman rhetoric in texts where "Rome" and "Romans" are not mentioned, except in properly biblical code — "Kittim," "Babylon," "Esau."

67. Barclay, *Jews in the Mediterranean Diaspora*, 381–95.

68. N. T. Wright, *The Climax of the Covenant: Christ and the Law in Pauline Theology* (Edinburgh: T. & T. Clark, 1991), 140–41.

69. Jewett, *Paul the Apostle to America*, 43.

overpowering. Wright, for example, persists in describing Paul's struggle against Israel's "meta-sin, the attempt to confine grace to race," to "treat the Torah as a charter of automatic national privilege."[70] In different ways, John Barclay and Daniel Boyarin regard Paul as an "anomalous" Jew, uniquely obsessed with the problem of a distinctive Jewish identity while his fellow Jews struggled to maintain that identity against Hellenizing and Romanizing pressures.[71] Decades ago Günther Bornkamm put this perspective in the starkest terms in his discussion of Romans: "Paul's opponent is not this or that section in a particular church, but the Jews and their understanding of salvation."[72]

F. C. Baur's dialectical reading of early Christian history posited a monolithic Jewish, and Jewish-Christian, front, including the Jerusalem apostles and Jewish Christians in Antioch and Galatia, against which Paul struggled throughout his apostolic career. That polarized reading, based on Paul's references to *Iudaismos* and the "traditions of the fathers" in Galatians 2, persists today, despite numerous efforts to correct it by pointing out the gentile identity of Paul's addressees and the broad agreement regarding circumcision that Paul shared with the Jerusalem apostles.[73]

S. R. F. Price and others have shown that first-century Asia Minor was characterized by an enthusiastic cultivation of emperor worship among the provincial elite. Romanization remained primarily an urban phenomenon, however, only beginning to penetrate into the countryside in Paul's day. Surely we can imagine that colonizing pressures would be experienced as a threat to native identity among non-elite residents of Asian cities and smaller towns. One likely response on the part of hard-pressed natives might be to want to affiliate, as quickly as possible, with an alternative ethnic identity that already enjoyed acceptance and considerable prestige in the empire, namely, Judaism. We should expect on this hypothesis precisely the sorts of behaviors that are reflected in Galatians: a rush on the part of former pagans (4:8) to be circumcised, for its value as a marker of ethnic identity (3:3; 5:2), and thus to avoid persecution (6:12; cf. 5:11); along with a reluctance to accept the full obedience to the Torah that any Jew would know circumcision required (5:3; 6:13). On these terms we could understand the Galatian controversy as the result of colonizing pressures and nativist counterpressures,

---

70. Wright, *The Climax of the Covenant*, 240–43, 248–51; for critiques see Fredriksen, "What You See Is What You Get," and Roetzel, "No 'Race of Israel' in Paul's Letters."

71. Barclay, *Jews in the Mediterranean Diaspora*, 381–95; Boyarin, *A Radical Jew*.

72. Günther Bornkamm, *Paul*, trans. D. M. G. Stalker (New York: Harper & Row, 1971), 95.

73. Johannes Munck's effort to concentrate attention on the gentile recipients of Galatians (*Paul and the Salvation of Mankind* [Atlanta: John Knox Press, 1977], 69–133) has been revived by Lloyd Gaston (*Paul and the Torah* [Vancouver: University of British Columbia Press, 1987]), but has won only limited acceptance. Baur's dialectical schema is given new life in a social-scientific commentary by Philip Esler, *Galatians* (Cambridge: Cambridge University Press, 1997).

rather than perpetuate a caricature of an aggressive and hypocritical Jewish proselytizing campaign as the necessary background to the letter.[74]

## A New Reading of Romans

As stated earlier, the scholarly preoccupation with Paul's supposed debate with Judaism tends to eclipse aspects of a more egalitarian social ethic, not least because of the perceived social conservatism in Romans, especially in 13:1–7. The view that Romans represents a summary of Paul's theology, and that his theology is developed there in fundamental contrast to Jewish thought, persists, for example, in James D. G. Dunn's magisterial volume  *The Theology of Paul the Apostle:*

> In the movement and dialogue of Paul's theologizing, his letter to the Romans is a relatively...fixed feature....It was written under prob-ably the most congenial circumstances of his mission, with time for careful reflection and composition. And, above all, it was clearly in-tended to set out and defend his own mature understanding of the gospel (1:16–17)....Romans is still far removed from a dogmatic or systematic treatise on theology, but it nevertheless is the most sustained and reflective statement of Paul's own theology by Paul himself.[75]

We have seen important alternative readings, however. In *A Rereading of Romans*, Stanley Stowers questioned the nearly ubiquitous tendency to import Jews or Jewish-Christian opponents into the interpretation of Paul's argument. The heart of the letter is Paul's appeal to the Romans to recognize his gospel as a means to achieve the goal of self-mastery that dominated first-century thinking in the Augustan age. Gerald Downing offered a similar reading of Romans as evidence for Paul's thorough acquaintance with and advocacy of Stoic and Cynic-like ethics.[76]

William S. Campbell, Mark Nanos, and Mark Reasoner have offered readings of the letter as Paul's confrontation with a Gentile-Christian ide-ology of supersession that denies the value of Jewish identity, an ideology linked to prevalent Roman views of the Jews as a subject people.[77] Although this context is widely recognized for Romans 11, the far more common in-terpretation today still reads the rest of the letter as Paul's defense of his law-free mission among Gentiles, over against Jewish "ethnocentrism" or

---

74. Gaston similarly attributes the Galatian legalism to "uncertainty" on the part of Gentiles (*Paul and the Torah*, 25).

75. James D. G. Dunn, *The Theology of Paul the Apostle* (Grand Rapids, Mich.: Eerdmans, 1998), 25.

76. Stowers, *A Rereading of Romans*, 21–33; F. Gerald Downing, *Cynics, Paul, and the Pauline Churches*, Cynics and Christian Origins II (London and New York: Routledge, 1998), 274–82.

77. Campbell, *Paul's Gospel in an Intercultural Context;* Nanos, *The Mystery of Romans,* 99–101; Mark Reasoner, *"Strong" and "Weak" in Romans 14–15* (Cambridge: Cambridge University Press, 1998).

"boasting" or "national righteousness." I have argued, as have others, that gentile Christian supersessionism is Paul's principal target in Romans.[78] Here it must suffice to offer a few exegetical observations suggesting that Paul's target is more closely connected with Roman imperialism than with any supposed Jewish "cultural imperialism."

First, Paul's declaration in 1:16, "I am not ashamed of the gospel: for it is the power of God unto salvation," is often read as the "thesis" of the letter, rather as if we were beginning an essay in dogmatics. But the declaration of shamelessness is a formal feature of the apology the faithful make before their impious accusers. We find it already in Socrates' defense before his fellow Athenians;[79] it sounds repeatedly from the lips of Jewish martyrs in this period.[80] The protest of innocence, of having nothing to put one to shame, is as frequent in Christian martyrologies.[81]

The contrast at the beginning of the letter is not between two ways of being righteous before God — through "faith" or through "works" (that contrast is not made until 3:20!) — but between the justice of God (*diakaiosune ton theou*, 1:17) and the utter injustice and impiety of human society (*adikia kai asébeia*, 1:18–32). Theologians of liberation have rightly seen that for Paul, as for Israel's prophets before him, social injustice, the desire to impose "dehumanized relations" on others, is the root of idolatry. Paul's concern is "the justice which the world and peoples and society . . . have been awaiting."[82] As we have seen, Georgi and Stowers argued that the most appropriate background for the indictment of wholesale human wickedness in Romans 1 is the vaunt of divine justice made by or on behalf of the Roman emperor. The poet propagandists of the Augustan principate hailed a "golden age," the banishing of War, the return of Faith and Justice to rule over the earth, the flourishing of Law and Right, a flood of piety — all embodied in the person of the Augustus, the *Sebastos* himself.[83] The theme of

---

78. Neil Elliott, *The Rhetoric of Romans: Argumentative Constraint and Strategy and Paul's "Dialogue with Judaism,"* JSNTSup 45 (Sheffield: JSOT Press, 1990); *Liberating Paul*, 73–75, 181–89, 214–26.

79. Meletus's accusations are "disgraceful" (*aischron*, Apology 24A); Socrates challenges an Athenian, "are you not ashamed" (*ouk aischynei*) to be careless regarding philosophy? (29D). He refuses to act disgracefully by pleading for his life (35A); at length, he declares he has been convicted on account of "lack of shamelessness" (*anaischyntias*, 38D).

80. When, in 4 Maccabees, the aged Eleazar defies Antiochus Epiphanes, he refuses to let his people or the Torah be put to shame (5:34–38); he renounces the "shamefulness" of submitting to the king (6:20). The youths whose martyrdoms follow refuse to put their ancestors to shame (9:23); the shame falls rather on the Greek king (12:11).

81. See Luise Schottroff, " 'Give to Caesar What Belongs to Caesar and to God What Belongs to God,' " in *The Love of Enemy and Nonretaliation in the New Testament,* ed. Willard M. Swartley (Louisville: Westminster/John Knox Press, 1992), 223–57.

82. José Porfirio Miranda, *Marx and the Bible: A Critique of the Philosophy of Oppression,* trans. John Eagleson (Maryknoll, N.Y.: Orbis, 1974), 160–79; Juan Luis Segundo, *The Humanistic Christology of Paul,* vol. 2 of *Jesus of Nazareth Yesterday and Today,* ed. and trans. John Drury (Maryknoll, N.Y.: Orbis, 1986), 28–29.

83. Georgi, *Theocracy;* Stowers, *A Rereading of Romans,* 52–58.

moral "self-mastery" which Stowers traces throughout Romans was a cornerstone of the Augustan reform — but note that it is also the philosophical theme of that script for resistance to empire, 4 Maccabees.[84]

Stowers notes that "Paul wrote Romans early in Nero's reign, when golden age ideology and hopes may have reached their highest peak since Augustus." No less than in Augustus's day, the "gospel" of the emperor's accession proclaimed the restoration of a "golden age," not only for the Roman people but for all peoples fortunate enough to be brought beneath the benevolent wings of empire. "Kindly Justice returns to the earth," hymns Calpurnius Siculus: "Peace in her fullness shall come"; the gods have brought "holy rites instead of war."[85] But as Stowers also shows, Roman propagandists were as concerned as any Jewish apocalyptist to lament the sinfulness of the age. "Full of sin, our age has defiled first the marriage bed, our offspring, and our homes," cried Horace, citing the new dances teenage girls are trying out as evidence that "the stream of disaster has overflowed both people and nation" (Third Ode). Even Virgil's buoyant Fourth Eclogue admits that although the final traces of Roman guilt shall vanish in the Augustan age, "some traces of ancient sin shall still survive" elsewhere, calling Romans forth to occasional wars of pacification. Paul's focus on sexually abusive behavior in Rom. 1:24–27 calls to mind the anxieties of Roman propagandists over the sexual machinations of women in the imperial household.[86]

These brief observations suffice to show that from its first chapter, the letter Paul directed to Rome is not a theological brief. It is a defiant indictment of the rampant injustice and impiety of the Roman "golden age." We know other similar repudiations of the empire's empty self-aggrandizement from Jewish and pagan sources.[87] The whole letter is structured around the contrast between the shameful deeds of the present dark age (1:18–32; 13:11–14), deeds of which Paul's readers are "now ashamed" (6:20–23),

---

84. Stowers, *A Rereading of Romans*, 124.

85. Calpurnius Siculus, *Bucolica*, and the *Einsiedeln Eclogues*, in *Minor Latin Poets*, trans. J. Wight Duff and Arnold M. Duff (Cambridge: Harvard University Press, 1954).

86. Velleius Paterculus, *History of Rome*, 2:99 (Julia); Tacitus, *Annals,* passim.

87. The bankruptcy of Rome's claims is a theme in other Jewish literature in the period, though usually expressed in code. In the *Commentary on Habakkuk* from Qumran, it is the "Kittim" who "march across the plain, smiting and plundering the cities of the earth"; they "inspire all the nations with fear. . . . All their evil plotting is done with intention and they deal with all the nations in cunning and guild" (1QpHab 3; Geza Vermes, *The Dead Sea Scrolls in English*, 3d ed. [New York: Penguin, 1987], 284). Genesis Rabban declares, "Just as a pig lies down and sticks out its hoofs as though to say 'I am clean,' so the evil empire robs and oppresses, while pretending to execute justice" (65:1); see N. R. M. de Lange, "Jewish Attitudes to the Roman Empire," in Garnsey and Whittaker, eds., *Imperialism in the Ancient World*, chap. 12.

The theme is also expressed in "pagan" literature. The Roman historian Tacitus provides a compelling anti-Roman speech on the lips of the Briton chieftain Calgacus: "to plunder, butcher, steal, these things [the Romans] misname empire; they make a desolation and call it peace" (*Histories* 4:17:2).

and the holiness and sobriety that is now possible "in the Spirit" (6:15–19; 8:4–17; 12:1–2). Victor Paul Furnish showed decades ago that the contrast between former shameful living and the new life in Christ, the "once — but now scheme" of early Christian preaching, gives the letter its underlying structure. His case is strengthened by Halvor Moxnes's observation that the contrast of honor and shame language is more pervasive than "justification" language in structuring the letter.[88]

I suggest that we have here the key to the coherence of Paul's argument in Romans: He seeks to move his gentile Christian readers away from a theological "boast" over a vanquished Israel (11:13–32) to the "sober judgment" (*sophrosune,* 12:3) that governs chapters 12–15.

Within these chapters lies the notorious passage 13:1–7, which threatens to shipwreck any but a politically conservative reading of the letter, and indeed of Paul's theology. These verses cannot be excised as an interpolation,[89] although as several scholars observed decades ago, tensions here resist harmonization with Paul's theology more broadly, and preclude generalization as Paul's "theology of the state."[90] When we recall Roman and provincial discussions, so prevalent in Paul's day, regarding public control through consent and coercion,[91] it must seem significant that Paul both describes ruling authorities as "God's ministers" and "servants" (13:4, 6), in no way a "ter-

---

88. Victor Paul Furnish, *Theology and Ethics in Paul* (Nashville: Abingdon, 1968), 105–6; Moxnes, "Honor and Righteousness"; "Honor, Shame."

89. Leander E. Keck offers an important warning to interpreters of 13:1–7: "What Makes Romans Tick?" in *Pauline Theology III: Romans,* ed. David M. Hay and E. Elizabeth Johnson (Minneapolis: Fortress Press, 1995), 3–29.

90. Ernst Käsemann, "Principles on the Interpretation of Romans 13," in *New Testament Questions of Today,* trans. W. J. Montague (Philadelphia: Fortress, 1969), 212–13; James Kallas, "Romans XIII.1–7: An Interpolation," *NTS* 11 (1964–5): 365–74; J. C. O'Neill, *Paul's Letter to the Romans* (London: Penguin, 1975), 209ff.

91. Perelman and Olbrechts-Tyteca observe that "the use of argumentation implies that one has renounced resorting to force alone," and that "recourse to argumentation assumes the establishment of a community of minds which, while it lasts, excludes the use of violence" (*The New Rhetoric,* 55). As the previously discussed extracts from Cicero show, however, within the context of imperialism, persuasive speech remains the prerogative of the ruling class, alongside other forms of political coercion, including overt violence. (See also Noam Chomsky's discussion of "Force and Opinion" in his analysis of modern (U.S.) imperialism: *Deterring Democracy* [New York: Hill and Wang, 1992], chap. 12.)

Jewish provincials could observe the relationship between persuasion and coercive force, but only in order to contrast them. Thus the Jewish heroes of 4 Maccabees repeatedly defy the coercive "appeals" of the Greek tyrant, while confessing their being "persuaded" by Torah. Both Philo and Josephus mark the difference between the Jewish *politeuma* of persuasion and government by force: thus, Philo contends, Moses resisted the temptation of "issuing orders without words of exhortation, as though to slaves instead of free men," which "savored of tyranny and despotism." Therefore "in his commands and prohibitions he suggests and admonishes rather than commands," with laws written "in order to exhort rather than to enforce" (*De Vita Mosis* 2:49–51). The same theme appears in Josephus's apology *Against Apion:* Moses, rather than creating a monarchy or an oligarchy, created a theocracy based upon persuasion, setting in supreme position the priests, "pre-eminently gifted with persuasive eloquence and discretion." The result is that each Jew is "firmly persuaded" personally to be willing "to brave all manner of suffering rather than to utter a single word against the Law" (2:164–67, 186–87, 218–19).

ror to good conduct" (13:3), and warns the Roman Christians to "submit" to them (13:2), not to oppose them, invoking the threat of the not-so-idle sword (13:4). To "conscience" Paul adds the fear of "wrath" as a motive for obedience; both honor and "fear" are due the authorities. These tensions suggest that Rom. 13:1–7 may be another example of the sort of cautious "hidden transcript" that we observed in Philo as well.[92]

The "boast" Paul opposes within Roman gentile Christianity is not a narrowly theological phenomenon; it coincides with more widespread currents of anti-Jewish prejudice in Rome, prejudice fueled by riots and disturbances in Alexandria, Palestine, and Rome itself.[93] It is no mere flourish when Paul construes the rhetorical situation as the opposition of two forms of worship: the shameful idolatry of the Roman world (1:18–32), which is at its root the surrender of one's body to the power of sin and injustice (6:12–20), and the "rational worship" *logike latreia* (12:1) practiced by Christians as they present their bodies for God's justice (6:19). Paul presents himself in Romans in sacerdotal terms: he introduces himself (in 1:9) as one who performs sacred service to God *latreuo;* at last (15:14–16) he sums up his "bold" exhortation to the Romans as his "priestly service of the gospel of God," the "offering up" of holy persons (*ierourgeia; prosphopa*). As William Cavanaugh has pointed out in a profound discussion of Paul's "body of Christ" language in the context of the modern torture state, Paul's language demobilizes Christians from the worship of Roman gods (the much-vaunted *eusebeia* of imperial rhetoric, *asebeia* to Paul) and enlists them in the spiritual worship of the God who raised Jesus from the dead.[94] The letter to the Romans is nothing less than a direct challenge to the ritual and ceremony of empire.

These remarks hardly exhaust the significance of imperialism for the study of ancient rhetoric. They may point us toward a program, however, in which "taking empire seriously" includes setting Paul's letters in the context of imperial propaganda and panegyric, and the voices of demurral and submission, or discontent and resistance, raised against it by Paul's Jewish contemporaries. The result may be a dramatically new appreciation of Paul.[95]

---

92. I have pursued this suggestion further in "Romans 13:1–7 in the Context of Imperial Ideology."

93. John G. Gager, *The Origins of Anti-Semitism* (New York: Oxford University Press, 1981), 63–88; Nanos, *The Mystery of Romans*, 99–101; Elliott, *Liberating Paul*, 215–16.

94. See William Cavanaugh, *Torture and Eucharist* (London: Blackwell, 1998).

95. I am grateful for the comments of fellow scholars at a session of the Pauline Epistles Section at the 1996 annual meeting of the Society of Biblical Literature, at which an earlier form of this essay was read. I am particularly grateful to Robert Jewett, Allen Callahan, and Elisabeth Schüssler Fiorenza, my fellow panelists at this session, and to Richard A. Horsley, who conceived and organized it.

# 2

# PAUL AND THE POLITICS OF INTERPRETATION

*Elisabeth Schüssler Fiorenza*

⌐⌐⌐⌐⌐⌐⌐⌐⌐⌐

K RISTER STENDAHL at one point made an ingenious proposal for a "Department of Public Health" in biblical studies. My own work has
sought to heed his call and to develop his proposal, albeit from a quite
different social location and theoretical perspective. I will first outline a
rhetorics of inquiry and ethics of interpretation as an interdisciplinary field
of study that can investigate the "public health" aspects of biblical writings.
In a second step I will discuss the noxious "public health" problem caused
by the rhetorics of "othering" inscribed in Pauline writings.

To further exemplify such an ethics of interpretation that investigates the
"public health" aspects of biblical texts and interpretations, a third step will
explore one of the most promising directions in Pauline studies, the political analysis of Paul's writings. It seems the hermeneutics of identification
continues to determine Pauline interpretation, even within this emerging political paradigm stressing the imperial context of Paul. Finally, I will discuss
the political hermeneutics of *ekklēsia* as an alternative strategy and matrix
for both exegetical and interpretive readings of Paul's letters.

## The Ethics of Interpretation

In a very significant but not well-known article on "Ancient Scripture in the
Modern World," Stendahl pointed out that biblical scholars and theologians
are usually seen as "sales people" who "often rightly speak about the good
wares we have." Instead of developing this "sales people" approach in defense of the Bible, he called on the basis of his own experience for a public
health department of biblical studies:

> A few years ago, when I was in Germany for some discussions, a
> woman who had seen my bibliography asked me a question about
> something to which I had never given much thought. She said: "I

looked at your bibliography, and it seems that there are two things you are constantly mentioning, constantly thinking about, and constantly writing about — women and Jews. How come? And what do women and Jews have in common for a New Testament scholar?"[1]

Stendahl observed that this question was not so difficult to answer:

> From a New Testament scholar's point of view, these are two rather striking issues on which the Christian tradition, and in the case of women, the whole scriptural tradition has had a clearly detrimental and dangerous effect. There is no question that the way the New Testament material speaks about Judaism contains within itself the seeds of much anti-Judaism; and that the male community has found aid and comfort in its chauvinism in the name of the Bible is relatively easy to document in western culture. (204)

Stendahl goes on to say that he began then to understand his teaching situation in terms of what he called the "Public Health Department." Using a metaphor from atomic power he insisted that biblical interpretation must be concerned with an interpretation of the scriptures that does not produce "a harmful fallout":

> I have come to believe that the problem calls for frontal attention to what I have called the public health aspect of interpretation. How does the church live with the Bible without undesirable effects? I would guess that the last racists in this country, if there ever be an end to such, will be the ones with Bible in hand. There never has been an evil cause in the world that has not become more evil if it has been possible to argue it on biblical grounds. (205)

Stendahl considered the public health aspect of biblical interpretation to be the task of "application" (205), since he subscribed to a hermeneutical model that subsequently has been (mis)used to strengthen scientistic interpretation. His famous article on biblical theology in which he spelled out his hermeneutical program conceptualized interpretation as divided into descriptive exegesis and relevant application.[2] Yet, whereas in his earlier presentation of this hermeneutical model scientific exegesis had the task of exegetical-historical description, he argued later in his 1982 contribution that "applied" theology had to be concerned not only with "sales," that is, persuasion, but also with "public health," that is, with a critical analysis of the consequences of biblical texts and discourses.

---

1. Krister Stendahl, "Ancient Scripture in the Modern World," in *Scripture in the Jewish and Christian Traditions: Authority, Interpretation, Relevance*, ed. Frederick E. Greenspahn (Nashville: Abingdon Press, 1982), 204. Subsequent page references appear in the text.

2. Krister Stendahl, "Biblical Theology, Contemporary," in *Interpreter's Dictionary of the Bible*, vol. 1, ed. G. A. Buttrick (Nashville: Abingdon Press, 1962), 418–32.

However, Stendahl's proposal for a "public health" inquiry did not explicitly address the new liberationist voices in biblical studies, theology, and ethics such as African American or black, feminist, or Latin American, African, Asian, and Jewish liberation theologies which were emerging in the 1970s on the academic scene, voices that are crucial to the work of the Paul and Politics Group of the SBL. If he had done so, he might have been challenged to question the hermeneutical model that he had proposed twenty years earlier.

More recently, Gerd Theissen, albeit in a German-European context, has addressed the hermeneutical problem posed by such liberationist approaches. He proposes a division between scientific exegesis (e.g., textual criticism, historical-critical, linguistic, intertextual, literary critical, social-scientific, archaeological methods as well as the history of interpretation), engaged reading forms (*engagierte Lektüreformen;* e.g., existential, depth-psychological, materialist, feminist, Latin American, Jewish interpretation), and practical communicative forms (e.g., preaching, meditation, art, bibliodrama, interactional Bible study, narrative exegesis, dance and music).

According to Theissen the scientific methods of exegesis are disinterested and *applikationsfern* in contrast to the engaged reading methods whose expressed goal supposedly is application. The practical forms in turn, according to Theissen, have the function to mediate both scientific and engaged forms of interpretation. Despite its good intentions, this proposal relegates the "engaged hermeneutical approaches" to the nonscientific realm and thereby reinscribes the prevalent prejudice that considers them unscientific. He thus privileges the positivist model of academic interpretation as the only "scientific" one.[3]

In contrast to such a separation of scientific exegesis and interpretation on the one hand and practical application and communication on the other, I have sought to develop Stendahl's proposal for a public health department by reconceptualizing biblical studies as a rhetoric of inquiry and ethics of interpretation. To envision the rhetoric and ethic of interpretation as a new interdisciplinary area of biblical studies aims to overcome the constructed dichotomy between engaged scholarship (e.g., feminist, postcolonial, African American, queer, and other subdisciplines) and "scientific" malestream interpretation.[4] Whereas the former allegedly utilizes ethical criteria, the latter is said to live up to a scientific ethos that gives precedence to cognitive criteria. I would argue, however, that a truly scientific ethos demands both ethical and cognitive criteria, theory and practice, which must be reasoned out in

---

3. Gerd Theissen, "Methodenkonkurrenz und hermeneutischer Konflikt: Pluralismus in Exegese und Lektüre der Bibel," in *Pluralismus und Identität,* ed. Joachim Mehlhausen (Gütersloh: Chr. Kaiser Gütersloher Verlagshaus, 1995), 127–40.

4. I have taken over the expression "malestream" from feminist theorists. It is not a pejorative but a descriptive term, since most of our cultural and religious texts, traditions, and institutions have been and are still determined by elite (white) men.

terms of intersubjectively understandable and communicable knowledge. To split off rationality from ethic and praxis opens the door for irresponsible scholarship that can nevertheless from a subjective point of view be quite ethical.

As an intellectual discipline the ethics of interpretation must be distinguished from the ethics of a text, for example, the ethics of Paul or of the Christian (New) Testament on the whole. In my view a Christian Testament (CT) ethics has the task to investigate and systematize the ethical or moral contents of biblical writings. The ethics of interpretation, in turn, is a second-order reflection both on biblical writings and on the ethos and morals of biblical studies. "Ethics" is understood here in the general sense as "morality rendered self-conscious" whereby morality names a "pervasive and often only partly conscious set of value-laden dispositions, inclinations, attitudes, and habits."[5]

Thus the "ethics of interpretation" is best understood as a critical scientific rather than as a positivistic scientist metatheory. As a new interdisciplinary area of critical reflexivity and research, the ethics of interpretation studies the "pervasive and often only partly conscious set of value-laden dispositions, inclinations, attitudes and habits" of biblical studies as an academic discipline. Such a critical exploration of the ethos and morality of biblical scholarship, or of what it means to work scientifically and ethically, has as its goal scholarly responsibility and accountability as an integral part of the research process. In other words, the ethics of interpretation seeks to articulate a professional ethics for biblical studies.

Since I understand my work as a part of this direction, I am interested here in refining rather than debunking the scientific program of biblical studies. Whereas in my book *Rhetoric and Ethic* I have explored the implications of the ethics of interpretation for biblical theology, here I want to demonstrate the significance of a "public health" inquiry for the hermeneutics of Paul's writings and I will do so by focusing on the rhetorical practices and hermeneutical assumptions at work in Pauline scholarship.[6]

It was Krister Stendahl who was in the forefront of inaugurating a paradigm shift in Pauline studies in the 1960s. In his landmark paper, "The Apostle Paul and the Introspective Conscience of the West," Stendahl exposed the Augustinian and Lutheran interpretive tradition that focused on individual conscience and conceived of Paul as the first great Christian theologian over and against Judaism.[7] Whereas Paul's concern was the in-

---

5. Wayne A. Meeks, *The Origins of Christian Morality: The First Two Centuries* (New Haven: Yale University Press, 1993), 4.

6. Elisabeth Schüssler Fiorenza, *Rhetoric and Ethic: The Politics of Biblical Studies* (Minneapolis: Fortress Press, 1999).

7. Krister Stendahl, "The Apostle Paul and the Introspective Conscience of the West," *HTR* 56 (1963): 199–215; reprinted in Stendahl, *Paul among Jews and Gentiles, and Other Essays* (Philadelphia: Fortress Press, 1974), 78–96.

clusion of Gentiles in the messianic community, later Western exegesis was concerned with the existential question: "How can I find a gracious G*d?"

This European-Lutheran reading of Paul, which was individualistic and often anti-Jewish, Stendahl argued, must give way to a reading of Paul that understands him more as a Jewish rather than as an anti-Jewish Christian theologian who was more concerned with salvation history than with individual sin and salvation. Contemporary scholarship understands Paul as a great early Christian theologian who was wrestling with heterogeneous social groups and religiopolitical directions and was seeking a way of survival for "his" communities exposed to the death-dealing powers of Roman imperialism.

While Stendahl's paper was written as an address to the American Psychological Association and emphasized salvation history as an alternative hermeneutical framework, Pauline scholars today utilize sociology, anthropology, and ethnography to illuminate Paul's writings. Social world studies have argued that the situation of Paul's communities was not like an American public square where different Christian confessions have built their churches side by side but must be imagined as being much more similar to social movements or religious sects (e.g., John Gager, Douglas Meeks, and Robin Scroggs).

Cultural and literary studies, in turn, have highlighted the social metaphors and symbolic universe constructed by Paul rather than seeking to reduce them to essentialist theological statements (e.g., Norman Peterson, Dale Martin). Others have underscored the formal rhetorics of Paul's correspondence but have often done so in terms of the classical rhetorical textbooks (H. D. Betz, Margaret Mitchell) rather than in an ideology-critical fashion (Elizabeth Castelli, Cynthia Briggs Kittredge).

Moreover, liberationist scholars have underscored the oppressive as well as the liberative aspects of Paul's rhetoric. Feminist and postcolonial scholars in turn have pointed to the ideological deformations of Pauline texts that are often reinscribed by malestream Pauline scholarship. Political historical studies (Richard Horsley) and political theology (Jacob Taubes) stress the importance of Roman imperialism and Jewish messianism as the context of Paul's writings.

However, a full paradigm shift from an individualistic Euro-American malestream framework of interpretation to a fully political and communal paradigm of Pauline studies has not yet been accomplished. The reason for this, I suggest, is the hegemonic politics of interpretation. The rhetoric of Pauline interpreters continues not only to identify themselves with Paul but also to see Paul as identical with "his" communities, postulating that Paul was the powerful creator and unquestioned leader of the communities to whom he writes.

The difference such a paradigm shift to the political study of Paul would make comes to the fore when one engages a rhetoric of inquiry for examining the noxious effects of the hegemonic politics of Pauline studies. Constitutive elements of such a malestream rhetorics and politics of inquiry are the politics of otherness and othering, and its tendencies of marginalization and vilification, and the politics and logics of identity and identification.

## The Pauline Politics of "Othering"

One of the negative legacies of Pauline discourse is its inscribed politics of "othering." Such a politics and rhetorics of othering establishes identity either by declaring the difference of the other as the same or by vilifying and idealizing difference as otherness.[8] It justifies relationships of ruling[9] by obfuscating structures of domination and subordination as "naturalized" differences. Hence, this politics of othering can be changed only when it is understood not as a universal transcultural binary structure or given revelation but as a historical political practice.

The politics of othering and vilification permeates the discourses of Paul himself,[10] as scholarship on the so-called opponents of Paul's diverse letters indicates. Its relentless othering engenders the strategies of marginalization and silencing that are inscribed in the Pauline text and reinscribed by contemporary exegetical and theological scholarship. Not just religious studies but all modern theories of political and moral life are shot through with the politics of othering, that is, with ideologies of sexism, colonialism and racism, the systems and discourses of marginalization, vilification, and dehumanization.

This politics of othering is indebted to the classic anti-democratic discourses of Plato and Aristotle, as well as those of modern democratic philosophers such as Locke, Hobbes, Rousseau, and Hegel, which position the "civic public" and the "impartial and universal point of view of normative reason" as opposite to the private realm that encompasses the family as the domain of women, of "the body, affectivity and desire."[11] Hence, it is important that Pauline scholarship is aware of these theoretical discourses when investigating Paul's rhetorics.

Ancient and modern Western philosophies have developed such a "politics and rhetorics of otherness"[12] that justifies why not all members of the

---

8. Cf. Sandra Lee Bartky, *Femininity and Domination: Studies in the Phenomenology of Oppression* (New York: Routledge, 1990).

9. For this expression see Dorothy E. Smith, *The Conceptual Practices of Power: A Feminist Sociology of Knowledge* (Boston: Northeastern University Press, 1990).

10. For instance, one needs only to read the invectives of Paul against those with whom he disagrees in Galatians or Philippians.

11. Iris Marion Young, "Impartiality and the Civic Public: Some Implications of the Feminist Critiques of Moral and Political Theory," in *Feminism as Critique*, ed. Seyla Benhabib and Drucilla Cornell (Minneapolis: University of Minnesota Press, 1985), 59. Kathleen Jones, *Compassionate Authority: Democracy and the Representation of Wo/men* (New York: Routledge, 1993).

12. For the development of the "political philosophy of otherness" as legitimizing patriar-

*polis* but only certain men can claim the rights of citizens, participate in democratic government, or deliberate in public. In its classic form this politics of othering is rooted in the practices of the andro-social Greek *polis*, its political-philosophical subtext is democracy, and its social formation is patriarchy or, in my terms, kyriarchy, that is, the governing dominance or supremacy of elite propertied men. The exclusion from democratic government of free-born propertied women, poor women and men, slave women and men, as well as barbarian women and men required ideological justifications. It needed to be argued why only free-born propertied Greek male heads of households could be full citizens if, as the Sophists maintained, all are equal by nature.[13]

The articulation of dualisms, such as human-animal, male-female, slave-free, native-alien, and the assertion of the "natural" inferiority of free-born women as well as slave women and men are ideological constructs that reproduce the politics of otherness in the various historical mutations of Western capitalist kyriarchy. They were reproduced in the discourses of political philosophy at the emergence of modern democracy, which advocated the Enlightenment construction of the "Man of Reason,"[14] and in colonialist rationalizations of racism. This Western political and philosophical rhetorics of otherness masks the oppressive relations of domination and exclusion in systemic patrikyriarchy. However, it must be recognized that this politics of othering does not elaborate generic man but rather the imperial Sovereign-Father or in black idiom, the Boss-Man, as the universal subject. Its totalizing discourse of male-female dualism masks the complex interstructuring of systems of exploitation and dehumanization in the kyriarchal domination of Western societies and religions.

This Western "politics of identity" and "rhetorics of othering" establishes identity either by comparison to the other as an inferior "same" or by emphasizing and stereotyping difference as the otherness of the other.[15] Such differences are established as "relationships of ruling,"[16] in which structures of domination and subordination are mystified as "naturalized" or "revealed" differences. This "politics of otherness" has found its way into the canon of Christian scriptures and permeates theological discourse in general and Pauline writings and their contemporary interpretations in particular.

It is no accident, therefore, that the majority of scholars have followed

---

chal societal structures of domination in antiquity, cf. Susan Moller Okin, *Women in Western Political Thought* (Princeton: Princeton University Press, 1979), 15–98; Elizabeth V. Spelman, *Inessential Woman: Problems of Exclusion in Feminist Thought* (Boston: Beacon Press, 1988), 19–56; and especially Page DuBois, *Centaurs and Amazons: Women and the Pre-History of the Great Chain of Being* (Ann Arbor: University of Michigan Press, 1982).

13. DuBois, *Centaurs and Amazons.*

14. Genevieve Lloyd, *The Man of Reason: Male and Female in Western Philosophy* (Minneapolis: University of Minnesota Press, 1984).

15. Cf. Bartky, *Femininity and Domination.*

16. For this expression see Smith, *Conceptual Practices of Power.*

Paul's example in reconstructing his arguments as "normative" over and against Paul's so-called Gnostic, libertine, or Jewish legalistic "opponents." Exegetical discourses continue to understand the Pauline writings either theologically, as documents of inner Christian struggles between orthodoxy and heresy, or they read them sociologically as records of opposing sectarian groups that are defined in contrast to the malestream church. In both instances, scholars valorize canonical voices as right and true but vilify their submerged alternative arguments as false and heretical.

In other words, the scholarly discourses on Paul's politics of meaning construct a series of dualistic religious, cultural, and political oppositions such as orthodoxy-heresy, apostle-community, honor-shame, mission-propaganda, and theology of the cross–libertine enthusiasm rather than underscoring that they are theological arguments over meaning and interpretation. This series of dualisms privileges the first terms of the opposition by reserving them either for Paul, orthodoxy, or Christianity on the whole and constructs the second terms as negative "other" by attributing them either to the opponents, to Hellenistic propagandists, to Jewish legalists, or to other outsider groups. Such interpretive dualistic oppositions muddle and play down the linking and connecting terms such as "audience, community, gospel" by subsuming them under either pole of the opposition rather than seeing them as a possibility for overcoming the argumentative dualism constructed by Paul.

The most telling dualistic construct is that of gender, which is already inscribed in the Pauline letters insofar as Paul understands himself as the "father" of the Corinthian community who is to present the community "as a pure bride to her one husband," Christ (2 Cor. 11:2–3). This gendering of the community has negative overtones since it is connected with a reference to the seduction of Eve. Such a symbolic construct of gender dualism at once coheres in and undermines the other dualistic oppositions insofar as it casts all speaking subjects (Paul, the opponents, contemporary interpreters, and so on) as masculine and construes their audience (the Corinthian community, Judaism, or contemporary readers, etc.) in feminine terms as passive, immature, and gullible.

## Pauline Studies and Its Politics of Meaning

Such an essentializing politics of othering, I suggest, also informs the politics of identification that reinscribes malestream relations of privilege and orthodox relations of exclusion by inviting readerly identification with Paul and his arguments. Such an identification with Paul's theological rhetoric, for example, with that of his fatherly authority allows ecclesial and academic "fathers" to claim Paul's authority for themselves. Moreover, by stressing an unbridgeable gulf between the past and the present, between Paul and himself, the exegete occludes the fact that Paul's meanings are present only in and through the words of interpreters. Thereby he, and it is still mostly

a he, surreptitiously claims Paul's theological authority for his own interpretation. Such a rhetoric of identification achieves its aim both by claiming
scientific authority for its own interpretations and by disqualifying the others
as biased, ideological, or as reading their own interests into the text.

Moreover, the rhetoric of radical difference between past and present
invigorates the rhetoric of identification insofar as it serves to construct
sameness between Paul and "his" communities.[17] It does so by identifying
Paul's discourses with those of the communities to whom he writes and
thereby suppressing and eradicating the historical voices and multiplex visions that differ from Paul's. Moreover, insofar as historical-critical studies
see Pauline texts and their arguments, that is, the rhetorical situation construed by Paul, as identical with the actual historical-rhetorical situation,
they obscure not only the difference between Paul's theological rhetoric and
that of his contemporary interpreters but also the rhetoric of early Christian
communities that Paul's text may misrepresent or silence.

By paying close attention to the rhetorics and politics of identification,
I argue, a "public health" approach to biblical studies is able to investigate the politics of meaning of Pauline discourses and to contribute to
the broader articulation of a political criticism in Pauline studies. Studies that read the Pauline discourses in political terms and understand their
rhetorical-historical situation as one determined by Roman imperial power
and violence lend themselves to such an investigation.

Obviously, I am not interested in undermining the political interpretive
paradigm by pointing out that it continues to be caught up in the politics of
identification. Rather, I am interested in showing what an ideology-critical
rhetorical analysis of the Pauline politics of meaning could contribute to the
fashioning of Pauline studies as political inquiry that is able to investigate
the "public health" aspects of Pauline discourses. In short, I am interested
in exploring how Pauline studies and their politics of meaning would benefit
from a critical rhetorical inquiry into the "public health" aspects of Pauline
discourses if they were to engage a hermeneutics of *ekklēsia* that can make
visible the limitations and possibilities of Pauline discourses.

If I single out the work of Richard Horsley and Neil Elliott, specifically
their contributions to the collection of essays *Paul and Empire*, I do so
because both scholars have pioneered Pauline studies as concerned with
political realities. As Horsley observes, "Since so little attention has been
devoted to the Roman imperial context of Paul's mission and his relations to
it, we are only at the point of attempting to formulate appropriate questions
and provisional research strategies."[18]

---

17. For an exploration of sameness and difference in Pauline interpretation see the intriguing
work of Elizabeth Castelli, *Imitating Paul: A Discourse of Power* (Louisville: Westminster/John
Knox Press, 1991), who utilizes Michel Foucault's theoretical framework for her analysis.

18. Richard A. Horsley, ed., *Paul and Empire: Religion and Power in Roman Imperial
Society* (Harrisburg, Pa.: Trinity Press International, 1997), 3.

Hence, I believe it is justified now to critically explore the politics of meaning and research strategies constituting this new field of study. Such an intervention seems to be called for because this new area of political biblical investigation is in danger of being conceptualized again in terms of "Paul's mission" and his "basic agenda," which is easily understood in terms of a rhetorics of othering and identification. My critical intervention has two goals. On the one hand I want to challenge hermeneutical approaches that focus primarily on Paul's rhetoric and not also on that of the different voices of *ekklēsia*. On the other hand, I hope to demonstrate how a "public health" investigation in Pauline studies has to be operative not just on the level of application but especially also on the level of critical exegesis and its processes of meaning production.

In his "1 Corinthians: A Case Study of Paul's Assembly as an Alternative Society," Horsley claims that in recent debates on Paul's injunctions to wo/men and slaves "little attention has been given to the wider horizon within which Paul understands the assembly's struggles," that is, the theological frame of crucifixion and resurrection or "to Paul's adamant opposition to Roman imperial society," that is, the political frame of Roman imperialism. He then goes on to show how "at certain points in 1 Corinthians Paul articulates ways in which the assembly of saints is to constitute a community of a new society alternative to the dominant imperial society."[19]

*First:* The picture that emerges from 1 Corinthians, Horsley argues, is not "one of a religious cult, but of a nascent social movement comprised of a network of cells" (245).

*Second:* According to Horsley, Paul not only urges group solidarity but also insists that the community is to be completely autonomous and independent of the "world." Hence, it should "maintain its ethical purity and group discipline" as well as "absolute independence from the established courts" (246).

*Third:* In Horsley's view the sharing of "food offered to idols" was for Paul not a question of ethics. Rather, for him the integrity and survival of the *ekklēsia* "as an exclusive community to the dominant society and its social networks" was at stake (248–49).

*Fourth:* Horsley points to Paul's refusal of support from the patronage of the community as an indication that Paul believed that "his assembly(ies) should embody economic relations dramatically different from those in Roman imperial society" (249). However, Paul was not able to develop an alternative economic vision for this alternative society.

*Fifth:* Horsley stresses that the collection for the poor is an economic aspect that is probably unique and without precedence in Greco-Roman

---

19. Horsley, "1 Corinthians: A Case Study of Paul's Assembly as an Alternative Society," in ibid., 242–52 (subsequent references appear in the text).

society. Paul used it as a tool to "maintain their solidarity as an exclusive community that stands against the larger society" (252).

Horsley's reading of the rhetorics of Paul in 1 Corinthians, which despite its contrary intentions tends to reinscribe the preconstructed opposition between community and world, is very perceptive and persuasive.[20] However, even if one agrees with it, one must point out that his analysis eschews asking the critical questions as to the ideological underpinnings of Paul's arguments and their implications for the "public health" aspects of the letter. In other words, rather than reinscribing Paul's dualistic arguments, an ethics of interpretation is called for that is able to critically question the politics of meaning that is produced in the process of interpretation.

Although Horsley is very much aware of the questions raised by feminist and postcolonial interpretations and seeks to heed their critical rhetorical and ideological analyses of Pauline discourses,[21] he nevertheless tends to focus on the rhetorics of Paul. Although much more than other scholars he seeks to allow for a critical intervention of the voices of the *ekklēsia* to which the letter was addressed, because of his focus on Paul's rhetoric, he does not always point out how Paul's rhetoric seeks to maintain his own authority by engaging the rhetorics of othering, censure, vituperation, exclusion, vilification, and even violence toward the community. Hence, Paul's politics of meaning often seems not very different from the hegemonic discourses of domination and empire, albeit it does not (yet) have the underpinnings of state power.

I want to stress, again, that I am not interested here in disagreeing with Horsley. Rather, because we are in agreement, I want to point out that a second step of critical reflection is necessary which explicitly moves to a metalevel discussion and ideology-critical examination of the interpretive frameworks and scholarly rhetorics that foster a hermeneutics of identification with Paul. Such an examination must critically interrogate the values and power relations that are inscribed not only in Pauline texts and but also in their interpretations. Before one can claim that Paul's politics of meaning is anti-imperial and that it advocates an alternative society, one needs to critically interrogate its rhetorical power as to how much it is reinscribing the authoritarian kyriarchal (imperial) discourse.

If one focuses on the marginal and powerless, such as slaves and wo/men, one is no longer able to argue that Paul's rhetoric calls into question rather than reinscribes the social values and dominant relations of Greco-Roman imperialism. It seems to me the case for Paul's anti-imperialism can only

---

20. See also Horsley's commentary on *1 Corinthians*, Abingdon NT Commentaries (Nashville: Abingdon Press, 1998), in which he reconstructs the voices in the Corinthian *ekklēsia*, critically exposes the vilifying tendencies of Paul's rhetoric, and discusses the dangers of not reading Paul critically.

21. See, for instance, Horsley, "Innovation in Search of Reorientation: New Testament Studies Rediscovering Its Subject Matter," *JAAR* 62 (1994): 1111–26.

be made if the silenced and submerged voices of the Corinthians are not heard in the process of interpretation. In order to hear these voices and their arguments, one must decenter Paul's voice. If one wants to understand their counterarguments, one needs to read the text "against the grain" and pay special attention to the contradictions and tensions inscribed in it.

The significance of this letter to the Corinthians as a major source of knowledge about the community is jeopardized, I argue, when commentators value Paul's response over and above the theological self-understanding and practice of the *ekklēsia*. In so doing, they risk dissolving the distinction between the rhetorical situation as construed by Paul and the actual historical situation in Corinth. Whereas exegetes today presuppose the canonical status of Paul and therefore give priority to his theological authority and rhetorical response, such claims to authority for Paul cannot be maintained for the original situation.

An ethics of interpretation must recognize that many things advocated by Paul are shared by the Corinthian community. If one assumes a broad theological movement of which Paul is a part, one can relativize the voice of Paul as one among many. Hence, in areas of disagreement one must give the benefit of the doubt to the submerged Corinthian voices rather than to that of Paul. Wherever Paul's rhetoric vilifies and belittles the Corinthian community one must resist his rhetoric rather than valorize it. Rather than seeing Paul as the authoritative pastor, one must seek to understand the debates in Corinth as legitimate discussions within the *ekklēsia*.

Only if one explicitly problematizes a hermeneutics of identification can one value the voices within the Corinthian community that Paul's rhetoric seeks to silence.[22] Then one can understand Paul as only one partner, although in retrospect a very significant one, in the theological debates between those who sought to live G*d's alternative society, the "new creation," and those who legitimate the patriarchal structures and imperialist values of Greco-Roman society in ideological terms. Hence, it is safe to assume that the members of the *ekklēsia* in Corinth understood Paul's letter differently depending on which side they took in the debate. In tracing Paul's arguments, one still may be able to hear the submerged voices of the *ekklēsia*.

In short, an ethics of interpretation that does the work of a public health department in Pauline studies would require that scholars problematize the hermeneutics of identification with Paul and critically investigate the "public health" aspects of Paul's rhetorics and politics of meaning. A truly political paradigm of Pauline studies must not in any way valorize Paul's rhetoric of othering but critically inquire into the politics of meaning inscribed in Pauline discourses as well as that of Pauline scholarship.

In the same volume on *Paul and Empire* Neil Elliott singles out a specific problem for investigation. He addresses the "notorious exegetical problem"

---

22. See my revised entry on 1 Corinthians in *Harper's Bible Commentary*.

and "theological scandal" that Romans 13:1–7 poses for us today.[23] Elliott seeks to show that this text, which is considered by some scholars to be a non-Pauline interpolation, makes sense in the overall theological argument of Paul's letter when read in the context of political rhetoric in the Roman Empire. Again, if I raise questions of an ethics of interpretation with respect to this article, I am not doing so because I am interested in deconstructing Elliott's liberationist interpretation and proposing my own exegetical reading instead. Rather, I want to point out that the politics of meaning constructed by Elliott needs to be investigated in terms of an ethics of interpretation and to be scrutinized as to its "public health" consequences.

Over and against the widespread understanding that Paul's letter to the Romans in general was written in defense of the gentile Christian church and that Rom. 13:1–7 in particular was best understood as a "theology of the state," Elliott argues that Paul's target is not Jewish boasting but gentile arrogance. Paul wrote the letter not only in order to oppose the gentile Christians "boasting" over Israel but also in order to challenge their indifference to the plight of Jews in Rome. Thus, Elliott's argument is two-pronged. On the one hand, he maintains that the function of Romans is to advocate for the safety of the Jewish community in the imperial capital. Popular unrest and the ensuing violence especially during tax revolts were easily deflected onto Jews. Jews were feared to bear the brunt of violence when tax riots broke out in the city. Romans 13 has to be understood as a prudent attempt to prevent such a situation.

On the other hand, Elliott seeks to trace and underscore the connections between the exhortation in 13:1–7 and other parts of the letter. In a careful comparison between Romans 8 and 13:1–7 he shows convincingly that both texts stress subordination. Since subordination is appropriate to the calling of Christians, they must subordinate themselves to the authorities who wield the threat of punishment. Nevertheless, they need not live in fear, despite the sufferings inflicted in the present age. Just as Christians know that "all things work together for good for those who love G*d" (8:28), so Christians must know that the authorities are G*d's servants "for the good" (13:4, 6). Elliott sums up his argument as follows:

> Against the keen eschatological tenor of his letters elsewhere, Paul's positive characterization of "the governing authorities" here appears a foreign body. Within the rhetorical structure of Romans, however, these remarks have an important function: to encourage submission, for now, to the authorities, rather than desperate resistance; and thus to safeguard the most vulnerable around and among the Roman Christians, those Jews struggling to rebuild their shattered community in the wake of imperial violence. (203)

23. Neil Elliott, "Romans 13:1–7 in the Context of Imperial Propaganda," in *Paul and Empire*, ed. Horsley, 184. Subsequent page references appear in the text.

For such a general climate of anti-Jewish sentiment Elliot refers to Tacitus's *Annals*, stating that Rome had recently expelled Jews from the city because of riots "at the instigation of Chrestos" (15.44). Somewhat later, during the time of Nero riots arose "because of exorbitant taxation" (185). Elliott concludes:

> There is also warning here, against arrogance, presumption, the scapegoating of the weak and the vanquished; and warning against any disruptive action that could bring crashing down on the poor community of Israel the ominous storm clouds of imperial power overhead. Only the pernicious twists of fate would later enlist these verses in the service of the empire itself. (204)

In short, by making palatable the rhetoric of Romans 13, Elliott reinscribes Paul's rhetorics of subordination. By seeing its function as a "fitting response" to the reconstructed rhetorical situation of danger, fear, and violence, he makes Paul's rhetoric not only understandable but also acceptable. Such an interpretation of Paul's discourse as "protective rhetoric" is not able to critically analyze the values and attitudes advocated by this rhetoric and to subject Paul's politics of meaning to the "health" inspection of an ethics of inquiry. It rescues the political discourse of Roman 13 as "fitting" into the overall picture of Paul's argument in Romans.

However, this reading only intensifies the "public health" problem posed by Romans 13 when it invites us to read Romans 8–15 as a rhetoric of subordination that stands in the ideological service of domination. Even when granted that Elliott's reconstruction of the inscribed rhetorical situation is accurate, it does not follow that Paul's construction of the rhetorical situation corresponds to the actual historical situation nor that the rhetoric of Romans 13 was the appropriate theoethical response. Instead of revalorizing Paul's rhetoric, one must theorize and develop a critical biblical rhetorical inquiry that would help to prevent scholarly identification with Paul and the exegetical reinscription of Paul's rhetoric of othering.

## The Political Hermeneutics of *Ekklēsia*

In order to replace the malestream hermeneutics of othering and identification, feminist liberationist scholarship has insisted on a rhetorics and politics of meaning that privileges the *ekklēsia* (Elisabeth Schüssler Fiorenza) or the "voices within Paul's voice" (Antoinette Clark Wire) rather than the master voice of Paul. Such a politics of meaning understood as inquiry into the "public health" aspects of Pauline texts and studies insists on a critical rhetorical, ideological, and historical analysis.

To undercut the hegemonic politics of meaning one must conceptualize not only early Christian communities and their discourses but also

contemporary practices of interpretation as *ekklēsia,* that is, as sites of communicative persuasion, competing discourses, emancipatory struggles, and
theological visions which are shared by all the participants. Such a recon-
ceptualization of *ekklēsia* as a pluriform congregation of fully responsible
"adult" voices who have equal standing becomes possible, I have argued,
only if one deconstructs the gendered identification between Paul and his
interpreters that underwrites the authority claims of biblical scholars. This
would require that one replace the politics of theological identification with
a radical democratic politics of *ekklēsia* which can comprehend the disputes
in the early Christian *ekklēsia* in terms of *parrēsia* — the free speech of citizens — rather than cast them in terms of confessional internecine altercations
or imperial market competition.[24]

My own work has sought to develop such a reconstructive historical
politics of interpretation that valorizes difference, plurivocity, argument,
persuasion, and the democratic participation of all those excluded from or
subordinated by theological discourses.[25] In her dissertation, Cynthia Briggs
Kittredge has pursued this approach in order to show that the discourse
of subordination goes back to Paul himself. To that end she examined the
rhetorics of obedience in the letters attributed to Paul and in particular has
focused on the rhetoric of Philippians and Ephesians. By distinguishing between the inscribed rhetorical and the possible historical situation, her work
is able to trace in these letters the struggle between a rhetoric of *ekklēsia* and
one of kyriarchal submission.

> In both Philippians and Ephesians, the authors use the language of
> obedience to respond to alternative languages and symbolic universes
> within early Christian communities. Evidence of these visions sur-
> vives in the early Christian traditions that Paul and the Pauline author
> employ in their arguments.[26]

Pauline interpretation that understands itself as a hermeneutics of *ekklēsia*
attempts to trace and revalorize the early Christian egalitarian traditions. At
the same time it seeks to displace the politics and rhetorics of subordination
and otherness which is inscribed in the "Pauline" correspondence with a
hermeneutics and rhetorics of equality and responsibility. It conceives of
early Christian writings as taking sides in the emancipatory struggles of
antiquity and conceptualizes early Christian community as a radical demo-

---

24. See Dieter Georgi, *Theocracy in Paul's Praxis and Theology,* trans. David E. Green
(Minneapolis: Fortress Press, 1991), for this expression. However, Georgi also operates with a
Lutheran hermeneutics of identification with Paul.

25. See my books, *In Memory of Her; But She Said; Jesus: Miriam's Child, Sophia's Prophet;
Sharing Her Word;* and *Revelation: Vision of a Just World.*

26. Cynthia Briggs Kittredge, *Community and Authority: The Rhetoric of Obedience in the
Pauline Tradition* (Harrisburg, Pa.: Trinity Press International, 1998), 178.

cratic assembly (*ekklēsia*) of differing theological voices and sociorhetorical practices.

Such a radical egalitarian politics of *ekklēsia*, I argue, must become an integral part of the emerging political paradigm of Pauline studies. The ethics of interpretation requires the articulation of a theology of the Divine *politeuma* as its theological grounds and theoretical frame for which it can draw on biblical resources. In Christian Testament writings such as Philippians or 1 Peter one can still trace the self-understanding of early Christians as foreigners and resident aliens whose citizenship is elsewhere.

For instance in Phil. 3:20 Paul asserts in dualistic terms that Christians' "citizenship" or "commonwealth" (*politeuma*) is "in heaven and it is from there that we are expecting a savior." As Carolyn Osiek points out:

> This is the second time in the letter that Paul draws upon the language of the city-state (see 1:27) to imply that all Christians, male and female, have the responsibility of full participation in the commonwealth in which they belong most appropriately. This is the basis for any vision of a discipleship of equals in the Pauline churches. In a world of social inequalities, Christians are to live in the consciousness of their heavenly equal citizenship here and now.[27]

The "*politeuma* in heaven" has usually been understood in dualistic terms as "pie in the sky" or as otherworldly spiritualized reality that has nothing to do with the reality and politics of the earthly Roman Empire. However, if one understands "otherworldliness"[28] and "heaven" not as negation of humanness and creation but as the site of G*d's justice and well-being that is traditionally called "salvation," then one can conceptualize the Divine *politeuma* as the theological location from where a radical critique of oppressive "earthly" structures becomes possible.[29]

Such a theoretization of the "*politeuma* in heaven" would allow the hermeneutics of *ekklēsia* to place Pauline rhetorics under the radical horizon of

---

27. Carolyn Osiek, "Philippians," in *Searching the Scriptures*, vol. 2: *A Feminist Commentary*, ed. Elisabeth Schüssler Fiorenza (New York: Crossroad, 1994), 246.

28. For such an attempt at redefinition see Vincent L. Wimbush, " 'Not of This World': Early Christianity as Rhetorical and Social Formation," in *Reimagining Christian Origins: A Colloquium Honoring Burton L. Mack*, ed. Elizabeth A. Castelli and Hal Taussig (Valley Forge: Trinity Press International, 1996), 23–36. However, Wimbush seems not to discuss that otherworldliness can have a critical function vis-à-vis political power relations as well as a conforming function to hegemonic oppressive power.

29. Ronald F. Thiemann, *Religion in Public Life: A Dilemma for Democracy* (Washington, D.C.: Georgetown University Press, 1996), 169, suggests a similar but different argument when he contends: "The engagement of the religious citizen with a democratic regime is perhaps best captured under the notion of 'pilgrim citizenship.' Recognizing the penultimate character of the public realm, believers will not seek their final resting place in this sphere of power and persuasion." I would add that the "heavenly" *politeuma* of believers must be re-visioned as a sphere of democratic power and persuasion if religious u-topia should fulfill its critical function.

G*d's alternative world.[30] As the hermeneutical-theological horizon of political Pauline studies, such a critical "otherworldliness" can acknowledge the kyriarchal deformations of the biblical text. It does not need to justify or explain away such kyriarchal Scriptural formations but can sustain a hermeneutics of suspicion with respect to all biblical texts and theological traditions. It can theologically explore the contradictions and conflicts inscribed in biblical texts and their interpretations.

Differences and contradictions in the rhetoric of early Christian sources point to sociopolitical conflicts and religiocultural tensions between "egalitarian" movements — be they Hellenistic, Jewish or early Christian — and their dominant kyriarchal sociopolitical-religious contexts. These differing and contradictory sociorhetorical formations also point to sociopolitical conflicts within early Christian communities which understood themselves as a "pneumatic democracy." Such rhetorical tensions can be traced between those who advocate the ethos of _ekklēsia_ both as a "_basileia_ discipleship of equals" and as "a community of freedom in the Spirit," on the one hand, and those that advocate the kyriarchal leadership of elite male power and the kyriarchal institutionalization of the _ekklēsia,_ on the other hand.

The kyriocentric arguments of a politics and rhetorics of submission seek to reintroduce into the _ekklēsia_ the dualistic split between the public and private spheres, between those who speak and those who are silent, between women and men, between slaves and free, between Jews and Greeks, between humans and nature. For instance, they insist on relegating married women to the private sphere, on restricting their activity to proper "feminine" behavior, and on limiting women to leadership over other wo/men. These arguments for the "ethics and politics of submission" not only place restrictions on women's leadership in the _ekklēsia_ but also promote acceptance of slave-women's sufferings and advocate the adaptation of the whole Christian community to hegemonic kyriarchal structures of superordination and subordination.[31]

In contrast, the hermeneutics and politics of _ekklēsia_ enable readers to displace both the "scientific" paradigm which reconstructs early Christianity in terms of sectarian conflict and exclusions and the doctrinal paradigm which defines it in terms of orthodoxy-heresy. It can do so by recontextualizing

30. In his lectures on the "Political Theology of Paul," the Jewish philosopher Jacob Taubes has argued that the "people of G*d" are to be envisioned as a historical community free of domination. The explosive power of the political theology of Israel consists in the fact that in it the people replace the king as the representative of G*d. However, in the horizon of Jewish thought the institutions of domination of people by people cannot and may not represent the Messiah. The messianic must not legitimate the political order but can only relativize and ultimately replace it. See Jacob Taubes, _Die Politische Theologie des Paulus,_ ed. Aleida Assmann and Jan Assmann (Munich: Wilhem Fink Verlag, 1993), 178–80.

31. For the fuller development of such an emancipatory reconstructive argument see my article, "A Discipleship of Equals: Ekklesial Democracy and Patriarchy in Biblical Perspective," in _A Democratic Catholic Church,_ ed. Eugene C. Bianchi and Rosemary Radford Ruether (New York: Crossroad, 1992).

early Christian debates within Greco-Roman and Jewish radical democratic discourses and by ceasing to articulate an unbridgeable gulf between past and present.

In such a new contextualization Pauline writings can be read as public arguments that seek to persuade and convince "citizens" who share common cultural worlds and religious visions of equality and freedom. Rather than map the historical rhetorical situation in terms of the rhetorical situation inscribed by Paul or in terms of the logic of identity and politics of otherness, a rhetorical radical democratic politics of meaning can understand Pauline discourses and their suppressed alternative voices as two sides of one and the same rhetorical "coin." Hence, it is able to reconceptualize the Pauline text as site of rhetorical-political struggle and an arena of competing cultural-religious practices.

Such a hermeneutics of *ekklēsia* no longer needs to privilege the authorial master-voice of Paul or that of any other canonical writer, but can position its own inquiry on the side of the historical victims whose subjugated knowledges have left traces in the canonical text. However, such a conflictive egalitarian politics of interpretation would be misapprehended if its re-visioning of early Christian life were read in dualistic terms either as linear development or as rapid and uncontested decline from *ekklēsia* as the discipleship of equals to *ekklēsia* as the kyriarchal household of God.

Instead, this model conceptualizes the struggles of the Christian movements known through Paul's writings as pluriform movements of women and men gifted by the Divine Spirit and engaged in an ongoing theological debate over equality, freedom, dignity, and full "citizenship" in the *ekklēsia*. If such a theoretical frame and reconstruction of the debates in the pneumatic *ekklēsia* is interfaced with an intercultural and interreligious reconstructive model of reading, one can show that such emancipatory rhetorical practices and sociopolitical religious struggles for freedom[32] and for the right of "citizenship" are not restricted to early Christianity but began long before the Christian movements emerged on the scene, and are still ongoing today. They have continued throughout Western history, although a kyriarchal politics of interpretation has failed to write the ongoing history of struggle. The recognition of the rhetoricity rather than the authority of Pauline discourses would allow scholars to position their research within the ongoing history of such struggles and their politics of interpretation.

---

32. Orlando Patterson, *Freedom*, vol. 1: *Freedom in the Making of Western Culture* (New York: HarperCollins, 1991), claims to be the first such emancipatory history of freedom. It seems not accidental that his historical reconstruction of the struggles for freedom in antiquity recognizes women's crucial participation and contribution to these struggles.

# 3

# RESPONSE

## EXEGETICAL SUPPORT FROM ROMANS
## AND OTHER LETTERS

*Robert Jewett*

𝖌𝖌𝖌𝖌𝖌𝖌𝖌𝖌𝖌𝖌

T HE PROVOCATIVE CHAPTERS by Elisabeth Schüssler Fiorenza and Neil Elliott open up some revolutionary vistas that could energize Pauline studies and provide answers to a number of conundrums in his letters. This volume represents a creative continuation of interpretive impulses developed by Krister Stendahl, to whom many of us are profoundly indebted. I am particularly sympathetic to the efforts to take the matter of democratic discourse seriously, understanding Paul's voice as one among a community of charismatic equals in the early church, voices grappling in different ways with the issues of social domination, imperialism, and cultural conformity.

Elisabeth Schüssler Fiorenza has been a leader on this point, using sophisticated methods to lift up a wide variety of voices in the early Christian movement. She has lent her formidable analytic skills to the task of clarifying the "pneumatic democracy" in some branches of the Pauline church, lifting up voices that were silenced by the canonical process. I have tried to develop what Schüssler Fiorenza calls "a critical emancipatory approach" to Paul that opens up an interactive dialogue with American culture. I affirm her efforts to view Paul's letters as evidence of "rhetorical-political struggle and an arena of competing cultural-religious practices."

I have been stimulated by Neil Elliott's books on the rhetoric of Paul's letters and his paper that deals with the imperial background of Pauline theology. Although disagreeing with his assessment of the authenticity of some passages, a matter on which there was significant debate at the time of the original presentation of these papers, I find his effort to "give empire its due" to be very fruitful. My work with the details of Paul's argument in Rom. 1:18–32 leads me to support in the strongest terms Elliott's view that it is a "defiant indictment of the rampant injustice and impiety of the Roman 'golden age.'" I resonate with his declaration that "Romans is nothing less than a direct challenge

58

to the ritual and ceremony of empire." I am intrigued with his fresh approach to being "ashamed of the gospel" in Rom. 1:16. His reflections on the relevance of rhetoric and coercion in the context of imperialism bring him rather close to Schüssler Fiorenza's interest in a politics of *ekklēsia*, where "communicative persuasion, emancipatory struggles and theological visions ... are shared by all the participants." I agree with both of them in understanding some of "the disputes in the early Christian *ekklēsia* in terms of *parrēsia* — the free speech of citizens," to use Schüssler Fiorenza's formulation.

Since Schüssler Fiorenza's chapter is primarily theoretical and Elliott's provides a review of literature and of Roman cultural evidence, I intend to respond to the issues primarily in the light of exegetical evidence drawn from the Pauline letters themselves.

## The Scope of the Pauline Evidence

At the 1996 SBL annual meeting of the Society of Biblical Literature, when these papers were first presented, the evidentiary premises that led to Schüssler Fiorenza's and Elliott's conclusions were clearly stated and formed the basis of controversial debate. In the current form, in the chapters of this volume some of these issues are sidestepped, but they remain crucial nevertheless. The matters of interpolation, literary unity, and redaction are crucial in any assessment of Paul and politics. If Paul wrote Rom. 13:1–7, as Elliott at times has doubted and as Schüssler Fiorenza and I assume, it has an important bearing on Paul's attitude toward the Roman Empire. If Paul wrote 1 Cor. 14:33b–36, as Schüssler Fiorenza assumes and as Elliott and I doubt,[1] it has a bearing on the question of Paul's commitment to democratic participation in the early Christian communities. Believing these words to be Paul's, Schüssler Fiorenza concludes that Paul advocated "hegemonic kyriarchal structures of superordination and subordination." Drawing the opposite conclusion on the basis of viewing 1 Cor. 14:33b–36 as an interpolation, Elliott presents Paul as a model of human liberation.

Another crucial case in point is Rom. 16:17–20a, the anti-heretical tirade that comprises the most notorious and explicit example of what Schüssler Fiorenza denounces as the "politics of othering." If this material was interpolated by later hands associated with those who created the Pastoral Epistles in order to counter Paul's inclusive admonition, "Greet one another with a holy kiss; all the churches of Christ greet you" (Rom. 16:16),[2] Paul's

---

1. See Robert Jewett, *Paul the Apostle to America: Cultural Trends and Pauline Scholarship* (Louisville: Westminster/John Knox Press, 1994), which develops the case for interpolation presented in "The Sexual Liberation of the Apostle Paul," *JAAR Supplement* 47 (1979): 55–87.

2. See Robert Jewett, "The God of Peace in Romans: Reflections on Crucial Lutheran Texts," in "Essays in Honor of Edgar Krentz," *Currents in Theology and Mission* 25, no. 3 (June 1998): 186–94; this argument on interpolation was first presented in my *Christian Tolerance: Paul's Message to the Modern Church* (Philadelphia: Westminster Press, 1982).

stance as an opponent of the politics of domination and exclusion would be clarified.

So how are we to adjudicate the question of how to assess the authenticity of documentary evidence in assessing Paul's view of the empire? In her original paper, Schüssler Fiorenza criticized interpolation theories as characteristic of "malestream defenses of Paul," motivated by hegemonic desire on the part of scholars to ensure "the symbolic coherence of Paul's theological argument." Chastened by postmodernist critiques, I continue to believe that a modest form of the scientific method offers a more promising approach. A properly scientific method looks for similar indications of authenticity, whether assessing the authorship of Plato's epistles or Shakespeare's sonnets, or deciding whether a contemporary will and testament was forged or amended. Evidence must be adduced and interpreted to develop a hypothesis, which must then be submitted to cross-examination and a decision in which some portion of the public is engaged. The acid test of scientific orientation is not some silly claim of objectivity but rather the willingness to subject one's claims to the possibility of disconfirmation on the basis of publicly accessible evidence. This method never produces absolute certainties, admitting in Paul's words that we all "see through a glass darkly." But the historical-critical method is more promising than a postmodernism that imputes hegemonic motives to dissenting participants and asserts theories and conclusions that must finally be accepted on authority.

A related issue is the evidentiary force of voices within the early church that have been inferred from the Pauline letters. The reconstruction of such voices is one of the most subtle and controversial achievements of the historical-critical method. Schüssler Fiorenza argues that such voices should always take precedence over Paul's own views, because, on the basis of her interpretation of the letters, Paul is an advocate of kyriarchy. "Whenever Paul's rhetoric vilifies and belittles [the community]," she writes, "one must resist his rhetoric rather than valorize it." I believe there is substantial evidence to confirm her insistence that the early church was at times engaged in "a radical egalitarian politics of *ekklēsia*." Elliott's reflections on the functions of persuasion within imperialistic contexts provide a framework for understanding what was at stake for the early church. I would like to suggest, however, that Paul's conversation partners were frequently on the imperialistic side of the ledger.

## Imperialistic Voices within the *Ekklēsia*

With regard to the Roman and Corinthian letters that provide most of the evidence for Elliott and Schüssler Fiorenza, it is Paul rather than the congregational voices who provides the strongest resistance against the politics of empire. In 1 Cor. 1:12, Paul cites some of these voices that make it clear that adherence to a particular patron was becoming a source of prideful separation: " 'I belong to Paul,' or 'I belong to Apollos.' " It is Paul who provides the argument against the divisive slogans that implied imperial superiority of one group over another. In 1 Corinthians 8 and 10 he struggles against the tendency of the "strong" to violate the consciences of the "weak" with regard to eating meat offered to idols. In 1 Cor. 11:17–34 he counters the habit of rich patrons arriving early at the love feasts, devouring the rich food and wine before the slaves and handworkers arrive, thus "humiliating those who have nothing." This seems to be an example of the habits of imperial privilege, such as Elliott and Schüssler Fiorenza have described, filtering back into the Christian community. Throughout 2 Corinthians, Paul is struggling against the superapostles, who bring an imperial style of leadership into the church. On the basis of the reconstruction by Dieter Georgi and others, their voices are certainly not on the side of egalitarian values. With bitter sarcasm, Paul exposes the congregation's complicity in their own submission under the pressure of the superapostles' employment of the standard habits of imperial domination: "For you bear it if a man makes slaves of you, or preys upon you, or takes advantage of you, or puts on airs, or strikes you in the face. To my shame, I must say, we were too weak for that" (2 Cor. 11:20–21). Paul's brilliant and penetrating analysis of this situation and his advocacy of an egalitarian theology of the cross leads to the rhetoric that Schüssler Fiorenza decries, identifying his leadership as marrying the congregation as "a pure bride of Christ" (2 Cor. 11:4) and taking "every thought captive to obey Christ, being ready to punish every disobedience" (2 Cor. 10:5–6). He batters and belittles the Corinthians who have subjected themselves to this new tyranny. In behalf of the principle of the equality of all persons in Christ, he acts as a representative of what Stendahl called the "Department of Public Health" in a corrosive, imperialistic environment.

In Rom. 14:1–15:7 Paul describes the mutually discriminatory behavior that marks the relations of these groups toward the others.[3] The voice of the "strong" is evident in Paul's admonition not to "despise" the members of the other groups who have a more conservative attitude toward the Jewish law; the voice of the "weak" surfaces in Paul's reference to their passing "judgment" on those who feel free from the law (14:3). Cultural, ethnic, and liturgical issues divide these groups, but it is Paul who develops the argument for mutual respect and welcome. The admonition in 15:7, "welcome one another, therefore, as Christ has welcomed you, for the glory of God," aims to replace these imperialistic habits of exclusion and domination.

The final chapter of the letter points in the same direction. The theological and cultural implications of the greetings of Romans 16 and their crucial role in the purpose of Romans have still not been fully credited in recent studies, despite the challenge posed by Terence Y. Mullins more than thirty

---

3. See ibid.

years ago.[4] The word *aspazomai* ["greet"] is repeated twenty-one times in Romans 16, more than the rest of the Pauline letters altogether. Paul's selection of the second-person plural imperative form, *aspasasthe* ["you should greet"], in 16:3–16 was surely intentional and should not be translated as "I send greetings to...."[5] As Otto Michel points out, "The ones being greeted are at the same time those whom the Roman congregation should grant recognition."[6] When one observes the random sequence of the requested greetings and the interweaving of established Christian cells (16:3–5, 10b, 11b, 14, 15) and isolated Christian leaders, it becomes clear that the recognition is to be mutual. In this context, to greet is to honor and welcome one another, probably with the hug, kiss, handshaking, or bowing that gave expression to greeting in the ancient world; the original meaning of the Greek term was to wrap one's arms around another.[7] All of the indications in this chapter point to Paul rather than the congregation itself as the one initially interested in this strategy of mutual welcome and inclusion.

## Overcoming the Legacy of Greco-Romans vs. Barbarians

An important indication of Paul's resistance to what Schüssler Fiorenza calls "the politics of othering" is Rom. 1:14, which explains the background of Paul's letter and its associated mission to Spain. It reveals his attitude toward "subject peoples," on which Elliott has provided rich social background. Paul describes his calling as an apostle to the Gentiles in a remarkable formulation describing his "obligation" to the hostile poles of ethnicity, class, and education. Although its importance has rarely been recognized, this verse is in several respects the "key to Romans," revealing the "situation of its composition."[8] "Greeks and Barbarians" is a stereotypical formula in which "Greeks" are typically mentioned first and "Barbarians" second. In the bilingual context of Rome, "Greek" meant "Greco-Roman"[9] while

---

4. Terence Y. Mullins expressed disquiet at the traditional view of the bearing of the greetings on the relationship between Paul and his audience as well as on the significance of the greetings for the understanding of Paul's argument in the letter in "Greeting as a New Testament Form," *JBL* 87 (1968): "The relationship between Paul and the congregation at Rome seems to be other than scholars have assumed, and no simple readjustment of our old notions is likely to bring it into focus.... [S]omething in our usual interpretation of Romans is wrong; and the way to straighten it out is to establish as much objective data as possible before using the evidence supplied by the contents of the letter" (426).

5. Barclay M. Newman and Eugene A. Nida, *A Translator's Handbook on Paul's Letter to the Romans* (Stuttgart: United Bible Societies, 1973), 291.

6. Michel, *Der Brief an die Römer*, MeyerK 4, 14th ed. (Göttingen: Vandenhoeck and Ruprecht, 1978), 474.

7. See Hans Windisch, *"aspazomai ktl,"* TDNT 1 (1946): 497.

8. Sigfred Pedersen, "Theologische Überlegungen zur Isagogik des Römerbriefes," *ZNW* 76 (1985): 47.

9. Fréderic Godet, *Commentary on St. Paul's Epistle to the Romans* (New York: Funk and Wagnalls, 1883, 1889; repr. Grand Rapids, Mich.: Kregel, 1977), 89, notes that Cicero in *De finibus* 2.15 joins Greece and Rome in antithesis to the *barbaria*.

"Barbarian" refers to alien tribes who cannot speak Greek or Latin and are uncultured, wild, crude, fierce, and in a basic sense, uncivilized.[10] Although there was a protest against this division of the human race by the geographer Eratosthenes (Strabo 1.4.9), Joseph Vogt reports that the antithesis "Roman/barbarian" was so widely accepted that the Germans who established their kingdom within the empire referred to themselves as *barbari*.[11] The triumph of Rome over the Barbarians was celebrated in public art and monuments, in victory parades, in the gladiatorial games, and on coins, thus revealing that this antithesis was basic to the imperial worldview. The comprehensive study of this phenomenon by Yves Albert Dauge shows that from the second century B.C.E. to the fifth century C.E., Barbarians were viewed by Romans as inherently "inhuman, ferocious, arrogant, weak, warlike, discordant, *unanitas*, unstable, etc."[12] These character traits were seen as the polar opposites of Roman virtues.[13] For the safety of the world and of civilization itself, Barbarians had to be subjugated by Rome, which received therein its appointed task from the gods. Of particular interest to Paul's letter that prepared the way for a mission to Spain, the Spaniards were viewed as Barbarians par excellence because so large a proportion continued to resist Roman rule, to rebel with frightening frequency, to refuse to speak Latin or to use the Roman names for their cities, streams, or mountains.[14] In view of this profound cultural antipathy, it is amazing that Paul dared to link Greeks and Barbarians with the connective *te kai*, used previously in 1:12 to imply an inclusion of opposites in the sense of "both and," and to use exactly the same connective with the next pair of opposites, thereby conveying the sweeping inclusivity of the gospel of Christ crucified for all.

The word *sophoi* can be used to describe a wise, competent person or a philosopher,[15] but in this antithesis to *anoêtoi* ("uneducated") rather than *aphrôn* ("fool"), it has the connotation of being educated in the Greco-Roman system.[16] The antithesis is close to "sophisticates and rustics," and since the Greco-Roman educational system concentrated on linguistic and

---

10. Hans Windisch, *"barbaros," TDNT* 1 (1964): 547–48; Joseph Vogt, *Kulturwelt und Barbaren: Zum Menschheitsbild der spätantiken Gesellschaft*, Abhandlungen der Geistes- und Sozialwissenschaftlichen Klasse 1 (Wiesbaden: Steiner, 1967): "[I]n east and in west the view prevailed that the barbarians were excluded and that the civilized people of the orbis Romanus simply represented genus humanum.... All who lived outside of the border fortifications were called barbarians.... [T]hey were to be opposed with every available means as enemies of culture" (12).

11. Vogt, *Kulturwelt und Barbaren*, 8–9.

12. Dauge, *Le Barbare: Recherches sur la conception romaine de la barbarie et de la civilisation*, Collection Latomus 176 (Brussels: Latomus, 1981), 472–73.

13. Ibid., 534–44.

14. See ibid., 175, 479, 489, 661, 733.

15. Ulrich Wilckens and Georg Fohrer, *"sophia ktl," TDNT* 7 (1971): 468–74; BAGD 760.

16. See Theodor Zahn, *Der Brief des Paulus an die Römer*, Kommentar zum Neuen Testament 6, 3d ed. (Leipzig: Deichert, 1925), 66; C. E. B. Cranfield, *A Critical and Exegetical Commentary on the Epistle to the Romans*, ICC (Edinburgh: T. & T. Clark, 1975–79), 84.

rhetorical competence in Greek and Latin, this antithesis roughly corresponds to "Greeks and Barbarians."[17] There is no doubt that the negative
pole, "uneducated," carried a heavy burden of opprobrium, because the
Greeks had developed the idea that education created what Werner Jaeger
described as

> a higher type of man. They believed that education embodied the pur-
> pose of all human effort. It was, they held, the ultimate justification
> for the existence of both the individual and the community.... And
> it was ultimately in the form of paideia, "culture," that the Greeks
> bequeathed the whole achievement of the Hellenic mind to the other
> nations of antiquity. Augustus envisaged the task of the Roman empire
> in terms of Greek culture.[18]

The educational system developed by the Greek sophists and carried forward in Roman times aimed at developing virtue and excellence needed for
public service, with the corollary that the uneducated person was perceived
to lack the capacity for either.[19] A person called *anoêtos* was therefore not
just "unwise, irrational," and "foolish," but not fully human.[20] This word
shares with "Barbarian" the contempt thought to be warranted for persons
and groups capable of great mischief but inherently incapable of construc-
tive contributions to the human enterprise. And since the relationship with
the divine was thought to be centered in knowledge, the "uneducated" were
viewed as profoundly impaired in religious capacity. For example, Philo
can query the person whose behavior blinds him to God, "Why is this
evil plight, thou uneducated?" (*Somn* 2.181). Titus 3:3 echoes this cultural
commonplace when it describes the condition of humans prior to conversion as "uneducated, disobedient, led astray, slaves to various passions and
pleasures.... "

As if the grouping of these two pairs of moral, ethic, and cultural opposites in a "both and" syntax were not scandalous enough, Paul employs
the expression that to all of the above, "I am obligated." This term reflects
an ethical system more prevalent in the Greco-Roman world than in the
Hebraic-Jewish world, where it is restricted to material indebtedness.[21] In
his *Laws* 4.417B, Plato explains that piety requires gratitude to parents and
the gods because "the debtor should pay back the first and greatest of debts,
the most primary of all dues, and that he should acknowledge that all that
he owns and has belongs to those who begot and reared him." This sense of

---

17. Otto Kuss, *Der Römerbrief übersetzt und erklärt* (Regensburg: Pustet, 1957–78), 19;
Ernst Kühl, *Der Brief des Paulus an die Römer* (Leipzig: Quell and Meyer, 1913) 28–29.
18. Werner Jaeger, *Paideia: The Ideals of Greek Culture*, trans. G. Highet (New York:
Oxford University Press, 1939, 1945), 1:xvii.
19. Ibid., 288–93.
20. Johannes Behm and E. Würtwein, *"noe...anoëtos ktl,"* TDNT 4 (1967): 961.
21. See Friedrich Hauck, *"opheilô ktl,"* TDNT 5 (1967): 560–61.

ethical obligation was particularly prevalent in Rome where *officium* ("obligation, duty") was required out of gratitude for gifts received from the gods, one's family, the state, or patrons.[22] Officials were bound to perform the duties of their *officium*, the technical term for a governmental post.[23] Cicero formulated the premise of this system in his essay *De officiis* ("The Duties, Obligations") 1.47: "For no obligation (*officium*) is more imperative than of proving one's gratitude." The prominence of these ideas in Rome, and particularly their likely embodiment in two of the Christian cells situated within the imperial bureaucracy (Rom. 16:10–11), may explain why Paul uses "obligation" in Romans more than in any other letter. In this context it has a socially revolutionary implication, as Paul S. Minear explains:

> Obligation to him who died [i.e., Christ] produces obligation to those for whom he died. This very "law" applies with special force to the particularity of Paul's call as an apostle. God's intention in bringing Paul to faith in Christ had been to send him as a "minister of Christ Jesus to the Gentiles" (15:16). To the extent that Paul was indebted to God for this call, to that very extent he was indebted to those Gentiles for whose sake God had called him.[24]

Thus while the Greco-Roman ethic of reciprocity would require obligations to the Greeks and the educated, who were perceived to have provided benefits for others, it was a complete reversal of the system to feel indebtedness to Barbarians and the uneducated. This correlates closely with the argument in 1:18–32, which Elliott rightly describes as "antagonism . . . to the propaganda and pretense" of imperial propaganda concerning Rome's virtue in comparison with Barbarians. In the light of the Roman civic cult, Rom. 1:14 is a highly distinctive expression of Paul's missionary orientation, confirming that Paul should be identified as a powerful opponent of the kind of "othering" that Schüssler Fiorenza decries.

## Obligations to an Empire Whose Sacred Canopy of the Roman Gods Has Been Replaced

The status and interpretation of Romans 13 plays a crucial role in both papers. The interpretation of this pericope has swung from abject subservience to political authorities viewed as virtually divine to critical submission on the basis of their advancement of justice. The virtually endless stream of

---

22. See Mark Reasoner, *The Strong and the Weak: Romans 14:1–15:13 in Context*, SNTSMS 103 (Cambridge: Cambridge University Press, 1999), 176–86.

23. Reasoner, *The Strong and the Weak*, 181, cites A. E. R. Boak, "Officium," *PW* 34.2045–56, for this technical usage that provides the linguistic background for the modern concept of "official, office."

24. Minear, *The Obedience of Faith: The Purpose of Paul in the Epistle to the Romans*, SBT 2 (Napierville, Ill.: Allenson, 1971), 104.

studies has been marked by advocacy of various appraisals of the role of government shaped by theological traditions.[25] Only recently have scholars begun to view this passage as an interaction with the Roman civic cult,[26] thus taking fuller account of the political and cultural context of Paul's letter and its missional purpose.

The anti-imperialistic implications of Rom. 13:1b–c, echoed and reinforced by verses 1a, 4a and d, and 6b (referring to governmental agents as servants of God), are most easily grasped when one compares Paul's statement with the Roman civic cult and takes account of the twelve chapters of argument that precede this pericope. Elliott has provided an excellent analysis of the former in its conviction that the gods had granted Rome its empire on grounds of their punctilious religious devotion. In that light the disparity with Paul's view assumes a large significance. In Romans 13 the God who grants authority to governmental agencies is not Mars or Jupiter, as in the Roman civic cult; nor is he represented by the pantheon of Greco-Roman deities that had been assimilated into the civic cult since the time of Augustus. The God of whom Paul speaks in chapter 13 of this letter is the same as announced in chapter 1, whose righteousness was elaborated for the next twelve chapters. It is the God embodied in the crucified Christ who is in view here, which turns this passage into a massive act of political cooptation. If the Roman authorities had understood this argument, it would have been viewed as thoroughly subversive. That the Roman authorities were ordained by the God and Father of Jesus Christ turns the entire Roman civic cult on its head, exposing its suppression of the truth. Its involvement in the martyrdom of Christ, crucified under Pontius Pilate, cannot have been forgotten by the readers of chapter 13 who knew from firsthand experience the hollowness of Rome's claim to have established a benign rule of law. The critique of the law in all its forms in the first eight chapters of this letter cannot have been forgotten, which explains why the proudest institution of the Pax Romana, the rule of law, goes unmentioned here. Nothing remains of the claim in Roman propaganda that its law enforcement system was redemptive, producing a

---

25. See the major accounts of the history of research: Fritz Hermann Keienburg, *Die Geschichte der Auslegung von Römer 13, 1–7* (Gelsenkirchen: Hertel, 1952, 1956); Ernst Käsemann, "Römer 13,1–7 in unserer Generation," *ZThK* (1959): 316–76; G. Scharffenorth, "Römer 13 in der Geschichte des politischen Denkens. Ein Beitrag zur Klärung der politischen Traditionen in Deutschland seit dem 15. Jahrhundert," dissertation, University of Heidelberg, 1964; Lutz Pohle, *Die Christen und der Staat nach Röm 13, 1–7 in der neueren deutschsprachigen Schriftauslegung* (Mainz: Grünewald, 1984); Vilho Riekkinen, *Römer 13. Aufzeichnung und Weiterführung der exegetischen Diskussion,* Annales academiae scientiarum fennicae: Dissertationes humanarum litterarum 23 (Helsinki: Suomalainen Tiedeakatemia, 1980), 8–202; Jan Botha, "Creation of New Meaning: Rhetorical Situations and the Reception of Romans 13:1–7," *JTSA* 79 (1992): 24–37.

26. In addition to the two papers currently under discussion, see Dieter Georgi, *Theocracy in Paul's Praxis and Theology,* trans. D. E. Green (Minneapolis: Fortress, 1991), 81–102; Neil Elliott, "Romans 13:1–7 in the Context of Imperial Propaganda," in *Paul and Empire: Religion and Power in Roman Imperial Society,* ed. R. A. Horsley (Harrisburg, Pa.: Trinity Press International, 1997), 184–204.

kind of messianic peace under the rule of the gods "Justitia" and "Clementia." Christ alone is the fulfillment of the law (10:4), not the emperor or the Roman gods. And nothing remains of the specious claim in the civic cult that the empire had been given to Rome because of its superior virtue and piety, a matter that had been demolished by 1:18–3:20. What remains is the simple fact of divine appointment, "ordained by God," a matter justified not by the virtue of the appointee but in the mysterious mind of God who elects whom she will as the agents of her purpose (9:14–33, 11:17–32). Submission to the governmental authorities is therefore an expression of respect not for the authorities themselves but for the crucified deity who stands behind them.

That Paul does not intend to enforce a subordinationist stance is confirmed by the section that follows Rom. 13:1–7, which neither paper takes into account. In 13:8 Paul writes, "Owe no one anything, except to love one another; for the one who loves the other has fulfilled the law." The admonition to love one another begins with the theme of obligation developed in 13:7. The maxims in these two verses follow the pattern of "antilogical *gnômai*" found in classical Greek collections.[27] Whereas 13:7 urged "Render to all what is obligated," 13:8 insists that believers should "owe no one anything." The expression "owe no one anything" employs a conventional expression for monetary or social indebtedness as the parallels indicate.[28] Adolf Strobel pointed to a striking parallel in a grave inscription that celebrated a Roman woman of pagan background who "lived well and owed no one anything."[29] This widely shared value of being free of debts is also expressed in a letter from a young man to his mother: "Don't you know that I would rather become a cripple than to owe a man even an obolos?"[30] Paul's admonition extends this traditional reluctance to incur indebtedness into all areas of life with the word *mêden* ("anything"), which includes the list of taxes, customs, respect, and honor owed in verse 7. These and all other obligations are to be met, taken care of, paid off, so that Christians are free to devote themselves to their new relationships. This implies the avoidance of falling under the control of creditors or remaining entangled with patrons who might erode the capacity of the members of house and tenement churches to shape their common life in Christ. This counsel is consistent with Paul's preference to avoid dependency relations, except for radical dependency as a slave of Christ, visible in 1 Corinthians 9, in 1 and 2 Thessalonians, and in Philippians 4. He wants Christians to be slaves of no human, if they can avoid it,[31] indebted only to mutual love. Their former

27. See John Barns, "A New Gnomologium: With Some Remarks on Gnomic Anthologies, II," *CQ* 45 (1951): 3, discusses Plutarch, *Quomodo adolescens poetas audire debeat* ¶4 (page 20C) who presents "opposite points of view on a given subject" as an educational technique.

28. See Friedrich Hauck, "*opheilô ktl,*" *TDNT* 5 (1967): 559–60; BAGD, 598–99.

29. Cited by Strobel, "Verständnis von Rm 13," 92 from *IGRom,* 1.104.

30. Cited from BGU II 846 by Ulrich Wilckens, *Der Brief an die Römer,* EKKNT 6 (Zürich: Benziger; Neukirchen-Vluyn: Neukirchener Verlag, 1978–82), 3.67.

31. See Jewett, *Paul the Apostle to America,* chapter 6.

social obligations are to be replaced by a single new obligation to meet the needs of fellow members in the church.

The puzzle about the admonition in 13:8a is whether the exception clause was meant to be understood antithetically ("but you ought to love one another") or inclusively ("except to love one another"), which is the more natural and convincing option. A new obligation is to replace the social dependency on patrons or families, namely, "to love one another." It is crucial for the interpretation of this pericope to clarify the social context of Paul's formulaic obligation. That Paul has in mind the new obligation to love the members of one's house or tenement church as the new fictive family in which believers are embedded is strongly indicated by the wording of this verse and close parallels elsewhere in the Pauline letters (1 Thess. 3:12; 2 Thess. 1:3, 4:9; Gal. 5:13). Similar "one another" sayings occur repeatedly in Romans (1:12; 12:5, 10, 16), referring to fellow Christians, as in the later sayings (Rom. 14:13, 19; 15:5, 7, 14; 16:16).

The theme of mutual love recurs in 13:10, which I translate "The agape does no evil to the neighbor; therefore law's fulfillment is the agape." The persistent deletion by commentators and translators of the article in connection with love in this verse serves to generalize the admonition and drive it in a theoretical, legalistic direction not intended by Paul. This entails a significant misunderstanding of the function of the article in Greek, which serves "to distinguish the subject noun from the predicate noun," thus establishing the topic of the sentence.[32] By the emphatic positioning of *hê agapê* ("the love") as the first and last words in the sentence, and by repeating the article twice in this carefully constructed verse, Paul makes clear that that the specific and distinctive form of love as experienced by early house and tenement churches is the topic.[33] The logical social corollary to "the love" in this verse is the agape meal otherwise known as the love-feast, the common meal shared by most sectors of the early church in connection with the Lord's Supper. The repeated arthrous use of "love" in this verse justifies the translation "the agape." If this translation is correct, it follows that the entirety of Romans 14–16 deals with the question of inclusion of outsiders and members of other ethnic groups into the local love-feasts in Rome. A new empire of inclusion is here seen to be replacing the empire of privilege, power, and domination.

---

32. David Sansone, "Towards a New Doctrine of the Article in Greek: Some Observations on the Definite Article in Plato," *CP* 20 (1993): 200.

33. See BDF, ¶252, where *hê agapê* is rendered "Christian Love," with reference to John 1:21. For a discussion of the fact that the Greek article derives from the demonstrative pronoun and retains its deictic quality of pointing to a specific or previously named topic, see Robert W. Funk, "The Syntax of the Greek Article: Its Importance for Critical Pauline Problems," dissertation, Vanderbilt University, Nashville, 1953, 31–56. He discusses the arthrous use of *agapê* as "a good example of an abstract that has been thoroughly Christianized" on 106–12.

## The Hope of Global Conversion and Pacification

The global reach of Paul's mission, which the consideration of Paul and the politics of empire stimulates us to confront, is elaborated in Rom. 15:9–13. The LXX version of Deut. 32:43 is cited to show how the Gentiles will take up the melody of the cosmic chorus of praise. As James Dunn points out, the LXX had expanded the Hebrew wording of the song of Moses and mitigated the triumph over the Gentiles with the phrase Paul cites here, "with his people,"[34] implying that both Jews and Gentiles will join in the same chorus. The Masoretic text, in contrast, has "O Gentiles, praise his people." By selecting this line from the LXX and avoiding the other references in Deut. 32:43 to avenging "the blood of his children, and . . . vengeance on his adversaries" among the Gentiles, Paul drives forward his thesis of ethnic mutuality in Christ.[35] Consistent with his avoidance of the Rabbinic custom of giving precedence in a *Haraz* to Pentateuch texts, Paul not only places Deuteronomy after a Psalm text but recontextualizes and reinterprets it in the light of Christ's welcome of Jews and Gentiles alike (15:7). And in contrast to the broad tradition of anticipating gentile conversion as a form of social and political subordination to Israel, bringing their gifts to the Jerusalem temple, Paul envisions all nations rejoicing together, with each other rather than above or below each other with respect to honor, lending their varied voices to the cosmic chorus of praise.[36]

The theme of inclusive praise is reinforced by the citation of Ps. 117:1, which includes the parallel references to "all the Gentiles" and "all the nations." As C. E. B. Cranfield observes, "With its repeated use of *pas*, it stresses the fact that no people is to be excluded from this common praise of God."[37] The citation is slightly altered by moving the first phrase ahead in the sentence, lending additional emphasis on the inclusion of the Gentiles. The citation refers to the Gentiles in the third person because the missionary goal of reaching beyond the already converted Gentiles in Rome to the yet unconverted Gentiles in Spain is in view. Their voices will be added to the voices of Jewish Christians in the eschatological chorus, as the wording of 15:11b makes plain. In the context of Paul's argument, the phrase "all the peoples" includes the Jews among the other peoples of the world. This scriptural warrant reinforces the emphasis of the preceding citation concerning ethnic groups rejoicing with each other rather than at each other's expense.

Paul cites Isa. 11:10 (LXX) at the end of his catena. Because the larger context of Isaiah 11 conveys the eschatological vision of the restoration of

---

34. James D. G. Dunn, *Romans 9–16*, Word Biblical Commentary 38B (Dallas: Word, 1988), 849.

35. See Wilckens, *Der Brief an die Römer*, 3:107–8.

36. As Richard B. Hays shows in *Echoes of Scripture in the Letters of Paul* (New Haven: Yale University Press, 1989), 71, this passage embodies "his vision for a church composed of Jews and Gentiles glorifying God together."

37. Cranfield, *Romans*, 746.

the lost tribes of Israel, the chauvinistic potential of Israel's military dominance over the Gentiles needed to be eliminated by the placement and content of the three preceding citations. Paul cites from the LXX, eliminating the phrase "in that day." If the deletion was motivated by the desire to preserve "that day" as a reference to the final judgment as in 2:5, 16 and 13:12,[38] it also allows a recontextualizing of the citation as a prophecy of missionary fulfillment rather than a threatened day of judgment in which the Gentiles would be forced to acknowledge their subordination under Israel's messiah. The Masoretic text, once again, was much less suitable for Paul's purpose, referring to the shoot of David standing as an "ensign" to the Gentiles, that is, as a battle flag symbolizing Israel's military predominance.[39] While *hriza* meant "root" in Rom. 11:16–18, here it seems to refer to a "shoot" that springs up from the root. In Christian Maurer's words, "From the pitiable remnant of the house of Jesse there will come forth, as from the remaining stump of a tree, a new shoot which will establish the coming kingdom."[40] It appears likely that "shoot of Jesse" was a traditional messianic title, both for Judaism and early Christianity. Here Paul returns to the same Jewish-Christian credal tradition with which the letter began, referring to Jesus as "born of the seed of David" (1:3). Even the expression "from the resurrection of the dead" (1:4) is echoed in the wording the LXX supplied for the shoot of Jesse who "who rises up" to fulfill his messianic role.[41] The expression *archein ethnōn* is a typical Hellenistic Jewish expression for ruling the Gentiles. The *Epistle of Aristeas* refers to "the multitudes whom you rule" while Mark 10:42 refers to "the ones recognized to rule the Gentiles." The same verb was used to describe the goddess Isis as "having great power and ruling in the world." Without the recontextualizing provided by the preceding citations, by the insistence on mutual welcome between ethnic groups, and by the entire earlier argument of Romans that eliminates any basis for cultural or political predominance, this reference would simply remain an expression of Jewish cultural and political imperialism. But if Jesus is the long-expected "shoot of Jesse," his lordship has the quality of servanthood that 15:8 reinforced by means of the term *diakonos* ("servant"). Christ died for his enemies rather than subjugating them by force. On the basis of this revolutionary transformation of Jewish messianism, Paul is able to cite the final line of Isa. 11:10, "in him will the Gentiles hope," because the rule of Christ is not simply another form of despotism.

---

38. Dunn, *Romans 9–16*, 850.

39. See the discussion of this predominantly military symbol by Fabry, *"nes," TWAT* 5 (1985): 468–73. Typical Old Testament parallels are Exod. 17:6; Num. 26:10; Isa. 5:26, 18:3, 30:17, 31:9; Zech. 9:16; Ps. 74:4. If the Hebrew text had been used here, it probably would have evoked the battle flags of the Roman legions familiar to the hearers of Paul's letter in Rome.

40. Christian Maurer, *"hriza," TDNT* 6 (1968): 986.

41. See Heinrich Schlier, *Der Römerbrief*, HThKNT 6 (Freiburg: Herder, 1977), 425; Dunn, *Romans*, 850.

The Gentiles hope for their own conversion in the context of global pacification, an eschatological hope centered in Christ. Since Paul's purpose is to elicit support for the gentile mission, he ends the citation at this point, rather than continuing on to the ingathering of Jewish exiles in Isaiah 11:11.

# Conclusion

Returning to the starting point where the chapters by Schüssler Fiorenza and Elliott seem to converge, I believe that a great deal of exegetical evidence can be adduced in support of interpreting Paul's letters in the light of the imperial context. This stimulates me to reach for a further elaboration of what Paul calls the Christian *politeuma*. There is a global sweep to Paul's view of the gospel mission; it reaches, particularly in Romans, to the end of the earth, to Spain (Rom. 15:24, 28). The exclusive claims of both Jews and Gentiles are countered and transformed by this gospel. It is Paul in particular who wishes the new community to be marked by persuasion rather than coercion. He stresses that its Lord is the crucified one, not the emperor; he exults that its citizens are mostly the rank and file of men, women, and children, both slave and free; its sustenance is the love-feast rather than the imperial dole granted to privileged citizens; its liturgy centers on the crucifixion and resurrection of Jesus rather than on the triumph over enemies in the civic cult and the theater; its honor comes through the imputation of righteousness rather than through the advantages of birth and achievement; it is more committed to *agapē* than to order; and its reach includes Barbarians as well as Greeks and Romans, Gentiles as well as Jews. This expands and broadens Elliott's suggestion that the "key to the coherence" of Romans is to "move his Gentile-Christian readers away from a theological 'boast' over a vanquished Israel." The critique of the gentile side is visible in Romans 11, which Elliott lifts up, but in chapters 14–16 both sides are urged to overcome their "contempt" and their "judging" of opponents. Paul urges each branch of the splintered church in Rome to welcome others into the love-feasts that he hopes to extend to the Barbarians in Spain. Paul's mission implies an alternative vision of the path toward global reconciliation. It runs neither through Roman propaganda and imperial rule nor through conversion to a single ethnic identity or theological orientation.[42] His reconciling gospel reveals that gentile contempt is as problematic as Jewish judging. On the premise of the cross and resurrection of Christ, all nations have fallen short and entered into deadly competition with divinity. Since God's grace is equally available to all, no claim of superiority remains valid and therewith the basis for every kind of imperialism has been removed.

---

42. It thus becomes clear that it is Paul's interpreters rather than Paul himself to whom Daniel Boyarin should address his complaint of ethnocentrism, cited by Elliott.

# — 4 —

# RHETORIC AND EMPIRE — AND 1 CORINTHIANS

### Richard A. Horsley

🔲🔲🔲🔲🔲🔲🔲🔲🔲

K RISTER STENDAHL persistently pressed theologians and biblical scholars to consider the particular context Paul was addressing in formulating an argument. He sharply challenged the reductive "introspective" individualism that "plagued" Western culture in general and Pauline interpretation in particular. This individualistic interpretation also focused almost exclusively on Paul's thought, neglecting the concrete issues confronted by Paul and the communities of the movement he was called to catalyze. Over against the tendency to Christianize Paul, Stendahl also steadfastly insisted on a Jewish Paul, solidly grounded in the traditions of Israel and concerned for the historical situation of his people.[1] The recent resurgence of rhetorical criticism in New Testament studies has aided appreciably in discerning the argumentative forms Paul uses and the local "rhetorical situation" he addresses. The Greco-Roman rhetoric that Paul utilizes, however, belonged not simply to the realm of culture favored by modern Western interpreters, but to the broader political context of the Roman imperial order over against which Paul carried out his mission. Moreover, as can be seen in 1 Corinthians, Paul exhibits a distinctive perspective and particular forms of argument that derive from a source other than the standard Greco-Roman forms of rhetoric recently adduced to explain his arguments.

## Rhetorical Forms and Political Discourse in 1 Corinthians

A revived rhetorical criticism has opened a fuller and more sensitive understanding of the rhetorical situation and Paul's arguments in 1 Corinthians.[2]

---

1. Krister Stendahl first issued the challenge to the dominant introspective Western Protestant understanding of Paul in "The Apostle Paul and the Introspective Conscience of the West," *HTR* 56 (1963): 199–215, then expanded the critique and its implications for interpretation of Paul in *Paul among Jews and Gentiles, and Other Essays* (Philadelphia: Fortress Press, 1976), in which the article is reprinted.

2. The key studies laying the groundwork are Elisabeth Schüssler Fiorenza, "Rhetorical Situation and Historical Reconstruction in 1 Corinthians," *NTS* 33 (1987): 386–403, and

Intensive and detailed recent studies focusing on the form and contents of the letter have made several significant points. In rhetorical form 1 Corinthians consists of a series of deliberative arguments aimed at persuading the hearers to take a particular course of action.[3] The deliberative rhetoric of the letter corresponds to its context of reading/hearing, the *ekklēsia* gathered to discuss its situation and course of action.

In rhetorical content, key terms pertaining to civil concord versus civil discord govern the arguments of 1 Corinthians. In the opening statement of the main body of the letter in 1:10–12 Paul uses "technical language derived from political oratory and treatises concerning political unity" (*tō autō legein/phronein; schisma, en tō autō noi, homonoia, eris*).[4] This language signals the principal concern of the letter, which is thereafter dominated throughout by key terms used in advocating political unity versus political divisions. Among the most significant of these are the appeal to what is advantageous for the common interest of the community (*sympherein*, 6:12; 10:23; 12:7; adj. 7:35 and 10:33), the metaphor of "building up" the body politic (3:9–17; 6:9; 8:1, 10; 10:23; 14:3–5, 12, 17, 26), and the analogy of cooperation of members of the body, one of the most common paradigms for concord and cessation of divisions in Greek political rhetoric.[5] In his argument for common advantage and the building up of the *ekklēsia*/community, moreover, Paul utilizes rhetorical devices common to political rhetoric such as setting forth ancestors or himself as the example that the audience should imitate (*ancestors:* in addition to 10:1–13, see 5:6–8; 6:16–17; 9:8–10, 13; 10:18; 14:21; *himself:* e.g., 4:8–13; 8:13; chaps. 9 and 13).[6]

Recognizing the deliberative rhetorical form and political content of 1 Co-

---

Antoinette Clark Wire, *The Corinthian Women Prophets: A Reconstruction through Paul's Rhetoric* (Minneapolis: Fortress Press, 1990).

3. For example, Margaret M. Mitchell, *Paul and the Rhetoric of Reconciliation* (Louisville, Ky.: Westminster/John Knox Press, 1992), 23, explains that 1 Corinthians is classified as deliberative rhetoric insofar as it is characterized by four things: (1) focus on future, (2) appeal to what is advantageous (*to symferon*), (3) proof by example, and (4) appropriate subject for deliberation such as factionalism and concord.

4. Ibid., 65–81; Lawrence L. Welborn, "On the Discord in Corinth: 1 Corinthians 1–4 and Ancient Politics," *JBL* 106 (1987): 86–87, 89, 107, surveys all the terms that refer to strife in the ancient *polis*.

5. Mitchell, *Paul and the Rhetoric of Reconciliation*, 99–100, points out that Vielhauer minimizes the Greek background of the building metaphor because it does not appear in a religious sense, but that it is precisely the political background on which Paul is drawing. On the body metaphor see 158–64. But notice how Paul turns it around in application from the usual Roman application that manipulated the lower orders to acquiesce in the supposed common interest rather than to press their own grievances against the elite.

6. Ibid., 42, 45, 49–51. In this case, however, Paul is reinforcing the notion that the assembly is an exclusive community that must hold itself distant and distinct from surrounding peoples/society, as the Israelites had to do to attain their goal. And on presenting himself as *paradeigma* which the audience is to imitate, note how he turns the tables on the usual rhetorical strategy, since he presents himself as the embodiment of the virtual opposite of the honorable aristocratic values (on which see further below).

rinthians, however, is far from sufficient as a basis for understanding the argument of the letter.[7] In 1 Corinthians Paul is utilizing the standard deliberative forms and the standard terms of Greco-Roman political rhetoric to argue for the unity and concord of the *ekklēsia*, the term Paul uses for the body politic he is addressing. *Ekklēsia*, of course, is another standard political term, referring normally to the deliberative assembly of the Greek city-state that constituted one of the fundamental forms of self-government, or "politics" of the *polis*, the other being the smaller *boulē*, or council. Evidently, however, the *ekklēsia* that Paul is writing to is different from and stands over against the established *ekklēsia* of the *polis* of Corinth to which political rhetoric of concord would ordinarily have been addressed. In 1 Cor. 6:1–11 he insists adamantly that his addressees avoid the civil courts, and in 1 Cor. 10:1–22 he forbids them participation in the sacrificial temple banquets by which the overlapping networks of social relations that constituted the body politic were ritually constituted. Paul thus employs the standard deliberative rhetoric of unity and concord to advocate disunity and discord in the *polis* of Corinth. Since "the present form of this world is passing away," he tells his hearers to live as if they had no dealings with the world (1 Cor. 7:29–31). Paul is using the deliberative rhetoric of political unity and concord for the virtual opposite of its usual purpose. It is clearly necessary to investigate the functions (as well as the forms) of political rhetoric in Roman imperial society in order to understand Paul's rhetoric in 1 Corinthians.

## Functions of Rhetoric in Roman Imperial Society

Rhetoric was the most important cultural form in urban life of Western antiquity. "Hellenistic culture was above all things a rhetorical culture, and its typical literary form was the public lecture."[8]

> The one art in which cultivated people commonly expressed their cultivation, from the fifth century B.C. to the fifth century A.D.... was *eloquentia*.... All other arts save poetry were left to slaves or to the lower classes.... This art...engaged the idle hours of an aristocracy forever dabbling...in literature.[9]

---

7. Such a recognition, for example, does not prevent theological interpreters from reverting to the modern Western assumption of a separation between politics and religion, suggesting that Paul was persuading the Corinthians to focus on a theology of the cross instead of "playing politics" (Welborn, "On the Discord in Corinth," 109–10). But where do 1:26–30 and 2:6–8 fit in such a reading of 1 Corinthians 1–4?

8. H. I. Marrou, *A History of Education in Antiquity* (New York: Sheed and Ward, 1956), 187, 195; David E. Aune, *The New Testament in Its Literary Environment* (Philadelphia: Westminster Press, 1987), 12–13.

9. Ramsay MacMullen, *Enemies of the Roman Order* (Cambridge: Harvard University Press, 1966), 15. Among New Testament scholars, E. A. Judge some time ago pointed out that one "could hardly exaggerate the importance of rhetoric in shaping antiquity's own under-

Rhetoric has often been understood and discussed as a "cultural" phenomenon, certainly in the recent rediscovery of rhetoric by New Testament studies. Recent treatments by classics scholars, however, suggest that this understanding is far too narrow, indeed that it misses the point. Rhetoric was political as well as cultural.[10] Cultivated people in Roman antiquity "could see a relation almost hidden from us between their politics and what we would call their culture, and defended it as an extension of their freedom."[11]

Drawing on the work of anthropologists and cultural historians, classics scholars have opened new avenues toward an understanding of the workings of the Roman Empire and the role of rhetoric as one of the principal means of social control and cohesion. The far-flung and extremely diverse Roman Empire operated with only limited military forces and at the outset with virtually no imperial bureaucracy. Other mechanisms of social control provided the coherence of the empire. Only recently, as questions of the imperial coherence are posed in more explicit form, is it becoming evident that the imperial power relations were constituted by social and cultural forms as well as by politics. Stated somewhat differently, our modern Western habit of categorizing reality into separate spheres of politics, economics, culture, and religion has been blocking our understanding of ancient realities. Rhetoric was one of four interrelated forms by which power relations in Roman imperial society were maintained, indeed by which they were constituted.

First, of course, came military conquest, although its importance as a mechanism of social control declined after the time of initial conquest, particularly in the most "civilized" areas of the empire such as the area of Paul's mission in the cities of Greece and Asia Minor.[12] "The most striking feature of the Julio-Claudian system of imperial security was its economy of force."[13] The legions were not deployed as an occupying army across the empire, but as a mobile striking force for purposes of internal as well as external security. In areas more recently conquered, such as greater Judea, where resistance to the full impact of conquest and tribute continued, the legions posed a deterrent threat, what modern political scientists call "forceful suasion."[14] If the subjected people rebelled, the legions could be sent on reconquest, a repeat performance of the devastation of villages, slaughter

---

standing of itself." "Paul's Boasting in Relation to Contemporary Professional Practice," *ABR* 16 (1966): 42.

10. Simon Swain, *Hellenism and Empire: Language, Classicism, and Power in the Greek World, A.D. 50–250* (Oxford: Clarendon, 1996), 88.

11. MacMullen, *Enemies of the Roman Order*, 15.

12. "Let it be your work, Roman, to rule the peoples with your sway — these shall be your arts: to impose the habit of peace, to spare the conquered and put down the proud [*pacere subiectis, et debellare superbos*]" (Vergil, *Aeneid* 6.847–53).

13. Edward A. Luttwak, *The Grand Strategy of the Roman Empire* (Baltimore: Johns Hopkins University Press, 1976), 13.

14. Ibid., 17–19, 33. Recent brief treatment of rebellions in Martin Goodman, "Opponents of Rome: Jews and Others," in *Images of Empire*, ed. Loveday Alexander (Sheffield: JSOT, 1991), 222–38.

and enslavement of their inhabitants, and general terrorization of the population by such means as public display of hundreds of the ostensible "rebels"
executed by torturous crucifixion. In areas such as Greece and Asia Minor,
on the other hand, there were only vestiges of the military in the form of
colonies such as at Philippi and Thessalonica. In such areas military conquest functioned primarily as a memory, as in the devastation of Corinth
nearly two centuries before the time of Paul's mission there.

Military action in previously conquered areas intensified in the late Republic, of course, as the Roman civil war involved virtually the whole
empire. After Octavian's great victory at Actium, however, "peace and security" were imposed on the empire by its savior and the "good news"
spread far and wide via a burgeoning emperor cult, the second major means
by which the empire was held together. In the decades after Actium many
Greek cities established imperial cult in multiple forms. The emperor cult has
been taken seriously neither as genuine religion, because it did not match the
Christian model of personal belief in God, nor as effective politics, since it
appeared to rationalist modern scholars as merely empty ritual forms. With
a broader understanding of religious forms and a recognition of the reality
of ancient "civil religion," we can begin now to appreciate how effective
the emperor cult may have been as a means of social cohesion. Public space
in the "city centers" became virtually pervaded by the imperial presence in
the form of temples that dominated the agora, imperial statues and shrines,
public inscriptions, and images on coins. Almost the entire population of
cities participated in annual or semiannual festivals honoring the emperor —
perhaps the only occasion on which the poor would ever eat meat. Cities
and provinces competed with one another in staging the most extravagant
festival or building the most impressive temples or even the most grandly
redesigned public space in which the imperial temples were the focus of attention. The Greek cities thus integrated the emperor as a new and uniquely
powerful divine presence into their traditional civil religion.[15]

In the third, closely interrelated form of imperial power relations by
which the empire held together, the very sponsors of the imperial cult were
the local elite who cultivated close relations with the emperor (or imperial
family) as their patron in a rapidly extending system of patronage. Indeed,
their sponsorship of the imperial cult and other euergetism in their native
cities, and even abroad, was the means by which they consolidated their
own power. In return for their beneficence to their cities, the latter honored

---

15. Fully documented in S. R. F. Price, *Rituals and Power* (Cambridge: Cambridge University
Press, 1984); see also particularly Paul Zanker, *The Power of Images in the Age of Augustus*
(Ann Arbor: University of Michigan Press, 1992); and Richard Gordon, "The Veil of Power:
Priesthood, Religion and Ideology," in *Pagan Priests: Religion and Power in the Ancient World*,
ed. Mary Beard and John North (London: Duckworth, 1990), 199–232. Selections from all
three in Richard A. Horsley, ed., *Paul and Empire: Religion and Paul in Roman Imperial Society*
(Valley Forge, Pa.: Trinity Press International, 1997).

them with election to the most prestigious public offices and civic or imperial priesthoods.[16]

While we have to look for sources that explicitly articulate the roles of the imperial cult and the patronage system as forms of imperial control and coherence, Latin and Greek literature make no secret of the importance of rhetoric, the fourth means by which the Roman imperial order was maintained. Already under the late Republic, Roman leaders understood that the two basic motives for conformity to the dominant order were fear and consent. Fear, particularly important among the masses, was evoked by force or coercion. Consent, on the other hand, was evoked by persuasion.[17] In maintaining order, of course, the wise statesman would have recourse both to rhetoric, which provides training in shame, and to the evocation of fear. According to Cicero, "The governing statesman strengthens this feeling in commonwealths by the force of public opinion and perfects it by the inculcation of principles and by systematic training so that shame deters the citizen from crime no less effectively than fear" (*Rep.* 5.6). Not long after the battle of Actium Velleius Paterculus articulated Roman candor about coercion and persuasion as their twin means of social control: "justice, equity, and industry, long buried in oblivion, have been restored to the state. . . . Rioting in the theater has been suppressed; all citizens have either been impressed with the wish to do right, or have been forced to do so by necessity" (*History of Rome* 2.126). In the late Republic and early empire the Romans still believed that since, blessed by Fortune, their conquests were what had brought glory to them and compelled the whole world to yield to their commands, war was to be more highly valued than rhetoric (Cicero, *pro Murena* 21ff.). By the time of Nero, toward the end of Paul's mission, Roman nobles realized that rhetoric could be a practical substitute for making war. Seneca even has his imperial patron Nero, reflecting on his absolute power, declare how remarkably effective he intended persuasion to be: "With me the sword is hidden, nay, is sheathed" (*Clem.* 49). Of course, when persuasion failed in areas such as Judea — we may think of the speech to the exasperated Jerusalemites set into Agrippa II's mouth by Josephus (*J.W.* 2.350ff.) — the sword did not remain sheathed for long, as in the unrelenting Roman reconquest and devastation of the land and slaughter and enslavement of the people.[18]

---

16. On the patronage system that developed toward the end of the Republic and into the early Empire, see especially Richard Saller, *Personal Patronage under the Empire* (New York: Cambridge University Press, 1982); Andrew Wallace-Hadrill, *Patronage in Ancient Society* (London: Routledge, 1989); and the concise treatment in Peter Garnsey and Richard Saller, *The Roman Empire: Economy, Society, Culture* (Berkeley: University of California Press, 1987). On the extension of the patronage network into Corinth, see John K. Chow, *Patronage and Power* (Sheffield: Sheffield Academic Press, 1992), chap. 1. The last two are excerpted in *Paul and Empire,* ed. Horsley.

17. Neil Elliott, "Romans 13:1–7 in the Context of Imperial Propaganda," in *Paul and Empire,* ed. Horsley, 202–3.

18. The candor of ancient Roman writers such as Cicero and Velleius Paterculus would appear to exceed the political realism of scholars of "the new rhetoric" such as Chaim Perel-

It is not difficult to discern, however, that persuasion worked in close collaboration with both the imperial cult and the patronage system in which the local and provincial elite operated as clients of their imperial patrons. In the heyday of Athenian imperialism perhaps rhetoric had still been an effective instrument of civil cohesion. Rhetoric developed, of course, as an instrument of politics, the art of persuasion practiced in the city assembly (*ekklēsia*) gathered for deliberation or litigation or the whole body politic assembled for celebrative occasions. But rhetoric simultaneously articulated power relations of domination — by the elite educated male heads of households, whose wives and slaves labored to facilitate the leisure (*scholē*) of their lords to make the very public policy that sanctioned slavery, diminished women's rights, and denied political rights to resident aliens.[19] When cities became components of Hellenistic empires, however, rhetoric was adapted as an instrument of imperial civilization. Under the Roman Empire both the Greek and Roman elite further developed rhetoric to serve the Greek oligarchy and the imperial order in its steady erosion of the Greek democracy in which it had originated.[20]

Indeed, the resurgence of classical rhetoric in the Greek cities went hand-in-gloved-hand with the Roman restoration of Greek oligarchies to firm control of their cities under Augustus and his successors. This can be seen early in the process in a statement by Dionysius of Halicarnassus, active in Rome, 30–8 B.C.E.

> The ancient, sober Rhetoric has been restored to her former rightful place of honor, while the brainless new ["Asiatic"] Rhetoric has been restrained from enjoying a fame which it does not deserve and from living in luxury on the fruits of another's labors. ... The cause and origin of this great revolution has been the conquest of the world by Rome, who has thus made every city focus its entire attention upon her. Her leaders are chosen on merit, and administer the state according to

man and L. Olbrechts-Tyteca, who suggest that "the use of argumentation implies that one has renounced resorting to force alone" and that "recourse to argumentation assumes the establishment of a community of minds which, while it lasts, excludes the use of violence" (*The New Rhetoric: A Treatise on Argumentation*, trans. John Wilkinson and Purcell Weaver [Notre Dame, Ind.: Notre Dame University Press, 1969], 55). One of the reasons that oratory was "persuasive" is surely that behind it lay the threat of coercive force.

19. See further Jennifer Tolbert Roberts, *Athens on Trial: The Antidemocratic Traditions in Western Thought* (Princeton: Princeton University Press, 1994), 30; Cheryl Glenn, *Rhetoric Retold: Regendering the Tradition from Antiquity through the Renaissance* (Carbondale: Southern Illinois University Press, 1997), 1–2; Elisabeth Schüssler Fiorenza, *Rhetoric and Ethic: The Politics of Biblical Studies* (Minneapolis: Fortress Press, 1999), 62.

20. Burton L. Mack, *Rhetoric and the New Testament* (Minneapolis: Fortress Press, 1990), 29: "Rhetoric was now in the service of culture." That is a partial truth. But as Swain says precisely about developments toward the "Second Sophistic," " 'cultural' is far too innocent and passive a word" (*Hellenism and Empire*, 88). The following sketch of rhetoric as a principal means by which the oligarchies in the Greek cities protected their own position and interests in the Roman imperial order draws on Swain and the shorter earlier study by E. L. Bowie, "Greeks and Their Past in the Second Sophistic," *Past and Present* 46 (1970): 3–41.

the highest principles. They are thoroughly cultured and in the highest degree discerning, so that under their ordering influence the sensible section of the population has increased its power and the foolish have been compelled to behave rationally. (*On the Ancient Orators* Pref. 1–3, Loeb)

The conflict to which Dionysius refers is more than a mere cultural controversy between two styles of rhetoric.[21] He is writing from the perspective of the philo-Roman oligarchies in the Greek cities. Waves of discontent among the lower strata and the Roman civil wars had severely shaken their hold on power in the first century B.C.E. Athens itself, for example, produced a successful democratic insurrection against the philo-Roman oligarchy (Pausanius 1.20.5) and political unrest continued there at various times under Augustus.[22]

The Roman aristocracy, who always "detested democracy," repeatedly assisted the oligarchies in restoring order and fostered revival of the old Greek ideals of patriotism, justice, responsibility and reverence, and moderation. Under imperial Roman rule, then, the last vestiges of democracy were undermined, as the oligarchies gained control of or simply abolished the city assemblies, gradually destroyed the law courts (*dikasteria*), and by attaching liturgies to magistracies, established a property requirement for holding public office.[23] Under Augustus it was precisely magnates from among the aristocratic families who cultivated the imperial family as client "friends" of Caesar and sponsored the emperor cult and imperial festivals in their respective cities. And it was Dionysius's successors among the aristocracies of the Greek cities who revived rhetoric as an instrument of social control and cohesion.

With the weakening or abolition of the assemblies and law courts, two of the traditional functions of rhetoric disappeared. Rhetoric's political role had simply changed. The demise of the *dikasteria* did not eliminate the need for

---

21. See the discussions in Emilio Gabba, "The Historians and Augustus," in *Caesar Augustus: Seven Aspects*, ed. Fergus Millar and Erich Segal (Oxford: Clarendon Press, 1984); and Karl Galinsky, *Augustan Culture* (Princeton: Princeton University Press, 1996), 341.

22. M. Hoff, "Civil Disobedience and Unrest in Augustan Athens," *Hesperia* 58 (1989): 267–76.

23. Evidence and analysis in G. E. M. de Ste. Croix, *The Class Struggle in the Ancient World* (Ithaca, N.Y.: Cornell University Press, 1981), 300–326, with a summary on 344: "Rome made sure that Greece was kept quiet and friendly to her by ensuring that the cities were controlled by the wealthy class, which now had mainly given up any idea of resistance to Roman rule and in fact seemed to have welcomed it for the most part, as an insurance against popular movements from below." Rome also helped secure the economic basis on which its alliance with local oligarchies rested: "the chief [economic] effect [of the Roman Empire] was to promote an ever increasing concentration of land in the hands of its governing aristocracy at the expense of the population at large" (A. H. M. Jones, *Roman Economy: Studies in Ancient Economic and Administrative History*, ed. P. A. Brunt [Oxford: Blackwell, 1974], 135). This is confirmed for Achaia, of which Corinth was the capital and economic center, by Susan Alcock, *Graecia Capta: The Landscapes of Roman Greece* (Cambridge: Cambridge University Press, 1993).

judicial rhetoric. The courts simply became instruments of the wealthy and powerful,[24] with judicial rhetoric playing a corresponding role. Gradually stripped of any significant power, city *ekklēsiai* deliberated about matters that served to reinforce the established power relations, such as voting additional honors to the emperor and election of local magnates to office in return for their liberal benefactions in sponsoring a festival or underwriting expenses for a public building.[25] And of course the Greek aristocracies under the Roman Empire provide the classic example of how epideictic rhetoric was especially important for "those who . . . defend the traditional and accepted values," to cite a generalization by Perelman and Olbrechts-Tyteca.[26] The agora and the theater were indeed places to give and hear an interesting speech, and eloquence was required at civic festivals.[27] Public declamation became one of the principal forms of public entertainment and could be heard throughout the Greek- and Latin-speaking areas of the empire in lecture halls and temples as well as theaters.[28] But the established, well-connected orators who delivered declamations and other public speeches were men of wealth, status, power, and influence who were heavily invested in politics, the courts, and civic honors — in contrast to mere philosophers, who often criticized such aristocratic values in favor of wisdom as the true wealth, power, and honor.[29]

An extensive recent study of "Language, Classicism, and Power in the Greek World" explains the function of rhetoric as revived under the Roman Empire:

> The study of rhetoric was the commonest form of higher education followed by the elite. Many of its members would have gone through

---

24. Peter Garnsey, *Social Status and Legal Privilege in the Roman Empire* (Oxford: Oxford University Press, 1970). A. H. M. Jones, *The Later Roman Empire 284–602* (Oxford: Norman, 1964), 1:517, 519, offers a summary of how the built-in disposition of Roman law and law courts to favor the wealthy and powerful became more institutionalized during the Principate: "There was one law for the rich and another for the poor," although in the purely civil sphere "it was not so much the law that was at fault, as the courts."

25. Mack claims that "rhetoric provided the rules for making critical judgments in the course of all forms of social intercourse" (*Rhetoric and the New Testament*, 29, 31). Under the Roman imperial order, however, "What should be done" had already been decided before a public orator began to speak.

26. Perelman and Olbrechts-Tyteca, *New Rhetoric*, 55 (section on "Argumentation and Violence"). For the situation in ancient Greek cities by the late first century, see further Bowie, "Greeks and Their Past," esp. 4–6.

27. Mack, *Rhetoric and the New Testament*, 31. That "Formal education may have been costly and thus not available to many" is an understatement. The role of the general public — *idiōtes* with regard to rhetoric — was to listen to representatives of the aristocrats.

28. M. L. Clarke, *Rhetoric at Rome: A Historical Survey* (London: Cohen and West, 1953), 85–86; Donald L. Clark, *Rhetoric in Greco-Roman Education* (New York: Columbia University Press, 1957), 216; Stephen M. Pogoloff, *Logos and Sophia: The Rhetorical Situation of 1 Corinthians*, SBLDS 134 (Atlanta: Scholars Press, 1992), 52–53.

29. See Swain, *Hellenism and Empire*; Bowie, "Greeks and Their Past," esp. 3–6, 36–39; Pogoloff, *Logos and Sophia*, 57–64.

the stage of learning the basic exercises (or *progymnasmata*). . . . These exercises revolved round continuous reading and writing from the classical texts. More advanced training was available after the *progymnasmata* stage to those who wanted it. For though opportunities for public speaking were diminished in comparison with the democratic Athens of the classical period, there remained many occasions when the educated class were obliged or pleased to speak in public. Speeches of welcome to dignitaries, memorial or funeral orations, addresses at weddings, speeches honoring the gods, competitions at festivals, in other words the types of speech filed under the heading "epideictic" or display oratory were always needed. The two other advanced categories of speech-making defined in classical times, judicial oratory and political or deliberative oratory, also remained in use. As a work like Plutarch's *Political Advice* makes clear, politicians might not be free to say what they wanted to the people, but public speech was the primary method of ruling them.[30]

The most prominent theme in the oratory and related literature of the early imperial period "is that of peace, established and maintained by the emperor throughout the whole world and bringing an end to *stasis* and civil war, which also develops into a recognition that the empire provides its inhabitants with *asphaleia*, security against external attack."[31] That reflects the position the orators held and the stake they had in the established social order, which would have been threatened by any eruption of party strife and discord. But it also reveals the uneasy awareness among the elite that they were the beneficiaries of the "exploitation and inequality upon which the ancient economy depended."[32] They well knew that, as Aristotle and a host of other classical writers had stated, "party strife is everywhere due to inequality" (*Pol.* 5.1.6 1301b27).

Finally, insofar as rationalist modern biblical interpreters seem uneasy about Paul's apocalyptic frame of mind as somewhat fantastic, the aristocratic Greek practitioners of rhetoric in the early empire were living in a fantasy world, an imagined world constructed selectively out of the glories of the heroic ancient Greek past. "The fictitious forensic or deliberative cases which so appealed to the elite . . . drew their subjects from Greek history" peopled by stereotyped figures and the heroes of yesteryear. In this "rhetorical city" the rich often saw themselves

---

30. Swain, *Hellenism and Empire*, 90. Cf. the shorter, earlier survey of "the second sophistic" by Bowie, "Greeks and Their Past."

31. V. Nutton, "The Beneficial Ideology," in *Imperialism in the Ancient World*, ed. Peter Garnsey and C. R. Whittaker (Cambridge: Cambridge University Press, 1978), 210–11, with references.

32. See the fuller discussion by Welborn, "On the Discord in Corinth," 94–96.

as protectors of the city and were, after all, essential to its well-being. They no doubt derived immense satisfaction from the benefactions which they made to the citizens [who], as Dio of Prusa puts it, could acclaim them "all day long as war-heroes, Olympians, saviours, and feeders." ... Practicing the role of civic protector in the schools [of rhetoric] was an entertaining way of practising for the real life of a superior. Historical declamations allowed the elite not only to practice as leaders but to practice as the leaders of the great age of Greece.[33]

From this survey of the function of rhetoric in the Greek cities of the Roman Empire, it is clear that Paul, the "assembly" he helped get started in Corinth, and the communications between them, such as 1 Corinthians, were embedded in a system of power relations that were constituted and maintained by public oratory, in close collaboration with the emperor cult, both of which were sponsored by the urban elite as clients of the imperial house.[34] The next task is to investigate how Paul and the people he addressed in Corinth may have related to that network of power relations, particularly in their own discourses as evident in 1 Corinthians.

## Complicating Rhetorical Criticism to Comprehend a Complicated Rhetorical Situation

First Corinthians, which features so many parallels to public rhetoric, should thus be read in the context of the functions of public rhetoric in the Roman imperial order. Methodologically, however, while rhetorical criticism leads us to focus on the concrete rhetorical situation Paul addressed in 1 Corinthians, that situation was far more complex than previously acknowledged, requiring that our approach to and analysis of it be correspondingly complex.

Rhetorical analysis offers a radically specific orientation to and focus on a particular concrete rhetorical situation. According to principles of rhetorical analysis, the persuasive work that a speech or letter does is inextricable

---

33. Swain, *Hellenism and Empire*, 92. Similarly Bowie, "Greeks and Their Past."

34. Like S. R. F. Price, I am working with the understanding of power as power relations articulated by Michel Foucault, summarized in *Power/Knowledge* (New York: Pantheon, 1980), 78–208 (chap. 5: "Two Lectures"). "Power means relations, a more-or-less organised, hierarchical, co-ordinated cluster of relations" (198–99). "Power is exercised rather than possessed ... the overall effect of its [the ruling class's] positions ... it exerts pressure upon [the people], just as they themselves, in their struggle against it, resist the grip it has upon them" (*Discipline and Punish: The Birth of the Prison* [New York: Pantheon, 1979], 26–27). Elizabeth A. Castelli, "Intrepretations of Power in 1 Corinthians" *Semeia* (1991): 197–222, applies the concept to Paul's discourse in 1 Corinthians. The contents of Paul's subsequent correspondence with the Corinthians (esp. 2 Corinthians 10–13), however, suggests that in writing 1 Corinthians Paul had not "exercised" very much power in Foucault's sense. As Christian scripture, of course, 1 Corinthians has exercised power, one mark of which is the resistance to it that many of us are now offering.

from its particular historical circumstances. Indeed, the communication or persuasion that takes place is a function of the contingent local people party to the communication and their background, circumstances, and interests. One of the principal reasons that rhetorical criticism is so attractive is that it "can place a writing at the juncture of social history and read it as a record of some moment of exchange that may have contributed to the social formations we seek better to understand."[35] However, "the social circumstances of the early Christian movements do not correspond to the traditional occasions for each type of speech."[36] Moreover, Paul's aims and the interests of his audience differed radically from those of the Greek elite who cultivated classical rhetoric. Most fundamentally, contrary to common claims in Pauline studies, Paul was not involved in public oratory but in small-group teaching and letter writing connected with separatist communities.[37]

To pursue rhetorical analysis in any depth, it is thus necessary to consider the purpose and effects of arguments in the concrete rhetorical situation. Perhaps because they were trained to focus on exegesis of pericopes taken out of their broader literary and historical context, New Testament scholars have tended to focus on the types and devices of rhetorical forms. Even the great Latin master Quintilian, however, downgraded the importance of rhetorical theory in favor of the contingencies of circumstances (*Inst. Ora.* 2.13.15–17). Speeches and letters were direct responses to particular historical-political situations and problems. "Actual speeches could be more complex and eclectic than the rhetorical handbooks might suggest."[38] Letters were even more flexible and eclectic in adaptation of cultural forms.[39] Since the social circumstances of Paul's mission do not correspond to the traditional occasions of Greek rhetoric and since he has mixed and significantly adapted the basic rhetorical forms in composing his letters, therefore, we should attend less to the formal types of rhetoric than to the rhetorical situation. In Paul's letters form is subsumed to function in the act of communication and persuasion.[40]

The rhetorical situation in Corinth addressed in 1 Corinthians, the func-

---

35. Mack, *Rhetoric and the New Testament*, 17.

36. Ibid., 35. Moreover (p. 37), the formal rhetorical categories such as the "final topics" were utterly "empty of specific content, for the level of abstraction excludes any indication of what may have been considered 'right' or 'lawful' at a given juncture in a social history."

37. Stanley K. Stowers, "Social Status, Public Speaking and Private Teaching; The Circumstances of Paul's Preaching Activity," *NovT* 26 (1984): 59–82.

38. Aune, *New Testament in Its Literary Environment*, 199.

39. Note the sensitivity to this flexibility of form in Stanley K. Stowers, *Letter Writing in Greco-Roman Antiquity* (Philadelphia: Westminster Press, 1986).

40. Formal, structural rhetorical analysis of 1 Corinthians 15 and 1 Corinthians 9, for example, do not reveal much about what the issues were or what Paul was attempting to accomplish in either argument; cf. Mack, *Rhetoric and the New Testament*, 56–58, 60–63; and Vernon K. Robbins, *Exploring the Texture of Texts* (Valley Forge, Pa.: Trinity Press International, 1996), 57. See further Rollin Ramsaran, *Liberating Words* (Valley Forge, Pa.: Trinity Press International, 1996), 26–27, 78–79, with nn. 8–9.

tion of the letter, and our approach to the letter, moreover, present a far more complicated set of problems than is usually assumed in rhetorical criticism, in at least two major ways.

First, as is commonly recognized in analysis of classical oratory, rhetoric was tethered to a *sensus communis*, a common cultural heritage, including the standard rhetorical forms, dominant and organizing concepts and metaphors, and historical references.[41] As becomes unavoidably evident in the Corinthian correspondence, far more than in Paul's other letters, Paul did not share much of a common cultural heritage with his audience. At points in 1 Corinthians it would appear that he and the addressees were virtually talking past one another. Having been shaped by a different cultural background than were the Corinthians, Paul worked in Corinth only about eighteen months, and other missionaries, Apollos in particular, who had a different message and viewpoint, worked there after he left. Paul's situation in Corinth resembles that of a modern European Christian missionary in a colonial situation, only in reverse. In modern times missionaries from the imperial metropolis and dominant culture went to colonized people in order to "convert" them to the colonizers' metropolitan religion and culture. By contrast, although he had previous experience in the dominant culture, in cities such as Corinth and Ephesus Paul was a missionary from a subjected "backward" people and culture attempting to "evangelize" people who shared the culture of the imperial metropolis. In such circumstances rhetorical analysis must be supplemented with a little sociology of knowledge, particularly the concepts of "socialization," "secondary socialization," and "resocialization."[42] As scholars now recognize after generations of intensive analysis of Paul's language and thought patterns, after his own "socialization" or "secondary socialization" in Jerusalem scribal circles, he understood reality in a way very similar to that articulated in Judean apocalyptic literature. In contrast, the Corinthians he addressed, by virtue of their socialization in the Romanized Hellenistic metropolis of Corinth, worked from a very different orientation toward reality, a very different sense of personal and social life. That made communication between them far more difficult than usual in the practice of Greek oratory and makes rhetorical analysis far more complex and difficult for 1 Corinthians than, for example, for a speech of Dio Chrysostom.

While much analysis of 1 Corinthians has explored this highly complex and confused "rhetorical situation" through Paul's arguments — how he uses, qualifies, twists, and/or rejects terms and principles of some of the Corinthians — most recent rhetorical analysis has not taken this, and previ-

---

41. Pogoloff, *Logos and Sophia*, 29; Swain, *Hellenism and Power*, chap. 3, is highly instructive for rhetoric in the Greek cities under the empire.

42. Peter Berger and Thomas Luckmann, *The Social Construction of Reality* (Garden City, N.Y.: Doubleday, 1966).

ous analysis of it, into account.[43] It is likely that the goal and the result of persuasion were significantly different for Paul in 1 Corinthians, who was writing to people whose disagreements with him were rooted in a very different worldview, than it would have been for orators addressing audiences who shared common cultural heritage as well as the same basic worldview. Paul's subsequent correspondence with the Corinthians (see especially 2 Corinthians 10–13) suggest that his attempt in 1 Corinthians to persuade the Corinthian "spirituals" of his viewpoint was not all that successful.

The rhetorical situation of 1 Corinthians was even further complicated by the activity in the Corinthian community of Apollos, known in Acts 18:24 as "a Jew from Alexandria, eloquent and well versed in the scriptures." It does not take much of a hermeneutics of suspicion to detect that Paul was not happy about the effects of Apollos's ministry in Corinth (see especially 3:10–15, 9:12a). In that connection, it is surely significant that nearly all of the language and principles that Paul seriously qualifies, twists into his own formulations, or rejects outright can be paralleled in the Wisdom of Solomon 6–10 or the treatises of Philo of Alexandria. It seems most likely that in 1 Corinthians Paul was arguing with a religiosity of individual spiritual transcendence focused on personal devotion to and/or possession of heavenly Sophia, very similar to that articulated in such Hellenistic Jewish texts. The structure of the rhetorical situation of 1 Corinthians is, therefore, far more complicated than that of a speech by a public orator in a Greek city. The latter presupposes and draws on a common cultural heritage to persuade people who share a common worldview to stand in concord with the dominant social-cultural order. Using some of the same rhetorical forms and terms, Paul attempts to persuade people — some of whom have a very different cultural heritage and worldview — not only to take the action he recommends but to think about reality more in the way he does and to disengage from the dominant social-cultural order.

Second, in an important discovery and innovation, rhetorical criticism has been used to reconstruct the multiple voices involved in the newly founded community *ekklēsia* in Corinth that can be discerned in Paul's arguments in 1 Corinthians.[44] Recent rhetorical studies thus supplement and refine earlier, less sophisticated studies that discerned understandings of Jesus, wisdom, transcendent spirituality, ecstatic prophecy, and theology in the Corinthian community that were different from what Paul espoused.[45] Insofar as the

---

43. The rhetorical analyses of 1 Corinthians 15 by Mack (*Rhetoric and the New Testament*, 56–59) and Robbins (*Exploring the Texture of Texts*, 56–58), for example, include no hypothesis about what it is that Paul is arguing against, as articulated in the statement "there is no resurrection of the dead." But how can we begin to analyze or understand his argument without some sense of what he is arguing against, what position he is addressing — and how, as elsewhere in the letter, he is using language of the Corinthians addressed in his formulations?

44. See especially Schüssler Fiorenza, "Rhetorical Situation and Historical Reconstruction," 386–403; and Wire, *The Corinthian Women Prophets*.

45. Birger A. Pearson, *The Pneumatikos-Psychikos Terminology in 1 Corinthians*, SBLDS

letter in which Paul referred to but overwrote these views and practices in arguing for his own views later became authoritative as Christian scripture, these other voices, other discourses, became subjugated. Thus the original hearers/readers with whom Paul was arguing were a construction of Paul. It seems possible now, with tools such as rhetorical criticism, precisely by discerning their difference from and conflict with Paul's views, to reconstruct these alternative voices and to examine their relation to the power relations of Roman imperial society.

Insofar as Paul's 1 Corinthians became Christian scripture — that is, was included in a "Pauline" collection of letters, then underwent a canonization process, and has been understood predominantly according to Christian theological interpretation — Paul's own discourse in 1 Corinthians also became subjugated. Ironically, Paul's formulations and arguments in 1 Corinthians became subjugated by a later Christian/"Pauline" viewpoint that seems closer in certain respects to the views of the Corinthians (and/or Apollos) that Paul was arguing against than to his own argument.[46] Not only is Paul to a degree a construction of his hearers/readers, as he tried to explain himself in their terms, but also, insofar as subsequent readers of 1 Corinthians read with an understanding similar to the Corinthians he was addressing, Paul's arguments became all the more a construction of his Corinthian-like later readers. Paul's discourse continues to be subjugated by modern Western cultural hegemony when discussed only in terms of religion — such as translating *ekklēsia* as "church" — or when it is simply assumed that he and his Corinthian addressees were involved in a religion we call Christianity, which of course did not yet exist.

Our task thus is to attempt to discern the subjugated discourses of both Paul and the Corinthians in and through 1 Corinthians. Partly because we have his other letters for comparison, Paul's arguments in 1 Corinthians are surely far more readily reconstructible than the alternative views and practices subjugated in the letter. Since we have access to the alternative

---

12 (Missoula, Mont.: Scholars Press, 1973); Richard A. Horsley, "*Pneumatikos vs. Psychikos:* Distinctions of Spiritual Status among the Corinthians," *HTR* 69 (1976): 269–88; Horsley, "Wisdom of Word and Words of Wisdom," *CBQ* 39 (1977): 224–39; Horsley, "How Can Some of You Say, 'There Is No Resurrection of the Dead'? Spiritual Elitism in Corinth," *NovT* 20 (1978): 203–31; Horsley, "Gnosis in Corinth: 1 Cor. 8:1–6," *NTS* 27 (1980): 32–51.

46. For example, Paul's attempt to substitute Christ for heavenly Wisdom (Sophia) became subjugated by the identification of Christ with Sophia and the theological characterization of Christ as Sophia. Later "Pauline" and Christian readers and theologians thus read 1 Cor. 8:6 as a doctrine of a preexistent Christ and 10:4 as if Christ were a preexistent divine agent active in Israel's history, instead of as rhetorical devices to displace the Corinthians' focus on heavenly Sophia. Or more generally, Paul's attempt to counter the Corinthians' spiritualized personal transcendence was itself spiritualized in subsequent "Pauline" and canonical and scholarly readings. Later readers, including modern exegetes and commentaries, thus read 1 Cor. 2:6–16 as if Paul really did have a special "wisdom in a mystery" that he taught only to a spiritual elite rather than as part of a rhetorical technique of *sarkasmos* by which he mocks what he constructs as the Corinthians' spiritual elitism, which becomes clear in the "put-down" of 3:1–4.

voices only through Paul's arguments, however, it is all the more important for us as critical interpreters to recognize that Paul's views may need to be separated from the canonized and theological "Pauline" understanding in ways somewhat similar to those in which we discern the Corinthians' (and/or Apollos's) views through Paul's arguments.

## Personal Spiritual Transcendence of Imperial Power Relations

Judging from how Paul qualifies or bluntly rejects certain terms, concepts, principles, actions, or figures, they can be discerned as expressions of the position or practices of Corinthians that Paul opposes. These Corinthians were excited about attaining a spiritual status as "wise, powerful, nobly born," "filled, rich, and kingly," "mature" versus "babes" and *"pneumatikoi"* versus *"psychikoi"* (1:26, 4:8–10, 2:6–3:4). This special spiritual status, moreover, apparently came from a close relationship with heavenly wisdom (Sophia; 1:18–24; 2:6; note also that the predications Paul applies to Christ in 8:6 and 10:3–4 ordinarily were applied to Sophia in Hellenistic Jewish literature). The wisdom possessed by the wise included eloquent speech (1:17–20; 2:1–5). The persons who had become "wise, powerful, mature" were regularly caught up into a state of ecstatic prophecy, experiencing such "spiritual things" (*pneumatika*) as tongues and an insight or "word of *sophia*" or "word of *gnōsis*" (12:1, 8; 14:2, 7–9, 14, 23, 27–28, 37). The scriptural archetype or paradigm of the wise, perfect *pneumatikos*, moreover, was the *anthropos* created according to the "image of God" in Gen. 1:26–27 or "the man from heaven," whereas that of the mere *psychikos* was the lower "man from the earth" and "of dust," created later in Gen. 2:7 (15:44–49).

The true self of the *pneumatikos* that experienced this transcendent spiritual status was apparently the soul (or mind), which was thus secured in its "immortality" and "incorruptibility," as separate from the body, which was "corruptible" and "mortal," that is, "dead" (15:42, 52–54; 15:12). The immortal self or soul of the *pneumatikos* was thus thought to have transcended the body and its various aspects, which now belonged to a separate sphere of existence. For example, "Food is meant for the stomach and the stomach for food" (6:13). Complete devotion to heavenly Sophia, however, entailed sexual asceticism, to the point of separating from one's spouse so as to disengage from sexual activity: "It is well for a man not to touch a woman" (7:1, 5). Young, unmarried women were to remain "virgins' (7:25, 36–38). With regard to the wider society, the spiritually wise/powerful/mature person stood firm in the conviction that "all things are possible/authorized for me" (*panta moi existin;* 6:12=10:23). This personal ethical "authority" or "liberty" was rooted in the possession of theological *gnosis*, by which the enlightened one knew that "no idol in the world really exists" and that "there is no God but one" (8:9, 1, 4). Possession of this *gnosis* that the gods supposedly represented by the idols did not really exist, a knowledge that made the "consciousness" "strong," meant that one was free to "eat food offered to idols" in the various temples of the city (8:1, 7, 10).

Virtually all of this language, including the principles of theological *gnosis*, is paralleled in the Wisdom of Solomon and the treatises of Philo of Alexandria.[47] For the only terms that are not explicitly paralleled in Philo's writings, *pneumatikos* and *psychikos*, the basic distinction expressed by those terms between two types of people is paralleled in Philo, along with their scriptural archetypes or images in Gen. 1:26–27 and 2:7 respectively.[48] Thus, all of Paul's arguments in 1 Corinthians, with the possible exception of 11:3–16, which may be a later interpolation, can be understood as addressed to a religiosity of personal spiritual transcendence similar to that expressed in Wisdom 6–10 and Philo, including his portrayal of the Therapeutrides and Therapeutae, the ascetic mystical Jewish group near Alexandria. The striking and comprehensive parallels between the language and possibly the religiosity of the Corinthians addressed in 1 Corinthians and Philo and Wisdom 6–10, moreover, may have a direct link in the person of Apollos. Paul's not-so-subtle subordination of Apollos's work in Corinth to his own and the implied threat of divine judgment on that work in 1 Cor. 3:5–15 in the context of his rejection of the Corinthians' exalted spiritual status, high valuation of eloquence, and focus on Sophia (cf. Apollos mentioned as connected with the divisiveness at the outset of the argument, 1:10–12 and again in 3:21–23) indicate that Paul viewed Apollos as connected with the views he is arguing against. The tradition transmitted in Acts 18:24 indicates that Apollos was a Jew from Alexandria, "an eloquent man, well-versed in the scriptures." It is difficult to avoid the conclusion that Apollos, who worked in the Corinthian assembly after Paul had left for Ephesus, must have influenced the particular forms that the piety of some of the Corinthians had taken.

How such Hellenistic Jewish discourse that had apparently resonated so significantly with many members of the assembly Paul had helped found in Corinth related to the system of power relations in Roman imperial society supported by public oratory is complicated but at least minimally discernible. The Sophia/wisdom that constituted both the agent and the content of salvation was known from spiritual (allegorical) interpretation of Jewish scriptural traditions (under the cloud, passing through the sea, spiritual food, drink, rock, 1 Cor. 10:1–4 — all symbols from the exodus-wilderness narrative). Thus the source of wisdom and the salvation it offered

---

47. For fuller elaboration and documentation on the following, see my articles cited above in n. 45 and my *1 Corinthians*, Abingdon NT Commentaries (Nashville: Abingdon Press, 1998).

48. With somewhat different emphases, Pearson, *Pneumatikos-Psychikos Terminology*; and Horsley, *"Pneumatikos vs. Psychikos."*

was the cultural tradition of a people subjected by the empire. Insofar as that cultural tradition was spiritualized and wisdom personified and reified as a divine figure, Sophia, that transcended the world, a close relation with her brought a personal transcendence of mundane social-political reality. That found expression in several interrelated forms that inverted or devalued fundamental aspects of social and even personal life as understood in the dominant culture.

Whereas the imperial propaganda, mediated into urban social affairs by public oratory, advocated the conception and nurture of children in patriarchal families, the Corinthian *pneumatikoi* (like the Therapeutics) in their exclusive devotion to heavenly Sophia and possession of *gnosis* experienced a newly attained "authority" over their own bodies, some women even withdrawing from sexual relations with their spouses. Now faithful to a transcendent mate, their bodies were no longer available for reproductive labor in service of the imperial program.[49] Indeed, the bodies of the Corinthian slaves, freed slaves, and artisans generally were controlled by the imperial order in the onerous productive labor expected through the patronage pyramids into which most were swept by their poverty and powerlessness. But their true selves, their souls, had attained transcendence of the mundane world and a secure immortality and authority subject to no one. In the tradition of late prophetic and Hellenistic Jewish critique of the gods of their imperial rulers, the Corinthians, in their newly gained *gnosis*, simply dismissed the gods of the dominant imperial order as mere idols, as simply nonexistent. Thus the ritual sacrificial meals by which the gods were worshiped and the social order maintained were merely harmless social gatherings.

Most interesting perhaps is the inversion of meaning in the Corinthian *pneumatikoi*'s spiritualized use of time-honored terms for the aristocratic values of classical Greek and Roman imperial society dominated politically, economically, and culturally by the oligarchies who held highest status by heredity as the nobly born, powerful, rich, honored, and wise. Again the Corinthian "spirituals" appear to parallel the Wisdom of Solomon 6–10 and Philo and their readers. As Hellenistic Jews, the latter, despite their subordination to the empire as second-class inhabitants (noncitizens lacking certain rights and privileges) of the cities in which they lived, could attain a spiritually aristocratic status as "nobly born, powerful, rich" through their possession of Sophia. Similarly, poor, lowly, despised Corinthian artisans, slaves, or descendants of freed slaves who had been sent as colonists to Corinth a century before could now enjoy the excitement of similar spiritual

---

49. As Wire, *Corinthian Women Prophets*, 72–97, demonstrates, Paul designed his argument in 1 Corinthians 5–7 to persuade women in the Corinthian community to use their bodies as a means of controlling men's drive toward *porneia*, although presumably this did not include submission again to the imperial program of reproduction in the service of patriarchal families that formed the basis of the whole civil and imperial system.

status as the truly "wise, nobly born, honored, and rich" through their newly acquired wisdom and devotion to Sophia.

## Paul's Use of Political Rhetoric in Opposition to Empire

Examination of Paul's arguments in 1 Corinthians in the context of the imperial power relations supported by contemporary public oratory indicates how Paul opposed both the function of standard Greco-Roman rhetoric and the Roman imperial order it served.[50]

Although he used its devices, Paul bluntly rejected the high value that the dominant culture placed on rhetorical persuasion (1:17–20; 2:1, 4; 4:19).[51] He also diametrically opposed Greco-Roman rhetoric substantively even where he utilized its typical techniques and devices in offering himself as an example of the behavior he was advocating. An orator presented not just an argument but also his own character (*ethos*) to lend authority to his message. Paul offered himself as a paradigm of what he argued for in most of the major arguments of 1 Corinthians (see esp. 1–4, 8–10, 12–14). The *ethos* or "character" he presented, however, was virtually the antithesis of the epitome of aristocratic virtue and values standard in Greco-Roman rhetoric. This is not simply a matter of his denial of his own eloquence (2:1–4), which offers at least a superficial resemblance to Greek orators' self-deprecations. It is rather that Paul presented himself as the very opposite of the Greco-Roman standard: weak, foolish, poor (and working with one's hands for a living), lowly, and despised, rather than powerful, wise, wealthy (living from others' labor), noble, and honored (4:8–13), and compelled by necessity rather than living by one's own free will (9:15–19). An orator might well "boast," but he would hardly boast of being a "fool" or the "dregs of all things." Paul played his and the Corinthians' lowly social status to the utmost (e.g., in 1 Cor. 4:8–13). But as he surely understood, in the Roman-Hellenistic cultural context he carried the stigma both of working with his hands (1 Thess. 1:9, 4:11) and of being a Jew — the

---

50. In declining support from one of the aspiring patrons involved in the assembly he helped start in Corinth (1 Cor. 9:3–15) which would have made him a house apostle, Paul apparently also opposed the pattern of patron-client relations by which the imperial order was constituted. See further Victor Furnish, *II Corinthians*, AB (Garden City, N.Y.: Doubleday, 1984); and Peter Marshall, *Enmity in Corinth: Social Conventions in Paul's Relations with the Corinthians*, WUNT 2/23 (Tübingen: Mohr Siebeck, 1987). But Paul appears also, in effect, to have fostered a patronage network of his own in the Corinthian assembly, in his special relations with Stephanus and Phoebe (1 Cor. 16:16; Rom 16:1), as I suggest in "1 Corinthians: A Case Study of Paul's Assembly as an Alternative Society," in *Paul and Empire*, ed. Horsley, 249–50.

51. Hans Dieter Betz, "The Problem of Rhetoric and Theology according to the Apostle Paul," in *L'apôtre Paul, personalité, style et ministère*, ed. A. Vanhoye (Louvain: Louvain University Press, 1986), 36–37, points out that while "demonstration" (*apodeixis*) figures prominently in ancient rhetorical theory, "for Paul it is constitutive of a rhetoric different from the art of persuasion."

Roman elite looked upon Jews, like Syrians, as good for nothing other than enslavement.[52]

Besides opposing the function of public oratory, Paul used key terms and symbols of Greco-Roman rhetoric and Roman imperial ideology to oppose the Roman imperial order ordinarily supported by that rhetoric and ideology.[53] In pressing for the solidarity of the Corinthian *ekklēsia* in his own movement that stood sharply over against the dominant imperial society, Paul used the standard political rhetoric of unity, concord, and common advantage versus civil strife, in effect, to subvert the established "political" order. Even more striking is the way in which the terms and their historical referents most fundamental in 1 Corinthians and the rest of his letters directly oppose the same terms and their referents in the Roman imperial order and its political culture. As noted briefly at the outset, Paul apparently understood the *ekklēsia* which he urged to maintain unity and concord as an alternative assembly set sharply over against the established *ekklēsia* of Corinth.[54] Insofar as he insisted on the solidarity of his assembly in Corinth, therefore, he was subverting the unity and concord advocated in public oratory that formed the very basis of the Pax Romana in the Greek cities. He even instructed the alternative *ekklēsia* to conduct their own community affairs separate from the dominant society, specifically to deal internally with whatever conflicts emerged and to avoid the civil courts, and in general, when they had to deal with the world, to do so "as though they had no dealings with it" (1 Corinthians 5; 6:1–11; 7:29–31). He further adamantly forbade members of the new alternative *ekklēsia* to participate in the very sacrificial meals that constitute the overlapping networks of communal relations in Corinthian society (see esp. 1 Cor. 10:14–22).[55]

Most striking of all in Paul's use of "loaded" political language is *euangelion*.[56] In Greek cities such as Corinth, *euangelion* was the "gospel" of the "salvation" and "peace and security" established by the imperial savior Au-

---

52. So also Stowers, "Social Status," 74.

53. Dieter Georgi outlines how Paul does this more or less throughout his letters in *Theocracy in Paul's Praxis and Theology*, trans. David E. Green (Minneapolis: Fortress Press, 1991). See further Helmut Koester, "Imperial Ideology and Paul's Eschatology in 1 Thessalonians," and Neil Elliott, "The Anti-Imperial Message of the Cross," in *Paul and Empire*, ed. Horsley, 158–66 and 167–83, respectively.

54. As noted by Mitchell, *Paul and the Rhetoric of Reconciliation*, 101 n. 219, Werner Jaeger saw that "[t]he apostle Paul wrote to the Christian community at Corinth, a state within a state, which had to be 'edified,' i.e., literally constructed like an edifice, so that its members would join together to form an organic whole." *Werner Jaeger: Five Essays*, trans. A. M. Fiske (Montreal: Casalini, 1966), 140. For a sketch of Paul's construction of his *ekklēsia* as an alternative society, see Horsley in *Paul and Empire*, chap. 14.

55. See further Horsley, "1 Corinthians: A Case Study of Paul's Assembly," 247–49; Horsley, *1 Corinthians*, 115–24, 139–46; and Stanley K. Stowers, "Greeks Who Sacrifice and Those Who Do Not: Toward an Anthropology of Greek Religion," in *The Social World of the First Christians: Essays in Honor of Wayne Meeks*, ed. L. M. White and L. Yarbrough (Minneapolis: Fortress Press, 1995), 293–333.

56. Concise review of the uses of the term *euangelion* with references to scholarly discussions

gustus and his successors. The imperial savior had brought "salvation" and "peace and security" precisely by terrorizing means of "forceful suasion" such as crucifying subjects who had the audacity to resist Roman rule. This gospel was proclaimed on coins and inscriptions and celebrated in imperial city festivals in honor of the emperor. As part of the celebration of the gospel of the imperial savior, sacrifices of gratitude were offered in the temples and shrines that dominated public space in the city-centers of Corinth and other Greek cities. Paul taught an alternative gospel, that of a leader of a subject people who had been crucified for his resistance to the imperial order. Such a gospel of the crucified was not only foolishness, as the opposite of the dominant aristocratic values affirmed in every public speech. To speak a gospel of the crucified was also "foolish" in the sense of politically suicidal, because it would bring the Romans down on one's head — to maintain the peace with military violence when persuasion and intimidation did not suffice.

Paul's anti-imperial gospel, moreover, also insisted that Jesus Christ had been vindicated by God, raised from the dead and exalted as the heavenly Lord (the "Lord of Glory," 2:8, 15:3–4; cf. the pre-Pauline hymn in Phil. 2:6–11). In the Roman imperial context, however, that meant that Christ had assumed the position of the emperor whose death was merely a transition into his apotheosis. In 1 Corinthians in particular, as also in Philippians 3, furthermore, Paul explicitly articulated the anti-imperial political implications of Christ's heavenly enthronement as the true Lord or "emperor" of the world. In the Roman crucifixion of Christ the political "rulers of this age" had doomed themselves to destruction (1 Cor. 2:6–8).[57] Equally outrageous was Paul's assertion that Christ, vindicated by God and now "reigning" in heaven — where presumably only the greatest Greek heroes and deified Roman emperors joined the great gods in celestial glory — was about to "destroy every rule and every authority and power" (1 Cor. 15:24–28). In his use of key terms and symbols from political public oratory and imperial ideology, Paul was thus proclaiming an alternative gospel of an alternative emperor as well as building an alternative assembly in the city of Corinth.[58]

---

in Helmut Koester, *Ancient Christian Gospels* (Philadelphia: Trinity Press International, 1990), 1–6.

57. In the continuing subjugation of Paul's discourse, theologically determined Christian exegesis has habitually read these rulers through the deutero-Pauline Colossians and Ephesians as cosmic or demonic forces. Such a depoliticizing reading, however, cannot be sustained against the usual meaning of *archontes* as political rulers. Similarly, Paul's statement in 1 Cor. 15:24–28 cannot be assimilated to, but must be differentiated from, the later deutero-Pauline spiritualization of political rulers into cosmic powers. See further Wesley Carr, "The Rulers of This Age — I Corinthians II.6–8," *NTS* 23 (1976): 20–35; and more fully, Carr, *Angels and Principalities* (Cambridge: Cambridge University Press, 1981); and Neil Elliott's critique of reading of 1 Cor. 2:6–8 and 15:24 in terms of Colossians 1 in *Liberating Paul* (Maryknoll, N.Y.: Orbis, 1994), 114–24.

58. That representation of Christ as the true "emperor" is not simply a coincidental outburst in 1 Corinthians, inconsistent with the rest of Paul's letters, is clear from Paul's political and

Paul's redeployment of key terms from Roman imperial ideology, however, meant that he "reinscribed" imperial images and relations within his arguments aimed at reinforcing the discipline of an anti-imperial movement. In offering his assembly an alternative to Caesar, Paul in effect presented Jesus Christ as the true emperor, the true Lord and Savior who was in the process of subjugating all things to himself! Such imperial language could only reinforce relations of subordination within the assembly. It would not have been difficult for the emergent monarchic polity of the Christian movement to appeal to and build on Paul's imperial counterimperial language. Already in the deutero-Pauline letters the implications of such language for relations within the movement and its adjustment to the dominant social order are abundantly evident. In its imagery of Christ as the true emperor, the Christian church was already well prepared for its own establishment under Constantine.

## The Anti-Imperial Apocalyptic Background and Orientation of Paul's Opposition to the Roman Imperial Order

Paul's portrayal of the crucified Jesus' vindication through resurrection was rooted in Judean apocalypticism. So also is the focus of his gospel on a figure executed by the imperial rulers. In addition to acknowledging the imperial context of apocalyptic literature and indeed all Jewish life and literature in late Second Temple times, it is significant to note how other Jewish writers responded to the imperial situation in which they lived as subject people before noting that a principal concern of (most extant) Judean apocalyptic literature was to insist on the eventual independence and restoration of a subject people, Israel, in a persistent resistance to imperial domination.

Since the Babylonian conquest of Judea and destruction of Jerusalem and Solomon's temple, the great watershed event in ancient Judean history, Judean life and literature had been dominated by one empire after another for centuries, with the exception of a brief interlude under the Hasmonean dynasty.[59] The Second Temple and its high priestly regimes were sponsored by imperial regimes. The Jewish diaspora in general was the result of imperial manipulations and movement of subject peoples. This is generally

---

imperial characterization of Christ at the climax of the end of his argument in Philippians 3: "Our government (*politeuma*) is in heaven, and from there we expect a Savior, the Lord Jesus Christ. He will transform [us] by the power that also enables him to make all things subject to himself."

59. My attempt to draw attention to the importance of the "imperial situation" of Second Temple Judean society and its implication for understanding Jesus in *Jesus and the Spiral of Violence: Popular Jewish Resistance in Roman Palestine* (San Francisco: Harper and Row, 1987), esp. chaps. 1–2, have been followed by little discussion, with the exception of John Dominic Crossan, *The Historical Jesus* (San Francisco: HarperCollins, 1991), part 1, who emphasizes key features of the cultural influence of the Roman Empire for understanding Jesus.

ignored or obscured because of the theological interests and focus of Christian biblical scholarship. The effect, however, is that Christian scholarly construction of "Judaism," like modern "Orientalism" more generally, conspires with ancient empires to subjugate the discourses of ancient Judean apocalyptic and other literatures. This is particularly true with regard to how ancient Jews responded to imperial rule.

The most pointedly anti-imperial of Jewish literatures was Judean apocalyptic literature. Indeed, the whole purpose and function of Judean apocalyptic writing was to bolster Judean scribal circles and others in their adherence to the traditional Jewish way of life, in resistance to overt and covert pressures to conform to the dominant imperial politics and culture.[60] This basic purpose of Judean apocalypses is often obscured precisely because of the theological categories that determine their modern Christian theologically oriented interpretation, which tends to focus on heavenly journeys, "dualism," "supernatural" powers, and fantastic portrayals of "cosmic catastrophe." Such features, however, would appear to be instrumental or secondary matters in most Judean apocalyptic literature. For example, far from being central to the visionaries' message of hope for a future free of imperial domination and courage to resist imperial repression, "cosmic catastrophes" were part of the rhetoric by which they embellished how "awesome" God's eventual intervention on behalf of the oppressed people would be.

Most of the extant Judean apocalyptic literature from late Second Temple times focuses on the crisis under the Seleucid emperor Antiochus Epiphanes, which eventually touched off the Maccabean Revolt (The Apocalypse of Weeks and the Animal Apocalypse in *1 Enoch* 93:1–10 + 91:11–17 and 85–91; the several apocalyptic dreams/visions in Daniel 7, 8, 9, 10–12; the *Testament of Moses*). Most of these documents also place their main concern, surviving the violent suppression of the traditional Judean way of life under Antiochus Epiphanes, in the broader context of the long history of Judean subjection to one empire after another. In their struggle to understand and persist in the historical crises in which they were caught, moreover, the authors of apocalyptic literature recalled their people's previous situations that had been free of imperial domination, whether their deliverance from slavery in Egypt, the exploits of archaic heroes, or the glorious days of Judean kings. Indeed, their struggle to discern the significance of their people's long subjugation to empire and especially the threat to the

---

60. Recent treatments of the "social world/setting" of "Jewish apocalypticism" focus mainly on the world/setting within "Judaism," with little attention to the imperial situation; e.g., Lester L. Grabbe, "The Social Setting of Early Jewish Apocalypticism," *JSP* 4 (1989): 27–47; Philip R. Davies, "The Social World of Apocalyptic Writings," in *The World of Ancient Israel: Sociological, Anthropological, and Political Perspectives: Essays by Members of the Society of Old Testament Study*, ed. R. E. Clements (Cambridge: Cambridge University Press, 1989), 251–71.

very survival of the Judean people drove the scribal circles that produced this literature to explore the significance of the whole sweep of universal history since the very creation.[61] However mythic and fantastic their images seem to modern rationalists, the apocalyptic visionaries were able critically to demystify the pretensions and practices of the dominant imperial regime, at least for the scribal circles who produced and read apocalyptic literature. And they insisted on the integrity and independence of their own society and its traditional way of life, over against attempts by the imperial regime to impose a dominant metropolitan culture and/or politics. Most important, the scribal circles that produced this literature were able, through their revelations, creatively to envision a future for their society in freedom and justice beyond their present oppression under imperial rulers and/or their local client rulers.[62]

The fundamental message of most of this Judean apocalyptic literature, usually articulated relatively briefly in general but vivid imagery appropriate to visions, focused on future deliverance from imperial domination. The basic message (the core of what has often been referred to as apocalyptic eschatology) focused on two or three interrelated future events:[63] In God's final intervention, (1) the oppressive rulers would be judged or destroyed, (2) the people would be delivered and/or restored, and (3) those who had been martyred for their persistence in the traditional way of life and resis-

---

61. Amos Wilder, "Eschatological Imagery and Earthly Circumstance," *NTS* 5 (1958–59), commented that "eschatology includes the history.... It is ... a vision of history as a whole, a transfiguration of the given world, not an escape from or a denial of it" (235). Wilder's sensitivity to the rhetoric of apocalyptic literature served as an important antidote to the tendency to portray Judean apocalyptic literature as somehow alienated from history.

62. As Amos Wilder said of the relation of "Eschatological Imagery and Earthly Circumstance," the "visionary state ... represents a genuine cognition and affirmation.... The transcendental imagery does not lend itself to our spacial distinctions between mundane and supramundane" (234). Similarly, "The eschatological myth dramatizes the transfiguration of the world and is not mere poetry of an unthinkable a-temporal state" (231). The rhetoric of Judean apocalypses is usually concrete even in dream imagery, often explicitly historical in envisioning a transformation not of "the world," but of the present Hellenistic or Roman imperial order of injustice and oppression, while the future known only through visions is portrayed in vaguer, sometimes fantastic images, often by analogy with past experiences of deliverance such as the exodus.

63. Sketched in Horsley, *Jesus and the Spiral of Violence*, 157–60, cf. 129–45; and more recently in "The Kingdom of God and the Renewal of Israel: Synoptic Gospels, Jesus Movements, and Apocalypticism," in *Encyclopedia of Apocalypticism*, vol. 1: *The Origins of Apocalypticism in Judaism and Christianity*, ed. John J. Collins (New York: Continuum, 1998), 304–9. See also the concise survey of Judean apocalyptic literature by John J. Collins, "From Prophecy to Apocalypticism: The Expectation of the End," in *Encyclopedia of Apocalypticism*, 1:129–61. My more concrete and specific reading of the basic message of Judean apocalyptic literature is consistent with treatments by specialists on such material: John J. Collins, "Genre, Ideology and Social Movements in Jewish Apocalypticism," and George W. E. Nickelsburg, "The Apocalyptic Construction of Reality in *1 Enoch*," in *Mysteries and Revelations: Apocalyptic Studies since the Uppsala Colloquium*, ed. John J. Collins and James H. Charlesworth, JSPSS 9 (Sheffield: Sheffield Academic Press, 1991), 11–25, 51–64, emphasize "eschatological/coming judgment" (which encompasses both judgment of rulers and restoration of the people) as central to the worldview and message of the Judean apocalypses.

tance to oppression would be vindicated and/or be resurrected in order to join in the finally restored life of the people. (*Apocalypse of Weeks*, Animal Apocalypse, Daniel 10–12, *Testament of Moses* have all three; Daniel 7 and 8 lack the third.) Especially significant as the background to the way in which Paul and others understood Jesus is the particular way in which the vindication of martyrs for the cause was symbolized and its relation to the judgment of the imperial rulers and the restoration of God's people (in the Animal Apocalypse, Daniel 10–12, and *Testament of Moses*). While a collective resurrection symbolizes the renewal of the people generally in some texts (Isa. 26:19), in Daniel and others it symbolizes the way those martyred for their persistence in resistance to imperial repression will be vindicated and/or join the restored people (e.g., Dan. 12:2; *1 Enoch* 51:1–2). Exaltation to heavenly places/glory is also a principal symbol of vindication (Dan. 12:3; *T. Moses* 10:8–10). It is precisely against the background of this relatively consistent pattern of three interrelated events in which the fulfillment of history is represented in Judean apocalyptic literature as God's (plan for the) overcoming of imperial rule that Paul's anti–Roman imperial stance and anti–Roman imperial rhetoric can be understood.

## The Apocalyptic Pattern in Paul's Anti-Imperial Rhetoric

Rhetorical criticism of Paul's letters must take into account the content of his arguments as well as their rhetorical forms and devices. To take just one example, not only does an appropriate reading of 1 Corinthians 15 depend on at least a rough sense of what the Corinthians addressed may have meant by "there is no resurrection of the dead," but Paul shifts the focus from the reality of the resurrection (15:12–34) to the manner of the resurrection (15:35–49).[64] When we do so with Judean apocalyptic literature in mind, then we may notice some significant patterns as well as motifs for understanding what Paul was arguing in 1 Corinthians.

Interpreters commonly observe that Paul's thinking is similar to Jewish apocalypticism, even though terms and motifs from Judean apocalypses do not pervade his letters. Amid his Greek rhetorical patterns and Hellenistic concepts, the Judean apocalyptic terms and symbols are hardly prevalent, although they are distinctive and significant. In 1 Corinthians, for example, in addition to the resurrection discussed in chapter 15, God's "mystery," or his plan for the fulfillment of history (deliverance of the people from imperial domination; 2:6–8, 15:51–52; cf. Daniel 2; Rom. 11:25–27), and the conviction that, at "the day of the Lord," "this age" will be superseded by a new age or the "kingdom of God" (1:20, 2:6–8; cf. Gal. 1:4; *1 Enoch* 71:15; *4 Ezra* 7:12–13, 50, 112–13, 119; 8:1; *2 Baruch* 14:13,

---

64. That shift remains unaddressed, for example, in the incisive formal analyses by Mack, *Rhetoric and the New Testament*, 56–59, and Robbins, *Exploring the Texture of Texts*, 52–58.

15:8, 44:8–15, 83:4–9) are the most striking. Most significant, however, is that Paul shares the same basic historical-eschatological orientation to reality as Judean apocalypticism, in which God intervenes in a history under the sway of imperial powers (and even of superhuman powers) to judge the oppressive powers and to deliver his people and to vindicate the martyrs.[65]

Paul's letters also display some significant differences from Judean apocalyptic literature in two principal regards, while retaining the same basic historical-eschatological orientation toward God's overcoming of empire and deliverance of the people. Whereas the Judean apocalypses eagerly await God's intervention, Paul proclaims that God has already inaugurated the decisive intervention in the crucifixion and resurrection of Christ. In this regard, Paul displays a similarity with certain of the Dead Sea Scrolls, in which the appearance of the Righteous Teacher and the advent of the priestly-scribal community to the wilderness at Qumran to "prepare the way of the Lord" are understood as the inauguration of the decisive events at the fulfillment of history. Second, at some point, perhaps in his own revelatory experience (*apokalypsis*, Gal. 1:15–16), Paul became convinced that God's final deliverance inaugurated in the imperial execution and divine vindication of Jesus Christ included not just the children of Israel but all peoples of the world. In this second respect, he simply picks up on the Israelite-Jewish tradition that in the fulfillment of the promise to Abraham-Israel all peoples were to receive blessings (see especially the argument in Galatians 3), which continued into some late prophetic books, such as the later chapters in Isaiah, cited frequently by Paul. He understood his own commissioning by Christ (Gal. 1:13–18), of course, as a programmatic attempt to implement precisely this eschatological fulfillment of history that has been running primarily through the history of Israel, the subject people, not through the history of Rome, the imperial power.

Because Paul believed that God's final deliverance and restoration of the people had already begun in Jesus' faithful act of martyrdom and his divine vindication by resurrection, the principal agenda of Judean apocalypticism became far more intricately interrelated and the sequence somewhat altered in Paul's gospel. While some apocalyptic literature had attributed a sustaining salvific effect to the faithful deaths of the martyrs, the final deliverance and restoration of the people was to come only when/after God came in judgment to terminate the rule of empire, at which time the faithful martyrs and other righteous would be resurrected in order to join in the finally

---

65. Despite all the serious inadequacies and Christian theological agenda of Pauline interpretation from Schweitzer and Bultmann to Käsemann and Beker (see the rambling critique by R. Barry Matlock, *Unveiling the Apocalyptic Paul: Paul's Interpreters and the Rhetoric of Criticism*, JSNTSup 127 [Sheffield: Sheffield Academic Press, 1996]), there remains a fundamental similarity between Paul's orientation to reality and the "distinctive world-view" constituted by the "common content" of Judean apocalypses. On the latter, see Collins, "Genre, Ideology, and Social Movements," 15–17.

restored people. Paul believed that God's righteous act of deliverance had actually begun in Jesus Christ's faithful death as indicated precisely in his resurrection-vindication by God, in which the general resurrection of the dead had also begun, with Christ as the "down payment" or "first-fruits" (1 Cor. 15:20). The effect was to "mix up" the principal components in the apocalyptic agenda of fulfillment. Deliverance and restoration of the people had already begun in anticipation of the final judgment, which was now associated with the vindicated Christ who was coming imminently in "the day of the Lord." Nevertheless, these principal components from Judean apocalyptic visions of historical fulfillment are all still present in Paul's letters.

When we look closely at the content of the several major sections of 1 Corinthians, these three events or motifs, the fundamental counterimperial agenda of Judean apocalyptic literature — martyr death and vindication, renewal of the people, and divine judgment of imperial rulers — appear as the underlying structuring components of Paul's arguments, whatever the particular point of the arguments may be ostensibly. This is most striking in the opening and closing main arguments, that is, chapters 1–4 and chapter 15, but is evident in other arguments as well. It is hardly possible in the brief sketch to develop the case in detail.[66]

First Corinthians 1–4 presents an argument for unity of the assembly instead of divisiveness, which is integrally connected with argumentation against boasting in exalted spiritual status attained by possession of Sophia and in favor of focus on the crucified Christ and the humiliated status of those who are called. Twice in the first major step of the argument (1:18–2:5) and once again in the second (2:6–3:4), however, Paul structures his argumentation in terms of how, according to his revealed plan, God acted to defeat (shame, destroy) the imperial rulers, along with the dominant imperial values and aristocracy, and to save people in the rulers' execution of Christ and God's calling of those humiliated in the imperial order. The key is the reference to God's *mystērion* (= *raz* in Hebrew, cf. Daniel 2) in 2:7, that is, God's plan for the resolution of the historical crisis of imperial rule. *Mystērion*'s apposition with *sophia* in 2:7 provides the key to the meaning of "the wisdom of God" in the otherwise unintelligible play on words in 1:21; for in Paul's Judean apocalyptic background, "wisdom" was a virtual synonym for God's "mystery" (cf. *1 Enoch* and some Dead Sea Scrolls). The structure of 1:18–21 is thus a prophecy and fulfillment of God's plan to destroy or make foolish the "wisdom of the wise/of the world," which by innuendo points to the high evaluation and self-interested deployment of eloquence/persuasion (the "wisdom of word" of the "debaters of this age," 1:17, 20; 2:1). Similarly in the next paragraph, 1:26–31, Paul refers to the

---

66. For fuller exposition of Paul's main arguments in 1 Corinthians, albeit with less explicit emphasis on their apocalyptic background, see Horsley, *1 Corinthians*.

inauspicious social position of the Corinthians themselves in pointing out that precisely by calling weak and lowly people into the new movement, God has shamed and reduced to nonexistence the aristocracies of the world who prided themselves in their exalted social-economic-political position. Most explicitly of all, in 2:6–10 (–3:4), he declares that in the execution of Jesus by the imperial rulers ("of this age") God has doomed those imperial rulers to destruction and begun the redemption of the people, for the crucified one turned out to be "the Lord of glory," vindicated by God in resurrection and exaltation. The final judgment, which is only implicit in 2:6–10 with regard to the "rulers of this age," becomes explicit in the third and fourth major steps of Paul's argument (3:5–23, 4:1–21), only with regard to the mission in progress in Corinth by which the people are being saved. "The Day" of God's judgment, "the time" of "the Lord's coming," looms imminently ahead. Paul leaves it unsaid that in that "Day" the "rulers of this age" who are already doomed by their crucifixion of "the Lord of glory" will finally be "destroyed" (2:6). In the structure of his overall argument, however, the judgment stands also as the ultimate sanction on the work of the apostles as well as the behavior of the Corinthians (3:10–17, 4:2–5), beyond which, at the very end of his argument as well as the very end of God's plan, stands the ultimate goal of a restored human society, "the kingdom of God" (4:20).

First Corinthians 15 is an argument for the reality and manner of the resurrection of the dead addressed to some who deny it, apparently as unintelligible according to their understanding of reality. Paul uses the tradition of the crucifixion-resurrection creed as the basis of his argument but also elaborates on the subjugation of the imperial rulers and the transformation of humanity that the crucifixion and resurrection inaugurated. In the first half of the argument, for the reality of the resurrection of the dead, he really does not (cannot?) make an argument that adequately addresses the presuppositions of the skeptical Corinthians. He simply reasserts his gospel of the crucifixion and resurrection and draws the "logical" conclusion which makes sense only to someone who already believes in the reality of general resurrection (15:1–19). First Corinthians 15:20–24 is really the center and substance of his argument—and, *in nuce,* a full world-historical apocalyptic scheme of God's anti-imperial fulfillment of history in the renewal of humanity. In the death and resurrection of Christ God has inaugurated fulfillment of history in a new humanity/society beyond the original humanity begun in Adam, which is under the power of Death as well as the imperial rulers. Imminently the rest of the general resurrection will be completed and Christ who, since his resurrection, is in effect the real emperor will subject all things, all rulers as well as Death, to himself and then to God. In the second half of the argument, 15:35–57, Paul makes more of an effort to argue in terms intelligible to the Corinthians, utilizing their own key terms and symbols. He must know, however, that in their terms an immortal and imperishable body would have been an oxymoron, absolute nonsense as a contradiction in terms (15:42, 53–54). His persuasiveness, if he even cares about it, really depends upon the "mystery" that he proclaims in an almost ecstatic outburst at the end of his argument, the mystery about the fulfillment of a new humanity at the very end of the eschatological events, 15:51–52.[67] In 1 Corinthians 15 the apocalyptic agenda as well as symbols provide the underlying structure as well as the substance of Paul's argument.

In all of the other arguments of 1 Corinthians (with the possible exception of chapters 12–14), the basic assumption, explicit and implicit, is that the Corinthian community is part of the broader restoration of the people, or rather the building of a wider, international people of God now under-way since the crucifixion and resurrection of Christ. Paul regularly mentions or alludes to the crucified and resurrected Lord or Christ (e.g., 5:7; 6:13–14, 20; 7:12, 22; 8:11; 9:1, 12; 11:23–26; 12:3). The very structure and substance of his arguments in chapters 5, 6, 7, 8–10, and 11:17–34, how-ever, are keyed to the imminent divine judgment and imminent end of "the present form of this world." The implication for the life of the assembly as the people of God under construction is that they must maintain solidarity over against the dominant imperial society.

This is clearest perhaps in 6:1–11 and in 5:1–13 read in the light of 6:1–11. The assembly members, the "saints," will soon be involved in the final judgment of "the world." That, if nothing else, should make absolutely clear that they are to conduct their own community affairs as an alternative society independent of the larger society, having no dealings with institu-tions such as the civil courts. Meanwhile, the assembly itself has authority under the Lordship of Christ to deal with its own conflicts and other af-fairs. Chapter 7 focuses on marital and sexual relations. But even there Paul cannot resist reference to "the impending crisis," that "the appointed time has grown short,... for the present form of this world is passing away." Therefore let "those who deal with the world [act] as though they had no dealings with it." First Corinthians 10:1–13, 14–22 form the center of the long argument in chapters 8–10 that the Corinthians cannot participate in the sacrificial meals that constitute the various overlapping kinship, civil, and imperial groups or communities that comprise the dominant Corinthian and Roman imperial society. Paul argues in 10:1–13, 14–22 that the new inter-national redemption inaugurated at the end of the ages in the Christ events

---

67. This is close to what Amos Wilder must have meant by "an ecstatic apprehension of immediate vindication," "Eschatological Imagery and Earthly Circumstance," 237. Wilder characterized the rhetoric of apocalyptic discourse as "symbolic realism" (as opposed to an idealist aesthetic): "its symbols are not merely rhetoric and decoration. They are real media of power and life" (235–36). One could compare Paul's characterization of his own gospel/preaching in 1 Cor. 2:4 (cf. Gal. 3:1–5; 1 Thess. 1:8) as "manifestations of power." How would a "symbolic realist" such as Paul "explain" his vision to a literalistic or idealist thinker? In oxymorons and intentional contradictions in terms, such as "spiritual/incorruptible body" or "demons" and insistence that "non-existent idols really do exist" (cf. 1 Cor. 10:20–21 and 8:5 in context of the "dialogue" with the Corinthians).

stands in continuity with Israel, that judgment looms ahead, and that the people in process of redemption must maintain solidarity over against the dominant society. Finally, 11:17–34 focuses on the basis of the assembly's solidarity and its stand over against the dominant society: "proclaiming the Lord's death until he comes" (11:26).

A more complicated rhetorical analysis of Paul's arguments in 1 Corinthians, one that takes into account the broader "rhetorical situation" of the Roman imperial order as well as the particular rhetorical situation of the community in Corinth in which both Paul and Apollos had worked, thus uncovers at least two discourses that stand opposed to the Roman imperial order and its culture. In their devotion to heavenly Sophia, the Corinthian *pneumatikoi* simply transcended the dominant social order by means of a spiritual trans-valuation of aristocratic values. Devalued people, such as women, slaves, freed people, and lowly artisans, found a transcendent identity that liberated them from cultural attitudes and even social roles in which they were regu-larly demeaned. In order to understand some of the other "voices" evident in Paul's arguments in 1 Corinthians, rhetorical criticism needs to explore how what may have appeared as the rhetoric of spiritual transcendence in Hellenistic Jewish and other texts may also have aided and abetted ordinary people's resistance to the dominant imperial order.

Paul's own arguments display a composite rhetoric. He used the standard forms and devices of Greco-Roman rhetoric. Yet he used these forms that were ordinarily deployed in reinforcing the cohesion of the Greek cities as part of the overall Roman imperial order to try to reinforce the solidarity of a movement that stood over against the dominant imperial order. This is all the clearer when we note that he also used the central symbolism of the Roman imperial cult to articulate his own alternative "gospel" of an alternative "Lord" and "Savior" whose crucifixion, exaltation, and parousia meant the imminent termination of the imperial order. The structuring perspective and agenda of his arguments in 1 Corinthians, however, appear to resemble and to be heavily influenced by the fundamental agenda evident in Judean apocalyptic literature, a principal purpose of which was resistance to the Hellenistic and Roman Empires that were threatening the faithful pursuit of the traditional Judean (biblical) way of life. In order to understand the arguments of 1 Corinthians, and probably other Pauline letters, in their broader historical context, rhetorical criticism must expand its repertoire to include the rhetoric of Judean apocalyptic literature and the ways Paul draws on that tradition in which, apparently, he had been "resocialized" prior to his calling as an apostle of Jesus Christ.

In the history of later Christian appropriation of both the spiritual tran-scendence of the Corinthian *pneumatikoi* and Paul's anti-imperial use of imperial language, their quests for alternatives to the Roman imperial order became obscured. Already in the deutero-Pauline letters, spiritual transcendence became the way of adjusting to the imperial order while replicating its social patterns within the churches. And after the establishment of the church in the empire, Paul's representation of the exalted and reigning Jesus Christ as Lord and Savior would be used to consolidate the imperial order. The same images that Paul borrowed to represent the martyred messiah as the emperor of the world, over against the dominant order, could easily be deployed by an established and triumphal Christianity in installing its divine Lord as emperor of the dominant order.

# — 5 —

# CORINTHIAN WOMEN PROPHETS AND PAUL'S ARGUMENTATION IN 1 CORINTHIANS

*Cynthia Briggs Kittredge*

ANTOINETTE CLARK WIRE, Elisabeth Schüssler Fiorenza, Elizabeth Castelli, and other feminist critics have challenged students of Paul to interpret his letters not simply as reflecting conflict between an orthodox Paul and heretical or heterodox opponents, but as rhetorical arguments that can be read with a method that makes audible different voices who participate in debates about early Christian beliefs and self-understandings.[1] These interpreters have made significant methodological contributions to the discussion of "Paul and Politics" in the study of Paul's letters. Three of their insights have a vital place in this discussion. First, they have not read Paul's rhetoric at face value but have read it "against the grain" in order to distinguish between the rhetorical situation constructed by Paul and the historical situation.[2] To do so they have used the insights of modern rhetorical theory as well as identifying the ancient rhetorical forms within Paul's arguments.[3] Second, they have pointed to a consideration of gender as a central category

---

1. See Antoinette Clark Wire, *The Corinthian Women Prophets: A Reconstruction through Paul's Rhetoric* (Minneapolis: Fortress Press, 1990). See also Elisabeth Schüssler Fiorenza, "Pauline Theology and the Politics of Meaning," in her *Rhetoric and Ethic: The Politics of Biblical Studies* (Minneapolis: Fortress Press, 1999), 175–94; see also her essay in this volume. Elizabeth Castelli, *Imitating Paul: A Discourse of Power* (Louisville, Ky.: John Knox Press, 1991). It is with deep appreciation for Krister Stendahl's work on the theological questions raised by the texts on Paul and women that the present essay is contributed to this volume in his honor.

2. Elisabeth Schüssler Fiorenza, "Rhetorical Situation and Historical Reconstruction in 1 Corinthians," *NTS* 33 (1987): 386–403. Shelly Matthews employs this method in "2 Corinthians," in *Searching the Scriptures*, vol. 2: *A Feminist Commentary*, ed. Elisabeth Schüssler Fiorenza (New York: Crossroad, 1994), 196–217. See also Cynthia Briggs Kittredge, *Community and Authority: The Rhetoric of Obedience in the Pauline Tradition*, HTS (Harrisburg, Pa.: Trinity Press International, 1998).

3. For discussions of the modern and ancient rhetoric see Wire, *Corinthian Women Prophets*, 197–201. See also Jan Botha, *Subject to Whose Authority? Multiple Readings of Romans 13* (Atlanta: Scholars Press, 1994). See also Elisabeth Schüssler Fiorenza, "Challenging

in analysis. They understand women as historical agents who contributed to the formation of early communities of Christ-believers, rather than as "topics" addressed by biblical writers. And third, they have not assumed Paul's authority but recognized the role of the letters in developing that authority. All three points are extremely relevant for the interpretation of 1 Corinthians, a letter whose "situation" and "opponents" have been notoriously difficult to profile and in which the complex of sexuality, marriage, prophecy, asceticism, and authority is clearly of central importance.

Antoinette Clark Wire demonstrates this approach in her study of 1 Corinthians. She analyzes the many indications in the letter that the prophets are women, and she recognizes their gender to be key to understanding how they experience baptism to raise their status and allow them access to God through the activity of the Spirit.[4] Her reconstruction of their position through a critical analysis of Paul's rhetoric in 1 Corinthians has insights with important consequences for reading Paul and the politics of the *ekklēsia* in Corinth.

The challenge posed by Wire and other interpreters should be taken more thoroughly into account by those who read Paul in light of Roman imperial ideology.[5] Sympathetic to issues of liberation and the use of Pauline texts in repressive ways throughout the history of interpretation, Neil Elliott and Richard Horsley have highlighted Paul's radical stance in opposition to Roman imperial order and practices.[6] For example, Richard Horsley argues in his commentary on 1 Corinthians that in that letter Paul presents the *ekklēsia,* organized by egalitarian principles, as an alternative society to the Roman patronage system.[7] Neil Elliott, sharpening the political sting of Paul's apocalypticism, has argued persuasively that Paul anticipates the rule of Christ to destroy all earthly rulers. Both have argued that Paul's symbolic language should be read in its contemporary imperial context rather than in terms of existentialism or gnosticism.[8] Horsley and Elliott move away from a dichotomous reading of 1 Corinthians as a debate between Paul and opponents and focus on reading Paul against a more overarching "opponent" in the Roman imperial system. Paul's disagreements with "internal" "opponents" are understood to be consonant with his critique of the empire,

---

the Rhetorical Half-Turn: Feminist and Rhetorical Biblical Criticism," in *Rhetoric, Scripture, and Theology,* ed. Stanley Porter and Thomas Olbricht, JSNTSup 131 (Sheffield: JSOT, 1996).

4. Wire, *Corinthian Women Prophets,* 1, 63–71, 202.

5. Neil Elliott, *Liberating Paul: The Justice of God and the Politics of the Apostle* (Maryknoll, N.Y.: Orbis, 1994); Richard A. Horsley, ed., *Paul and Empire: Religion and Paul in Roman Imperial Society* (Valley Forge, Pa.: Trinity Press International, 1997); Richard A. Horsley, *1 Corinthians,* Abingdon NT Commentaries (Nashville: Abingdon Press, 1998).

6. For clear elaboration of the interpretive effects of Paul's rhetoric in modern political contexts and the effect of the canon of Paul's letters on the interpretation of Paul, see especially Elliott, *Liberating Paul,* 3–54.

7. Horsley, *Paul and Empire,* 213. For example, Horsley, *1 Corinthians,* 163–65.

8. Elliott, *Liberating Paul,* 110–14; Horsley, *Paul and Empire,* 144, 148.

that they are spiritual elites seeking to take advantage of their freedom over the common good of the *ekklēsia*. Within this reconstructed picture of the situation, Paul's recommendation of subordination of women to men is seen to be anomalous, ironic, or less important than his overall radical position with respect to Roman imperial society.[9]

By viewing Paul's first letter to the Corinthians in light of imperial ideology rather than focusing upon Paul's relationships with other members of the *ekklēsia,* these critics have successfully highlighted the political dimension of Paul's language with respect to the imperial environment outside the *ekklēsia*. But they have not acknowledged explicitly enough the way that same political language shapes the internal organization of the *ekklēsia*.[10] Thus, this perspective still has not adequately articulated the relationship between Paul's apocalyptic critique of imperial system and proclamation of its replacement by the rule of God with the insistence, made most direct in the disputed verses 14:34–35, that certain elements of that system, particularly patriarchal marriage, must remain in effect. I want to point out how a perspective such as Wire's, in which Paul's voice is not considered to be the authoritative center of the letter, may complement, make more complex, or, in some instances, correct their reading.

An approach that reads the letter as a rhetorical argument that builds a symbolic universe in which gender relations are constructed can more adequately show how Paul uses imperial language to both subvert and reinscribe the imperial system. To illustrate, I will discuss the portion of Paul's argument for the resurrection at the culmination of 1 Corinthians in which he presents the apocalyptic scenario of the end time, 1 Cor. 15:23–28. These verses are replete with language of political relationships: "rule" (*archē*), "authority" (*exousia*), "power" (*dynamis*), "to reign" (*basileuō*), "to be subjected" (*hypotassesthai*). Neil Elliott has argued that these verses, along with the parallel verse 2:8, should be read within the Roman imperial context in which God's ultimate rule destroys every ruler of this age.[11] Elliott's argument corrects an overspiritualized interpretation of these verses in 1 Corinthians and makes the case that apocalyptic language did have a sociopolitical dimension when used by Paul.

---

9. The complex issue of whether to take 14:34–35 as a later interpolation or as an original part of the letter is a crucial factor in the way one reads Paul's argument. Both Horsley and Elliott consider these verses to be an interpolation. On the basis of the flow of the argument, Horsley also questions the originality of 1 Cor. 11:2–16. If the disputed verses in 1 Cor. 14:34–35 are judged to be original, it intensifies the problem of Paul's insistence on traditional patterns of subordination in marriage in the *ekklēsia*.

10. Horsley acknowledges explicitly the way that Paul's rhetoric at times tends to "reinforce the very patriarchal and authoritative social relationship that the alternative society he was building was ostensibly attempting to transform" (*1 Corinthians*, 38). He also notes the irony that with some in Corinth, Paul may have established his own patronage system (*Paul and Empire*, 255). Nevertheless, because his emphasis is on Paul's critique of empire, the significance of this fact is minimized.

11. Elliott, *Liberating Paul*, 111.

However, within these verses is Paul's argument that the son will be subjected to the father.[12] "When all things are subjected to him, then the son himself will also be subjected to him who put all things under him, that God may be everything to every one" (1 Cor. 15:28).

What may appear to be an exegetical fine point about divine relationships with little concrete relevance becomes more important when it is examined within the overall movement of Paul's rhetoric in which he constructs relationships between himself and members of the Corinthian community as well as between Christ and God, husband and wife.[13] While this language confronts the imperial system by envisioning its replacement by the reign of God, it also culminates Paul's argument with an image of the subjection of Christ to God. This image resonates in a letter that in many of its arguments is concerned with the proper order of relationships within the *ekklēsia,* particularly the husband and wife relationship and the relationship of the Corinthian community and Paul.

The verb *hypotassesthai,* which occurs in this verse and originates in the quotation of Psalm 8, is one element in the field of political terminology that recurs within 1 Corinthians. Political language includes "rulers of this age" (2:8), "reigning or being king" (4:8), and "be subject" (14:33, 15:23–28, 16:16). All this language speaks of relationships of unequal power in which one of superior strength rules over another. The one who rules occupies the position above the one who is subjected. Philo and Josephus and other Greek authors contemporaneous with Paul use the language of being the subject of a ruler in the contexts of political and marital subjection.[14] In 1 Corinthians, in addition to appearing here in 1 Cor. 15:27–28, the same verb occurs in 1 Cor. 14:32, in 14:34 (the prohibition of women speaking in churches), and in 1 Cor. 16:16 (in Paul's commendation of Stephanus). Paul uses this identical political term in 1 Corinthians to speak of relationships between members of the *ekklēsia* and between Christ, God, and all things. Paul's insistence that Christ will be subjected to God at the end must be read in light of the other points in which Paul is concerned to establish the proper ranking of individuals, whether on the divine or human plane. For instance, in 1 Cor. 3:23, at the conclusion of his discussion of the relationship between himself and Apollos, Paul asserts the priority or primacy of God: "all are yours, and you are Christ's and Christ is God's." To the situation of division in the community, the series of genitives presents a picture in which God encompasses Christ, Christ encompasses the addressees, and "you" encompass all. In a second example, in 4:14, 16, Paul describes himself as becoming the father in Christ of the Corinthian community. And in 11:3 Paul presents a chain linked with the word *kephalē,* "the head of

---

12. Gordon D. Fee, *The First Epistle to the Corinthians,* New International Commentary on the New Testament (Grand Rapids, Mich.: Eerdmans, 1987), 754–60.

13. Wire, *Corinthian Women Prophets,* 165–66.

14. Kittredge, *Community and Authority,* 37–51.

every man is Christ, the head of a woman is her husband, and the head of Christ is God."

In each of these instances, Paul constructs a series of linked elements in an implied hierarchy in which the element in the middle position is essential to mediate between the other two: in 3:22, you-Christ-God; in 4:14, children-father–in Christ; and in 11:3, woman-man-Christ-God. In comparison with these examples, then, the proper order between Christ and God in the apocalyptic scenario in 1 Cor. 15:28 is not an exegetical afterthought, but the culminating image of subordination in which the son must occupy an intermediary position between the Father and all things. In the symbolic universe of the letter, God's subjection of Christ is the ultimate symbolic legitimization of the father's position between the children and Christ and the husband's position between his wife and God.[15]

Now having observed the way that Paul describes relationships within the letter, let us look at this feature of his argument within the social context of the imperial system. Seen in the perspective of the imperial context, the pattern of linked hierarchical relationships that are elaborated throughout the letter resembles the social relationships established through the patronage system. Recent studies of society of Roman Corinth have contributed to our understanding of the patronage system as the way of integrating the empire. John Chow has described the network of relationships in Corinth as a hierarchy made of up the emperor, Roman officials, local notables, and the populace. Chow defines a patron-client tie as "an asymmetrical exchange relationship." "Patronage was one of the ways through which society in Corinth was organized. Because of such relationships, people at different levels, from the emperor down to a citizen in a town, were linked together, even though their interests might not be the same."[16]

In his reading of 1 Corinthians, Richard Horsley argues that Paul constructs his community in opposition to the patronage system by building the *ekklēsia* on egalitarian principles, preventing Christians from bringing their disagreements to the courts, and by refusing to accept support for his apostolic work.[17] In Horsley's reconstruction, the members of the community with whom Paul disagrees understand themselves to be the spiritual elite who are caught up in replicating the values of high status. Thus he reads Paul's critique of empire as consistent with his disagreement with his internal "opponents." Much about this reading is both exegetically persuasive and attractive theologically.

However, the many points in Paul's argument where Paul constructs a chain of authority in which the middle element is essential causes us to question whether Paul is simply opposing the patronage system or is funda-

---

15. Wire, *Corinthian Women Prophets*, 36–37.
16. John Chow, "Patronage in Roman Corinth," in *Paul and Empire*, ed. Horsley, 107, 119.
17. Horsley, ed., *Paul and Empire*, 217.

mentally shaped by it. Such an observation might be unexceptional except for the strong case made by Wire that other Christ-believers in Corinth may have understood Christ as their key link with God through baptism, rather than as a middle term in a chain of subordination. When contrasted with this reconstruction of the women prophets' position, Paul's insistence that the son must be subjected to God called directly upon the pattern of the patronage system as the proper order of relationships. From this perspective, it is Paul who reinforces the language of subordination typical of the patronage system and it is those with whom he argues in Corinth whose symbolic universe most threatens the imperial system.[18] Note that this analysis focuses on 1 Cor. 15:23–28, in which the language of *hypotassesthai* is used, and a pattern of argumentation throughout the letter; it does not depend solely on the disputed verses 14:34–35.

The language of other Christ-believers within the community, such as the Corinthian women prophets, may contribute positively to our understanding of *ekklēsia* in relation to empire. But this possibility can only be seen with a methodological perspective that can sympathetically reconstruct the position of those with whom Paul disputes and whom Paul's rhetoric constructs as "the other."[19] Such a method requires that one not read Paul's characterizations of those with whom he debates as being a complete or accurate historical picture of them. Rather one must read traces of their positions in Paul's letters and must compile and critically interpret evidence of women's prophecy and asceticism within the early Christian tradition and in the wider Greco-Roman world.[20]

The contributions of those scholars who have focused on gender as a central category in 1 Corinthians make the situation of Paul in the Roman imperial context more complicated than simply Paul as radical, his opponents misguided, and his conservative attitudes about gender relations an ironic capitulation to imperial language or a mistaken impression caused by later interpolators. Their work points to further work that needs to be done on the interrelationship between gender hierarchy and imperial system in the ancient world.

Those who seek to interpret Paul in an imperial context have thus far restricted themselves to emphasizing Paul's radical stance and underplaying the ways in which Paul's language replicates and reinscribes imperial power relations. In doing so they continue to operate with the traditional paradigm in which Paul's position, now "correctly" interpreted within his imperial

---

18. Wire, *Corinthian Women Prophets*, 38, 187. Her argument about the women prophets' understanding of baptism is made on pp. 167–69.

19. In his 1 Corinthians commentary, Horsley shows awareness and sympathy for other voices within the community (*1 Corinthians*, 34, 37) but overall he takes Paul's voice as normative.

20. See Wire's appendices in *Corinthian Women Prophets* on "Women Who Speak for God," 237–69. See also the work of Ross Shepard Kraemer, *Her Share of the Blessings* (New York: Oxford University Press, 1992).

context, is the only important one and other voices must be subordinated to his. The strength of this paradigm testifies to the effectiveness of Paul's rhetoric as it has been amplified throughout the history of interpretation. Within the contemporary politics of Pauline interpretation their decision to do this may be justified because of the undeniable power that Paul's position, however it is reconstructed, continues to have in Christian theological contexts. However, the critique posed by Wire and others presents another way to proceed in a reconstruction of the diverse languages and self-understandings of those in early Christian communities, both women and men, as well as the languages of the imperial system. Such an exploration would provide a basis for ethical and theological evaluation of the adequacy of those diverse Christian perspectives within the first-century context and in dialogue with contemporary theological and political positions.

# PAUL ON
# BONDAGE AND FREEDOM
# IN IMPERIAL ROMAN SOCIETY

*Sheila Briggs*

## Introduction

S LAVERY IN THE ROMAN EMPIRE was, like all historical systems of slavery, a process of domination.[1] Yet, slavery was not just one aspect
of Greco-Roman society; the Roman Empire was a slave society.[2] Slavery
pervaded materially and ideologically the whole sociocultural domain and
therefore was integral to social functions and cultural productions that in
nonslaveowning societies are implemented in other ways. It existed as a
multifarious system, comprising slave systems of different origins which co-
existed and coalesced, and which were overlaid by newer uses of slavery,
such as the deployment of slaves in the imperial administration. Slavery as
both fundamental structure and texture of the Greco-Roman world led to
the complexity — the ambiguities and contradictions — that modern scholars have noted about it. We must expect to find this complexity reflected in
Paul's writings.

Because slavery is a process or set of processes of domination, it is always
related to the signification of power and powerlessness in the cultures where
it exists. However, under slavery the discourse of power has a "double,"
what I will call here the discourse of evasion. The raw exercise of power,
the display of the unlimited subjugation of the slave, can only be sustained
if it is embedded in a broader field of social relations that stubbornly resists
the coercive character of slavery becoming the focus of attention. We find
both discourses in Paul, and they correspond to whether Paul was talking

---

1. For the groundbreaking study of slavery as a process of domination, see Orlando Patterson, *Slavery and Social Death: A Comparative Study* (Cambridge: Harvard University Press,
1982).

2. K. R. Bradley, *Slavery and Society at Rome*, Key Themes in Ancient History (Cambridge:
Cambridge University Press, 1994), 10–30.

about the social institution of slavery or using slavery as a metaphor in his theological rhetoric. In 1 Corinthians Paul at once addresses and evades the social institution of slavery and also employs it metaphorically. I will be concentrating in this essay on the former, but will also indicate briefly what the implications are of a discourse of evasion in dealing with the social institution for the metaphorical use.

## Paul's Treatment of the Social Institution of Slavery

Paul intended his advice to slaves in 1 Cor. 7:21–24 to be an example of his basic principle of the right Christian attitude to one's social status — "In whatever condition you were called, brothers and sisters, there remain with God" (7:24; cf. 7:17). In fact, the previous example concerning circumcision served his purpose better than slavery, since Paul assumed and accepted that manumission was a real possibility for many slaves (7:21c). The difficulties of interpreting *mallon chrēsai* in 7:21d need to be mentioned here. The debate is engaged over whether we are to complete the phrase as "better use freedom" or "better use slavery." Was Paul encouraging slaves to avail themselves of the opportunity to become free or exhorting them to remain in slavery even if offered freedom? In contemporary scholarship the balance has shifted toward the interpretation of the phrase as "use freedom." The reason for favoring "use freedom" has much to do with the actual practice of manumission in Roman slavery, which, since S. Scott Bartchy's work, has been seen as the key to understanding what Paul meant within his own social context. Roman urban slaves had a reasonable hope for manumission, because this was often a financial advantage to their owners while also being a typical reward slaveowners gave their slaves for loyal service.

Slaves often had the opportunity to accumulate savings, their *peculium*, out of which they might purchase their freedom. Slaves who were trying to earn the purchase of their freedom were likely to work more diligently and more profitably for their owners, who also stood to be handsomely recompensed for the loss of their slave at manumission through the slave's savings. Furthermore, manumission did not bring an end to the obligations of the former slave to his or her owner. Freedpersons were bound to their former owners who were now their patrons. Under Roman law freedpersons were required to perform services (*operae*) for their patrons. Since some slaves held positions of responsibility within the households of wealthy owners, setting such slaves free, who would continue working for their patrons, made financial sense when their legal status as freedpersons would allow them to be more effective business agents for their former owners. In the Greek east

---

3. S. Scott Bartchy, *Mallon Chrēsai: First-Century Slavery and the Interpretation of 1 Corinthians 7:21*, SBLDS 11 (Missoula, Mont.: Society of Biblical Literature for the Seminar on Paul, 1973), 88–91.

the historical development of slavery had been different than in the Roman context. In the classical period manumission was not common in Greece but increased in later Hellenistic society.[4] However, the obligations that a freed-person owed his or her former owner were often more burdensome than in the Roman context. A *paramonō* contract stipulated that the manumitted slave had to "remain" (*paramenein*) with his or her former owner or other beneficiary of the contract for a specified period of time. These contracts be-came over time more restrictive of freedpersons' liberty, often obliging them to serve until the death of the beneficiary and comply with every demand at the pain of physical punishment or even being reduced once again to slav-ery. In cases where the stipulations of the *paramonō* contract were harsh, the line between slavery and freedom was thin.[5]

J. Albert Harrill, in his recent and major study of the Corinthian pas-sage, warns us against making certain modern assumptions about the nature of ancient slavery in the debate over the meaning of *mallon chrēsai*. He criticizes Bartchy for the latter's depiction of Roman slavery as one that promoted the humane treatment of slaves and therefore their contentment with their lot.[6] Bartchy completed his study before the publication of M. I. Finley's *Ancient Slavery and Modern Ideology* and therefore relied partly on the work of Joseph Vogt and those who followed him.[7] Finley's attack was aimed especially at Vogt and sought to refute the conception of ancient slav-ery as predominantly humanitarian.[8] The frequency of manumission among the Romans was not the result of humane attitudes toward slaves but part of an elaborate system of social control, which ensured the survival and sta-bility of the slave society. K. R. Bradley comes to the following conclusion about the role of manumission in the Roman slave system:

> Everything combined to produce subordination in the slave to the mas-ter during slavery and to create a situation in which total domination over and exploitation of the slave were feasible. The long-term incen-tive of freedom did not automatically convert itself for the slave into the final reward, and was not necessarily supposed to, so that as with the family lives of slaves, it was the element of uncertainty which sur-rounded manumission, which made freedom an effective form of social manipulation.[9]

---

4. Yvon Garlan, *Slavery in Ancient Greece*, trans. Janet Lloyd (Ithaca, N.Y.: Cornell University Press, 1988), 74.

5. Ibid., 78–80.

6. James Albert Harrill, *The Manumission of Slaves in Early Christianity*, HUT 32 (Tübingen: J. C. B. Mohr [Paul Siebeck], 1995), 96–101.

7. Bartchy, *Mallon Chrēsai*, 68ff.

8. M. I. Finley, *Ancient Slavery and Modern Ideology* (New York: Viking Press, 1980); Joseph Vogt, *Ancient Slavery and the Ideal of Man*, trans. Thomas Wiedemann (Cambridge: Harvard University Press, 1975).

9. K. R. Bradley, *Slaves and Masters in the Roman Empire: A Study in Social Control* (New York: Oxford University Press, 1987), 112.

Another misconception about ancient slavery that Harrill seeks to dispel is that social conservatives in antiquity opposed manumission.[10] Since slavery was not under fundamental attack in the ancient world, freeing slaves was not placed in the context of a condemnation of slavery and a call for its abolition. Even if one sees Paul as a social conservative, this would not have been expressed as opposition to slaves' obtaining their freedom, since manumission underpinned rather than subverted the ancient social order. Paul's primary concern in 7:21–24 was not with the social status of slave and free per se but with the attitude adopted by Christians to their social status. He urged slaves not to worry about their status and hence situates his statements on slavery and freedom within the broader context of 1 Corinthians 7, where Paul's main topic is marriage. His later remarks about being free of anxiety about the affairs of the world in 7:32–35 are addressed first to those considering marriage. Yet, they are of broader application since they follow his more general plea "that those who deal with the world be as though they had no dealings with it" (7:31). Paul was exhorting slaves not to make the prospect of manumission the overriding concern of their lives. If concern over Christians' anxieties about their worldly existence motivated Paul in 1 Corinthians 7, then the "use slavery" hypothesis becomes contextually less plausible. No one in the Greco-Roman world, including Paul, could reasonably believe the slave's existence was free of anxiety. Slaves could at the wish and whim of their owners be separated from those they considered their family, beaten for the most trivial cause, or forced to perform the most degrading or body-breaking labor. Fear was the emotion most commonly associated with the slave.[11] Paul also would have had an implicit understanding of manumission as a mechanism of social control, which K. R. Bradley identifies in the quotation above. Paul is, therefore, not rejecting manumission, but warning against being ruled by the uncertainty which the prospect of manumission produced and which internally controlled the slave.

Paul's admonition in 7:23 that Christians not become the slaves of human masters is directed as much at slaves as at the free. Paul is reiterating in part the well-known Stoic topos that true liberty is inner freedom, which is therefore not dependent on life circumstances and hence accessible to slaves as well as the free. However, the ground of Christian freedom from enslavement to the external things of this world is not a recognition of the inner autonomy with which nature endows human beings. Rather, it is the acceptance of an obligation to God that overrides all others, including those to owners and patrons (7:22). There may also be an oblique reference in 7:23 to the practice of selling oneself or one's family members into slavery as a means of securing or improving a livelihood. Although voluntary enslavement has been stressed by some New Testament scholars, there is no evidence

---

10. Harrill, *Manumission of Slaves*, 74–75.
11. See Bradley, *Slaves and Masters*, 113–37.

that this was more than an insignificant source of slaves.[12] Nonetheless, Paul would have been aware of the practice and may have encountered among the members of the Corinthian and other communities those who had undergone voluntary enslavement. The life of the unpropertied free was also one of insecurity. Slaves were housed, fed, and clothed by their owners. Some were given training in skilled occupations, gained expertise in commercial ventures, or even received a liberal education. For the free who were destitute or who lacked other means of social advancement, enslavement under some circumstances provided material survival or even improvement. Taking into account this background for interpretation, then, both slave and free were being urged by Paul not to let social mobility become the guiding motivation of their lives, whether that was emancipation from or entering into slavery. Paul was therefore addressing the specific anxieties over their material well-being of the urban poor, whether slave or free.

Even in 1 Corinthians 7 Paul's metaphorical use of slavery is prominent. When I speak of Paul's use of slavery as a metaphor, I mean metaphor in the strongest sense. Slavery was not a simile for the Christian's relationship to Christ and God. Paul was not making an analogy between one aspect of two otherwise dissimilar relationships. Rather, he was speaking of an identical relationship in two dissimilar realms wherein enslavement to Christ and God displaced the social institution. Hence, Paul's warning in 7:23, "Do not become slaves of human masters," may have been intentionally ambiguous, referring both to the practice of voluntary enslavement and to the submission to the world's affairs, which should have now been marginalized for the Christian. The phrases in 7:22, "freed person belonging to the Lord" and "slave of Christ," were intended by Paul to inculcate in Christians the same sense of dependence on and obligation to Christ that were owed by a slave to a slaveowner or by a freed person to his or her patron.

First Corinthians 7:21–24 is not the only passage in this letter to deal with the concrete social reality of slavery. In the previous chapter Paul condemns the behavior of male Christians who visit prostitutes. Paul contrasts being united with the body of a prostitute and being united with the spirit of Christ (6:16–17). The two are incompatible, and Paul once more uses the metaphor of slavery to remind Christians that they do not own themselves and their bodies (6:19–20). Prostitutes were usually slaves and therefore coerced into what was seen as a dishonorable occupation.[13] Yet Paul did not mention or condemn prostitution as resting on the sexual coercion of slaves. In fact,

---

12. For those who stress the role of voluntary enslavement, see Dale B. Martin, *Slavery as Salvation: The Metaphor of Slavery in Pauline Christianity* (New Haven: Yale University Press, 1990), 41–42; Bartchy, *Mallon Chrēsai*, 46–48. For a more skeptical assessment see Harrill, *Manumission of Slaves*, 96.

13. For an extensive study of 1 Cor. 6:12–20 in the light of ancient prostitution, see R. Kirchhoff, *Die Sünde gegen den eigenen Leib. Studien zu porne und porneia in 1Kor 6,12–20 und dem sozio-kulturellen Kontext der paulinischen Adressaten*, SUNT 18 (Göttingen: Vandenhoeck and Ruprecht, 1994), 37–68.

nowhere in Paul's letters can one find a reference to or prohibition of the sexual use of slaves, although this was one of the most common features of ancient slavery. I am not arguing that Paul approved of the sexual coercion that was integral to slavery as a process of domination. However, because Paul did not reject slavery as a process of domination, it would have been difficult to argue against its sexual form. The body of the slave, including its sexual and reproductive capacities, belonged to the owner.

The link between slavery and prostitution raises the further question of whether social status could prevent a person from being accepted into the Christian community. Obviously, large sectors of the slave population had no opportunity to come into contact with first-century urban Christianity: those who worked on the farms, in the mills, in the mines, all those who labored under harsh conditions, distant from urban life. For this vast underclass of slaves the system of slavery was neither benign nor did it offer upward social mobility. Contemporary scholars, like Paul himself, have focused upon the urban and upwardly mobile slave, but even in the cities the slave underclass was present. If a slave prostitute were able to leave her brothel (and in some cases prostitutes were chained to their brothels), would she have been allowed to join the Christian community? Put in the language of 1 Corinthians 6, could the body of a slave prostitute be "a temple of the Holy Spirit" and could she become "one spirit" with Christ?

Sexual exploitation of slaves, if it occurred within the Christian community, would raise several problems for Paul. He linked his discussion of marriage in 1 Corinthians 7 to his condemnation of visiting prostitutes in the previous chapter by bidding each man, who is unable to remain celibate, to have his own wife *dia tās porneias* (7:2). The direct addressee here is the free male Christian. Certainly, the urban and upwardly mobile male slave could have aspired to the same ideal of marriage. Paul was not just talking about the narrower legal definition of marriage, which would have excluded the liaisons of slaves and many of the low-status and unpropertied free, but the wider practice of social monogamy in the Greco-Roman world. It is also the case that slave as well as free men frequented the brothels. Paul's prohibition of visiting brothels would have affected poor men, slave or free, more than prosperous men, because the former would not have had the resources (nor often, in the case of the slave, the owner's permission) for social monogamy. The wealthier men, however, would have had the sexual use of their slaves and therefore their sexual activity would have been less restricted by not visiting brothels. Paul's statement in 1 Cor. 7:4 that both wife and husband have control over each other's body indicated that the free male did not have unrestricted use of his body and therefore implied that, since his own body in relationship to his wife has become a slave's body, his own sexual use of slaves' bodies has become illegitimate. This conclusion, however, Paul never makes explicit.

One can argue that early Christian exhortation to *sōphrosynē* and Paul's

own insistence in 1 Corinthians on *enkrateia* (cf. 9:25) would have dis-
couraged the sexual use of slaves. These virtues, although widely embraced
in the Greco-Roman world, did not affect conduct in ways that modern
interpreters might expect. The Stoic emperor in the next century, Marcus
Aurelius, could thank the gods for his sexual continence, because he did
not have sexual intercourse with the imperial concubine Benedicta or the
freedman Theodotus, both of whom were, it seems, the sexual partners of
his grandfather, Hadrian. In a slightly earlier passage he credits the sexual
abstinence of his youth to the fact that his upbringing in the house of his
grandfather's concubine was cut short.[14] There may be a parallel here to
the sexual liaison of a man with his "father's wife," condemned by Paul
in 1 Corinthians 5. Masters sometimes freed their female slaves in order to
take them as wives. In other instances the freedwoman became her master's
concubine. Both types of relationship could be covered by the designation of
the woman in 1 Corinthians 5 as the father's *gynē*. It is even possible that the
woman was not a freed concubine under Roman law but a slave who had
lived in a monogamous relationship with her master. If the woman had been
the legal wife of the father, then both law and custom in the Greco-Roman
world would have condemned the sexual liaison with the son. However, the
example of Marcus Aurelius shows that concubines and other less formal
sexual partners of a man's close male relatives were seen as sexually available
to him, at least after the kinsman's death. The man in 1 Corinthians 5 may
have become the woman's patron or owner at his father's death. Paul's rebuke of the Corinthian Christians in 5:2 reveals that many had been inclined
not to regard this sexual behavior as the serious offense Paul considered it
to be. The (former) enslavement of the woman in 1 Corinthians 5 may have
been the enabling factor for the man to have escaped moral censure for living
with her. If so, Paul did not acknowledge the role slavery played in promoting the sexual behavior he condemned. If the woman were slave or freed,
she may have had little choice in living with either the father or the son.
Again, the sexual exploitation of a slave or even freed woman's dependent
status may have prevented her from meeting the moral standards that Paul
wished to make a condition of membership in the Christian community.

An appeal to the virtues of self-restraint and moderation cast the bounds
of conduct wide. Paul was himself aware in 1 Corinthians 7 how formidable
the demand for *enkrateia* in the sexual realm was (7:9). He had been un-
willing in the previous chapter to issue a mere warning against *porneia*. The
avoidance of *porneia* was undoubtedly already embraced as a moral ideal
by the Corinthian community, but the word had such a broad semantic field
that its concrete import for behavior remained ambiguous. Surprising as it
may seem to us, an early Christian could have rejected the vice of *porneia*
without applying that to his own sexual intercourse with a *pornē*. For, al-

---

14. *Meditations*, 1.17.6 and 1.17.2.

though *porneia* indicated illicit sexual behavior, the recourse to prostitutes was neither morally or legally condemned. Under Roman law, especially after the marriage legislation of Augustus, a male citizen who had a sexual relationship with a free woman, who lived with him neither in marriage or a legally recognized form of concubinage, risked the criminal charge of committing a *stuprum*. However, his relationships with slaves and prostitutes were exempted from this category of legal and moral delict.[15] Paul made explicit the connection between eschewing *porneia* and shunning brothels. Paul recognized the limitations of relying on catalogs of virtues and vices in order to encourage or discourage specific forms of behavior. Paul could be quite precise in describing what behavior was compatible or incompatible with being a Christian. The sexual use of slaves was highly problematic for Paul's ideal of Christian behavior, but since it was intrinsic to the social institution that Paul did not wish to attack, he subjected it to no explicit criticism.

This discourse of evasion is a primary early Christian response to the social reality of slavery. There is no Pauline or New Testament passage that addresses the vulnerability of slaves to sexual exploitation or physical torture. In Paul's letter to Philemon there is perhaps the implication that Philemon should not physically punish Onesimus, if indeed Onesimus is a runaway slave at all.[16] However, Paul did not explicitly trespass on what he and his society understood as the prerogative of a slaveowner. The New Testament *Haustafeln* instruct slaveowners not to treat slaves harshly, but what constitutes harsh treatment is left undefined. It is unlikely that Paul or the *Haustafeln* intended to prevent owners from physically beating their slaves for what they perceived as disrespectful speech, laziness, tardiness, or lack of success in a task.

## Slavery as Metaphor in Paul

Paul avoided any direct discussion of what was integral to the ancient institution of slavery as a process of domination — the social degradation of the slave, which was accomplished through many means, including the infliction of physical pain, mutilation, and death, as well as sexual exploitation and coercion. These aspects of the social reality of slavery are transposed into the realm of theological metaphor. Paul's quotation of the Christological hymn in Philippians 2 exemplifies how the brutality of ancient slavery

---

15. Aline Rousselle, *Porneia: On Desire and the Body in Antiquity* (Oxford: Blackwell, 1988), 81.

16. For a denial of the hypothesis that Onesimus was a runaway slave, see Allen Dwight Callahan, *Embassy of Onesimus: The Letter of Paul to Philemon*, New Testament in Context (Valley Forge, Pa.: Trinity Press International, 1997), 4–19.

becomes a vehicle of Christian theology.[17] Jesus not only assumes the "form of a slave" but becomes vulnerable to the social degradation of slavery in its most extreme form. Crucifixion was the form of execution for slaves, and as such it was the most feared and despised form of capital punishment. Free persons of low status also suffered crucifixion and it represented their being stripped of what little social position and honor they had possessed. The rhetorical force of the Philippians' description of Christ taking on humanity is intensified by the enormity of a person of ultimate high status, one who is in the "form of God," being executed as a slave.

Christians share in the enslavement and extreme social degradation of Christ according to Paul. In Rom. 6:6 Paul reminded his audience, "We know that our old self was crucified with him so that the body of sin might be destroyed, and we might no longer be enslaved to sin." The whole of Romans 6 is indeed a transposition of what Orlando Patterson describes as the "social death" of the slave into theological metaphor.[18] In the social reality of slavery a slave is "dead" in the sense that she or he has no existence independent of her or his owner; the slave is legally without parentage and kinship group and without homeland or city. In Romans 6 all human beings are seen as enduring the equivalent of the social death of slavery and as being owned by sin. The escape from this state is not to be found through upward mobility, by becoming freedpersons of sin — or in extension of Paul's general argument in Romans — free under the law. Paul proposed a very different and very radical solution. The social death of slavery ended with the actual death of the slave. Baptism is crucifixion, and the most extreme degradation of the slave is the point of release from slavery. Nevertheless, baptism does not restore a preslavery identity and it does not return Christians to an original Adamic state prior to sin. Instead, what occurs is a transfer of ownership and Christians become "slaves of righteousness" since they "have been freed from sin and enslaved to God" (6:18, 22).

In both 1 Corinthians 6 and 7 we see the effect of the theological metaphor of slavery on Paul's injunctions to a Christian community. When addressing the use of prostitutes and the social status of slaves Paul reminded all Christians that they "were bought for a price" (6:20, 7:23). For Paul all Christians were theologically slaves. What is the connection of theological and social slavery? On the one hand, one could argue that when everyone is reduced to slavery before God, as owned either by sin or righteousness, then the social import of such a statement would be leveling and egalitarian. On the other hand, when salvation itself is seen as a process of domination, then the critique of social arrangements, resulting from processes of domination, is made, to say the least, more difficult. There is no evidence in Paul

---

17. Sheila Briggs, "Can an Enslaved God Liberate? Hermeneutical Reflections on Philippians 2:6–11," *Semeia* 47 (1989): 142–46.

18. Patterson, *Slavery and Social Death*, 35–76. Patterson recognizes the centrality of slavery to the symbolic system of Christianity, especially to the theology of Paul (70–72).

that he made a distinction conceptually or morally between theological and social processes of domination. The reality and validity of God owning the bodies and whole existence of Christians in the spiritual realm predisposed Paul not to question human beings owning the bodies and whole existence of others in the social world.

## Paul, Slavery in Ancient Literature, and the Discourse of Evasion

Paul and early Christians were not the only ancient writers to engage in a discourse of evasion about the social reality of slavery. I am going to discuss the discourse of evasion in other ancient literature especially through examples taken from Roman comedy, because this was a popular entertainment that reached an audience with a similar social breadth to the Christian community in Corinth. Corinth as a Roman colony in Greece had Latin cultural influences and the Roman comedians adapted Greek originals. Although dating from an earlier period, the Roman comedy of Plautus and Terence was still in vogue and performed in the first century.

Generally, in ancient literature we see a reluctance to confront the brutality of slavery; nonetheless it is depicted.[19] Ancient authors often remarked casually upon the brutality of slavery, which is not surprising since it was observed in everyday life. Yet the reader is not only spared a description of beatings, torture, and other humiliations, we are also distanced from the effects that these had on a slave. Nonetheless, there are moments when the sufferings or fears of slaves are expressed. Apuleius gives us a description of slaves in a mill branded, shackled, and almost naked, their backs scarred with floggings and their eyesight failing through working in smoke-filled darkness, but then he moves on to his next racy tale.[20] In Plautus's *Captivi* Philocrates and his slave Tyndarus are taken prisoners of war. Tyndarus swaps identity with his master, so that the latter is released as a messenger to the enemy. When Tyndarus's subterfuge is realized, he is condemned to the mines. At the end of the play, he is brought out and says, "I have seen a good many pictures whose subject was torture in hell, but let me tell you there is no hell that can match those stone quarries where I've been."[21] Even the upwardly mobile slave, being entirely in his or her owner's power, could be plunged into the brutalized existence of the slave underclass. In Terence's *Phormio* Geta fears the reprisal of his master for helping the master's son marry a free but low-status woman. He conjures up the "endless grinding in the mill, beatings, shackles, drudgery on the farms"

---

19. See William Fitzgerald, *Slavery and the Roman Literary Imagination*, Roman Literature and Its Contexts (Cambridge: Cambridge University Press, 2000), 32–41.

20. Apuleius, *Golden Ass*, 9.12.12.

21. Plautus, *Captivi*, 998–1000.

that can now befall him.[22] These sort of fears at displeasing an owner would not have been unknown to the Corinthian slaves in the Christian community.

The form of evasion that is primary in Greek and Roman popular literature is to deny that the social degradation of slavery can occur or occur permanently to those worthy of higher social status. A recurrent theme is that of free-born, indeed, high-born persons being enslaved as minors but their true identity being revealed in the plot, resulting in the restoration to their original social status and a happy marriage. The Greek romances, most famously Longus's *Daphnis and Chloe*, employ this plot line, but so do the Roman comedies. A favorite variation of this theme in Plautus's comedies is the enslavement of free-born and usually high-born women as infants who are saved from prostitution and other forms of dishonorable sexual use by the discovery of their true parentage (Selenium in *Cistellaria*, Palaestra in *Rudens*, Casina in the play of that name). Unlike the Philippians' hymn these fictions do not take the degradation of the slave out of the social realm, but nourish the idea that those who are worthy of honor will escape the slave condition.

A sure giveaway as to who is the enslaved aristocrat in Plautus's *Captivi* is when Hegio discovers Tyndarus's trickery in getting him to release the high-born and hence valuable prisoner of war Philocrates. Hegio (who will turn out to be Tyndarus's father) tells the slave that he will have him tortured in the most excruciating ways possible. Tyndarus replies, "The one who dies on account of virtuous action, does not perish utterly."[23] Tyndarus's justifiable claim to virtue indicates that he does not have a servile character. Orlando Patterson has noted that slave societies develop strong honor/shame codes and that the slave as a person with no standing in such a society is also characterized as a person without honor.[24] Greco-Roman society with its strong stratification and competition measured these in honor/shame categories. The popular representation that a person with honor could not be ultimately enslaved was accessible to the free-born, freedpersons, owners, and slaves. In the Corinthian community the exhortation to "imitate Christ" that we find in Philippians might have led some Corinthian slaves to think that their "true identity" as sons and daughters of God should also be reflected in their social status, thus giving them a theological motivation to seek their freedom. Paul in 1 Corinthians 7 may have been countering a theological argument for the manumission of slaves. He would, therefore, be expressing not opposition to manumission in principle but to specific theological assumptions which might motivate it.

---

22. Terence, *Phormio*, 248–50.
23. Plautus, *Captivi*, 690.
24. For his discussion of Greek and Roman societies, see *Slavery and Social Death*, 88–92.

## Conclusion: Slavery and Anxiety about Social Status

Paul, although a free Roman citizen, was not a member of the social elite. Most of the slaveowners among early Christians would have been of his social status or even lower. They belonged to the humble free-born or were themselves freedmen or freedwomen (possibly even slaves, since slaves could own other slaves). Their class experience and perspective on slavery differed from members of the social elite. Although Roman aristocrats upheld the distinction between poor free citizen and slave, they saw the lower-class free as sharing the same moral and intellectual deficiencies as slaves. Cicero distinguishes between those who exercise generosity as a virtue and those who are merely prodigal with their resources. In the latter category of squanderers he places those who provide entertainments for the gratification of the populace. He quotes Aristotle's opinion as his own, "This sort of amusement pleases children, silly women, slaves, and the free who are just like slaves [*servorum simillimi liberi*]."[25]

Paul and slaveowning Christians belonged to the ranks of the free and freed who were liable to be despised by the social elite as the "free who are just like slaves." They were small-scale slaveowners who did not possess slaves as luxury items but as workers in crafts and trade, in equally small-scale business enterprises. Their standard of living and of education was usually more similar to their slaves than to the social elite. Their economic dependence on their slaves would encourage them not to injure or maim them. The slaves could hope to be able to negotiate at some point their manumission, although since slaves had no legal rights, slaveowners could break such agreements, which obviously led to disputes and tensions between them. It is possible that Onesimus, if he were a slave running away from Philemon, sought out Paul initially to have him arbitrate an agreement on manumission, which he believed Philemon was reneging on. On the slaveowners' side, the regularity with which slaves became freedpersons blurred even further the concrete distinctions between slave and free. Paul and other nonelite, free-born Christians would suffer status anxiety as they competed with recent slaves, some well placed and wealthy through their connection to the imperial administration and aristocratic households.

Corinth in Paul's day was a Roman colony that had been founded by Julius Caesar in 44 B.C.E. and settled largely by Roman freedpersons. Depending on the form of manumission, the freed slave of a Roman citizen also acquired Roman citizenship. Freedpersons in a Roman colony like Corinth, therefore, obtained more rights than free-born noncitizen residents. Those who had become wealthy could aspire to civic offices and honors, allowing them to imitate aristocratic conduct. Some have identified the Erastus, mentioned by Paul in his greeting in Rom. 16:23 as a "*oikonomos* of the

---

25. Cicero, *De Officiis*, 2.16.

city," with the freedman *aedile* commemorated in a pavement inscription found in Corinth dating from the reign of Nero.[26] However, this claim has encountered skepticism on several counts. Erastus was not an uncommon name and "*oikonomos* of the city" is not necessarily the Greek equivalent of *aedile*, but can denote a low-ranking public slave as well as a leading municipal officer.[27] Whether the *aedile* Erastus was a member of the Christian community in Corinth or not, prosperous and influential freedpersons were probably to be found there. They were capable of providing financial support for Paul's ministry but its acceptance would have placed him in a patron-client relationship to them. In 1 Cor. 9:1–18 Paul asserts his entitlement to financial support as an apostle (9:3–7; 13–14) while at the same time stressing that he has not availed himself of this right (9:12, 15, 18). Dale Martin has investigated how Paul presents himself as a slave of Christ in 1 Corinthians 9.[28] Rather than undermining his authority, the self-description of Paul in terms of a slave *oikonomos* bolsters it. Paul is claiming a connection to the most powerful master, which far outdoes the connections of well-placed slaves and freedpersons to the imperial or aristocratic households. The obligations to a human patron are superseded by those to the divine master and patron. Although Paul's stance is theologically motivated by his desire to keep his proclamation of the gospel independent of all groups and factions in the community and therefore able to claim authority over all, this does not exclude that he felt resentment as a free-born citizen to being seen as a client of freedpersons. He thus undermines any potential subservience to a patron by claiming for himself the ultimate status, which a slave or freedperson might claim through association with the powerful.

Whatever rivalry over status that occurred between the humble free-born and the upwardly mobile slaves and freedpersons, they nonetheless shared a common social world. They were to each other business associates, coreligionists, marriage partners, and family members. The social elite, however, refused to entertain such familiarity with the servile and freed population. For them it was not a simply a matter of whether their personal social status would be devalued but of the preservation of the social order from corruption. Although the social elite were committed to the distinction of slave and free, their fear was not about slaves pressing for their freedom and thus making the social demarcation between the humble free and the upwardly mobile slave tenuous. Their more typical concern was about wealthy freedmen and freedwomen or their descendants infiltrating the social elite. Among his list of Nero's good deeds Suetonius commemorates that "For a

---

26. See, for example, Ben Witherington III, *Conflict and Community in Corinth: A Socio-Rhetorical Commentary on 1 and 2 Corinthians* (Grand Rapids, Mich.: W. B. Eerdmans, 1995), 33–34.

27. See Justus J. Meggitt, "The Social Status of Erastus (Rom 16:23)," *NovT* 38 (1996): 218–23.

28. Martin, *Slavery as Salvation*, 50–85.

long time he would not admit the sons of freedmen to the senate and he refused office to those who had been admitted by his predecessors." In the very
next section Suetonius also favorably mentioned that the emperor inflicted
punishment on Christians as a group of people adhering to a new and ma-
lignant superstition.[29] I am not suggesting that this juxtaposition of uppity
freedmen and dangerous Christians in Suetonius meant that he identified the
two groups. It does, however, indicate that both the dilution of social stratification and religious innovation were seen as socially corrosive. A Christian
community, which internally and theologically blurred the distinction between slave and free, could easily be seen by outsiders as subversive. First
Corinthians 7:21–24 is written from the perspective and in the interests of
free-born Christians from modest social backgrounds, who had status anxiety in relation to upwardly mobile slaves. Yet they had a further concern,
since they did not want to be identified as a malaise of the social order from
an elite perspective. They wanted to contain the theological metaphor of
slavery, suppressing some of the implications that could be drawn from it.
Christian freedom as children and heirs of God was not be perceived as a
challenge to the status quo by encouraging slave dissatisfaction with their
place in the social hierarchy of this world.

---

29. Suetonius, *Nero*, 15, 16.

# — 7 —

# RESPONSE

## THE POLITICS OF THE ASSEMBLY
## IN CORINTH

### *Antoinette Clark Wire*

▨▨▨▨▨▨▨▨▨▨

T HESE CHAPTERS by Richard Horsley, Cynthia Briggs Kittredge, and
Sheila Briggs take up the politics of the Christian assembly in Corinth as one aspect of a broader study of Paul and politics. Each person has
looked to Paul's rhetoric in 1 Corinthians to better decipher the politics of
that assembly and Paul's role in it.

Richard Horsley's essay provides an important corrective to present discussions of Paul's rhetoric by placing it in the context of the imperial rhetoric
used by the Greek and Roman elite in Hellenistic cities such as Corinth. He
argues that the way the local aristocracy spoke in city assemblies and at
festivals played the key role, alongside the emperor cult and the patronage
system, in maintaining imperial control once it was established by military
conquest. In these city assemblies the rhetoric was not democratic deliberation leading to substantive decision making but was celebrative praise of
local donors and especially of the supreme imperial donor of all peace and
security. This praise challenged its hearers to respond in unanimous gratitude and obedience to the emperor and to local leaders in his stead. Horsley
proposes that although Paul was at home in this Hellenistic world, he had
been "resocialized" into a Jewish-Christian apocalyptic worldview and applied his skills in persuasion to cultivate small communities committed to
an alternate gospel. This gospel concerned a man crucified by the empire in
its ignorance but now ruling with God and soon to appear to expose his
enemies and deliver his followers, both Jews and Gentiles, from imperial
domination. Horsley argues that 1 Corinthians begins and ends with the
apocalyptic mystery of God's wisdom that chooses the lowly, a mystery that
not only reverses all imperial claims but exposes his Corinthian opponents
who share the world's aristocratic values.

Granted that Paul uses apocalyptic rhetoric that was shaped in commu-

124

nities resisting imperial rule, as we can see it functioning in *1 Enoch* 1–16 and the *Apocalypse of John*, it is not clear that such anti-imperial rhetoric characterizes his discourse in this letter and distinguishes him from those he wants to persuade. When Paul speaks in the framework of this letter of the "rulers of this age" who "crucified the Lord of glory," and of "every ruler and authority and power" that Christ will destroy "before he turns the kingdom over to God" (1 Cor. 2:8, 15:24), he may be appealing to traditions he shares in common with the Corinthian Christians. But the persuasion that dominates the body of this letter is drawn, as Horsley (following Margaret Mitchell) has shown, from the rhetoric used in Hellenistic cities to belittle others for factionalism and self-seeking and to champion concord and order, a rhetoric also extended to defend the Pax Romana.[1] Horsley takes this to indicate that Paul's opponents in Corinth are assertive in the mode of a city elite. What he does not recognize is that it is aristocrats who practice this antifactionalist rhetoric against people who question their authority. In tarring the Corinthians with the brush of power-seeking, Paul is the one caught with the brush in his hand. And if Paul acts the aristocrat in his use of municipal rhetoric in this assembly, his protestations of modesty, simple speech, and service of unity are not counterindications but are recognizable elements in that rhetoric. Of course Paul appeals to Jewish and Christian traditions rather than local legends and customs when he adapts the rhetoric of concord to defend his once firm but now increasingly insecure position in the small Christian assemblies in Corinth. In response to charges that he does not demonstrate the wisdom of their new leaders, he responds that he wouldn't speak the world's wisdom even if he could (1:17–2:5), that he could speak God's wisdom but they aren't up to receiving it (2:6–3:4), and that his position as founder of their community makes him their father, which relegates other leaders to caretakers in his absence (3:5–4:21).

Who then is he seeking to persuade? This letter is not an appeal to Corinth's wise, powerful, and well-born, whom Paul in any case has said are few in the church. More likely he speaks in an eddy of the urban mix where people have little or no status and Paul can hope they will find his fatherly patronage a boon or at least good discipline. Whereas Horsley sees in them the pretensions of a spiritual elite who allegorize Israel's history as a means of individual cultivation as they circulate in the city's courts and festivals, I expect these are people who find in this community what they lack elsewhere. For many this may be the first chance to learn their origins, to speak in God's spirit, and to share the authority of God's children. If this is the case, the celibacy in this community needs to be read not by analogy to Philo's Therapeutes, who have set aside luxury in order to study alone and share in

---

1. See Horsley, "Rhetoric and Empire — and 1 Corinthians," in this volume, p. 91, drawing on Margaret Mitchell, *Paul and the Rhetoric of Reconciliation* (Louisville, Ky.: Westminster/John Knox, 1992).

occasional silent meals of bread and water, but by analogy to people such as "Jezebel" or Thecla or Maxmillia and Priscilla. These women appear to have left the restrictions of hearth and family in order to take active roles in a wider community, to inspire others with words from God, to eat with joy, even to eat sacrificed meat without fear to show that God is one.[2]

I sense that Horsley's articles written in the 1970s that characterize the Corinthians as connoisseurs of the Hellenistic wisdom tradition in the mode of Philo and Wisdom of Solomon continue to dominate Horsley's reading of the Corinthian church.[3] Recent research points toward city churches that included all classes except the elite and involved active participation of women and slaves, migrant artisans, and other alien residents. In this case Paul's rhetoric that mocks their claims to wisdom and honor cannot be read as a description of their high status. The wisdom they claim may bear some signs of Hellenistic-Jewish wisdom through Apollos's mediation — or, at least, Paul's counterattack may take clues from these rivals — but it is practiced by people largely without privileges to give up and is exercised not in speculative writing but as prophecy and prayer spoken in the assembly. Voices mediate God's words to the community in prophecy and voices mediate the people's words to God in prayer, the latter often moving into ecstatic speech. Such circulation or communication of multiple voices in God's spirit can threaten established leadership. Paul's concerted effort to restrict the quantity and simultaneity of such expressive speech and to privilege its interpretation and discernment shows his role as bearer of "decency and order" against disruption (1 Cor. 14:26–40). Horsley has shown that this rhetoric, when applied on the municipal level by local oligarchs, works in concert with imperial rule in the urban Roman east. How would its use in marginal communities be anti-imperial?

In order to show Paul's place as the anti-imperial voice in Corinth's church, Horsley not only stresses his opening and closing apocalyptic rhetoric over the rhetoric of concord he exercises in the body of the letter, but also he describes the Corinthian experience of God's wisdom or spirit in line with Hellenistic wisdom speculation as "personal transcendence of mundane social-political reality."[4] Yet there is every indication that Corinthians have experienced expansion of their social life and status through participation in the assembly. Whereas Paul saw their status when converted — "not many wise by human standards, not many powerful, not many well-born" — as God's reversal of human valuation, which they should continue to represent,

---

2. Philo, *On the Contemplative Life*; Rev. 2:20–23; *Acts of Paul and Thecla*; Eusebius, *Ecclesiastical History* 5.14–18.

3. Richard A. Horsley, "*Pneumatikos* vs. *Psychikos*: Distinctions of Spiritual Status among the Corinthians," *HTR* 69 (1976): 269–88; Horsley, "Wisdom of Word and Words of Wisdom," *CBQ* 39 (1977): 224–39; Horsley, "How Can Some of You Say, 'There Is No Resurrection of the Dead'? Spiritual Elitism in Corinth," *NovT* 20 (1978): 203–31; Horsley, "Gnosis in Corinth: 1 Cor. 8:1–6," *NTS* 27 (1980): 32–51.

4. Horsley, "Rhetoric and Empire — and 1 Corinthians," p. 89.

they saw it as God's choice to lift them up into wisdom, power, and honor through the practice of God's gifts in assemblies that reject the privileges of gender, caste, and nation (1 Cor. 4:7, 10; Gal. 3:28). The social reality of these changes can be seen in Paul's having to concede separation from husbands to women who claim it (7:11) and freedom to slaves who can acquire it (7:21) in order to restrict further changes in the assembly under the principle that all should live as they were when first called (7:17–24).

The question then becomes whether Paul's stance or the Corinthians' stance represents more threat to an empire established and sustained by class, caste, and gender privilege. If Paul in 1 Corinthians "reinscribed imperial images and relations within his arguments aimed at reinforcing the discipline of an anti-imperial movement,"[5] and that against opposition from within, I think Horsley greatly oversimplifies and even falsifies the picture to present Paul as the champion of what is anti-imperial and anti-elite in these urban churches. We have yet further steps to take to emerge fully from the Christian tradition of making the apostle the measure of virtue as we see it and the Corinthians the dark foil for its display.

Cynthia Briggs Kittredge's proposal can provide us a test case of whether Paul's rhetoric is effectively anti-imperial. She charts Paul's recurring uses of the verb "to be subject" and other re          1 Corin.. and concludes that the subjection    "Imperial Eschatology" rhetoric of 1 Corinthians 15 canno                    ..als w.. term to establish the proper ranki church. As she puts it, "God's subj   ..on of Christ is the .... legitimation of the father's position between the children and Christ, and husband's position between his wife and God."[6] She identifies these chain. of subjection with the rhetoric of the patronage system in its asymmetrical exchange relationships as recently studied for 1 Corinthians by John Chow.[7] And Horsley has named the patronage system alongside the imperial cult and the rhetoric of peace and concord as the three-legged stool of imperial ideology. Kittredge asks Horsley after her analysis "whether Paul is simply opposing the patronage system or is fundamentally shaped by it."[8]

Kittredge's challenge cannot simply be dismissed by saying that Paul must use the language of his world to affirm an alternate world. She puts in question whether Paul's alternate world is all that different from the one it means to replace, either in its social relations or its experience of the distant beneficent deity. Our task is to shake off what Horsley calls the subjection of Paul to being read as the authoritative expression of Christianity and

---

5. Ibid., 93.

6. See Cynthia Briggs Kittredge, p. 107 in this volume.

7. John Chow, "Patronage in Roman Corinth," in *Paul and Empire: Religion and Paul in Roman Imperial Society*, ed. Richard A. Horsley (Valley Forge, Pa.: Trinity Press International, 1997).

8. Kittredge, 108.

begin to read his voice alongside that of his opponents as the beginning of
our deliberating tradition, with serious arguments and strong rhetoric flying
both ways. Only then can we overcome the yet more virulent subjection of
our ancestors in Corinth, and since, to being dismissed as people without
authority. By this route we might even begin to shake the subjection of God
to the imperial mold.

Sheila Briggs's essay locates Paul's 1 Corinthians in imperial Roman society as a slave society, so identifying the fourth essential leg that holds up
the imperial throne — or rather the first: military force institutionalized in a
slave system alongside patronage relations, the emperor cult, and the rhetoric of gratitude and unity. She distinguishes two kinds of rhetoric that Paul
uses about slavery, the rhetoric of evasion when discussing the social institution of slavery and the rhetoric of power when using slavery as a metaphor
for following Christ. With the metaphor Paul claims that every believer is
as fully dependent on Christ and obligated to Christ as slave is to master,
whether this Christian is slave or free. I would like to hear her consider
further what this meant for the doubly obligated slave. How did she or he
become "a freed-person of the Lord" (7:22), having never been enslaved to
Christ? And how was that combined with being someone else's slave? If, as
Briggs says, "enslavement to Christ displaced the social institution," it must
either have been accompanied by an emancipation program so the person
was free to obey Christ, or the metaphor was itself a rhetoric of evasion
to the slave, promising a substitute slavery and delivering a double slavery.
This makes me wonder if Paul's theology of the cross was not essentially a
theology by and for the free, unsuitable to transform the life of the slave.
Or could it be meaningful in some sense for a slave to be challenged to
"take on the form of a slave" and identify with Christ in crucifixion (which
Briggs calls the ultimate brutality of ancient slavery), and hence to receive
exaltation with Christ?

Briggs focuses primary attention not on the slavery metaphor but on how
Paul addresses the institution of slavery with a rhetoric of evasion. She sees
that Paul in the Hellenistic city would have been in contact largely with upwardly mobile slaves because the poorest city slaves trapped in workshops
and brothels would be unable to come hear (or be unwelcome if they did),
and the mass of agricultural and mining slaves would never have heard of
Paul. Was Paul's rhetoric of evasion then geared to the slave with some skills
or other resources who might stand to lose from an attack on the master's
rights? Might that explain why Paul dissuades Philemon from physical punishment of Onesimus rather than challenging his right to torture a slave?
Could it explain why he prohibits Christian men from visiting prostitutes
rather than challenging the master's right to sexual coercion of a slave, personally and commercially? If so, Paul plays to the well-placed slave and to
his or her master by ignoring the great majority of slaves.

Briggs makes some intriguing suggestions about the consequence of Paul's prohibition of visiting prostitutes. She says it "would have affected poor men, slave or free, more than prosperous men because the former would not have had the resources (nor often, in the case of the slave, the owner's permission) for social monogamy."[9] Note that she has distinguished four groups of men here: free with resources and slave with resources, both of whom could have wives and homes if the slave's owner allowed, and slave and free without resources who resorted to prostitutes. Of course resources would be different for different people — strength, skills, looks, savings, clients, household, land, citizenship — and there would be a spectrum from being *with* to being *without* resources. This could be very fruitful. She also hints at a parallel four kinds of women when she says that the prostitute is probably a slave without resources rather than a skilled slave woman or a poor free woman. Perhaps in the future she will consider how some of these eight groups of people are featured not only vis-à-vis prostitution but in the movement toward sexual abstinence in the church, in the practice of eating sacrificed food, or in public prayer and prophecy in the assembly. Of course some questions won't be answerable, but none will be answered if not asked.

We are challenged by these colleagues to move more fully into the Hellenistic and Roman sources to learn everything we can about the imperial order that structured the lives of slave and free, male and female, and rich and poor in Roman Corinth. Their work is a good indication that we will finally be thrown back on the study of Paul's rhetoric because it is what gives us entry into the dynamics of this small assembly, its multiplex population, and their social and religious experience.

---

9. See Sheila Briggs, "Paul on Bondage and Freedom in Imperial Roman Society," in this volume.

# — 8 —

# PAUL AS THE NEW ABRAHAM

## *Pamela Eisenbaum*

𐎟𐎟𐎟𐎟𐎟𐎟𐎟𐎟𐎟𐎟

I N *Paul among Jews and Gentiles* (1977), Krister Stendahl argued convincingly for dispensing with the notion of conversion as applied to Paul's
religious experience, and for substituting the "call" of Paul.[1] Based on a compelling exegesis of Galatians 1, Stendahl demonstrated that Paul describes his
"vision" of the risen Christ like the call narratives of the Hebrew prophets,
particularly Jeremiah and Isaiah.[2] Rather than seeing Paul's missionary zeal
as the consequence of his conversion from Judaism to Christianity (which
did not yet exist as a definable religion), Stendahl demonstrated that Paul's
vision and his mission were inextricably linked from the start. The vision
was, in fact, a call to proclaim the word of the Lord, like the prophets
of old; the only difference was Paul's message would be directed not to
his fellow Jews, but rather to Gentiles. Paul believed it was time for the
final in-gathering of the nations, and he was being called to help carry
out the project. So persuasive was Stendahl that his interpretation became
the dominant understanding of Paul's religious experience and mission, at
least among Anglo-American scholars. The "call" is often understood as
foundational to the "new perspective" on Paul.

In recent years, however, Stendahl's model has been challenged. Perhaps
the most thoroughgoing challenge has come from Alan Segal. In *Paul the
Convert* (1990), Segal revives the conversion model, although he develops
a much more sophisticated notion of conversion based on sociological and
anthropological studies. Segal conceives of Paul as converting not from Judaism to Christianity, but from one form of Judaism (Pharisaism) to another
(belief in Jesus).[3] For Segal, Paul's switch from the former to the latter in-

---

1. Stendahl, *Paul among Jews and Gentiles, and Other Essays* (Philadelphia: Fortress Press,
1976).
2. See esp. Jer. 1:4–5; Isa. 49:1–6.
3. Although Segal frequently uses the language of Judaism and Christianity. See A. Segal, *Paul the Convert: The Apostolate and Apostasy of Saul the Pharisee* (New Haven: Yale
University Press, 1990).

volved a radical transformation, a transformation not fully appreciated by Stendahl and the scholars who have followed his lead.

The work of Stendahl and Segal has, generally speaking, marked out the principal options in recent Pauline studies. In arguing against the classical Lutheran understanding of the radical discontinuity between Paul's life before and after Christ, Stendahl had to emphasize strongly the continuity between Paul's life as a Jewish Pharisee and his life after his "call." Since Stendahl's landmark work, however, a bifurcation has arisen in Pauline scholarship. In general, those who follow the call model tend to emphasize continuity in Paul's life experience, while those who follow the conversion model tend to emphasize discontinuity. A correlation exists between, on the one hand, those who presuppose Stendahl's call model and therefore interpret Paul's theology and teachings as reflective of first-century Judaism and, on the other hand, those who presuppose some sort of conversion and thus understand Paul as fundamentally transformed and standing outside the bounds of Judaism.[4]

The issue of continuity in Paul's religious identity between his earlier life as a Pharisee and his subsequent life in Christ arises because of the mixed messages that seem to come through in his letters. Paul obviously understands himself as a Jew, both before and after his call. As he says in Gal. 2:15, "We are Jews by birth and not Gentile sinners." Statements such as this give a clear indication that Paul is just as Jewish after his call as before, and that his identity as a Jew distinguishes him from Gentiles. Yet, as many have shown, Paul speaks as if there is a huge disjuncture between his former life in Judaism and his life in Christ (Gal. 1:11–24; Phil. 3:7–8).[5] The ambiguity present in Paul's letters toward Judaism needs to be acknowledged. In Gal. 2:15, when he reminds his audience that he is a "Jew by birth," does he use the modifying expression "by birth" (*physei*) in order to qualify his Jewishness, or does he mean it more as a boast? To put it in modern terms, is Paul simply saying he is a Jew ethnically but not religiously, or is he saying he is a Jew through and through?

I align myself with the new perspective on Paul, and in this chapter I wish to build on Stendahl's work and that of other new perspective scholars, while at the same time taking seriously Segal's critique. I will offer an alternative paradigm for understanding Paul's experience of the revelation of Jesus and his religious identity. I believe Stendahl was right to use the language of "call," but the call that best reflects the apostle's experience is not so much

---

4. Scholars in the continuity camp include John Gager, Lloyd Gaston, and Mark Nanos; those in the discontinuity camp include E. P. Sanders, Francis Watson, and Stephen Westerholm. New perspective scholars like James D. G. Dunn and N. T. Wright fall somewhere in between, though see the critique of the new perspective by Nanos in *The Mystery of Romans* (Minneapolis: Fortress Press, 1996), 4–8.

5. Segal, *Paul the Convert*, 117–33; A. J. Hultgren, "The Self-Definition of Paul and His Communities," *Svensk Exegetisk Årsbok* 56 (1991): 78–100.

the call of the classical prophets as it is the call of Abraham, a figure who embodies both Jew and non-Jew. In what follows I will argue that Paul implicitly understands himself as an Abrahamic figure who establishes a new kind of family, one made up of Jews and Gentiles. I will first describe how the call of Abraham resembles Paul's mission and then explore who Abraham is for Paul in particular. It is my contention that the importance of Abraham for Paul is not as an example of faith to Gentiles. Rather, Abraham is a patrilineal ancestor who encompasses "many nations" and thus enables Jews and Gentiles to become kin. This understanding of Israel's patriarch mirrors Paul's self-understanding because Paul's mission is to create kinship ties between Jews and Gentiles as joint members of the family of God, as Stendahl's work on Romans has so ably demonstrated.[6]

## Paul and Abraham Share a Calling

To paraphrase Gen. 12:1–3, Abraham is asked to leave his homeland and separate from his kin with the promise that God will make of him a great nation; he will be blessed and through him "all the families of the earth will be blessed." Broadly speaking, this is what happens to Paul. He experiences a divine call described literally as God's revealing his son "in" him, though it is more typically translated "to" him (Gal. 1:15), which results in his migratory sojourn among foreign peoples, the Gentiles, so that he might preach the message God has told him to preach.

To be sure, the biblical language of Abraham's call is not present in Gal. 1:11–17, whereas the language of Jeremiah (1:4–5) or Isaiah (49:1–6), particularly regarding being set apart while in the womb, does appear. I do not wish to deny the resonance between the language of the prophets and that of Gal. 1:11–17, but I think that Paul's overall transformative experience is more akin to Abraham than to Jeremiah or Isaiah. The fact that Paul uses Abraham as a model figure in two of his epistles suggests that we look to Abraham as a model for Paul's own identity.[7] Although Paul is cer-

---

6. See most recently, Krister Stendahl, *Final Account: Paul's Letter to the Romans* (Minneapolis: Fortress Press, 1995).

7. Commentators frequently assume Paul made use of Abraham in his discussion in Galatians only because Paul's opponents invoked the great patriarch as part of their argument that the Galatians needed to be circumcised. J. L. Martyn is one of the most articulate defenders of this position; see "A Law-Observant Mission to the Gentiles: The Background of Galatians," *SJT* 38 (1985): 307–24, reprinted in *Theological Issues in the Letters of Paul* (Nashville: Abingdon Press, 1997). Some have made a similar kind of argument for Paul's use of Abraham in Romans; see the discussion of J. S. Siker, *Disinheriting the Jews: Abraham in Early Christian Controversy* (Louisville, Ky.: Westminster/John Knox, 1991), 52–76. I do not wish to dispute such claims in this essay, but my emphasis here is on Paul's perduring understanding of Abraham, apart from polemics. Much of my case depends upon an image of Abraham that would have been shared by various Jews (as well as god-fearers and proselytes). As J. M. G. Barclay has pointed out, it is quite likely that Paul shared much of the same vision of Abraham as

tainly familiar with the prophets and quotes from both Jeremiah and Isaiah, Abraham is a *person* to Paul in a way that Jeremiah and Isaiah are not.

The description of events in Gal. 1:11–17 has two essential components: (1) God's call (1:15) to Paul, which comes in the form of the revelation of his son and which presumably caused some sort of religious transformation, and (2) the commissioning of his task to go to the Gentiles, which results in the peripatetic existence that characterizes Paul's life thereafter. Two similar components appear in the opening verses of Genesis 12: (1) Abraham is called by God to leave his home and family, though no details are given as to how God revealed himself, and (2) this event leads not only to the blessing of Abraham's own family, but to the blessing of "all the families of the earth." The second effectively constitutes what Paul calls God's "promises" to Abraham. These promises are repeated and expanded as the story of the great patriarch moves along. Most significantly, God promises to give Abraham a land currently occupied by foreigners, the Canaanites, and to give Abraham a great progeny; Abraham will become the "ancestor of a multitude of nations" (Gen. 17:2–6).

While narrative details clearly differ for Paul and Abraham, their biographies share a similar pattern. Both are called by God to a purpose that benefits not only them and their families, but also the rest of humanity. Both Paul and Abraham become alienated from their communities of origin as a result of their experience. In Abraham's case, God literally calls him away from his family and kin; in Paul's case, God's call implicitly results in his alienation from the Jewish community of which he was once fully a part. Both Paul and Abraham become travelers among other peoples.

No doubt the call of Abraham in Gen. 12:1–3 is sketchy, but the portrait of Abraham popular in Paul's time resembles Paul's self-understanding in a more obvious way. Abraham's call is widely understood to have meant rejection of his former way of life.[8] Abraham turns from idolatry to worship of the one true God. In other words, Abraham is widely considered to be the first monotheist. Often this tradition includes a description of Abraham's original family as idolatrous and thus the reason for Abraham's separation from his people. Numerous texts can be mustered to illustrate this image of Abraham:[9]

---

the rival teachers, even if such commonality is obscured by the polemic about circumcision ("Mirror-Reading a Polemical Letter: Galatians as a Test Case," *JSNT* 31 [1987]: 73–93).

8. The characterization of Abraham in early Judaism is rich and varied, as surveys of the subject have shown, extending far beyond what I have covered here. Abraham was known for his hospitality, for having been given apocalyptic insights about the future of human beings, for having been an intermediary between God and others, and, perhaps most famously, for his faithful obedience to God. Because these qualities are either too generic or commonly attributed to other biblical figures, they are not terribly useful for my purposes in this essay.

9. James Kugel has collected many examples of postscriptural texts illustrating various facets of Abraham's call in *The Bible as It Was* (Cambridge: The Belknap Press of Harvard University, 1997), 133–48. The translations from the pseudepigraphic texts quoted here are his.

And the child [Abraham] began to realize the errors of the land that everyone was going astray after graven images and after impurity... and he separated from his father so that he might not worship the idols with him. (*Jub.* 11.16–17)

And when all those inhabiting the land were being led astray after their [idols], Abraham believed in Me and was not led astray with them. (Pseudo-Philo, *Liber antiquitatum biblicarum* 23.5)

He thus became the first person to argue that there is a single God who is the creator of all things, and that whatever any of these other things contribute to the good of the world, they are enabled to do so at His command, and not by any inherent force of their own.... Because of these ideas the Chaldeans and the other people of Mesopotamia rose up against him, and having resolved, in keeping with God's will and with His help, to leave his home, he settled in the land of Canaan. (Josephus, *Ant.* 1.154–57)

James Kugel argues that the tradition of Abraham as the first believer in the God of Israel may derive from Joshua:

And Joshua said to all the people, "Thus says the Lord, the God of Israel: 'Your ancestors lived of old beyond the Euphrates, Terah, the father of Abraham and of Nahor; they served other gods. Then I took your father Abraham from beyond the River and led him through all the land of Canaan.'" (24:2–3)[10]

Because Abraham's story begins with his being called away from home and involves many years of journeying, Philo allegorized the patriarch's life as the process of coming to ultimate enlightenment of the divine.[11] The very same reason that Abraham can be claimed as the originary ancestor of Israel requires that Abraham also be recognized as having been transformed from one sort of person to another. In other words, if Abraham is the first Israelite, then Israelites did not exist prior to Abraham, thus Abraham cannot have originally been an Israelite; he must have been something else first. Indeed, both Philo and Josephus consider Abraham the first proselyte, because Abraham was originally a Gentile who entered into a covenant with God by being circumcised only as an adult.[12] Furthermore, some ancient exegetes believed that Abraham came to monotheism through his precocious study of the stars, since the Chaldeans were famous for their skill at astronomy. In some strains of postbiblical tradition, the Israelite patriarch excels not only in the science of astronomy, but in wisdom and virtue generally, such that

---

10. Ibid., 133–34.

11. See *Migration of Abraham* and *On Abraham* 71.

12. See Philo, *Virt.* 212–17; Josephus, *Ant.* 1.7; 2.159–60. Abraham must be at least seventy-five years of age, which is how old he is when he leaves Haran, according to Gen. 12:4.

he becomes the mentor and teacher of other peoples like the Phoenicians and Egyptians.[13]

I do not wish to argue for Paul's direct textual dependence upon any of the postbiblical sources cited above. Because the traditions I have cited appear in a wide variety of sources and are therefore commonplace understandings, it is virtually certain that Paul was familiar with at least some of them. Significantly, however, one scholar has recently demonstrated that the tradition of Abraham "as the one who rejected idolatry and astral worship in favor of the worship of the creator God" is evidenced in Romans 4.[14] Obviously such an understanding of Abraham bears on the connection between Abraham and Gentiles that I will discuss momentarily. For now, I wish to emphasize that the notion of Abraham as one religiously transformed could well have functioned paradigmatically for Paul's self-understanding. Abraham's life as popularly conceived in Paul's time constitutes the closest biblical paradigm to Paul's experience. In other words, Abraham provides a model internal to Jewish tradition for a kind of religious transformation that results in sojourning among Gentiles and thus helps us to explain how Paul can sound so Jewish and yet so removed from his fellow Jews.

Just as Abraham is considered the quintessential hero whose divine call leads to his abandonment of a former way of life and wandering among foreign peoples who receive the benefit of his wisdom, so Paul can understand himself as fundamentally Jewish and yet transformed by his religious experience into someone who must go live abroad among foreign peoples and teach them God's wisdom. Paul speaks of his "former life in Judaism" (Gal. 1:13), often in direct contrast to his subsequent life in Christ, from which he counts all that came before as a loss (Phil. 3:4–7). Paul may be Jewish but he no longer lives among Jews, partly because of his own mission and partly because of their hostility.[15]

Paul's missionary travels not only alienate him from his home but also they are intended to benefit the other peoples (*ethne*) among whom he is destined to live. As Stendahl made clear, Paul's central identity is as the apostle to the Gentiles. This we know not just from Gal. 1:11–17, but from many

---

13. See the quotations of Pseudo-Epolemus and Artapanus in Eusebius, *Prep. Ev.* 9.17.3–4, 9.18.1; as well as Josephus, *Ant.* 1.167–68.

14. Edward Adams, "Abraham's Faith and Gentile Disobedience: Textual Links between Romans 1 and 4," *JSNT* 65 (1997): 55.

15. Cf. Segal, *Paul the Convert*, 122: "Paul recommends for everyone conversion to a life of spiritual transformation, not a life defined by ceremonial obligations. In so doing he takes the part of the gentile Christian community in which he lives. Paul's constant theme of the opposition of faith and law is a social and political justification for a new variety of community. It matches the opposition between Jewish and gentile Christianity." Of course, I do not think Paul universalizes his religious transformation and therefore expects it of others. Rather, if Paul models his religious transformation on Abraham, as I argue, then such transformation plays a unique role for him in his particular mission. Furthermore, it binds people of different sorts together, instead of separating them from one another.

texts.[16] In Gal. 1:23–24, Paul explicitly recalls how his religious experience has influenced other believers: " 'He who once persecuted us is now preaching the faith he once tried to destroy.' And they glorified God because of me." Paul positions himself as a model, hence his frequent exhortation, "Be imitators of me," to the non-Jewish peoples of the world in order to teach them how to be worshipers of the one true God.

Most important, Paul positions himself as a new kind of patriarch, capable of unifying the multitude of nations who are already potentially related to one another through Abraham. As I intend to show in the next section, Abraham is primarily *father* Abraham for Paul, as for most any other Jew. The difference, however, is that Paul emphasizes the biblical claim that Abraham was destined to become the father of a multitude of nations and not just the father of the Jews.[17] Paul thinks of his preaching to the Gentiles as a kind of spiritual birthing process, as indicated by his frequent use of parental imagery for himself, as well as his persistent use of kinship terms.[18] By his preaching, Paul makes willing Gentiles legitimate members of Abraham's family, which is the equivalent of making them children of God, as Gal. 3:26–4:7 makes clear. By informing Gentiles of the blessings promised to Abraham and his seed, they become heirs of the divine promises, and Paul, as the bestower of the inheritance, has become their father. Insofar as Paul establishes this newly constituted family of God, Paul functions as a founding father, just like Abraham.

## Abraham and the Gentiles

My argument that Paul thinks of himself as a kind of *Abraham redivivus* depends not only on Paul's self-description but also on Paul's particular understanding of Abraham, specifically, demonstrating that Paul understands the relationship between Abraham and believing Gentiles not as one of analogy but as one of kinship. The majority of scholars assume Abraham is an exemplary figure for Gentiles both in Galatians and Romans. Recently, however, some have begun to recognize that Abraham-as-ancestor may be more significant in Paul's thinking than Abraham-as-example.[19] As

16. E.g., Gal. 2:1–10; Rom. 1:1–6, 13; 15:15–21.

17. Although many ancient Jewish interpreters explicitly recognize that Paul is the father of many nations, this aspect of Abraham's identity more often than not lay dormant in Jewish exegesis. See W. D. Davies, *The Gospel and the Land: Early Christianity and Jewish Territorial Doctrine* (Sheffield: JSOT Press, 1994), 166–77.

18. See, e.g., Gal. 4:19; 1 Cor. 4:15; 1 Thess. 2:11. Although Paul's use of kinship terms is most often understood metaphorically, I believe such terms are theologically and socially significant.

19. See the excellent discussion of Stanley Stowers in *Rereading Romans: Justice, Jews, and Gentiles* (New Haven: Yale University Press, 1994), 227–50. Stowers points out that people who are kin are also expected to manifest the same characteristics as their ancestors, which may render the contrast between Abraham-as-example and Abraham-as-ancestor ultimately meaningless.

one writer avers, "The idea is that the Gentiles are blessed not simply like Abraham but because of Abraham. Abraham becomes the reason *why* Gentiles experience salvation, not the example of *how* an individual becomes saved."[20] To be sure, both letters introduce the discussion of Abraham with the famous quotation from Gen. 15:6 ("Abraham believed God and it was reckoned to him as righteousness"), but both letters use it to make the point that Abraham's righteousness is connected to his status as the great patriarch. Moreover, Paul argues that Christian believers can claim Abraham as their father and claim to be the rightful heirs of God's promises to Abraham. In polemical terms, Abraham is not just the father of the Jews but of Gentile believers also, and not just metaphorically or spiritually speaking. Abraham is just as much the patriarch of believing Gentiles as he is of Jewish believers.

Scholars have observed that Paul sometimes describes Abraham and Gentiles similarly. For example, Paul essentially labels Abraham a "former idolater and polytheist" when in Rom. 4:5 he indirectly calls the patriarch "ungodly" (*asebes*), a word commonly used of Gentiles and which Paul himself uses to emphasize the idolatrous state of Gentiles in Rom. 1:18.[21] Similarly, the beginning of Galatians 4 makes mention of "elemental spirits" (*ta stoicheia tou kosmou*; Gal. 4:3, 9) to which Gentiles were once enslaved. Although there exists much speculation about exactly what Paul refers to here, it is likely that this is an allusion to Abraham's attention to the stars prior to his conversion to monotheism. If so, Paul once again connects the Gentiles' former lives to Abraham's former life.[22]

While scholars take note of the descriptive connections between Abraham and Gentiles, they generally think of these connections as analogical and rhetorical. They argue that Paul manipulates his rhetoric so as to bolster his use of Abraham as an example of faith for Gentiles.[23] Paul's analogies between Abraham and Gentiles are not intended to prove a genetic or ancestral connection between the two. In contrast, I think the connections Paul makes are there to reinforce what he understands to be a relation of kinship, albeit one that needs to be formally acknowledged. People who are kin are supposed to be similar to one another; those who belong to the same family share important characteristics.[24] The emphasis for Paul, however, both in Galatians and Romans, is not on the way Gentiles can be *like* Abraham if

20. Michael Cranford, "Abraham in Romans 4: The Father of All Who Believe," *NTS* 41 (1995): 73, italics his.

21. Adams, "Abraham's Faith and Gentile Disobedience," 59. A similar observation is made by James Dunn, *Romans 1–8*, Word Biblical Commentary (Dallas: Word Books, 1998), 205.

22. Cf. Wis. 13:15 and see the discussion by J. L. Martyn, *Galatians*, AB (New York: Doubleday, 1998), 399–400.

23. In addition to those already listed, see Francis Watson, *Paul, Judaism, and the Gentiles: A Sociological Approach* (Cambridge: Cambridge University, 1986), 136–42.

24. That is, no doubt, why some Hellenistic and rabbinic authors were compelled to say that Abraham observed Torah, even though he lived long before Sinai. Since Jewish law is seen by such authors as essential to Jewish identity, they could not imagine that their ancestral patriarch did not observe Torah. See, e.g., Sir. 44:20.

they emulate his faith; the emphasis is on their existing *relatedness* to him which they can now claim.

I do not have space for a detailed exegesis of Galatians 3 and Romans 4, Paul's two lengthy discussions of Abraham, but I do want to highlight some texts, focusing particularly on those places where Paul refers to Abraham's being the "father of many nations" (Gen. 17:5) who are blessed because of him (Gen. 12:3).

> Because Abraham "believed God, and it was reckoned to him as righteousness," so you see, those descended of faith — they are the sons of Abraham. And scripture, foreseeing that God would justify the nations out of faith, proclaimed the gospel beforehand to Abraham, saying "In you shall all the nations be blessed," so that those who are descended of faith are blessed with faithful Abraham. (Gal. 3:6–9)[25]

The NRSV translates *oi ek pisteōs*, a phrase that occurs repeatedly in this context, as "those who believe," and the RSV translates "men of faith." These translations reflect the reigning assumption that the faith of individual believers is what counts for Paul, their faith should resemble the faith of Abraham, and by virtue of this similarity they can be called "sons of Abraham." According to this view, the relationship between Gentiles and Abraham is one of affinity. The language of kinship is the rhetorical or metaphorical means of making this point.

In contrast, I translate *oi ek pisteōs* as "those descended of faith," because the preposition *ek* means "out of" or "derived from" and can be used for a person's lineage.[26] Since the focus of Paul's concern here is defining who the true children of Abraham are, using language of descent is appropriate. If Paul meant to say "those who believe" are children of Abraham, he would not have used the phrase *oi ek pisteōs*.[27] But he would most likely have used the active participle, *oi pisteuontes*, or some equivalent, as he does elsewhere.[28] Rather, *ek* consistently connotes origins or derivation and points toward the source of something, and Paul's usage is no different. Thus, *ek pisteōs* means that "faith," at least in this case, does not refer to the personal interior belief of an individual but to an external source of faith from

---

25. Translation is mine, based on the NRSV.

26. Cf. John 1:13 and especially Rom. 1:3, *ek spermatos David*, translated in the NRSV as descended from David. See also the discussion in Stowers, *Rereading Romans* (225–26, 237–43), who finds that "[t]he article with *ek* is well known in Greek as a way of denoting origins, participation, and membership" (240). He cites Lucian, *Vit. Auct.* 43 as an example. Although Stowers's discussion focuses on Romans 3–4, not on Galatians 3, and I would probably not agree on all exegetical points in both texts, his work with regard to this issue is foundational to my own.

27. Cf. Segal (*Paul the Convert*, 119), who translates the phrase "those who are under faith, a phrase defining his audience sociologically, describing how they entered Christian community." I do not see, however, that such connotations are implicit in the preposition *ek*.

28. Cf. Rom. 3:22, 4:11.

which one derives benefit. Being a descendant of Abraham entitles one to certain benefits, namely, receiving the blessings as God promised, as Paul reminds his audience in verse 8. Therefore, it is not the believers' own faith to which Paul refers in this passage, but most likely Abraham's faith. This interpretation is corroborated by Rom. 4:16, where the expression *to ek pisteōs Abraam* appears, which I translate "those descended from the faith of Abraham."[29]

Just what does it mean to be descended from the faith of Abraham? I believe the answer can be found in Rom. 4:16–22, which happens to be the other place where Paul quotes Genesis to illustrate Abraham's ancestral connection to the nations:

> That is why it depends on faith, in order that the promise will be guaranteed according to grace to all his descendants, not only to those who are descended from law, but also to those descended from the faith of Abraham, who is the father of us all. As it is written, "I have made you the father of many nations" in the presence of the God in whom he believed, who gives life to the dead and calls into existence the things that do not exist. Hoping against hope, he believed that he would become "the father of many nations," according to what was said, "So numerous shall your descendants be." He did not weaken in faith when he considered his own body, which was already as good as dead (for he was about a hundred years old), or when he considered the barrenness of Sarah's womb. No distrust made him waver concerning the promise of God, but he grew strong in faith as he gave glory to God, being fully convinced that God was able to do what he had promised. Therefore his faith "was reckoned to him as righteousness."[30]

Here Paul makes clear that Abraham's quintessential act of faith is the conception of Isaac. Therefore, those who are "descended of faith" are those born of Abraham through Isaac. To be sure, Abraham is considered faithful in general, and many other of his actions could be labeled faithful, but this particular procreative act counts as *the* faithful act second only to Christ's act of faith because it aids God in fulfilling God's promises.[31] Abraham's act of faith is to start a family on behalf of God; he produces offspring that bear God's blessing. Put another way, Abraham's act of faith provides God with heirs, which, by the way, is exactly what Paul thinks he is doing.

What's more, the heirs include the "nations." Although it was not commonly emphasized, it was not unusual for Jewish interpreters to mention

---

29. My claim about Abraham resembles debates about whether *pistis xpristou* is a subjective or objective genitive, whether one is justified by Christ's own faithful act on the cross, or by one's own faith in Christ. See Richard B. Hays, *The Faith of Jesus Christ: An Investigation into the Narrative Substructure of Gal. 3:1–4:11* (Chico, Calif.: Scholars, 1983).

30. I have again modified the NRSV.

31. Cf. Stowers, *Rereading Romans*, 230, 243.

Abraham being the father of Gentiles.[32] In some cases, Abraham was understood to be the ancestor of certain Gentiles to whom Jews could then claim a kinship relation.[33] What is unusual, however, is that Paul explicitly connects the promise that Abraham will be the father of many nations to the conception of Isaac. Although this linkage is unprecedented, it makes exegetical sense, since the biblical story indicates that the promise for multitudinous progeny and heirs is fulfilled, at least initially, with the birth of Isaac. For Paul, Abraham's act of faith gives birth to Jewish and gentile heirs; it marks the beginning of a line of descendants who will fulfill God's promises.

The similarity between Romans and Galatians with regard to Abraham being the father of Jews and Gentiles means that Paul's claim in Gal. 3:29 that the Gentiles are "Abraham's offspring, heirs according to promise" need not be seen only as a metaphor in his argument with the Jewish-Christian teachers at Galatia, who purportedly claim that the Galatians need to be circumcised to belong to Abraham. I think Paul thinks the Galatians are just as much the offspring of Abraham as are Jews.[34]

Both Jews and gentile believers are descendants of Abraham, but their Abrahamic inheritance is dependent upon being properly "adopted." Contrary to popular belief, Paul's argument in Galatians and Romans does not assume Jews are biological descendants (*kata sarka*), while Gentiles become descendants by "adoption" (*uiothesia*). He uses the term explicitly of Jews in Rom. 4:9: "They are Israelites, and to them belong the adoption." When Paul speaks of *uiothesia*, he does not wish to emphasize the Gentiles' lack of physiological connection to Abraham. He simply means that the Gentiles are now in the process of claiming their inheritance, whereas Jews have already received it. The term means "to become a son," with all the rights and privileges thereof.[35] Having the claim of inheritance to one's father's estate is of far greater significance in determining familial status than mere biology.[36]

Part of the reason that the conception of Isaac is so important as Abraham's act of faith is that Paul understands the story as evidence that the claim to God's promises is required for descendants to be recognized as true heirs. As Paul says:

---

32. Even Ben Sira, who fundamentally thinks of Abraham as the father of the Jewish nation, introduces the patriarch by calling him "the great father of a multitude of nations."

33. In 1 Macc. 12:21 and Josephus, *Ant.* 12.226, Jews and Spartans are said to be related because both are descended from Abraham.

34. Cf. Daniel Boyarin, *A Radical Jew: Paul and the Politics of Identity* (Berkeley: University of California Press, 1994), 144. My work is very much indebted to Boyarin's, but my reading of Galatians 3 differs markedly from his.

35. Cf. Paul's use of the term in Rom. 8:14–15.

36. This is evident from Paul himself when he says in Gal. 4:7: "So through God you are no longer a slave but a son, and if a son then an heir." See also Carolyn Osiek, "Galatians," in *Women's Bible Commentary*, ed. Carol Newsom and Sharon Ringe (Louisville, Ky.: Westminster/John Knox, 1998), 424.

For not all Israelites truly belong to Israel, and not all of Abraham's children are his true descendants; but "it is through Isaac that descendants shall be named for you." This means that it is not the children of the flesh who are the children of God, but the children of the promise are counted as descendants. For this is what the promise said, "About this time I will return and Sarah shall have a son." (Rom. 9:6–9)

"Children of promise" are Abraham's descendants through Isaac, those born by God's action, and not merely human procreation. The problem with unbelieving Jews from Paul's point of view is that, while they were fully informed claimants to their divine inheritance through Abraham, they are now rejecting it. The problem with Gentiles is that they have not previously had a chance to claim their inheritance. That is where Paul, apostle to the Gentiles, comes in. As a "descendant of Abraham," one who already holds claim to the inheritance, Paul can declare Gentiles part of Abraham's legitimate offspring, able to grant them their rightful inheritance as "heirs according to the promise" (Gal. 3:29).

Paul makes clear that Abraham's family never was constituted *kata sarka*, but by means of spiritual descent, which is not dependent on biological birth and blood relations, but which is nevertheless a bona fide lineage. Turning again to Romans 4, I translate verse 1: "What shall we say? Have we found Abraham to be our forefather according to the flesh?"[37] The inferred answer is, of course, no! Paul's point is that physical descent does not make one a rightful child or heir. The same point is implicit in Paul's allegory of Sarah and Hagar in Galatians 4. Any Jews who consider themselves descendants of Abraham do not hold this privilege by virtue of physical descent; otherwise, Abraham's children by Hagar would be counted as heirs along with Sarah's, which neither Paul nor any other Jews of his time believed to be the case. Paul's argument in Romans 4 can be summarized as follows: If a Jew's status before God is not dependent on biological lineage, then surely such lineage is not required for Gentiles either.[38]

## Paul, Abraham, and the Gentiles

Virtually ubiquitous in current scholarship on Paul, at least for those who subscribe to the new perspective, is that the apostle wished to break down the barriers that divide people, specifically the barrier between Jews and Gentiles.[39] The essence of the new perspective on this question looks something like this: Paul as a Hellenistic Jew followed monotheism to its logical

37. Cf. Richard Hayes, "Have We Found Abraham to Be Our Forefather according to the Flesh? A Reconsideration of Rom. 4:1," *NovT* (1985): 79–86.

38. See Cranford, "Abraham in Romans 4," 75.

39. As N. T. Wright says, "The presupposition of Paul's argument is that, if there is one God — the foundation of all Jewish belief — there must be one people of God. Were there to be two or more peoples, the whole theological scheme would lapse back into some sort

conclusion.[40] Believing in the divine impartiality of God, and as a result of his experience of the risen Christ, Paul was led to abandon the idea of Israel's uniqueness in the pursuit of theological and anthropological universalism. Jews "by birth" no longer hold the privileges they once held. Paul spiritualizes the understanding of Israel, so that anyone who has faith, Jew or Gentile, can be part of Israel. According to this view, genealogy no longer counts in the makeup of one's identity. As one scholar has put it, Paul renders "all genealogies irrelevant."[41]

I, too, believe Paul's project consists in his trying to construct, or perhaps reconstruct, a single family made up of Jews and Gentiles. But, in contrast to others, I do not think Paul devalues genealogy; rather he restructures genealogical lines in order to reconfigure the boundaries that unite and divide people. As a Hellenistic Jew Paul knows implicitly that one's genealogy is not coterminus with biology.

Biology is never the sole factor in determining kinship relations. Social processes, such as marriage and adoption, always aid in the construction of family and genealogy, though such processes are manifest in as many different ways as there are different cultures. Cultures that construct genealogies through the patriline, that is, exclusively through the father's line extending back to a single male ancestor, tend to depend upon social structures even more. As sociologist Nancy Jay has shown, paternity must be explicitly constructed, since it cannot be observed; but, because it is constructed, it is a more flexible form of genealogical identity.[42] Usually, focus on a single male ancestor is designed to provide society with a coherent social identity. Furthermore, concern for patriliny appears most frequently in those societies in which families are part of more extended and complex kin groups, for example, clans, tribes, and where the transfer of property needs conscious attention.[43]

Claiming to be the descendants of Abraham, as Jews had done for centuries prior to Paul, was likely not taken as literally by the Jews of Paul's time as modern scholars often think. Rather, the focus on Abraham and patrilineal genealogies linking Jews to him probably indicates some anxiety about the fluid boundaries of Israel as a people and the need to establish

---

of paganism, with each tribe or race possessing its own national deities" (*The Climax of the Covenant: Christ and the Law in Pauline Theology* [Minneapolis: Fortress Press, 1992], 170).

40. As Paul says in Rom. 3:29, "Is God the God of Jews only? Is he not the God of Gentiles also? Yes of Gentiles also...."

41. Howard Eilberg-Schwartz, *God's Phallus and Other Problems for Men and Monotheism* (Boston: Beacon Press, 1994), 228. To be fair, he qualifies this comment later on the same page by stating, "Thus although Paul repudiates genealogy as the defining feature of the Christian community, he does not totally eliminate it. Jews by birth retain an identifiable status with distinctive practices."

42. See Meyer Fortes, "The Structure of Unilineal Descent Groups," *American Anthropologist* 55 (1953): 25–34.

43. Nancy Jay, *Throughout Your Generations Forever: Sacrifice, Religion, and Paternity* (Chicago: University of Chicago Press, 1992), xxiv, 34.

a coherent identity. Several reasons can be adduced to support this assertion. First, by this time, the possibility of conversion already exists.[44] Since
a person can become a member of the Jewish community, and since the
Jewish community collectively understands itself as descended of Abraham,
one not biologically related to Abraham can be made into a descendant and
a legitimate heir of the Abrahamic promises.[45] Second, some scholars have
recently argued that circumcision constitutes a blood sacrifice by which men
lay claim to their sons as members of God's covenant people, much as Jay
describes. Indeed, if Jews saw themselves as automatically legitimate descendants of Abraham, why perform the rite of circumcision, which includes the
blessing, "Blessed art thou, Lord our God, King of the Universe, who has
sanctified us by his commandments, and commanded us to admit him [the
child] to the covenant of Abraham our father"?[46] It seems fairly clear that
circumcision gave a Jewish father the ability to *make* his son a descendant
of Abraham, rather than having to depend on a preexisting biological condition.[47] I imagine this symbolic function became even more important once
Jewish identity was established by the matrilineal principle. Finally, there is
evidence in both ancient Jewish and Christian circles that men could claim
powers of reproduction through the dissemination of religious instruction,
rather than through fertility. Howard Eilberg-Schwartz, who quotes from
an array of rabbinic texts, says the following:

> Rabbis fathered "children" through the teaching of Torah. As the
> learning of Torah emerged as the paradigmatic religious act in the

---

44. I follow the opinion of Shaye Cohen that conversion most likely originates in the Maccabean period (*The Beginnings of Jewishness: Boundaries, Varieties, Uncertainties* [Berkeley:
University of California Press, 1999], 109–39). Certainly by Paul's time, we have a great deal
of evidence attesting to the existence of proselytes (*proselyte* essentially functions as the Greek
term for a convert to Judaism).

45. I realize the claim that proselytes are as much descended of Abraham as native-born
Jews is not unproblematic, given the well-known mishnaic text that claims that Jews cannot
say "O God of our fathers" when reciting prayers (*m. Bik.* 1.4). At the same time, the Talmud
declares the convert to be "like an Israelite in all respects" (*b. Yebam.* 47b). As Cohen argues
(*Beginnings of Jewishness*, 154–74, 324–40), proselytes form a lower caste within the Jewish
community, even as they are theoretically full members of the Jewish community. However,
that proselytes were sometimes treated as second-class citizens is not altogether different from
Paul's understanding of Gentiles in Christ. On the one hand, Paul claims there is no distinction
between Jew and Greek, and yet he also claims that the Jews are special, possessed of certain
privileges. In both cases, one who shares no kinship relations becomes officially integrated
into the kin group, even if initially the awareness that the person has other origins cannot be
ignored. This problem, however, seems to be overcome within a generation. As Cohen argues,
the rabbis seem to regard the progeny of proselytes (assuming marriage to a Jewish woman)
no longer as proselytes but as Jews, who in fact now have Jewish fathers.

46. See the discussion by L. Hoffman, *Covenant of Blood: Circumcision and Gender in
Rabbinic Judaism* (Chicago: University of Chicago Press, 1996), 64–154. The quotation of the
blessing is taken from Hoffman's detailed description of the rite of circumcision (70).

47. Cf. Roman society, the *paterfamilias* can reject a biological child if he so chooses. Conversely, he can fully adopt one to whom he has no biological relation and make him heir to
his property. In traditional Roman religion, the *paterfamilias* must ritually recognize his own
child in order for that child to be recognized legally and socially as a member of the family.

rabbinic community, it absorbed the symbolic capital which had earlier been invested in procreation. Concerns about reproduction and lineage were symbolically extended from the human body to Torah knowledge itself.[48]

Like the rabbis, Christians could understand their preaching and the making of converts as an alternate form of reproduction. Such an understanding is implicit in the oft-recited claim that Christians "are made, not born."[49] Christian asceticism led to the high valuation of virginity and sexual abstinence, along with the consequent devaluation of physical reproduction.[50] Yet Christians kept increasing their numbers. I contend that this attitude, namely the procreative use of teaching and preaching to increase numbers, is implicitly present in Paul. After all, as Eilberg-Schwartz has ably demonstrated, because the Jewish God did not create by copulation with a consort but rather through speech, and because of the common association made between creation and procreation, seeing the procreative potential of human speech is not much of a leap.[51]

Paul makes that leap in Rom. 4:17. In his description of the conception of Isaac, Paul refers to God as the one "who gives life to the dead and calls into existence the things that do not exist." Paul here draws an explicit connection between God as creator and Abraham as procreator. Paul's retelling of the conception of Isaac in Rom. 4:17–22 (quoted earlier) is ethereal and devoid of sexuality. By describing Abraham's body as being "as good as dead," Paul removes any image of virility that might connote sexual activity. He paints a picture of the conception as a faithful enactment of the divine promise, which makes it into an entirely mental endeavor on Abraham's part: "he grew strong in faith as he gave glory to God." The point is not only to communicate that this procreative act is really a form of divine, and not fleshly, action but also to emphasize that lineage does not depend on biology.

In conclusion, Paul's description of Abraham's procreative act of faith mirrors his self-understanding as apostle to the Gentiles. Paul creates Abrahamic descendants not through biological reproduction but through his preaching and teaching. He is a verbal progenitor, struggling to "form" Christ in his gentile "children" (Gal. 4:19; 1 Cor. 4:14–15). Just before he begins his discussion of Abraham in Galatians, Paul says, "Does the one who supplies

---

48. Eilberg-Schwartz, *God's Phallus*, 212–13.

49. See, e.g., Tertullian, *Apology*, 3.1.18.

50. The fifth-century Syrian Christian Aphrahat gives evidence that Jews charged Christians with abrogating God's command to be fruitful and multiply, because they valued sexual abstinence so highly. From their perspective, however, Christians were multiplying their numbers, even if not always through sexual reproduction. See the discussion in D. Boyarin, *Carnal Israel: Reading Sex in Talmudic Culture* (Berkeley: University of California Press, 1993), 7, 141.

51. See Eilberg-Schwartz, *God's Phallus*, esp. 199–242.

the Spirit to you and works miracles among you do so by works of the law, or by faith that comes from hearing?" (Gal. 3:5).[52] The NRSV translates the last phrase as "your believing what you heard," which again places the emphasis on the believer's personal faith. But it seems to me much more likely that the "faith that comes from hearing" refers to Paul (or, hypothetically, to any preacher of the gospel) transmitting information about the faith that has been enacted on their behalf, whether by Abraham or by Christ.[53] More specifically, the "information" is really the divine promises God made originally to Abraham and by extension his family. As Paul says in Gal. 3:14, "that in Christ Jesus the blessing of Abraham might come upon the Gentiles, that we might receive the promise of the Spirit through faith." Paul's proclamation of the divine promises transmits the Abrahamic inheritance to those willing to hear it, and those who accept that inheritance are now Abraham's heirs.[54] Once Paul's Gentiles become part of the lineage of Abraham, they not only *receive* God's promises, they help God *enact* God's promise to the great patriarch that he would become the "father of many nations." And helping God to realize God's promises is apparently what Paul really means by "faith."

Postulating Abraham as Paul's missionary model helps explain the seeming contradictions in Paul's understanding of himself. The figure of Abraham could simultaneously serve as the ultimate symbol of Israel and the point of contact between Israel and the rest of the peoples of the world. Paul, the apostle to the Gentiles, never stopped being a Jew, but because his mission took him into foreign terrain, he came to understand what it means to be an "other," so much so that he partly became an "other."

---

52. Another modification of the NRSV which reads, "Well then, does God supply you with the Spirit and work miracles among you by your doing works of the law, or by your believing what you heard?"

53. Cf. Rom. 10:14–17.

54. The analogy of the will in Gal. 3:15–18 is therefore most appropriate.

# — 9 —

# THE INTER- AND INTRA-JEWISH POLITICAL CONTEXT OF PAUL'S LETTER TO THE GALATIANS

## Mark D. Nanos

ᘁᘁᘁᘁᘁᘁᘁᘁᘁᘁ

K RISTER STENDAHL suggested that inherent in Paul's language of justification by faith is his announcement that the promised day, when God would legitimate the standing of representatives of the nations alongside Israel as promised to Abraham, had dawned in the death and resurrection of Christ. Gentiles could now be counted among the righteous ones: "I would guess that the doctrine of justification originates in Paul's theological mind from his grappling with the problem of how to defend the place of the Gentiles in the Kingdom — the task with which he was charged in his call."[1] What kind of reaction would this assertion have received among Paul's fellow Jews? More to the point for a reading of Galatians: how would Jewish communities in central Anatolia have responded to *Gentiles* claiming to be full and equal members of the communities of the righteous, on the basis of faith in Christ, apart from proselyte conversion?

The reaction might have been a mixture of resistance and acceptance: denial of the Gentiles' claim on its own terms, but acceptance of the Gentiles as candidates for proselytism — as liminals, on their way from idolatry to righteousness. And the Gentiles, in turn, might have decided that they were willing to take this path in order to gain indisputable status among the righteous ones. This would allow them to escape the continuing constraints of their present ambiguous status, which still obliged them as "pagans," according to the prevailing views of both the Jewish communities and the pagan communities within which they functioned, to continue to participate in such practices as the imperial cult, practices no longer acceptable for Pauline Gentiles after they had turned to God in Christ (cf. 4:8–10).[2]

---

1. Krister Stendahl, *Paul among Jews and Gentiles, and Other Essays* (Philadelphia: Fortress Press, 1976), 27.
2. This seems to be the kind of practice that these former pagans are returning to again

146

This scenario, I suggest, is the background for Galatians. Paul heard from afar that his converts were considering complying with this "other" way to negotiate the problem, and this letter contains his response.

Imagine that these Gentiles, as relative newcomers to the Jewish communities, originally had gathered around the teaching of a visitor, Paul, with no reason to regard him as anything but a representative Jew working within representative Jewish groups. As time passed, however, they began to be aware that within the larger Jewish communities Paul's followers were regarded by other Jews as something of a subgroup. They became aware of an edge to Paul's teaching, an "us" and "them" aspect in the way Paul's group — their group — spoke. Their group did not mix as readily with other groups in the larger Jewish communities. Although they went to the larger assembly on the Sabbath for the reading of the scriptures, these Gentiles were more attuned to the members of their own little group than to others around them; there was an emerging "us" in the midst of a larger "them."

Following Stendahl, we may suppose that during these months they internalized Paul's proclamation of their identity as righteous ones, entitled to full and equal membership within the people of God, though remaining non-Jews. They came to believe that this proposition was "real," revealed in scripture, beyond dispute.

But then Paul left. The Gentiles ventured into larger meetings of the Jewish communities, perhaps for a holiday celebration or to hear the scripture reading as their own kinship and patron relations are deteriorating. There they were welcomed by some proselytes, formerly non-Jewish townspeople, perhaps old friends or neighbors.

We may assume that these proselytes, as representatives of the larger communities, did not share Paul's view of the status of those Gentiles apart from proselyte conversion. When Paul's gentile converts boldly announced their new standing among the righteous, claiming for themselves the "righteousing" power of their faith in a Judean martyred by the Roman regime, they might have been treated as confused, but sincere. They might have been gently put in their place and extended a helping hand.

Imagine this "good" message: They could indeed gain the identity among the righteous that they sought, but they had not yet completed the course by which this identity was to be won. That course, the ritual process of proselyte conversion, would indeed grant them identity as children of the quintessential proselyte and righteous one, Abraham himself. They would

---

in view of their status ambiguity, and to which Paul objects since they are already known by God (cf. Troy Martin, "Pagan and Judeo-Christian Time-Keeping Schemes in Gal. 4:10 and Col. 2:16," *NTS* 42 [1996]: 120–32), although for reasons different than Martin proposes (cf. Mark Nanos, "The Intra-Jewish Context of Galatians: Identifying the Players and Situation Implied in Paul's Letter of Ironic Rebuke," dissertation, University of St. Andrews, 2000, 198–202, 234–43). On the relevance of this practice for understanding the sociopolitical dynamics of communities in Galatia, see S. R. F. Price, *Rituals and Power: The Roman Imperial Cult in Asia Minor* (Cambridge: Cambridge University Press, 1984).

be honored with the identity they now claimed, legitimately, however, and not as the result of some merely half-baked notion proclaimed by some suspicious teacher who had recently passed through town. The wonderful age of which Paul had spoken was awaited, to be sure, but it had not yet come. No, they were still to be guided by the trusted and proven traditions of the fathers, to which they should now entrust themselves, and so find the acceptance they sought.

Of course, this gentile group was disappointed, shamed really, for their claim to honor had not been publicly recognized by those who knew and represented the communal norms.[3] They faced misunderstanding at home as well, and much more among their neighbors and coworkers. For these Gentiles were intimately associating with the synagogue, with people who embraced "foreign ways," married only among themselves, refrained from participating in the imperial cult by which the competitive commercial and religious interests of the town were advanced. Their lack of enthusiasm and even withdrawal from normal and important communal activities, family and commercial gatherings was cause for grave suspicion. Wouldn't their behavior bring down the wrath of the town elders, if not the gods?[4] Their families and friends grew uncertain, defensive, fearful: Were these no longer of us?

These "righteous" *Gentiles* might have been able to bear these suspicions earlier because of the value they had put on a new identity: they had become the children of God, and they would make a new life among those with whom they shared this identity. But now they were informed that this was not necessarily so! They were not yet the "us" that they had imagined, but still "them." They were not entitled to consider themselves free from the constraints of their pagan identities as though full members of the Jewish communities; for example, they were not yet included among those who were freed from participation in the imperial cult by way of the daily sacrifice made in Jerusalem (cf. Josephus, *Ant.* 14.185–267).[5] What were they to do?

This other message sounded good. It offered full membership in the new community according to prevailing communal, scripture-based norms. And this course had obviously worked wonderfully for the proselytes whom

---

3. Cf. Julian Pitt-Rivers, "Honor," *International Encyclopedia of the Social Sciences* (New York: Macmillan, 1968), 503–11; Pitt-Rivers, "Honour and Social Status," *Honour and Shame: The Values of Mediterranean Society*, ed. J. G. Peristiany (Chicago: University of Chicago Press, 1966), 19–77, esp. 21–24, 72; Bruce Malina, *The New Testament World: Insights from Cultural Anthropology* (Atlanta: John Knox Press, 1981), 25–50.

4. Cf. Sandra Walker-Ramisch, "Graeco-Roman Voluntary Associations and the Damascus Document: A Sociological Analysis," in *Voluntary Associations in the Graeco-Roman World*, ed. John S. Kloppenborg and Stephen G. Wilson (London: Routledge, 1996), 133–34.

5. Cf. Wendy Cotter, "The Collegia and Roman Law: State Restrictions on Voluntary Associations, 64 B.C.E.–200 C.E.," in *Voluntary Associations in the Graeco-Roman World*, ed. Kloppenborg and Wilson, 74–89.

they had met. These proselytes were now honored among the leaders of the Jewish community.

I suggest that whatever disagreement had arisen over views concerning Jesus, the heart of the matter in the Galatian synagogues was halakhic (thus 5:11). Attention had focused on the Gentiles' apparent (mis)understanding of their status, that they were already to be counted among the righteous. These Gentiles might have deliberated, in Paul's absence, that the "good news" offered them — that is, the prospect of full membership through proselytism — was thoroughly compatible with the good news they had already accepted from Paul. They might have reasoned they did not have time to consult with Paul; perhaps, that they did not have need.

As the letter to the Galatians demonstrates, Paul found out nonetheless and responded in a way very different from what they might have anticipated.

## The Letter to the Galatians and the Political Context of Paul's Response

Paul begins his response with irony: "I am surprised that you are so quickly defecting from him who called you in [the] grace [of Christ] for a different good news, which is not another, except [in the sense] that there are some who unsettle you and want to turn upside-down the good news of Christ" (1:6–7). The verb *thaumazo* signals the feigned "surprise" appropriate to a formal letter of ironic rebuke, as clearly as our "Dear John" letters signal the nature of the message to come.[6] Paul feigned parental ignorance to express

---

6. Correspondence is noted with the ironic type of letter in Pseudo-Libanius, *Epistolary Styles*, [56] from Abraham Malherbe, *Ancient Epistolary Theorists* (Atlanta: Scholars Press, 1988), 74–75: "I am greatly astonished at your sense of equity, that you have so quickly rushed from a well-ordered life to its opposite — for I hesitate to say to wickedness. It seems that you have contrived to make, not friends out of your enemies, but enemies out of your friends, for your action has shown itself to be unworthy of friends, but eminently worthy of your drunken behavior."

See also the example of a letter of reproach in Pseudo-Libanius, and Pseudo-Demetrius, *Epistolary Types*, in Malherbe, *Ancient Epistolary Theorists*, 40–41. For social implications of these letter types see also Stanley Stowers, "Social Typification and the Classification of Ancient Letters," *The Social World of Formative Christianity and Judaism: Essays in Tribute to Howard Clark Kee*, ed. Jacob Neusner, Peder Borgen, Ernest S. Frerichs, and Richard Horsley (Philadelphia: Fortress Press, 1988), 78–90.

These observations regarding the letter type include insights from the works of, for example, Niels Dahl, "Paul's Letter to the Galatians: Epistolary Genre, Content, and Structure," unpublished paper presented to 1973 SBL Paul Seminar; John L. White, "Introductory Formulae in the Body of the Pauline Letters," *JBL* 90 (1971): 96; Terence Mullins, "Formulas in New Testament Epistles," *JBL* 91 (1972): 385–86; S. Stowers, *Letter Writing in Greco-Roman Antiquity* (Philadelphia: Westminster Press, 1986), 134, 139; G. Walter Hansen, *Abraham in Galatians: Epistolary and Rhetorical Contexts*, JSNTSup 29 (Sheffield: Sheffield Academic Press, 1989); Hansen, *Galatians* (Downers Grove, Ill.: InterVarsity Press, 1994).

A brief discussion of how to recognize irony in this period can be found in Quintilian, *Inst. Oratore* 8.6.54. The ironic theorists from which these insights have been informed, ancient and

his disappointment, a rhetorical approach that leaves little room for escape. His words combined sharp censure for the recipients — "who do you think you are!" (1:6–7) — with a polemical curse-wish on anyone who would bring such pressures to bear upon "his" children — "who do you think they are!" (1:8–9).

The victims would have burned with shame from such exposure, caught in the act of compromising the minority principles they once embraced for the undeniably seductive promise of majority acceptance. The pain of such exposure is palpable, but so, too, is the anguish of the one who is seeking by this drastic approach to thwart a feared betrayal.

Such ironic rebuke is insider language, the language of parents with their children. It presumes the authority to correct the wrongdoer; it intends to stun quickly and to restore the offender to the family's norms. It seeks healing, not harm, of the family fabric. Irony gains its edge from shared values.[7] Paul's response works from the assumption that the addressees should know that this "other" message is only apparent "good news," that it is really bad for them, that it subverts the good news of Christ.

Paul struggles to ensure that the authority with which he addresses his converts from afar will not be undermined by those nearby who are "unsettling" them: "Paul an apostle — not from human agents nor through a human agency, but through Jesus Christ and God the Father, who raised him from the dead ones" (1:1; cf. 1:10). How can his converts now question what he made so clear to them before (1:9, 5:3), speaking with the authority he had directly from God? Even if he himself had previously enjoyed the highest honors from similar human beings — that is, before he received a revelation of Jesus Christ — he in no way depends upon such esteem now (1:13–16).

We may wonder whether the proselytes who have so "unsettled" Paul's converts would accept the antithesis he sets out. Were they "merely" human agents? Had Paul considered himself to be merely a human agent in his "former" manner of life? One thinks in this connection of the later rabbinic story of Rabbi Eliezer who, confirmed in a particular halakhic judgment by miracles and the very voice of God from heaven, was nevertheless overruled since "in this age" such decisions were entrusted to the world of human agents and authorities, what Paul might have called "the traditions of the fathers" (*Baba Mezia* 59b). It would be anachronistic to stretch this apparent parallel, but the passage raises the issue of the authority of revelation compared with the authority of scripture, a live concern in this period.[8]

---

modern, are too many to list here. A full discussion is planned in a forthcoming Fortress book project and is available in Nanos, "Intra-Jewish Context of Galatians," 30–61.

7. Linda Hutcheon, *Irony's Edge: The Theory and Politics of Irony* (London and New York: Routledge, 1994).

8. Cf. 1:12, 2:2; 1 Cor. 2:7–10; 2 Cor. 3:18, 4:3; Acts 9:3–19, 22:6–21, 26:12–23; Rev. 1:1. The role of revelation in the interpretation of Torah or Scripture in this period varies. In

## *Who Are the "Influencers"?*

Paul does not name the ones influencing Paul's addressees, although he variously describes them. He and the addressees know to whom he refers. Later interpreters have labeled them variously: (1) "judaizers," (2) "opponents," (3) "agitators" or "troublemakers," (4) "teachers," among others.

(1) While *judaizing* is something that Gentiles seeking Jewish status may do, it is inappropriate for describing efforts to persuade Gentiles to seek Jewish status. As a reflexive verb it is inappropriate as a label for Jews.[9] Moreover, in view of its negative ideological valence it is inappropriate for historical critical application. (2) It is not certain that these people actually "oppose" Paul, even if he opposes them.[10] In view of his accusations, it is likely that his defensive posture is rather in anticipation of the response to his message should the addressees heed his instruction. (3) Calling these people "agitators" and "troublemakers" merely mimics Paul's value judgments; it does not advance interpretation of the situation. Such labels stereotype the motives and methods of the others in a limited and polemical way; they hardly clarify the others' identity. (4) Referring to these "others" as "teachers" avoids the value judgments implied by the other choices and describes at least a significant part of their activity.[11] But its occupational focus may be too restrictive.

I shall call these others *influencers*. We can be certain at least that they are "influencing" Paul's converts, just as Paul seeks in this letter to "influence" the addressees to resist them. Paul is worried that his addressees have already begun the alternate course of proselyte conversion (*metatithesthe*,

---

Ben Sira, wisdom is in Torah and revealed through the sages (24; 39.1–8). *First Enoch* 92–105, on the other hand, emphasizes the role of revelation in validating the proper understanding of Torah. The Qumran community possessed a revealed knowledge of the interpretation of Torah not shared by other Israelites, which was entrusted to the authority of the community leaders (esp. 1QS 5; 8), and this is revealed to and through the Teacher of Righteousness, as it had been with the fathers on behalf of Israel (CD 13; 1QpHab 7.18.3). Cf. George W. E. Nickelsburg, "Revealed Wisdom as a Criterion for Inclusion and Exclusion: From Jewish Sectarianism to Early Christianity," in *To See Ourselves as Others See Us: Christians, Jews, Others in Late Antiquity*, ed. Jacob Neusner and E. Frerichs (Chico, Calif.: Scholars Press, 1985), 73–82; C. Rowland, "The Parting of the Ways: The Evidence of Jewish and Christian Apocalyptic and Mystical Material," in *Jews and Christians: The Parting of the Ways A.D. 70 to 135*, ed. J. D. G. Dunn (Tübingen: J. C. B. Mohr [Paul Siebeck], 1992), 213–37; L. Thompson, "Social Location of Early Christian Apocalyptic," *ANRW* II.26.3 (Berlin: Walter de Gruyter, 1996), 2617–56; Marcus Bockmuehl, *Revelation and Mystery in Ancient Judaism and Pauline Christianity* (1990; Grand Rapids, Mich.: William B. Eerdmans, 1997).

9. Cf. Shaye J. D. Cohen, *The Beginnings of Jewishness: Boundaries, Varieties, Uncertainties* (Berkeley: University of California Press, 1999), 175–97.

10. Different, but sympathetic on this point, see, e.g., Robert Jewett, "The Agitators and the Galatian Congregation," *NTS* 17 (1970–71): 206–8; George Howard, *Paul: Crisis in Galatia: A Study in Early Christian Theology* (Cambridge: Cambridge University Press, 1979), 7–11; George Lyons, *Pauline Autobiography: Toward a New Understanding* (Atlanta: Scholars Press, 1985), 79.

11. J. Louis Martyn, *Galatians: A New Translation with Introduction and Commentary*, AB 33A (New York: Doubleday, 1997), 118.

1:6; cf. 3:1–5, 5:1–12, 6:12–13); he anticipates that they have already accepted as "good" this "other" message. Such actions Paul attributes to the "unsettling" influence of these people (*tarassontes*, 1:7, 5:10), their casting of the "evil eye" of envy (*ebaskanen*, 3:1), their seeking to "exclude" (*ekkleisai*, 4:17),[12] their "obstructing" of the course the addressees were running (*enekopsen*, 5:7), all in all, their seeking to "compel" proselyte conversion (6:12–13; cf. 3:2–3; 5:1–4, 10–13).[13]

We must distinguish, moreover, as Paul does, between the "others" in Galatia and the individuals he mentions in autobiographical comments about events in Jerusalem or Antioch. Any analogies with the Galatian situation or influencers that may have been drawn by the addressees in view of these narrative examples are not as clear as many interpreters suppose, as they depend upon prior knowledge that we no longer share. The latter are identified as "inspecting or informant [*kataskopēsai*] pseudo-brethren" in Jerusalem (2:4);[14] "ones from James," or "ones for circumcision," in Antioch (2:12); by implication, the "persecutors" in the allegory of Abraham (4:29). These are "influencers," too, but they are not the influencers *in Galatia.* In these references, Paul is drawing on past examples of situations elsewhere, which he and the other apostles resolved in order "that the truth of the good news might be preserved for you" (2:5).

The overwhelming consensus in modern interpretation is that these shadowy figures in Galatia were, or claimed to be, representatives or associates of the Jerusalem apostles. As such they represented "Jewish," "Jerusalem-" or "Palestinian Christianity." Paul's gospel message is imagined by most modern critics to be at the strongest variance with theirs — his is "Law-free," theirs is "Torah-observant." They promote what Paul regards as "another gospel," and Paul's mission and gospel remain steadfastly independent of their influence.

On this view, the letter is an attack on the error of mixing Jewish identity and behavior with the confession of faith in Christ. Recent interpreters hasten to add that Paul's criticism of things Jewish is not aimed at Jews outside of the Christ movement. This is purely an *inter-* and *intra-* "Christian" affair. Galatians is thus not really anti-Jewish.

Clearly, Paul asserts that non-Jews in Christ are not to become Jews.

---

12. Cf. Christopher C. Smith, " *'Ekkleisai* in Galatians 4:17: The Motif of the Excluded Lover as a Metaphor of Manipulation," *CBQ* 58 (1996): 480–99.

13. On the conversion process in antiquity see, e.g., Alan F. Segal, *Paul the Convert: The Apostolate and Apostasy of Saul the Pharisee* (New Haven: Yale University Press, 1990), 72–114; Thomas M. Finn, *From Death to Rebirth: Ritual and Conversion in Antiquity* (Mahwah, N.J.: Paulist Press, 1997).

14. This section and the identity of the parties involved are discussed in an unpublished paper presented at the 1997 International Research Consultation on Ideology, Power and Interpretation, Birmingham, England, entitled "Intruding 'Spies' and 'Pseudo' Brethren: The Intra-Jewish Context of 'Those of Repute' in Jerusalem (Gal. 2:1–10)"; and in "Intra-Jewish Context of Galatians," 133–49.

But does he really equate freedom in Christ for Jewish people with freedom from observance of the Torah, for Jews as well as for Gentiles? That is, does he really suggest that Jews are also to become non-Jewish? Moreover, is the sectarian identity of "Christianity" really as institutionalized as such approaches assume?

## Challenging the Consensus View

As I read Galatians, the central issue between Paul and the influencers within the Galatian synagogues is at once halakhic and eschatological. The question of how Gentiles are to be incorporated into the people of God receives different answers, determined by the way Paul and the influencers respond to a prior question: Has the age to come dawned in Jesus Christ, or not?

We should expect Paul and the Jerusalem apostles to agree on this prior question. To suggest that it divides Paul and the Galatian influencers means that these influencers stand at some considerable distance from the Jerusalem apostles and the "people of James" in Antioch. In contrast to the consensus view, which tends to align these three groups as something of a united front over against Paul's "law-free" gospel, I consider it crucial to isolate the data bearing directly on the identity of the influencers in the Galatian situation from the narrative discourses relating prior situations in Jerusalem and Antioch.[15]

This latter narrative material provides illustrative examples to support Paul's argument. This material includes the autobiographical remarks in 1:11–2:21; the discussion of Abraham and his rightful heirs in 3:6–24 (–4:7); and the allegory of Abraham's sons in 4:22–30. Situational discourse occupies the rest of the letter (1:1–10, 3:1–5, 4:8–21, 5:1–6:18).[16] Special attention should be given within this material to the epistolary opening (1:1–10), wherein Paul first sets the tone of letter in ironic rebuke, and the closing (6:11–18), where he summarizes his perspective on the influencers and reiterates the appropriate response for his addressees.

Paul's autobiographical comments in 1:11–2:21 form a self-contained narrative unit. Paul defines his own independent revelation of the good news of Christ in tandem with the independent revelation enjoyed by the Jerusalem apostles (1:11–13, 15, 18; 2:1–2, 5, 7–9). He is *not* concerned to oppose his apostleship, mission, or message to that of the Jerusalem apostles.[17] Indeed, Paul shows his dyadic self; his confidence "toward the Galatians"

---

15. I do not mean by this the rhetorical device common to forensic rhetoric labeled *narratio*, referring to that part of an oration which sets out the events that have brought the case to court (see the discussion by Philip Kern, *Rhetoric and Galatians: Assessing an Approach to Paul's Epistle*, SNTSMS 101 [Cambridge: Cambridge University Press, 1998], 104–5).

16. See also Dahl, "Galatians"; on the transitions see the linguistic approach of Jonas Holmstrand, *Markers and Meaning in Paul: An Analysis of 1 Thessalonians, Philippians and Galatians*, CBNTS 28 (Stockholm: Almqvist and Wiksell International, 1997), 145–216.

17. Sympathetic with this view are the findings of Paul E. Koptak, "Rhetorical Identification in Paul's Autobiographical Narrative: Galatians 1.132.14," *JSNT* 40 (1990): 97–115.

now is embedded in the mutual agreement already reached in Jerusalem on the terms of the truth of the gospel for Gentiles: Paul was not, and is not, "running in vain."

That agreement was based not on the traditions of the fathers but upon revelation (1:15–16; 2:2). God has shown all of them that Gentiles who believe in Christ are to remain Gentiles, yet to be regarded as equals with Jewish believers in Jesus (2:7–9). That is the "truth of the gospel" (2:5, 14). This agreement was satisfactory to all the apostles. When outside agents unexpectedly tested this consensus, they were turned back; Titus was not circumcised.

In Antioch, even insiders such as Peter occasionally let similar intimidation detour them from consistently honoring the coalition's "freedom."[18] Note, however, that *this is not freedom from the Law*, but freedom for Torah-observant Jews to reconsider the halakhic implications for themselves of the inclusion of Gentiles in the people of God as full equals. With the changing of the ages, the traditions of the fathers have not been dismissed, but their *application* has modified: from expectation to implementation, from an awaited future to the dawn of the age to come. This is the "good news" Peter failed to defend, and for this Paul confronted him (2:11–21).

The human agents to whom Paul opposes his apostleship and his gospel are not the Jerusalem apostles or their emissaries. They are rather interpreters of "the traditions of the fathers," "flesh and blood" agents with whom Paul does not confer (1:13–16). They thus must be distinguished from those who were apostles before Paul, with whom he did not consult immediately (1:17), but only in due course (1:18, 2:1–10). These human agents maintain the prevailing view that gentile believers in Christ must become proselytes if they are to acquire standing as full members of the Jewish communities (e.g., Titus, 2:3; in Antioch, vv. 12–14).[19]

---

18. Jeremy Boissevain, *Friends of Friends: Networks, Manipulators and Coalitions* (Oxford: Basil Blackwell, 1974), esp. 170–205, for general discussion of coalitions and group identities. His defining of coalition as "a temporary alliance of distinct parties for a limited purpose" is useful, especially the emphasis he develops on the temporariness implied in such groups in order to achieve a limited purpose, yet accumulating more tasks as time passes without yet achieving that purpose (171). "Coalitions may comprise individuals, other coalitions, and even corporate groups; and most show a concentric form of organization, with core and peripheral members" (173).

19. One finds this view to be common, for example, as it is variously expressed: by Paul in his opposition to it for his Gentiles in Romans, Galatians; by Luke in Acts; and in other Jewish writings of the period: 1 Macc. 1:15, 44–48, 60–61; 2:45–46; 2 Macc. 6:10; *Jub.* 15:25–34; Josephus, *Ant.* 1.192, 13.318–19, 18.34–48; *Ag. Ap.* 2.137, 140–42; Philo: *Mig. Abr.* 92; and in Greco-Roman literature, including Strabo, *Geographica* 16.2.37; Diodorus Siculus, *World History* 1.55; Petronius, *Satyricon* 68.8; 102.13–14; Persius, *Satires* 5.179–84; Martial, *Epigrams* 7.35.3–4, 82; 11.94; Tacitus, *Histories* 5.5.2, 8–9; Juvenal, *Satires* 14.96–106; Horace, *Satires* 1.9.60–72; Suetonius, *Domitian* 12. It is attested also in the later rabbinic material (y. *Meg* 3.2.74d; *Midr. Exod. Rab.* 30.12). The governing statement is, of course, Gen. 17:9–14. See also discussion in John Nolland, "Uncircumcised Proselytes?" *JSJ* 12 (1981): 173–94; John J. Collins, "A Symbol of Otherness: Circumcision and Salvation in the First

Paul reminds his readers of the good news in which they believe: that because of Christ the age to come has begun in the midst of the present age, and they can participate in this eschatological reality as Gentiles. That is "the truth of the gospel" that was at stake in the past events he narrates; it is at stake now as his Galatian converts find themselves facing the constraints imposed by the convictions of the larger Jewish communities and their controlling agents: "Titus was not circumcised, or the Antiochenes, and you must not be either!"

Paul tells his readers they should not be surprised to find their expectations at variance with those of the influencers in Galatia. What should they expect? The influencers are simply maintaining the traditional boundary definitions for full inclusion of Gentiles. Paul's readers know he used to promote these very practices (1:13), and they have already been warned to expect opposition as well (1:9). For announcing that they need not join other righteous Gentiles who pursue the normal course of proselyte conversion, Paul has been "persecuted" (5:11); what do they expect for themselves but "suffering"?

These believers have taken on an identity constructed within the subgroup communities of those believing in the gospel of Jesus Christ only to have it challenged or dismissed by other, seemingly more powerful courts of reputation. They have experienced shame, the refusal of the larger communities to confirm the place of honor they have claimed. They may have seen this as "persecution," but the larger communities and their representatives may have intended it as education, discipline, or punishment. Concern for one's reputation is honorable: failure to be concerned for honor or shame constitutes shamelessness, and it is just such "foolish" behavior of which the addressees have been accused (cf. 1:6–9, 3:1–5, 4:8–21, 5:7–12, 6:12–13).[20]

These Gentiles have apparently begun to accept the "influencers'" demand to define their status according to the membership norms of the larger Jewish communities within which their subgroups operate. Paul approaches them as already having begun to defect, even as he insists they will not now complete this course (5:10). We detect here Paul's anxiety that they have internalized this other "good news" and now want to be circumcised (1:6–7; 3:1–5; 4:11, 19–21; 5:2–18). He fears that they are being "persuaded"

---

Century," in *To See Ourselves as Others See Us*, ed. Neusner and Frerichs, 163–86; Segal, *Paul the Convert*, 72–109; Louis H. Feldman, *Jew and Gentile in the Ancient World* (Princeton: Princeton University Press, 1993), 153–58; Gary G. Porton, *The Stranger within Your Gates: Converts and Conversion in Rabbinic Literature* (Chicago: University of Chicago Press, 1994), 132–54.

20. Calling someone or their thoughts or actions foolish (*anoētos*) indicates that one has behaved unwisely, without properly perceiving the situation (cf. Rom. 1:14; Aristotle, *Rhet.* 1.10.4/1368b: "mistaken ideas of right and wrong"). This does not mean that they do not "know," but that they do not understand the implications of what they "should" know, indicated by their inappropriate behavior. In honor and shame terms they are shameless; they do not show proper concern for their honor or the honor of their group.

by the majority communities' norms, by which they believe they may escape their current disputable and thus marginal status (5:7–12, 6:12–13). Their actions reveal the social dimensions of identity: "*Identification* depends upon affective powers of attraction, in intimate dyadic relationships and in more collective or public contexts. Identification, of course, is related to the desire to stay in the good graces of others." The "influencers" have made inroads with these Gentiles precisely because the latter, as marginals, seek to overcome the ambiguity and uncertainty of their identity by conforming to the larger community's behavioral membership criteria. "Strong pressures encouraging conformity — with penalties attaching to deviance — may oppress most those whose membership or social identity is insecure."[21]

We may describe these Gentiles as "outgrouped insiders" who now seek the dominant ingroup's acceptance.[22] The influencers consider them liminals, righteous gentile guests who need to be adopted into the family, perhaps even preliminals. Paul's addressees may well regard completion of the ritual process of circumcision as a small price to pay, for the "rights" of membership that they previously considered theirs exist only to the degree that they are recognized.[23]

I emphasize that Paul's appeal is not a message proclaimed against Israel, or against Torah observance by Jews who do not share faith in Christ. It is the message of Torah, the source of wisdom; it expresses the plight of Israel in the midst of the nations, of the psalmist or the prophet in the den of his accusers. Only in the context of Paul's polemic against influencers who seek to conform (sub)groups of gentile believers in Christ to the halakhic group norms of the larger Jewish communities do Paul's negative comments carry weight. Otherwise, Jewish identity and Torah observance are considered an advantage: Paul maintains the privilege of being "a Jew by nature, and not a gentile sinner" (2:14). This assumption underscores his rhetorical approach and the addressees' interest in circumcision for themselves. If the Galatians do not know Paul as a Torah-observant Jew, then the rhetoric of 5:3 would have no bite: "I testify again to every man who receives circumcision that he is bound to keep the whole law." Otherwise, they might simply respond, "but we want only what you have: Jewish identity, without obligation to observe 'the whole law.' "

At the heart of Paul's rhetoric is the call to remain "in Christ," that is, within the Christ-believing coalition's reference group norms. Here his readers' status has already been legitimated, albeit at the price of disapproval

---

21. Richard Jenkins, *Social Identity* (New York: Routledge, 1996), 120, 124.

22. This may be described according to social identity theory as social mobility. For this approach versus the social change model (which in my view accounts for Paul's response, under the subcategory of social creativity), see the analysis of Michael Hogg and Dominic Abrams, *Social Identifications: A Social Psychology of Intergroup Relations and Group Processes* (London: Routledge, 1988), 51–61; used to argue a different conclusion by Philip F. Esler, *Galatians*, NTR (London: Routledge, 1998), 49–57.

23. Cf. Jenkins, *Social Identity*, 135.

within the dominant communities. He capitalizes upon their dyadic situation in 3:1–5, rebuking their "foolishness," that is, their shamelessness within the court of reputation of the Christ-believing subgroup and their deference to the shame attributed by the influencers. They have been seduced by the dominant community's message that they can avoid being "excluded" by conforming (4:17). Paul insists, to the contrary, that the benefits held out to them necessarily subvert the foundational principles of their faith in Christ, just as had been implied earlier at Antioch, when Peter's withdrawal because of "fear" of "the ones for circumcision" there threatened to undermine the meaning of the death of Christ (2:14–21).[24]

## The Implied Intra-Jewish Context of the Galatian Addressees

We see, then, that the Galatians whom Paul addresses are members of Christ-believing subgroups within larger Jewish communities (recognizing that this is a circular letter, 1:2). The "influencers" are most likely proselytes within these larger communities but not members of the Christ-believing subgroups. Paul refers to the latter in 6:13 as *hoi peritemnomenoi*, either "those who receive circumcision" / "have themselves circumcised," or "those who cause to be circumcised."[25]

If proselytes, the influencers are the most natural contacts for education and social integration. Having previously been accorded the status of righteous Gentiles by the synagogue, they have a vested interest in guarding and facilitating the ritual process that negotiates hierarchical distinctions between righteous Gentiles and proselytes. Ritual circumcision defines their sense of self- and group identity; it governs their social interaction; it defines their social reality and political worldview. They can empathize with the liminal situation of the addressees but not with their outlandish claim to have acquired already the equality of status that accords with proselyte conversion. Although they themselves have crossed the ritual threshold and gained new status as proselytes, they perhaps still experience the social insecurity associated with liminality.[26] Thus Paul accuses them of agonistic rivalry in the flesh and of having cast the evil eye of envy upon his addressees (3:1). From the perspective of the influencers, who do these "Johnny-come-lately" Gentiles think they are? This presents a classic case in which envy is aroused,

---

24. See my "Peter's Hypocrisy (Gal. 2:11–21) in the Light of Paul's Anxiety (Rom. 7)," in *The Mystery of Romans: The Jewish Context of Paul's Letter* (Minneapolis: Fortress Press, 1996), 337–71.

25. See full discussion in my "The Intra-Jewish Context of Galatians," 197–218, 246–51.

26. Implied in Philo's concern to confront the problem, cf. *Virtues* 212–27, esp. 218–19, 223; *Special Laws* 1.51–53, 308–10. See Cohen, *Beginnings of Jewishness*, 160–62; Anthony Cohen, *Self-Consciousness: An Alternate Anthropology of Identity* (London: Routledge, 1994), 128; Esler, *Galatians*, 216–17, 223. Porton, *Stranger within Your Gates*, traces the rabbinic evidence.

exacerbated to the degree that the influencers might once have shared status and kinship with the addressees.[27] Moreover, these influencers, Paul alleges, seek to avoid any "persecution" that might be required of them if they were to represent the addressees' appeal to the meaning of "the cross of Christ" to legitimate their claim to full membership while remaining Gentiles (6:12): the influencers are invested in the larger Jewish communities' norms, but not the norms of the Christ-believing subgroups to which Paul's gentile converts have committed themselves.

Paul appeals to his addressees to keep their "eyes" on the one "publicly portrayed as crucified" and thus negate the force of the evil eye (3:1). Instead of seeking honor in the court of reputation of this present evil age, "biting and devouring one another" like wild animals (5:13–15), they should identify with the one who suffered the shame of crucifixion, the one who chose the seemingly weak and failing route of public shame in the interest of serving the other.[28] "If we live by the Spirit, let us also conform to [the way of] the Spirit. We should not be vainly proud, challenging one another [for honor], envying each other" (5:24–26; cf. Phil. 2:3–8). They should rather serve one another, confident that God will bring justice for those who do right (6:1–10).

Instead of complying with the "influencers," Paul exhorts his readers to seek another way: to "stand fast, therefore" and "not submit" the "freedom" they have in Christ (5:1–4, 11–15); to "wait for the hope of righteousness" (5:5); to avoid being "unsettled," "obstructed," "subverted" by the influencers (5:7–12), or seeking honor and status according to the world (6:12–15). They are children of God. God's Spirit is at work among them; they should seek the other's interest (5:15–26). They should "restore" the other in gentleness (6:1); "bear one another's burdens" (6:2); "test one's own work," avoid "boasting over one's neighbor" (6:4), and "not grow weary

---

27. Aristotle, *Rhetoric* 2.10, explains the dynamics of envy along these lines. He notes it is most likely among those closest in status. Likewise, the evil eye is the result of envy, and is thought to harm the one upon whom this gaze falls (cf. Plutarch, *Moralia* 8.5.7). Thus Paul's accusation (or "warning") that the addressees have been evil eyed by the influencers suggests that the addressees have something that the influencers might envy, though the addressees had failed to suspect this at work in the present circumstances they "suffer" (3:4: *epathete*), or in the motives of the influencers toward themselves. That which Paul considers enviable appears to be the presence of the Spirit and miracles in their midst (3:5), which would seem to indicate that the influencers regard such things inappropriate for those who have not completed the ritual process of proselyte conversion. Further discussion of Paul's accusation and the evil eye belief system to which it appeals is available in Nanos, " 'O foolish Galatians, who has cast the evil eye [of envy] upon you?' (Gal 3:1a–b): The Belief System and Interpretive Implications of Paul's Accusation," paper presented at the 1999 Annual SBL meeting in Boston.

28. Cf. Pseudo-Quintilian, *Declamations* 274: "Whenever we crucify the condemned, the most crowded roads are chosen, where the most people can see and be moved by this terror. For penalties relate not so much to retribution as to their exemplary effect." This public display of shame (Philo calls it "show"; *Flaccus* 84–85) was designed to strike fear of deviance from the established norms (cf. Jerome H. Neyrey, *Honor and Shame in the Gospel of Matthew* [Louisville, Ky.: Westminster/John Knox Press, 1998], 139–40).

in well-doing." They should "do good to everyone" (6:9–10) and resist the pressure of those who would "compel" them to be circumcised (6:12–13).

Paul's addressees have believed in one who bore the shame of public execution as a pretender (3:1). They heard this message from another who suffered similarly to preserve the truth of the good news of Christ for them (5:11; 6:17). What else but suffering should they expect from the social control agents of the larger communities if they stand fast in their identity in Christ?

Paul brings in this letter an inter-Jewish communal perspective (i.e., between this Jewish coalition and the dominant Jewish groups who do not agree on the meaning of the death of Christ, whether in Galatia or elsewhere) to bear upon the unsettling intra-Jewish communal circumstances developing within the Galatian situation in which this "other" apparent "message of good" is being proposed. Paul has suffered to defend their place as Gentiles in view of the meaning of the death of Christ; he thus hopes that his addressees will resist the temptation to conform to the "traditional" view in order to gain undisputed status in the present age, and instead continue on the course they had begun, walking straight toward the truth of the good news of Christ, whatever the price.

# — 10 —

# PAUL'S GOSPEL AND CAESAR'S EMPIRE

## N. T. Wright

ᔕᔕᔕᔕᔕᔕᔕᔕᔕᔕ

T HE MOST EXCITING developments today in the study of Paul and his
thought are not, I think, the recent works on Paul's theology (though
I have contributed to such an enterprise myself, and still believe in it in
principle).[1] I highlight, instead, the quite fresh attempts that are being made
to study the interface, the opposition, the conflict between Paul's gospel —
the message about the crucified Jesus — and the world in which his entire
ministry was conducted, the world in which Caesar not only held sway but
exercised power through his divine claim. What happens when we line up
Paul's gospel with Caesar's empire?[2]

I begin with a brief sketch of a recent work that pinpoints exactly these
issues. I shall then comment on this discussion, locate it within the wider
world of Pauline studies, and explain why I think this is really the leading
edge of the subject. This will clear the ground for four exegetical studies,
three quite brief and one somewhat fuller, which will state my basic case
and lead to four concluding reflections.

## Paul and Empire: Current Thinking

I had already been thinking thoughts like these for about four or five years,
and had indeed attempted to express them briefly in various publications,

---

1. See, recently, James D. G. Dunn, *The Theology of Paul the Apostle* (Grand Rapids,
Mich.: Eerdmans, 1998); the four volumes of *Pauline Theology* emerging from the Pauline
Theology Seminar at the SBL; and, among my own works, N. T. Wright, *The Climax of the
Covenant: Christ and the Law in Pauline Theology* (Minneapolis: Fortress, 1991).

2. This chapter owes its origin to a lecture given at the Princeton Center of Theological
Inquiry on Wednesday, November 18, 1998. It was originally published, in a more abbreviated
form, as "Paul's Gospel and Caesar's Empire" in *Center of Theological Inquiry Reflections* 2
(Spring 1999): 42–65. I am very grateful to my hosts in Princeton both for their hospitality
and for their readiness to allow me to reprint this. I offer it gladly now in tribute to Krister
Stendahl, whose collegial friendship over twenty-five years has been a delight and inspiration.

when in November 1997 I discovered Richard Horsley's *Paul and Empire: Religion and Power in Roman Imperial Society*.[3] As with most exciting discoveries, my own hunches were not only reinforced but developed in ways I had not imagined. Horsley's fascinating collection of essays brings together between two covers, in a way that happens all too rarely, specialist studies from the world of Greco-Roman historiography and New Testament theology, liberation theology and detailed exegesis. Horsley himself, as the editor, provides substantial and important introductions to each section of the book and offers his own exegetical study of 1 Corinthians as a conclusion.

One thesis of this important book stands out starkly in my mind, and should challenge all students of early Christianity to fresh thought. The evidence now available, including that from epigraphy and archaeology, appears to show that the cult of Caesar, so far from being one new religion among many in the Roman world, had already by the time of Paul's missionary activity become not only the dominant cult in a large part of the empire, certainly in the parts where Paul was active, but was actually the means (as opposed to overt large-scale military presence) whereby the Romans managed to control and govern such huge areas as came under their sway. The emperor's far-off presence was made ubiquitous by the standard means of statues and coins (the latter being the principal mass medium of the ancient world), reflecting his image throughout his domains; he was the great benefactor, through whom the great blessings of justice and peace, and a host of lesser ones besides, were showered outwards upon the grateful populace — who in turn worshipped him, honored him, and paid him taxes. In all this, the book asks pertinently, were the emperor's subjects doing something religious, or something political? Surely both. But does not this answer make nonsense of the great divide between sacred and secular, religion and society that has run through not only scholarship but also whole societies?

With this rhetorical question ringing in our ears, the book invites us to approach what has been called Paul's theology, and to find in it, not simply a few social or political "implications," but a major challenge to precisely that imperial cult and ideology which was part of the air Paul and his converts breathed.[4] His missionary work must be conceived not simply in terms of a traveling evangelist offering people a new religious experience, but of an ambassador for a king-in-waiting, establishing cells of people loyal to this new king, and ordering their lives according to his story, his symbols, and

---

3. Richard A. Horsley, ed., *Paul and Empire: Religion and Power in Roman Imperial Society* (Harrisburg, Pa.: Trinity Press International, 1997). One of the other recent books in this area on which Horsley draws for two of his chapters is Neil Elliott, *Liberating Paul: The Justice of God and the Politics of the Apostle* (Maryknoll, N.Y.: Orbis, 1994).

4. Cf. Dunn, *Theology of Paul the Apostle*, 674–80. The index to Dunn's book does not mention Caesar, empire, imperial cult, politics, power(s), or state. This highlights the danger of treating a specific text (in this case Romans) as a template for one's systematic treatment — though, as we shall see, the main sections of Romans might perhaps have suggested a very different ordering of the subject.

his praxis, and their minds according to his truth. This could not but be construed as deeply counterimperial, as subversive to the whole edifice of the Roman Empire; and there is in fact plenty of evidence that Paul intended it to be so construed, and that when he ended up in prison as a result he took it as a sign that he had been doing his job properly.

So far, I am in more or less complete agreement with the thesis that the book propounds, and am grateful to Horsley and his colleagues for pointing us in this direction. Our own time (our contemporary culture, and the present state of scholarship) is ripe for a reconsideration of the imperial cultic context of Paul's work and thought, not simply as one topic among others but as a theme that will color and redirect the whole. I have a hunch that it is because these questions were almost entirely screened out that the lengthy discussions of Pauline theology that took place at the Society of Biblical Literature in the late 1980s and early 1990s remained quite inconclusive. I wish to open the question up in a way which I hope will stimulate further thought, fresh exegesis, and fresh constructions of Paul's agenda and theology.

I do have several reservations about some of the book's subtexts, however, and flag them here before returning to them at the end of the essay. First, by no means all the contributors have abandoned what seems to me the quite misleading method of study whereby the classical world is combed for parallels to Paul which are then used to "explain" him.[5] Many Pauline scholars gave this up many years ago, but the alternative has not always been helpful either: a combing of the Jewish world, instead, for parallels that can then "explain" Paul. Paul himself explains himself rather differently; he is a Jewish apostle to the Gentiles, a man "in the Messiah" who believes the Messiah to be the crucified and risen Jesus of Nazareth. Unless we simply relativize Paul's self-description, neither of those simplified history-of-religion models will do; Paul's own self-understanding speaks of radical innovation from within a tradition, and of radical head-on confrontation with other traditions. The rather static explanatory models offered by traditional history-of-religions work, which seek to produce an almost evolutionary diagram for everything, screen out precisely such new moves. Indeed, if we are to be true to the vital insight that the modernist split between sacred and secular is fantastically distorting for understanding any first-century movement, we cannot be content merely to plot Paul's place on something that calls itself, or operates under the old rules of, history of religion. The early Christians, Paul among them, would not have recognized themselves and their movement under the Enlightenment's shrunken definition of "religion." Why not history of empire? Of humans? Why not simply "history"?[6]

---

5. A protest against this procedure was registered long ago by S. Sandmel, "Parallelomania," *JBL* 81 (1962): 1–13; similar protests should be lodged against the Hellenistic equivalents.

6. This puts a question mark against a recent, very stimulating book: Rodney Stark, *The*

Second, the book's blurb, and many of its contributions, emphasize that this way of reading Paul avoids the continuance, even within the so-called post-Sanders "new perspective" on Paul, of the way of understanding Paul's major emphases that appears to set him over against Judaism.[7] Paul emerges within Horsley's construct as someone opposed not to Judaism but to Caesar's empire. In this light, Sanders does not appear to have gone far enough in opposing the Lutheran model of Paul; Paul may not have had as much of a critique of Judaism as Protestant thought had supposed, but he was still to be understood, in Sanders's model, as fundamentally in dialogue with, and hence in a sense over against, the Jewish tradition, whereas he was in fact first and foremost in confrontation with the Roman world. I suspect that Sanders might have some comments to make on this by way of reply, but one can acknowledge an important point. However, this emphasis of Horsley and the other contributors, easily comprehensible within the sensitivities of a post-Holocaust Western world, and to my mind fundamentally right-minded in that it takes Paul's self-description as apostle to the Gentiles at face value, allowing it to determine and shape our view of how his thought actually works, still does not do justice to Paul's view of non-Christian Judaism and his own project in relation to it.

Just because some people have overdrawn and wrongly highlighted Paul's challenge to his own tradition, that does not mean that he did not challenge it at all. And just because his fundamental target was paganism and empire, and just because he used Jewish-style weapons to attack that target, that again does not mean that he did not challenge his fellow (but non-Christian) Jews.

One more question before moving rapidly to the central substance of this essay. While mainstream studies of Paul in the last generation have attempted to read him within his Jewish tradition, a good deal of work has still continued to locate him within the wider Greco-Roman world. One thinks, of course, of Wayne Meeks and Abraham Malherbe, and more recently the continuing project of Gerald Downing, and of other similar work.[8] But this has tended to focus on the location of Paul within a historical setting, rather than specifically on the confrontation between Paul and the pagan world

*Rise of Christianity: A Sociologist Reconsiders History* (Princeton, N.J.: Princeton University Press, 1996). Stark writes as a sociologist of *religion*, proposing hypotheses on that basis, which he then seeks to back up from historical sources. For a well-informed protest against splitting the ancient world up in the regular fashion, see the seminal work of S. R. F. Price, *Rituals and Power: The Roman Imperial Cult in Asia Minor* (Cambridge: Cambridge University Press, 1984), chap. 1.

7. Famously expressed in E. P. Sanders, *Paul and Palestinian Judaism: A Comparison of Patterns of Religion* (Philadelphia: Fortress, 1977).

8. Wayne A. Meeks, *The First Urban Christians: The Social World of the Apostle Paul* (New Haven: Yale University Press, 1983); Abraham J. Malherbe, *Paul and the Popular Philosophers* (Minneapolis: Fortress, 1989); Troels Engberg-Pedersen, ed., *Paul in His Hellenistic Context* (Edinburgh: T. & T. Clark, 1994); F. Gerald Downing, *Cynics, Paul and the Pauline Churches* (New York: Routledge, 1998).

he addressed.[9] Again, a fundamental issue in the historical study of Paul emerges here. For most of the last century it has been assumed that when a writer alludes to or echoes a theme or idea, this must imply agreement. Paul himself, of course, explicitly states the opposite ("taking every thought captive to obey Christ," 2 Cor. 10:5), but the steamroller of would-be deterministic historiography has rumbled on, insisting either that Paul employed non-Jewish ideas because he was a non-, or even an anti-Jewish thinker, or conversely that because he was a Jewish thinker he must have only used "Jewish" concepts. Theological and hermeneutical issues are never separable from the historical task, of course, but when the wires get crossed in this fashion we are simply no longer hearing what is being said.

It is, of course, much easier to highlight Paul's confrontation with some aspect of his world when the aspect in question is one that is currently so very deeply out of fashion. To say that Paul opposed imperialism is about as politically dangerous as suggesting that he was in favor of sunlight, fresh air, and orange juice. What we are faced with throughout his writings, however, is the fact that he was opposed to paganism in all its shapes and forms; not, however, as we shall see, with a dualistic opposition that could recognize nothing good in non-Jewish or non-Christian humans and their ways of life but with the settled and unshakeable conviction that the God of Abraham, Isaac, and Jacob, who was now revealed in and as Jesus of Nazareth, stood over against all other gods and goddesses, claiming unique allegiance. Paul, in other words, was not opposed to Caesar's empire primarily because it was an empire, with all the unpleasant things we have learned to associate with that word, but because it was Caesar's, and because Caesar was claiming divine status and honors which belonged only to the one God. This is not to say that Paul would have approved of that of which we disapprove; only that his political sensibilities were driven by his theological ones, not vice versa. All of which leads us to the text of Paul, and to our four specific issues.

## Jesus Christ Is Lord: Exegetical Studies in Paul's Counterimperial Gospel

### Gospel

I begin with the word *gospel* itself. As I have argued at some length elsewhere, it should now be a commonplace that the word *gospel* carries two sets of resonances for Paul.[10] On the one hand, the contexts within which

---

9. Meeks, *First Urban Christians*, chap. 6, is a partial exception to this. I have myself begun to address the question in *What St. Paul Really Said* (Grand Rapids, Mich.: Eerdmans, 1997), chap. 5.

10. N. T. Wright, "Gospel and Theology in Galatians," in *Gospel in Paul: Studies on Corinthians, Galatians and Romans for Richard N. Longenecker*, ed. L. Ann Jervis and Peter

the word is used indicate that for Paul the gospel he preached was the fulfillment of the message of Isaiah 40 and 52, the message of comfort for Israel and of hope for the whole world, because YHWH, the god of Israel, was at last returning to Zion to judge and redeem. On the other hand, again and again the context into which Paul was speaking was one where *gospel* would mean the celebration of the accession, or birth, of a king or emperor; and, though no doubt petty kingdoms might use the word for themselves, in Paul's world the main *gospel* that might be heard was the news of, or the celebration of, one or another of the Caesars.

Despite the way Protestantism in particular has used the phrase — making it refer, as Paul never does, to a supposed proclamation about justification by faith — for Paul "the gospel" is the announcement that the crucified and risen Jesus of Nazareth is Israel's Messiah and the world's Lord. It is, in other words, the thoroughly Jewish (and indeed Isaianic) message that challenges the royal and imperial messages abroad in Paul's world.

It is not difficult to see how this "gospel" functions for Paul. Theologically, it belongs completely with Isaiah's ringing monotheistic affirmations that YHWH and YHWH alone is the true god, the only creator, the only sovereign of the world, and that the gods of the nations are contemptible idols whose devotees are deceived, at best wasting their time and at worst under the sway of demons. Politically, it cannot but have been heard as a summons to allegiance to "another king," which is of course precisely what Luke says Paul was accused of saying (Acts 17:7). Practically, this means that Paul, in announcing the gospel, was more like a royal herald than a religious preacher or theological teacher. The appropriate response to this "gospel" can be stated in terms of "belief": after all, the announcement included the claim that the true God had raised Jesus from the dead. Or it can be stated in terms of "obedience"; after all, it was a direct summons to abandon other allegiances and give total loyalty to this Jesus. Or, as in Rom. 1:5 and elsewhere, these two can be combined, as Paul speaks, without feeling the need to cover his back against misinterpretation, of "the obedience of faith," *hypakoe pisteōs.*

How, then, does this "gospel" cohere with Paul's teaching of "justification by faith"? This is an important topic to which we shall return. For the moment we must look to the more basic content of the gospel, specifically, the claims Paul is advancing in it about Jesus himself.

---

Richardson (Sheffield: Sheffield Academic Press, 1994), 222–39; Wright, *What St. Paul Really Said,* chap. 3. The main evidence for the pagan use of *euanggelion* is the famous inscription from Priene (quoted frequently in the secondary sources: primary text in W. Dittenberger, ed., *Orientis Graeca Inscriptiones Selectae,* 4 vols. (Leipzig, 1903–5), vol. 2, no. 458, lines 30–52). The relative scarcity of other occurrences should not obscure the importance of this one.

## Jesus: King and Lord

The question of Paul's Christology has regularly been raised in terms of whether or not Paul thought Jesus was "divine," and if so in what sense. This is important, but no more important as the prior question: did Paul think that Jesus was Messiah, and did he make this thematic in his theology?

For generations now the received wisdom has been that Jesus' messiahship plays little or no role in Paul's thinking. Granted, he uses the word *Christos* all the time, but most have reckoned that it had become for him a mere proper name, with only one or two occurrences, such as Rom. 9:5, where the old Jewish meaning peeped out of hiding. This essentially de-judaized reading of Paul's use of *Christos* gained its apparent force from the following history-of-religions argument, explicit or implicit: Since Paul was the apostle to the Gentiles, and since the gentile world was looking for a cult figure, a kyrios, a Lord, there would have been no interest in a Jewish Messiah, and Paul himself had in any case left such Jewish notions, bound up as they were with a narrow ethnocentric theology, far behind. Even those who in other respects have challenged similar history-of-religions arguments often seem happy to let this one stand.[11] Alternatively, it is easy to suggest that, because the notion of messiahship carried overtones of violent military struggle, Paul wanted nothing to do with it.

I have elsewhere argued in some detail that this construal is entirely wrong.[12] It makes far better sense of passage after passage to understand *Christos* as specifically "Messiah," and to see, for instance, Paul's use of "in Christ" and "body of Christ," and similar language, in terms of membership within the royal family, the Messiah-people. Israel's king sums up his people in himself; what is true of him is true of them. Out of many arguments and many passages I here select only one of each: an argument from Paul's adoption of a central piece of Jewish self-understanding, and a passage in which Paul tells us in clear and unambiguous terms what precisely his "gospel" actually is.

The argument goes back to Isaiah and the Psalms, including some passages that Paul himself uses at key point in his arguments. What the older history-of-religions argument failed to reckon with was the Jewish understanding that, precisely because of Israel's status within the purposes of the creator god, Israel's king was always supposed to be the world's true king. "His dominion shall be from one sea to the other; from the River to the ends of the earth."[13] "The root of Jesse shall rise to rule the nations; in him shall

---

11. E.g., Martin Hengel, *The Son of God: The Origin of Christology and the History of Jewish-Hellenistic Religion*, trans. John Bowden (Philadelphia: Fortress Press, 1976); Hengel, *Studies in Early Christology* (Edinburgh: T. & T. Clark, 1995).

12. Wright, *Climax of the Covenant*, chaps. 2, 3. It should perhaps be noted that, for Paul as for the rest of Second Temple Judaism, "Messiah" carries no connotations of "divinity."

13. Ps. 72:8, looking back to Exod. 23:31, and to such "fulfilments" as 1 Kings 4:21–24; and across to other passages such as Ps. 80:11, 89:25–27; Zech. 9:10.

the nations hope."[14] This is part of the general eschatological scheme, familiar from many Jewish writings: because Israel's god is also the creator, when Israel's god finally does for Israel that which Israel longs for, the nations will be brought into the action, either for judgment or blessing — or both. There is every reason to suppose that Paul endorsed this train of thought and believed it to have been fulfilled in Jesus. However much, then, Paul knew perfectly well that Jesus of Nazareth was quite unlike the other would-be Messiah figures who flit to and fro through the pages of Josephus — think of Simon and Athronges, or Simon bar-Giora, or, from the next century, Simeon ben-Kosiba[15] — it is precisely part of the peculiar and characteristic tension of his whole theology to claim that this crucified Jesus was and is the Jewish Messiah promised in scripture. And this, for the reasons stated, is actually not a hindrance, from his point of view, to the gentile mission, but in fact its starting point. What the Gentiles need and long for, whether they know it or not, is the Jewish Messiah, who will bring the just and peaceful rule of the true God to bear on the whole world.

Romans 15:12, where the Isaiah passage just mentioned is quoted, is right at the final climax of the long argument of Romans. This is often ignored, partly because Romans 12–16 often receives short shrift from expositors already exhausted by the previous eleven chapters, but also because of the assumption that messiahship is irrelevant to Paul's theology. The quotation, however, closes the enormous circle that began with Rom. 1:3–4, where Paul looks for all the world as though he is giving a deliberate summary of what his "gospel" actually contains.

This passage, too, is often marginalized, for a similar reason: expositors are eager to get into what has been seen as the real meat of Paul's argument. The fact that the passage is so obviously messianic has caused it to be set aside, with frequent though very inconclusive speculation about whether the verses are or contain a pre-Pauline formula. The impression is given that Paul might have quoted such a thing, with or without his own modifications, not in order to say what he himself believed but in order simply to capture his audience's attention and perhaps goodwill. Leaving aside the peculiar logic of such a suggestion, I want to emphasize that the text as it stands summarizes, in formulaic terms no doubt, what Paul means by "the gospel"; and that, at the heart of this announcement, we find the Davidic messiahship of Jesus.

The phrase "son of God," though pregnant with other overtones that Paul will later cash out, has Davidic messiahship as its primary meaning, with echoes of Ps. 2:7 and 2 Sam. 7:14 in the background. The resurrection has installed Jesus of Nazareth as the Messiah of Israel, Paul insists, and

---

14. Isa. 11:10; cited Rom. 15:12 (see below).

15. On these, see my *The New Testament and the People of God*, vol. 1 of *Christian Origins and the Question of God* (hereafter *NTPG*) (Minneapolis: Fortress, 1992), 170–81.

therefore also the Lord to whose allegiance the world is now summoned. That is the burden of his song, the thrust of his *euangelion*. However unexpected, however shocking, however scandalous to Jews and foolish to Gentiles, this is the royal announcement that, from Paul's point of view, fulfills the prophecies of scripture and subverts the imperial gospel of Caesar. I propose that this reading of Rom. 1:3–4, though always in fact exegetically the most likely, receives substantial support when we set it in the wider context of the realization that Paul's gospel was a royal proclamation aimed at challenging other royal proclamations. Put Paul's theology in its political context, and it will make a lot more sense than if it is put merely within something called "religion." Religion is thrown in, of course, and soteriology, spirituality and all sorts of things; but if the matter is approached from the other end the reader may well omit — and many in our traditions have indeed omitted — something that was fundamental to Paul himself.

If Jesus is Messiah, he is also Lord, *kyrios*. It should now be apparent that the proper contexts for this term, too, are its Jewish roots on the one hand and its pagan challenge on the other. Taking them the other way around for the moment: the main challenge of the term, I suggest, was not to the world of private cults or mystery religions, where one might be initiated into membership of a group giving allegiance to some religion's "Lord." The main challenge was to the lordship of Caesar, which, though "political" from our point of view as well as in the first century, was also profoundly "religious." Caesar demanded worship as well as "secular" obedience: not just taxes, but sacrifices. He was well on his way to becoming the supreme divinity in the Greco-Roman world, maintaining his vast empire not simply by force — though there was of course plenty of that — but by the development of a flourishing religion that seemed to be trumping most others either by absorption or by greater attraction. Caesar, by being a servant of the state, had provided justice and peace to the whole world. He was therefore to be hailed as Lord and trusted as Savior. This is the world in which Paul announced that Jesus, the Jewish Messiah, was Savior and Lord.[16]

We shall presently examine a key passage, Philippians 3:20–21, in which that claim is made in all its starkness. Before we get to that, however, we must note the Jewish setting which forms one of the "echo chambers" within which Paul uses the word *lord* of Jesus. At one level he is drawing on the biblical portrait of the truly human one. In 1 Cor. 15:25–28 he combines Pss. 110:1 and 8:7 in order to predicate of Jesus the Messiah that which Psalm 8 says of the human being. God has put all things under the feet of the human figure; so, too, of the Jewish Messiah. But the Lordship that Jesus has thereby attained is not simply that promised to humans in the beginning.

---

16. A further theme that could have been tackled here, if space had allowed, is that of the "parousia," which, as Koester points out (*Paul and Empire*, 158–59), is itself replete with imperial/political overtones.

It is quite clear in several passages that, when Paul ascribes Lordship to Jesus, using the word *kyrios*, he has in mind very specifically the Septuagintal use of the word to stand for the unsayable Tetragrammaton, YHWH. Again and again Paul quotes biblical passages in which "the Lord" is indubitably YHWH, but of which, for him, the subject is now indisputably Jesus.[17] And, in a justly famous passage to which we shall return, Paul declares, through a deliberate quotation of Isaiah, that what YHWH had claimed as unique, the prerogative only of the creator and covenant god, was now shared with Jesus. "To me, me alone," says YHWH, "every knee shall bow, every tongue swear." Maybe, says Paul, but now "at the name of Jesus every knee shall bow."[18]

Was the clash with Caesar, then, the cause of Paul's elevation of Jesus to this extraordinary position? Non-Christian Jewish apologists have long maintained that Paul's high Christology is a function of his break with Judaism and his borrowing of categories from paganism; does the confrontation with Caesar provide a new version of this charge? By no means. It is not that, in order to oppose or upstage Caesar, Paul has invented a non-Jewish divine Jesus. The way he develops his Jesus-and-God language elsewhere rules this out completely.[19] Rather, Paul has arrived, on quite other grounds, at the belief that in Jesus of Nazareth, who has been shown to be Israel's Messiah in the resurrection, the one God of Israel has been personally revealed, such that Jesus himself is now part of the meaning of the word *God*. It is precisely in order to express this, a new and unexpected flowering from within Jewish monotheism, that he develops the father-son language, which prior to this point in Jewish tradition had to do, if anything, with Messiahship but which now becomes the vehicle of a new, high and deeply Jewish Christology.[20] Paul's most frequent language for Jesus, then, remained rooted in his Jewish traditions, asserting on the one hand that Jesus was the Messiah, long promised in the prophetic scriptures, bringing Israel's destiny to its God-ordained climax, and on the other that Jesus was Lord, both in the sense that he had embodied God's appointed destiny for the human race and in the sense that in him Israel's unique God had become personally present, accomplishing that which in scripture only God can accomplish. Simultaneously, and precisely because of the inner dynamic of this same Jewish tradition, Paul was announcing that Jesus was the true King of Israel and hence the true Lord of the world at exactly the time in history, and over exactly the geographical spread, where the Roman emperor was

---

17. E.g., Rom. 10:13, quoting Joel 3:5 LXX.

18. Phil. 2:10, alluding to Isa. 45:23. On the passage see my *Climax of the Covenant*, chap. 4, and below.

19. See my *Climax of the Covenant*, chaps. 4–6.

20. Unless we are to count Jesus' own usage: see N. T. Wright, "Jesus and the Victory of God," in *Christian Origins and the Question of God*, vol. 2 (Minneapolis: Fortress, 1996), chap. 13.

being proclaimed, in what styled itself a "gospel," in very similar terms. The mainstream Jewish monotheistic critique of paganism, of all its idolatry and immorality, found in Paul's day a more focused target and in Paul's theology a sharper weapon.

## God's Justice Revealed in the Gospel: Romans

The third of our exegetical studies takes us once more to Romans, this time to address the question left over earlier: in what way does the gospel, seen now as the royal announcement of Jesus as Messiah and Lord, lead to Paul's doctrine of justification by faith? The answer Paul himself supplies is this: because in the gospel God's righteousness is unveiled. The long-awaited apocalypse, the revelation of God's future, has occurred in Jesus, and occurs again whenever the gospel is proclaimed. What is revealed, as the curtain is drawn back by the gospel announcement, is "the righteousness of God." Rooted totally in Paul's world of apocalyptic Judaism, it stakes a claim to be the reality of which Caesar's world offers the parody.

In Rom. 1:16–17, Paul declares that the gospel unveils God's righteousness, the *dikaiosynē theou*. The Jewish context of Paul's work makes it absolutely certain[21] that he here refers not to a status that God imputes, imparts, or otherwise bestows upon humans, but to God's own righteousness, meaning God's faithfulness to the covenant with Israel, the Abrahamic covenant reaffirmed in Deuteronomy and elsewhere. (The question of the Mosaic covenant is, notoriously, one of the points of inner tension in his thinking, but we do not advance this discussion by denying his deliberate rootedness in the Abrahamic covenant.) According to this covenant faithfulness, as we can see in the analogous theological wrestlings of *4 Ezra*, the God of Israel must somehow not only be true to the covenant promises but also remain impartial, with no favorites. This God must also not only deal properly with evil but rescue the helpless.[22] This God must, in other words, act as the righteous judge in the cosmic law court. Things must be put to rights.

But this shows that the other obvious meaning of *dikaiosynē*, namely "justice," is not so far away as has often been supposed. We may doubt, in fact, whether Paul would have seen very much of a hermeneutical gap between what we mean by "righteousness" and what we mean by "justice." Not only did the same Greek word cover both. The sense of covenant faithfulness and the sense of things being put to rights belong together in the

---

21. N. T. Wright, "On Becoming the Righteousness of God: 2 Corinthians 5:21," in *Pauline Theology*, vol. 2, *1 and 2 Corinthians*, ed. David M. Hay (Minneapolis: Fortress, 1993), 200–208; Wright, *What St. Paul Really Said*, chap. 6; "Romans and the Theology of Paul," in *Society of Biblical Literature 1992 Seminar Papers*, ed. Eugene H. Lovering (Atlanta: Scholars Press, 1992), 184–213.

22. On *4 Ezra* and its parallels with Paul see Bruce W. Longenecker, *Eschatology and the Covenant in 4 Ezra and Romans 1–11*, JSNTSup 57 (Sheffield: Sheffield Academic Press, 1991).

mind of a Jew like Paul — however much they were held apart within both Reformation and Enlightenment thought, under such headings as "theology and ethics" or "salvation and politics." Just as the Messiah was destined to be Lord of the world, so, and for the same reasons, God's covenant with Israel had always been intended as the means of putting God's world to rights. In the rabbinic saying, God called Abraham to reverse the sin of Adam.[23] When, therefore, God's righteousness was unveiled, the effect would be precisely that the world would receive justice, that rich, restorative, much-to-be-longed-for justice of which the Psalmists had spoken with such feeling.[24]

But we need to remind ourselves where Paul's great letter was sent.[25] Debate about the situation of Romans has oscillated between those who suppose it to be simply "Paul's Last Will and Testament," summing up his gospel and theology before making his last great journey, and those who search in the Roman church, or in its relations with its non-Christian neighbors, for specific issues that Paul may have been addressing.[26] I have taken part in those debates, and I think the latter solution is broadly correct. But looming up behind all such discussions is quite a different issue, though commentators do not normally notice it. Paul was coming to Rome with the gospel message of Jesus the Jewish Messiah, the Lord of the world, claiming that through this message God's justice was unveiled once and for all. Rome prided itself on being, as it were, the capital of Justice, the source from which Justice would flow throughout the world. The Roman goddess Iustitia, like the Caesar-cult itself, was a comparative novelty in Paul's world: the temple to Iustitia was established on January 8, C.E. 13, and Iustitia was among the virtues celebrated by Augustus's famous *clipeus virtutis*, the golden shield set up in the Senate-house and inscribed with the emperor's virtues (27 B.C.E.). So close is the link between the new imperial regime and the virtue Iustitia that this goddess sometimes acquires the title "Augusta."[27] So, without losing any of its deep-rooted Jewish meanings of the covenant faithfulness

---

23. *Gen. Rab.* 14.6. I have explored this theme in various places, e.g., *Climax of the Covenant*, 21–26; *NTPG*, chap. 9.

24. Ps. 67:4, 82:8, and so on.

25. This point, though it was developed independently, has close analogies with the argument of Elliott, *Liberating Paul*, 190–92. See too Dieter Georgi, *Theocracy in Paul's Praxis and Theology* (Minneapolis: Fortress, 1991), chap. 4, excerpted in *Paul and Empire*, ed. Horsley, 148–57. Georgi seems to me to underplay the point about Iustitia in favor of other points equally worth further exploration, such as about fides/*pistis*. Perhaps his translation of *dikaiosynē* as "solidarity," and the rejection of its meaning of "justice" within the Jewish Bible as relevant to Paul, has led him to overlook the point. I agree with him (*Theocracy in Paul's Praxis and Theology*, 85) that Paul's *dikaiosynē* has its roots in the Jewish Bible, but one of my main themes here is that there is no need to refuse a concept a Greco-Roman setting or target just because its history-of-religions origin is Jewish.

26. See the discussions in the commentaries; and, e.g., K. P. Donfried, ed., *The Romans Debate*, rev. and expanded (Peabody, Mass.: Hendrikson, 1991).

27. On Iustitia, the Roman equivalent of the Greek *dike*, see, e.g., Ovid *Epistulae ex Ponto* 3.6.25; the *Acts of Augustus*, chap. 34.

of the creator God, with all that this means for God's dealing with sins and justification of those who believe, Paul's declaration that the gospel of King Jesus reveals God's *dikaiosynē* must also be read as a deliberate laying down of a challenge to the imperial pretension. If justice is wanted, it will be found not in the *euaggelion* that announces Caesar as Lord but in the *euaggelion* of Jesus.

Nor is this just a hint, a shot across Caesar's bows, to be quickly forgotten as the theme of the letter winds through its remarkable course. If Rom. 3:21–4:25 concludes that God has been faithful to the covenant with Abraham, Romans 5–8 concludes that God has thereby been true to the implicit covenant with the whole of creation. It is in 8:18–27 (more or less ignored, significantly enough, in much standard Pauline theology) that Paul finally shows how what God has done in Jesus the Messiah, in fulfillment of the covenant with Abraham, has addressed and in principle solved the problem of the whole world. God's covenant faithfulness has put the world to rights. Nothing Augustus or his successors could do, bringing their much-vaunted Pax Romana wherever they went, could compete with that; this is real justice, justice flowing from the throne of Jesus to the whole world. Seen from this point, Romans 9–11, while having as its main theme the paradoxical ways in which God's covenant faithfulness to Israel has worked out, are also concerned to bring a proper and just balance to the relationships within the wider community, advocating in particular a proper respect by Christians for their non-Christian Jewish neighbors. And Romans 14–15 is best read as urging a proper balance in the Christian community between Christians of different backgrounds.[28]

The problem of Rom. 13:1–7, seen within this wider context, is not so difficult as it has sometimes appeared. Paul's main aim, within the broad-brush ethical exhortations of chapters 12–13, is to point out that loyalty to Jesus does not mean anarchy in the state, and that however much the emperor may proclaim himself to be sovereign, without rival in the divine as well as the human sphere, he remains answerable to the true God. Despite what has often been suggested, reminding the emperor's subjects that the emperor is responsible to the true God is a diminution of, not a subjection to, imperial arrogance.[29]

The gospel of the true God, then, unveils the covenant faithfulness of this God, through which the entire world receives health-giving, restorative justice. That is the context within which, according to Romans, those who believe the gospel — who respond to the proclamation, that is, with "the obedience of faith" — are marked out by that faith, and by nothing else, as the eschatological people of God, the people whose sins have been dealt

28. Another theme we could study at this point is that of Pax/*eirene*; see Georgi, *Theocracy in Paul's Praxis and Theology*, 96–98 (though Georgi does not develop this very far).
29. On Romans 13 see Elliott, *Liberating Paul*, 214–26 (=*Paul and Empire*, ed. Horsley, chap. 11).

with on the cross, the people now assured of salvation/glorification. Nothing that I have said about what we might call the political dimension of Paul's argument in Romans should obscure for a moment that the message of the gospel is good news for sinners.

Rather, that emphasis should be highlighted and celebrated within the framework of God's triumph in Christ over all the principalities and powers. Nothing, not even Caesar's system, can separate us from God's love shown in the Messiah, Jesus.

All of which leads us to my fourth and final exegetical study. I have referred or alluded more than once to the third chapter of Philippians. I now want to propose a new way of reading that chapter as a whole.

## Paul's Coded Challenge to Empire: Philippians 3

The third chapter of Philippians presents the exegete with at least five interlocking puzzles. What is the target of Paul's polemic? How, more specifically, does the critique of the Jews in verses 2–7 cohere with the use of imperial language to describe Jesus in verses 20–21? Why does Paul tell the Philippians to imitate him (v. 17), since they, not being Jews, cannot travel by the route he has described as his own in verses 4–11? How does verse 1 belong with the chapter as a whole, if it does? And how does chapter 3 as a whole, which should probably be taken to include 4:1, belong with the letter as a whole, if it does?

I want to offer a reading of the chapter that I think throws a striking light on all these problems, and advances considerably the thesis I have been arguing overall about Paul's gospel and Caesar's empire, as well as the broader discussion about Paul's agendas vis-à-vis Caesar on the one hand and Judaism on the other.[30]

We may begin with the point that is frequently made (though not yet by all commentators) about 3:20: "Our citizenship is in heaven, and from it we await the Saviour, the Lord Jesus, the Messiah." These are Caesar-titles. The whole verse says: Jesus is Lord, and Caesar isn't. Caesar's empire, of which Philippi is a colonial outpost, is the parody; Jesus' empire, of which the Philippian church is a colonial outpost, is the reality.[31] And the point of having "citizenship in heaven" is not that one might eventually retire and go home to the mother city; no Roman colonial expected to do that, since one of the reasons Rome established colonies was overcrowding in the capital and the desire to spread Roman civilization in the rest of the empire. The point was that, if things were getting difficult in one's colonial setting, the

---

30. In addition to the commentaries, I have been much helped on Philippians (despite some continuing disagreements!) by the work of my former student Peter Oakes, whose book *Philippians: From People to Letter* is shortly to be published by Cambridge University Press in the SNTS Monograph Series.

31. Cf. Horsley, in *Paul and Empire*, ed. Horsley, 141: "The Philippians would hardly have been unaware that since the battle of Actium they already had a savior who was their lord."

emperor would come from the mother city to rescue and liberate his loyal subjects, transforming their situation from danger to safety.[32] Paul's description of Jesus, and his future saving activity, thus echoes what can be called imperial eschatology, even while being obviously derived from the same Jewish sources as was 1 Cor. 15:25–28. Indeed, verse 21 carries multiple echoes of several other Pauline passages (cf. Rom 8:29; 1 Cor. 15:43–53; 2 Cor. 3:18; Eph. 1:19–22). As so often, when Paul sums up a train of thought, particularly when it concerns Jesus, he brings together a familiar range of topics in a glittering finale to the argument.

What was the immediate significance of this Jesus-and-Caesar contrast? It was a challenge to an alternative loyalty. Jesus was the reality, Caesar the parody. It was the legitimation of the Christian church as the true empire of the true Lord. And it was the outworking of the great poem in the previous chapter; indeed, the very close linguistic and thematic links between 2:5–11 and 3:20–21, and the way the latter builds so naturally on the former, constitute one of the many good reasons for seeing Philippians, despite its jerkiness at certain joining points, as a single letter.[33] The poem in chapter 2 has exactly the same shape as some formulaic imperial acclamations: Jesus, not Caesar, has been a servant and is now to be hailed as *kyrios*. The fact that the poem, in its context in chapter 2, undergirds what we have been accustomed to call an ethical appeal should not blind us to the fact that Paul is here setting up themes he will later exploit. In any case, of course, the unity of the church for which the first half of chapter 2 is such an eloquent appeal is far from being a mere secondary question for Paul. If Jesus is Lord of the whole world, those who give him allegiance must be united, otherwise the claim will be seriously compromised. But if chapter 3 thus concludes with such a clear evocation of and challenge to imperial ideology and eschatology, how does this fit with the earlier parts of the chapter, for so long simply read as just another Pauline outburst against Jews in general or Jewish Christians on the other? Generations of exegetes have puzzled over this; we now hear less than once we did of the way in which Paul's eschatology challenges something called "perfectionism," and the way in which prognostic ideas flit to and from through the polemic, but the puzzle remains.[34]

The solution I propose is that Paul, for neither the first nor the last time, has Judaism and paganism, particularly, in this case, the Caesar-cult, simultaneously in mind, and is here using warnings against the former as a code for warnings against the latter. Paul's main concern here is not to warn the Philippians against Judaism or an anti-Pauline Jewish-Christian mission.

---

32. Cf. Elliott, *Liberating Paul*, 197; Georgi, *Theocracy in Paul's Praxis and Theology*, 72–78; Horsley in *Paul and Empire*, ed. Horsley, 140–41.

33. See my *Climax of the Covenant*, chap. 4 — though I managed in that entire chapter to ignore the Caesar dimension of Phil. 2:6–11, which now seems to me of great importance.

34. See H. Koester, "The Purpose of the Polemic of a Pauline Fragment (Philippians III)," *NTS* 8 (1961–62): 317–32.

We have, after all, no hard evidence that this danger threatened the churches in Greece as it had those in Asia. His concern is to warn them against the Caesar-cult and the entire panoply of pagan empire. But his method of warning them, and of encouraging them to take a stand for the counterempire of Jesus, is given for the most part in code. He tells them his own story, the story of how he had abandoned his status and privileges in order to find the true status and privilege of one in Christ, and he encourages them to imitate him. Read this way, the chapter gains both in coherence and in subtlety.

First, coherence. "To write the same things," he says in verse 1, "is no trouble for me, and it is safe for you." Why "safe"? Because nobody reading verses 2–16 would at once deduce that the recipients of the letter were being encouraged to be disloyal to Caesar. This is the coded message of subversive intrigue. The main thrust of the chapter is not to present a stark contrast between the two Lords of the world but to provide the Philippians with a powerful train of thought and to encourage them to live within it. "Join in imitating me," Paul says in verse 17; but, not being Jews, they cannot. Indeed, even if they had been Jews, they could hardly match Paul's top-drawer level of Jewishness (vv. 4–6). The rhetoric of the chapter does not simply give them orders; it encourages them to think their way into Paul's situation and then to transfer what he says about himself and his own privileges to their own position and status. Paul is not, in fact, shifting his target; he is using a warning about one thing as a way of issuing a different warning, all the more powerful for its being coded.

Second, subtlety. Paul builds up in verses 2–11 the argument that will then resound through to verse 21, with 10–11 anticipating the final climax of verses 20–21. There follows the famous warning against complacency, the danger to which recognition of the future hope is the antidote, in verses 12–16, to be followed by the final appeal, negatively in verses 17–19 and positively in verses 20–21. By this time, of course, both themes, "the warning against Judaism, and the warning against Caesar's empire and its blasphemous parody of Jesus' Lordship," have come together, so that, as expositors have noticed, it is possible to read verses 17–19 almost equally well as a scathing denunciation of non-Christian Jews (with "belly" and "shame" being perhaps euphemisms for the genitals which, from Paul's point of view, seemed to play an inordinately large role in non-Christian Jewish self-definition)[35] or, of course, as a more obvious denunciation of the pagan world that was all too familiar both to the Philippians and to the well-traveled apostle to the Gentiles.

All this raises some huge questions. First, what precisely are verses 2–11

---

35. See C. Mearns, "The Identity of Paul's Opponents at Philippi," *NTS* 33 (1987): 194–204. But cf. G. Fee, *Paul's Letter to the Philippians* (Grand Rapids, Mich.: Eerdmans, 1995), 317 n. 36, who describes Mearns's view as "a massive misreading of the evidence."

saying? Against whom are they warning, overtly as well as covertly, and what is the more precise logic of that warning?

The old debate as to whether Paul was opposing Judaism per se or a form of Jewish Christianity akin to that of the Galatian "agitators" is skewed in recent discussion[36] by the anxious attempt to protect Paul from saying anything apparently derogatory about Jews, and the equally eager attempt in some quarters to have him say as many snide things as possible about some of his fellow Christians. These contemporary concerns have often obscured the underlying thrust, which is both interestingly subtle in itself and fascinating when we come to apply it to the wider polemic the chapter is offering. Once again, part at least of the clue is found in the way in which these verses, too, look back to 2:5–11. There should be no doubt that Paul intended the first level of meaning of verses 3:2–6 to be about Jews, rather than Jewish Christians. Of course, the Galatian "agitators" would have come into the frame as well, but as a subset of a larger group: the dogs, the evil workers, the mutilation people. The first two of these epithets could have applied to pagans, of course, not least Cynics, as some have suggested. But the third, though clearly a pagan term, by generating the counterassertion of verse 3, shows that it is Jews who are in mind. Yes, but Jews seen now as a form of paganism.

The shock that greets such an announcement in our contemporary world should be blunted by two compelling factors. First, this is by no means the only time where Paul makes exactly this move. In Gal. 4:1–11, in line with the letter as a whole, he warns the young church that if they submit to circumcision they will not only not escape from the paganism they have rejected in becoming Christians, but will actually be returning to it in a subtler form. They will be returning to the realm of the flesh, of the principalities and powers. In Colossians 2, Paul warns the young church, not indeed against an actual syncretism or threatening new religion, but against Judaism described in terms of paganism.[37] This is a familiar trick. From Paul's Christian point of view, those Jews who do not embrace Jesus as their Messiah are thereby embracing instead an identity marked out by blood and soil, by ancestry and territory, in other words, by the "flesh." They are, therefore, subject to the same critique as paganism.

Nor is this a Pauline invention. Before we pick up the stones of our post-Enlightenment sensibilities to throw at Paul, or at any interpreter who dares to suggest that he might have done any such thing, we should recall that

---

36. See my recent essay, "The Letter to the Galatians: Exegesis and Theology," in *Between Two Horizons: Spanning New Testament Studies and Systematic Theology*, ed. Joel Green and Max Turner (Grand Rapids, Mich.: Eerdmans, 2000), 205–36.

37. I do not share the opinion that this is post-Pauline, and indeed the attempts within the new reading of Paul to suggest that Colossians and Ephesians represent a softening of Paul's opposition to Caesar strike me as absurd. See N. T. Wright, *The Epistles of Paul to the Colossians and to Philemon*, TNTC, n.s. (Grand Rapids, Mich.: Eerdmans, 1986); J. D. G. Dunn, *The Epistles of the Colossians and to Philemon* (Grand Rapids, Mich.: Eerdmans, 1996).

precisely this move was a standard way in which many Jewish groups in the Second Temple period would define themselves over against one another. We are the true Jews, say the Pharisees, say Qumran, say this or that revolutionary group; you are compromisers, *apikorsim,* no better than *goyim.* One example must suffice. When the original enthusiasm for the Maccabean revolt, and the resultant Hasmonean regime, had given way to disillusionment, some unknown writer appended to the Book of Daniel a further story, that of Susannah, in which the villains are now not the pagan rulers but the new Jewish ones, who are no better than pagans. This is simply the other side of the coin of doing what Paul is manifestly doing, despite our desire that he should not, in verse 3, namely, defining Christians not even as "the true circumcision," but simply as "the circumcision," *he peritome,* in contemptuous contrast to "the cutoff people," the "mutilation," *he katatome.* Paul is thus not only located on the map of Second Temple history, but, by employing an inner-Jewish rhetorical strategy in which one's opponents were cast as pseudopagans he is able to use the device in a quite new way, setting up precisely this polemic so as to serve a new purpose, namely, his anti-Caesar message.

Within this overall strategy, however, Paul is by no means saying, as some might too quickly conclude, that Judaism per se is bad and to be rejected. This is where the model of 2:5–11 becomes so important. The crucial point is that the Messiah did not regard his equality with God as something to be exploited; he did already possess equality with God and did not abandon it, but interpreted it as committing him to the path of suffering and death, a decision that was then vindicated in his exaltation and Lordship.[38] The fact that 3:7–11 is modeled on 2:5–11 suggests that we read Paul's autobiographical account as follows. Paul did not regard his covenant membership in Israel as something to be exploited. It did not entitle him to adopt a position of effortless superiority over the lesser breeds without the law. But nor did he therefore regard covenant membership itself as unimportant or to be jettisoned. He was not opposed to the idea of Judaism per se, nor indeed could he be; he was claiming the high ground that this, indeed, was what Judaism had always been supposed to be, the historical people whose identity and destiny were now revealed in the crucified Messiah. Just as the Messiah had obeyed the covenant plan of God and was now identified as the Lord of the world, so the Messiah's people were to find their covenant identity precisely "in" the Messiah, in his dying and rising, in his faithfulness, in the covenant membership that would be God's gift bestowed upon faithfulness.[39] Verses 10 and 11 sum up the train of thought; this, Paul is saying, is what it means to be the Israel of God, the circumcision. The fact

---

38. Cf. my *Climax of the Covenant,* chap. 4.
39. Note the very close parallel to this in Gal. 2:19–21.

that the crucified and risen Jesus is the Messiah has unveiled the truth about God's covenant plan for God's people.

Paul's warning, then, is not against so-called Judaizers, better perhaps simply described in terms of the Galatian situation as "agitators." It is a comparatively straightforward exposition of a standard Second Temple Jewish position; God has redefined Israel through certain climactic and revelatory — in other words, apocalyptic — events, and all forms of Judaism that do not recognize this and conform are at best out of date and at worst dangerous compromises and parodies.

This is not the central point of the chapter. The central point is now to argue: as I, Paul, have rethought my Jewish allegiance in the light of the crucified and risen Jesus, so you should rethink your Roman allegiance in the same light. The transitional passage, verses 12–16, turns the self-description of verses 4–11 into an example and exhortation, with the key transition coming in verses 15–16.

Eschatology is indeed the key here, but not in the way it is sometimes imagined. Just as Paul's covenant pilgrimage, his following of the Messiah through suffering and death to resurrection, is not yet complete, nor is the pilgrimage of the Philippians. This does of course rule out certain types of superspirituality, but I see no need to postulate that this is Paul's primary concern or even an important side issue. The important point is that the Philippians, like Paul, must find their whole identity in the crucified and risen Messiah and nowhere else.

The final appeal, in verses 17–21, is then to be understood as follows. It is, to begin with, primarily a warning against sheer paganism. The fact that verses 18 and 19 can be read as a coded warning against some types of Judaism may well be deliberate, but I do not think it is the main thing Paul is aiming at.[40] Rather, he is building up to saying: do not go along with the Caesar-cult that is currently sweeping the Eastern Mediterranean. You have one Lord and Savior, and he will vindicate and glorify you, if you hold firm to him, just as the Father vindicated and glorified him after he had obeyed.

But the model of Paul's self-description in verses 2–11 does not allow us to treat this appeal as a simplistic rejection of everything to do with Caesar's empire. Paul is no dualist. Think for a moment of his regular ethical appeals; just because all things are new in Christ, that does not mean that Christians do not share with their non-Christian pagan neighbors a broad perception of things that are good and things that are evil (Romans 12). Just as it is wrong to suppose that either Paul was anti-Jewish or he had no critique of any other Jews, so it would be wrong to suppose that either he was opposed entirely to everything to do with the Roman Empire or he was a quisling, a compromiser, going with the flow of the new regime. Once again, things are

---

40. See, e.g., Peter Oakes, *Philippians: From People to Letter* (Cambridge: Cambridge University Press, 2000).

not so straightforward. Here, too, the logic of his argument shows that, as in Colossians 1, the Paul of Philippians would be quite prepared to say that the creator God has made all things in Christ, including the principalities and powers that then need to be defeated and reconciled. Paul himself used his Roman citizenship to good advantage, not to set himself up as superior to noncitizens, nor yet, like Naaman the Syrian, to excuse a bit of paganism on the side, but as a way of getting to Rome to announce the revelation of God's justice in the Messiah, Jesus. Perhaps we might, then, treat his appeal as follows.

God has unveiled in Jesus his true kingdom, his true empire. It stands to all other empires, Caesar's included, somewhat as true covenant membership stands to that Judaism which remains opposed to the gospel message of the Messiah. The parallel may be uncomfortable for us at both ends, but we must follow it through; only so can the code, which is "safe" for the Philippians, have its full force. There is nothing specifically wrong with being a citizen of a country or of its wider extension, just as there is nothing wrong with being Jewish. But when the gospel of Jesus is unveiled it reveals the true empire, the true citizenship, and in that light all the pretensions of empire, not least the arrogant and blasphemous claims of the emperor himself, are shown up, just as those who pride themselves on their circumcision are shown up as being "the mutilation." This is neither complimentary nor dualistic — a position in which Paul's interpreters have always found it hard to imitate him. But the closing exhortation of the passage says it all: this is the way you are to stand firm in the Lord (4:1).

What then does Paul want his hearers to do? Should they renounce their citizenship? Presumably not; Paul did not renounce his. In any case, as sociological studies of Philippi have shown, by no means all the residents of the city and its surrounding area would have been Roman citizens, and hence it is likely that many of the young church there would not have had that privilege.[41] But the city as a whole prided itself on its colonial status, and even noncitizens might expect to derive benefit from such an intimate association with Rome, and hence with Caesar, the lord, the savior, the great benefactor. Paul is warning them not to compromise their allegiance to Jesus, and to be prepared, by refusing to take part in cultic and other activities, to follow their Messiah along the path of suffering, knowing that Jesus, the one true Lord, was the true Savior who would rescue them and give them the only glory worth possessing. Verse 21 indicates clearly enough, partly by its close association with 2:10–11 and partly by its parallel with the fuller statement in 1 Cor. 15:23–28, that the time will come when Caesar and all who fol-

---

41. Even if "belly" and "shame" are to be read as euphemisms, the natural primary application would be to the phallic symbolism of some pagan cult, not to a spurious emphasis on circumcision (or, for that matter, on sexual libertinism).

low and worship him will be humbled before the throne of the true Lord of the World.

What then can we say about the passage in Philippians 3 which has normally been the focus of attention, namely verses 2–11? Have we, by arguing that it functions as a coded warning and summons to a church faced with a different threat, thereby relativized its surface value, both as critique of non-Christian Judaism and as a statement of Christian identity? By no means.

First, there can be no doubt that here Paul is denying, in the strongest terms, that membership in the eschatological people of God can be demarcated by the regular boundary markers of non-Christian Judaism. Equally, there is no doubt that Paul is affirming that Judaism — he does not even say *true* Judaism or *fulfilled* Judaism (cf. Rom. 2:29) — is now defined in terms of the Messiah, Jesus. This is clearly a classic piece of Second Temple Jewish self-definition, claiming the high ground of the true fulfillment of God's purposes and denying that ground to all others. In particular, of course, Paul is denying it to his own previous mode of existence, his Pharisaic past. But we should note both what he does not say and the grounds for the claim he makes. He does not say that Pharisaic Judaism is silly, guilt-ridden, the wrong sort of religion. Rather, he says that it is a way of life characterized by *sarx*, flesh, and by trust in such flesh. We need the fuller statements of Galatians and Romans, of course, to make sense of this critique. But the key thing is that the death and resurrection of Jesus the Messiah have inaugurated the new, messianic age in which the messianic events of Jesus' suffering, death, and resurrection are now the defining characteristics of his people. Paul's argument, then, is basically eschatological and messianic: the events concerning Jesus have God's stamp upon them, declaring that the long-awaited new age has begun. Being the people of God is no longer defined according to the flesh, but according to the Messiah. Though this is as strong a critique of non-Christian "perhaps we should say, nonmessianic" Judaism as Paul offers at any point in his writings, it is essentially a critique from within. It is not a criticism of Judaism per se, merely of what happens when the Messiah comes and some Jews fail to acknowledge him.

Second, how does Paul's statement of Christian identity function? It is again notably Messiah-centered. Verses 7–11 are often cited in discussions of "justification by faith," to which topic indeed they contribute. But their primary emphasis is on being in Christ, belonging, that is, to the people of the Messiah. It is when one is "in the Messiah" (v. 9) that one possesses already the status of being the righteous people of God, a status which has nothing to do with possession of Torah, and hence nothing to do in and of itself with being ethnically Jewish, and everything to do with covenant faithfulness. Again we need the fuller statements of Galatians and Romans to understand the dense statement of verse 9; indeed, the dense and unexplained nature of this statement is itself an indication that Paul is not intending here to tell his audience something they do not in principle know already. In the light of fuller explanations elsewhere, I regard it as likely that *dia pisteōs Christou* in verse 9 should be understood as "through the faithfulness of the Messiah," and that the last phrase of the verse should be glossed as "the covenant status bestowed by God upon faithfulness." This messianic faithfulness is not, ultimately, something other than the "obedience" of the Messiah, outlined in 2:5–8. As verses 10 and 11 of the present chapter make clear, the messianic events of Jesus' suffering, death, and resurrection are the defining, because redeeming, features of the people of God; to belong to God's people is to be defined in terms of them. This definition can be stated in terms of knowledge (8, 10), gaining the Messiah (8), being found in him (9), being conformed to him (10), and attaining his resurrection (11).

Paul's doctrine of justification is not simply about how individuals find salvation. It is not about the rejection of an abstract moralism or Pelagianism and the embracing of an alternative scheme of abstract trust, nor about rejecting ritualism and relying on a purely spiritual approach to God. It is about the definition of the community by Jesus the Messiah.

We may note, in concluding this brief study of Philippians 3, that if verses 2–11 are really intended to function as a coded challenge to Caesar's empire, telling Paul's story of renouncing his past and embracing the Messiah in order to encourage the Philippians along an analogous path, they also function sequentially within the consecutive logic of the chapter. It is precisely because they are assured that they are indeed the people of the one true God, formed in the Messiah through his death and resurrection, that the Philippians will have courage and confidence to trust him as savior and lord and so to renounce the imperial claims of Caesar. And in doing so they will find the warnings of Paul resonating at various levels. If he can renounce his unrivalled privileges, so can they.

## Concluding Reflections

First, we may stress that Paul's critique of Caesar's empire was firmly grounded in his Jewish heritage. Discovering the pagan history-of-religions parallels to Paul does not mean suggesting that Paul did not remain a thoroughly Jewish thinker. What he does with the Caesar-cult stems directly from what Isaiah does with the Babylonian cult, which in turn looks back to Deuteronomy's rejection of all paganism in favor of the stern monotheism of the creator and covenant god. The rediscovery in our day of the pagan context and target of Paul's thinking should not mean for one minute that we go back on the great gain of the last generation, the rediscovery that Paul was and remained a thoroughly Jewish thinker.

Second, the Jewish thinking that formed the center and driving force of his rejection of Caesar's empire was expressed in terms of Paul's very high Christology. Philippians 3:20–21 is based firmly on 2:5–11, which articulates in poetic formulations, unlikely to have been composed then and there, a view of Jesus that claims for him nothing less than equality with, and thereby identity with, the one God of Jewish monotheism. In this passage and several others Paul therefore marks the beginning of the process that led eventually to what we know as Trinitarian theology, that view that marks differentiation within the one God. There has been a fashion in some circles for regarding later trinitarianism as one sign of the process whereby, so it is said, the church climbed down from its earlier political confrontation with the empire and arrived at a compromise, an accommodation. Whatever the truth of that, Paul's opposition to Caesar and adherence to a very high, very Jewish Christology were part of the same thing. Jesus was Lord — kyrios, with all its Septuagintal overtones — and Caesar was not.

Third, neither the recognition that Paul's main target was paganism, and the Caesar-cult in particular, nor the equal recognition that he remained a thoroughly Jewish thinker, should blind us for a moment to the fact that Paul still held a thorough and stern critique of nonmessianic Judaism. Though based on Paul's eschatological belief that the God of Israel had acted in Jesus to fulfill the covenant and usher in the long-awaited new age, this critique was not simply a matter of Paul's thinking that, since salvation was in Christ, it seemed not to be in Judaism after all. Paul remains at this point on the map of Second Temple Judaism. Believing that God had acted to remodel the covenant people necessarily and Jewishly meant believing that those who refused to join this remodeled people were missing out on God's eschatological purpose. As post-Holocaust thinkers we will be careful how we say all this. As historians of the first century we will recognize that it must be said. As Pauline theologians we will recognize that it contains no shadow, no hint, of anything that can truly be called anti-Judaism, still less anti-Semitism.

Fourth, the argument I have mounted indicates clearly enough that whatever it was Paul was heralding as he went around the Mediterranean world, our post-Enlightenment category of "religion" is far too restricted to handle it. Since that category was designed to exclude politics, among other things, and since Paul's proclamation clearly carried a political message at its heart, not merely as one "implication" among many, we should refuse to allow the study of Paul to be confined within what is normally thought of as the history of religion. This has large-scale implications for the organization of our disciplines. Was the Caesar-cult a matter of religion or politics? Perhaps Paul should be taught just as much in the politics departments of our universities as in the religion departments.

Fifth, if Paul's answer to Caesar's empire is the empire of Jesus, what does that say about this new empire, living under the rule of its new Lord? It implies a high and strong ecclesiology in which the scattered and often muddled cells of women, men, and children loyal to Jesus as Lord form colonial outposts of the empire that is to be: subversive little groups when seen from Caesar's point of view, but when seen Jewishly an advance foretaste of the time when the earth shall be filled with the glory of the God of Abraham and the nations will join Israel in singing God's praises (cf. Rom. 15:7–13). From this point of view, therefore, this counterempire can never be merely critical, never merely subversive. It claims to be the reality of which Caesar's empire is the parody; it claims to be modeling the genuine humanness, not least the justice and peace, and the unity across traditional racial and cultural barriers, of which Caesar's empire boasted. If this claim is not to collapse once more into dualism, into a rejection of every human aspiration and value, it will be apparent that there will be a large degree of overlap. "Shun what is evil; cling to what is good." There will be affirmation as well as rejection, collaboration as well as critique. To collaborate without compromise, to criticize without dualism — this is the delicate path that Jesus' counterempire had to learn to tread.

On the day I sat down to draft this essay, an editorial came to my eye that nicely summed up the first of these: what is desired is "a model for churches and theologians to contribute to the ordering of society, without being Christianly imperialistic."[42] Equally, we need a model for churches and theologians to contribute to the critique of society, without being Christianly dualistic. Paul points the way to this finely balanced agenda, and we who live with the legacy of two thousand years of the church getting it sometimes right and often wrong would do well to return to our roots to learn fresh wisdom.

---

42. W. M. Jacob, in *Theology* 101 (1998): 402.

# RESPONSE

## SOME ASPECTS OF CONVERSION AND IDENTITY FORMATION IN THE CHRISTIAN COMMUNITY OF PAUL'S TIME

### Alan F. Segal

[g g g g g g g g g g g]

K RISTER STENDAHL'S work is responsible for our seeing Paul's attempts to bring Jews and Gentiles together in the church in a new and more positive light.[1] He pointed out, in his now-famous article, "Paul and the Introspective Conscience of the West," that Paul's behavior should not be considered the result of a crisis of guilt.[2] Stendahl was speaking against a certain understanding of religious psychology and a certain understanding of Paul's Jewish past. Having taken the force of that critique, I suggested that the term *convert* could be rehabilitated and applied to Paul, provided one understood Stendahl's critique. Recognizing that it is a modern comparative term and not one that Paul used of himself, I suggested that the term *convert* applies to Paul and that the dynamic of conversion, which we know from modern social-psychological studies, could add to Stendahl's perception. Indeed, Paul does not use the term *convert* to refer to himself. To the contrary, he assumes that *metanoia* (let us call it conversion) is something that does not apply to him. I speculated that Paul was reticent to use it because of exactly what Stendahl maintains about him, that he had a robust conscience. *Metanoia* is the standard Greek translation for the Hebrew *teshuva* (repentance) and Paul is quite clear that he is a good Pharisee

---

1. Krister Stendahl's many accomplishments and contributions to the study and understanding of Paul certainly are in no need of emphasis. But it is a great pleasure to contribute these comments to a volume in honor of Krister Stendahl's eightieth birthday, recognizing publicly how important his work has been.

2. Krister Stendahl, "Paul and the Introspective Conscience of the West," *HTR* 56 (1963): 199–215, reprinted in Krister Stendahl, *Paul among Jews and Gentiles, and Other Essays* (Philadelphia: Fortress Press, 1976).

and blameless under the law: "as to righteousness under the law blameless" (Phil. 3:6).[3]

But we miss something important if we do not recognize that Paul is a convert in the basic sociological sense of that term — a person who changes religious communities. That does not necessarily have to apply to changing from one religion to another. It can also include changing from one sect to another. And this is the sense in which I applied it to Paul. In doing so, I tried to show that Paul's Christianity is very much based on his visionary, mystical, and apocalyptic Jewish experience and is quite different from the Christians who understood Christianity as completing their Judaism.[4] They would have continued to practice the Jewish law and not have seen the contradictions between their prior and current life. That does not mean that Paul never used Hellenistic rhetorical devices or relied on a proverb known from Greco-Roman antiquity. But, religiously, Paul was first a Pharisee, and probably a very conservative one since he was a persecutor of the church. This change of religious groups brought with it a firm break with his prior life:

> But whatever gain I had, I counted as loss for the sake of Christ. Indeed I count everything as loss because of the surpassing worth of knowing Christ Jesus my Lord. For his sake I have suffered the loss of all things, and count them as refuse, in order that I may gain Christ and be found in him, not having a righteousness of my own, based on law, but that which is through faith in Christ, the righteousness from God that depends on faith. (Phil. 3:7–9)

Of course, Paul continues to be a Jew and he continues to believe that his new faith is part of Judaism. But he sees that it implies some large changes; it quite overthrows his Pharisaism. Yet Paul does not forget his Pharisaic training and remains a skilled exegete of the Torah throughout his career. Indeed, forgetting the Christian assumption from which his exegesis comes, we can recognize the kinds of arguments that he uses from rabbinic literature that appeared two centuries later. Thus Paul becomes important evidence for the description of Pharisaism in the first century even after he left it, provided one is careful to distinguish between his training and his new commitments.

It may be that Paul was not entering a fully defined Christian community. Certainly that community was not as clearly defined as it was going to be when Christianity became a separate religion. But there were identifiable Christian communities during Paul's life. Though Christianity had not fully separated from Judaism during Paul's life or even quite some time afterwards, there was already enough of a Christian community for Paul to be concerned about it when he was a Pharisee. And, of course, after his con-

---

3. See my *Paul the Convert: The Apostolate and Apostasy of Saul the Pharisee* (New Haven: Yale University Press, 1990), especially 3–34.

4. Ibid., 341–50.

version, he spent many years in that community before writing his major letters, pointing up Paul's long association with the issues in Christianity before he wrote.

This learning process, it seems to me, is the most important aspect of applying the admittedly modern term *convert* to Paul's religious life. Paul usually understands himself in very modest terms: "For I am the least of the apostles, unfit to be called an apostle, because I persecuted the church of God. But by the grace of God I am what I am, and his grace toward me was not in vain. On the contrary, I worked harder than any of them, though it was not I, but the grace of God which is with me" (1 Cor. 15:9–10). But, when pressed, Paul uses terms about himself that resemble prophecy: "But when he who had set me apart before I was born, and had called me through his grace" (Gal. 1:15). Paul is certainly not just a prophet but an eschatological prophet (for instance, 2 Thessalonians 4 and 1 Corinthians 15).

Pamela Eisenbaum suggests that Paul used Abraham as a model in many areas, not least for his own role, and I agree heartily with her analysis. Abraham is called a "prophet" in Gen. 20:7. Paul and Abraham certainly both share a calling, as she says. And I think we all agree that Paul is not merely trying to dissolve Judaism into a wider universalism, though he does want to suggest that the claims of Judaism are different than he once thought.

Mark Nanos's chapter on the parties in Galatia illustrates that the situation is far more complicated than previously acknowledged. Clearly Paul is talking to the gentile converts of that place, arguing that they need not be circumcised. The more subtle question is the identity of the opponents. Like many, I had suggested that the opponents are Jewish Christians. Nanos suggests that they were Jews. It seems to me that Nanos's suggestion has great merit provided it is not understood as exclusively Jewish or Jewish Christian. Either Jew or Jewish Christian is possible; it is the position that counts, not the ethnic identity per se. We shall see that sometimes Paul's opponents must be Christians as well as, presumably, Jews. I would include in that category gentile Christians who had already been circumcised, making them Jews for all intents and purposes. They certainly would have ample motivation to ask the same very high commitments of their fellow converts.

What seems to me to be obvious is that Paul sees the terms of the choice to be starker than many other Jews would have seen it. As a Pharisee Paul says that once one accepts circumcision, one should accept the whole law:

> Now I, Paul, say to you that if you receive circumcision, Christ will be of no advantage to you. I testify again to every man who receives circumcision that he is bound to keep the whole law. You are severed from Christ, you who would be justified by the law; you have fallen away from grace. For through the Spirit, by faith, we wait for the hope of righteousness. (Gal. 5:25)

These terms are the terms of a Pharisee converted. For him the choice is Pharisaism or Christianity — there can be no lukewarm observance of law. For Paul the whole Torah means the Oral Law and the Pharisiac interpretations, not just the lesser biblical requirements, which was obviously the stance of some of his Jewish opponents in Galatia:

> It is those who want to make a good showing in the flesh that would compel you to be circumcised, and only in order that they may not be persecuted for the cross of Christ. For even those who receive circumcision do not themselves keep the law, but they desire to have you circumcised that they may glory in your flesh. But far be it from me to glory except in the cross of our Lord Jesus Christ, by which the world has been crucified to me, and I to the world. For neither circumcision counts for anything, nor uncircumcision, but a new creation. (Gal. 6:12–15)

Paul's comment that his opponents just want to avoid persecution "for the cross of Christ" suggests that the opponents are Christians who are afraid of public censure. Clearly they are Jews as well or they would not insist on circumcision. Of course, we may also suspect that some had nobler motives than Paul ascribes to them, but polemic was the dominant rhetorical style of the day. In any event Paul's polarized sense of the choices available marks him as a Pharisee. Other Jews could have recommended that converts enter Judaism without the expectation that they had to do all "613 commandments." Paul retains his preconversion superiority to those who do not keep the law as the Pharisees do. Both this passage and the archaeological evidence suggest that the Jews of Anatolia practiced Judaism in a largely non-Pharisaic way.

But, of course, Paul's solution to the question of law, which has become the standard solution in later Christianity, must have been a minority opinion in his own day. The issue is at first circumcision, but that is settled. The issue of circumcision does not affect one's salvation in later rabbinic Judaism, as Luke has some of the Pharisees suggest. Such rabbis did exist; they followed Rabbi Eliezer and not Rabbi Joshua:

> Rabbi Eliezer said: "All the nations will have no share in the world to come, even as it is said, 'the wicked shall go into Sheol, and all the nations that forget God' [Ps. 9:17]. The wicked shall go into Sheol — these are the wicked among Israel." Rabbi Joshua said to him: "If the verse had said, 'The wicked shall go into Sheol with all the nations,' and had stopped there, I should have agreed with you, but as it goes on to say 'who forget God,' it means there are righteous men among the nations who have a share in the world to come." (*t. Sanh.* 13.2; also see *m. Sanh.* 10, *Sanh.* 105a, *Sifra* 86b, *b. B. Qam.* 38a)

The issue is discussed and Rabbi Eliezer's position is left behind. The rabbinic position is only that circumcision is the marker for entrance into the Jewish covenant (cf. Acts 15:5), not that circumcision is necessary for salvation (cf. Acts 15:1). That position is most characteristic of apocalypticism in first-century Judaism (the Book of Jubilees on the twenty-eighth Jubilee). Indeed, the discussion in the early Christian community is only one further demonstration that such issues existed in the first century when the subject was inclusion, not exclusion.

Once the issue of circumcision was settled, the other, lesser laws become more troublesome. Indeed it is the settling of the issue of the inclusion of uncircumcised Christians into the community that makes the next step necessary because that makes them the equivalent of resident aliens. Acts makes clear that the Jerusalem church felt that the Gentiles in the church needed to observe certain rules against idolatry so that the Jews and Gentiles could be one community (Acts 15:20, 29; 21:25). This certainly must have contradicted Paul's thinking but, if Acts is correct, it appears as though he accepted this limitation on his converts' freedom for the sake of peace in the community. This is because he understood Christian freedom to include even the free choice not to take that freedom, if the unity of the church were at stake.[5]

So the issue is not the salvation of the Gentiles, either for Paul or for the rabbis, as is quite often assumed. Even as recently as Daniel Boyarin's extremely stimulating book on the radical Paul, it is assumed that he voted for universalism over particularism.[6] It seems to me that the original issue both for Paul and for the rabbis was not the salvation of the Gentiles but the making of one community with them. Paul saw that the survival of Christianity, even for the short time Paul anticipated before the consummation, depended on Jews and Gentiles making one community while the rabbis granted all righteous people salvation, though they could never be truly one community with them. Both are universalistic solutions, given the age they lived in. They do assume a different social situation and, indeed, they were later affected by Christianity's role as an imperial religion and Judaism's role as a tolerated guest, mostly in the Parthian and Sassanian empires. There was nothing inevitable about the outcome.

The differences between the rabbis and Paul in their models for universalism, I suggest, also come from their respective origins. Christianity was at first an apocalyptic sect that learned to live in this world for as long as it took before the Christ returned. Rabbinic Judaism was never that. It flirted with apocalypticism throughout its long history but never succumbed to it. But this only underlies the difficulty of these arguments both in our own day

---

5. See ibid., 187–224.

6. Daniel Boyarin, *A Radical Jew: Paul and the Politics of Identity* (Berkeley: University of California Press, 1994).

and in Paul's. It seems clear to me that Paul never doubted that he remained Jewish and part of the Jewish community. Nor did he ever doubt that his new community was part of God's plan. The problem is that the wider community of Jews did not agree with him, just as they did not entirely agree with each other.

N. T. Wright, with his characteristically powerful prose, suggests that one area in which Paul would not have been prepared to compromise was in the area of the imperial cult. I think he is correct in this assessment and I have no doubt that he is correct in the major thrust of his research. Though I consider myself part of the new "history of religions" school of historians of this period, I would certainly agree that we must never simply assume that Paul took some Jewish or pagan Hellenistic religious form and applied it to the story of Christ to come up with a new religion. For one thing, if I am right about the community Paul joined, he was only spelling out the spiritual experiences he had, certainly not consciously authoring religion. Nor is it clear to me that he had many followers at first. His letters give us a clearer sense of the extent of his enemies than they give us of the strength of his congregations. The gospels, written later, do not seem overly influenced by Pauline thought. Indeed, if anything, they sometimes seem to be defending against it, especially his view of the "spiritual body" resurrection. His letters had their greatest effect generations after his death. So, if he were trying to start a religion, he was not terribly successful at first. It is only generations later, when the church was largely Gentile, that the formulas he worked out seemed to make sense to everyone.

This bears emphasizing one more time: Paul's own religious experience was the undeniable bedrock on which he launched his mission. Paul was a man who had extremely powerful, life-changing religious visions. Even if Acts' description of his "conversion" is to be distrusted, Paul himself tells us that he has had visions and revelations of the Lord (2 Cor. 12:1, Galatians 1).

It seems clear, as Wright tells us, that Paul's critique of Caesar's empire was firmly grounded in his Jewish heritage. I have no doubt that Paul would have allowed himself to have been martyred rather than to have admitted that Caesar was "Lord" in the divine sense that Jesus was. Jews of all types knew that they must steel themselves to the same decision, were such demanded. And, of course, Jews were threatened with this dreaded choice during the reign of Caligula, as were Christians thereafter. No one would want to gainsay the holiness of the martyrs of either faith. And I think that Paul's high Christology must also have Jewish roots, though I would seek them in the biblical traditions of God's principal angelic mediator.

But I do not believe that religion ever excluded politics in the Roman Empire. That many in the Jewish community may have hoped for a political solution to any problems between it and the Roman Empire was only natural. Evidently many Christians felt similarly. We have the records of those in the Revelation of St. John and in various Jewish sources who could not avoid making the choice. If church tradition is correct, Paul was himself among them. Ironically enough, Paul's sense of unity of the church, centuries later, could also be put to the service of establishing and maintaining an imperial religion.

Wright's stirring final statements raise the issue of Paul's understanding of the place of Israel in God's plan and the significance of Romans 9–11. It seems clear that Paul foresees that the unity of all will (ultimately) be in Christ, in contradistinction to the "two covenant" position. So I agree with Wright over against the "two covenant" position interpretation of Judaism and Christianity as to what Paul said in Romans 9–11.

This is not a pleasant conclusion for me. I fight it at every opportunity. I do remember, however, a very significant conversation with Krister Stendahl one bright but cold afternoon in Cambridge several years ago.[7] In it, he showed me that his own position (i.e., Stendahl's) was not quite what I had understood when I put him squarely with Gager and Gaston. Stendahl showed me that his own position was more ambivalent than the one that I had attributed to him, a position closer to the ambiguity I see in Paul. I would like to believe and wish there was a way for modern Christian interpreters to distinguish between what was for Paul a wish or estimation on the one hand, and visionary certainty on the other. That is, I do not believe that Paul was given a revelation about the Jewish role in salvation in Romans 9–11. I believe it was his personal opinion. Of course, I wish Paul had clearly said that Jews and Christians could find their own way separately to the consummation. I do not think that Paul exactly said that. But I welcome the necessity of ambivalence and ambiguity in this matter. I frankly think that Paul was mostly expressing his surprise at the way in which God had chosen to fulfill his promises, not predicting what God would do.[8] As I expressed at the end of my *Paul the Convert*, I felt that Paul was too true a man of faith to have proclaimed as fact what God had not yet brought to pass. Paul knew that God would keep faith with Israel. But, since he had already been surprised by God's grace, he was unprepared to specify how.

---

7. I cherish that one brief afternoon in which I became Krister Stendahl's student and hope for many more such moments for all of us.

8. For this insight I was originally indebted to Professor Stendahl's Scandinavian colleague. Nils Dahl, "The Future of Israel," in his *Studies in Paul: Theology for the Early Christian Mission* (Minneapolis: Augsburg, 1977).

# — 12 —

# COLLECTION FOR THE SAINTS AS ANTICOLONIAL ACT

## IMPLICATIONS OF PAUL'S ETHNIC RECONSTRUCTION

*Sze-kar Wan*

᙭᙭᙭᙭᙭᙭᙭᙭᙭᙭

F IRST IN HIS LANDMARK 1963 article, "The Apostle Paul and the Introspective Conscience of the West," and later in his 1976 *Paul among Jews
and Gentiles,*[1] Bishop Krister Stendahl pioneered, then reinforced, what has
become scholarly standard in New Testament studies: far from suffering the
type of guilty conscience characteristic of the Protestant West, Paul was in
fact blessed with a rather robust self-image. Not only was he not plagued
with an excessive sense of personal shortcoming, he was proud of his previous accomplishments in Judaism, accomplishments he never hesitated to
recount for his readers (see, e.g., 2 Cor. 11:22, Gal. 1:13–14, Phil. 3:4–6).
Students of Paul owe a great debt to Bishop Stendahl who, in shifting their
productive attention from Paul the Christian to Paul the Jew, has been the
inspiration, at least in part, to many of the major publications on Paul in
the last quarter century.[2]

In spite of the attention on Paul's Jewishness, recent scholars have tended
to treat ethnicity more as a cultural artifact than a socioanthropological
construct.[3] Most seem to make the facile assumption that group identity is

---

1. Krister Stendahl, "The Apostle Paul and the Introspective Conscience of the West," in
*Paul among Jews and Gentiles, and Other Essays* (Philadelphia: Fortress Press, 1976); the
original article was a lecture delivered in 1961 which was later published in *HTR* 56 (1963)
199–215. See other essays in the same volume.

2. One need only mention E. P. Sanders, *Paul and Palestinian Judaism: A Comparison
of Patterns of Religions* (Philadelphia: Fortress Press, 1977); Alan Segal, *Paul the Convert:
The Apostolate and Apostasy of Saul the Pharisee* (New Haven: Yale University Press, 1990);
and Daniel Boyarin, *A Radical Jew: Paul and the Politics of Identity* (Berkeley: University of
California Press, 1994).

3. The partial exception is Boyarin, who is subtly nuanced in his discussion of Jewish ethnic
groups but nevertheless displays the tendency of treating Paul's own cultural identity statically.

defined by cultural values or essences that are inherently stable. In reality, this is rarely the case. One could depart from accepted cultural norms but still insist on being a member of an ethnic group. By the same token, once an ethnic group fixes its boundaries, it can incorporate with relative confidence new cultural elements into the group through structured interactions with outsiders. This, of course, was precisely Bishop Stendahl's enduring contribution to Pauline studies: in rejecting circumcision and dietary restrictions as sine-qua-non identity markers of Judaism, Paul nevertheless felt he could still insist on his membership within Judaism, albeit a Judaism reconfigured by means of reinterpreting the Abrahamic narrative (Romans 4; Galatians 3–4). Paul's self-consciousness of his own Jewishness gave him an in-group identity that his Christ-centered message did not take away, at least not yet in the early days of the fledgling Christ-worshiping movement. The central task of his ministry can therefore be seen as an attempt to stretch the group boundaries of Judaism to include gentile converts — boundaries, however, no longer defined by the signs of circumcision and dietary laws.

All this would indicate to us that we need a more flexible concept of ethnicity to evaluate Paul's program, one that is based not so much on a static notion of cultural essence as on the maintenance of group boundaries that are a function of internal and alterable self-definitions. Only such a notion of ethnicity as social construct can do justice to the controversies Paul had with his fellow missionaries over how the Jewish ethnic boundaries ought to be redrawn and whether Gentiles could be admitted into this newly constituted group. This approach has already been applied, with fruitful results, to the analysis of Galatians;[4] it can cast light on the collection for the Jerusalem saints as well. The collection was obviously important to Paul's ministry around Asia Minor, Macedonia, and Greece, since Paul makes reference to it in every one of his major letters (Rom. 15:25–28, 1 Cor. 16:1–4, 2 Corinthians 8–9, Gal. 2:10). Yet why was Paul so determined to carry out the collection, to the point of even risking his own life (cf. Rom. 15:31)? I will argue below that the collection lay at the heart of Paul's concern with redefining Jewish group boundaries to include gentile converts. In so doing, he constructed an all-embracing sociopolitical order that stood in contradistinction to and in criticism of colonial powers.[5]

---

See appreciative reviews by Mark G. Brett, "Interpreting Ethnicity: Method, Hermeneutics, Ethics," in *Ethnicity and the Bible*, ed. M. G. Brett (Leiden: Brill, 1996), 16–21; Mark G. Brett, "The Implied Ethics of Postcolonialism," *Jian Dao* 8 (1997): 1–13; John M. G. Barclay, " 'Neither Jew nor Greek': Multiculturalism and the New Perspective on Paul," in *Ethnicity and the Bible*, ed. Brett, 197–214.

4. Philip F. Esler, "Group Boundaries and Intergroup Conflict in Galatians: A New Reading of Galatians 5:13–6:10," in *Ethnicity and the Bible*, ed. Brett, 215–40.

5. My reading here is not strictly postcolonial, but in some aspects it does coincide with the goals of postcolonial studies in which ethnic integrity, self-determination, anti-colonial and anti-imperial concerns are all inextricably intertwined. See R. S. Sugirtharajah, *Asian Biblical Hermeneutics and Postcolonialism: Contesting the Interpretations* (Maryknoll, N.Y.: Orbis,

# A Chronology of the Collection

In a polemical narrative of the Jerusalem Council (Gal. 2:1–10),[6] Paul tells his readers that the council had reached a mutually beneficial resolution to the dispute between missionaries to Jews and Gentiles: to divide the mission field between those ministering to "the circumcised" and those whose prime responsibility it was to evangelize "the uncircumcised" (vv. 7–9). To Paul, in all likelihood, this was a momentous decision and represented a certain concession by the Jerusalem "pillars," since he took it to be a legitimation and formalization of the Gentiles' place in the young movement. That seems to be the very intent of using the Jerusalem proceedings to anchor his apostolic apologia in his emotional letter to the Galatians (Gal. 2:1–10). Almost as an afterthought, Paul adds, the council also resolved that Paul and Barnabas (cf. 2:1) do one more thing: remember the poor (2:10a). The exceptionally prominent position of the phrase "only the poor" in Paul's formulation (*monon tōn ptōchōn hina mnēmoneuōmen*) cries out for attention. Yet, after the readers' curiosity is piqued, the rest of Galatians passes over the subject in total silence. Why Paul makes no further mention of "the poor" in Galatians, intriguing as it is, we can consign to the realm of speculation. But if "the poor" plays no role in Paul's argument in the rest of Galatians — there seems to be none — and if there is no external pressure on Paul to recount this part of the Jerusalem Council — again there seems to be none — why does he feel compelled to mention it in an otherwise polemical context?

A ready answer is that Paul takes the charge of "remembering the poor" seriously as an integral part of his apostolic mission. Since his readers already knew this, so goes the argument, he felt confident that he need only mention it in passing. This certainly would not be wrong. From 1 Cor. 16:1–4 we know that he had evidently given his Galatian converts instructions to put aside some money on the first day of each week for the purpose of the collection (vv. 1–2). Once collected, the sum would be sent to "the saints" in Jerusalem (vv. 1, 3). At the time of his writing, Paul had not decided whether or not to accompany the entourage to Jerusalem (v. 4). The term used here, *logeia* (vv. 1, 2), was commonly used for money collected for religious or cultic purposes,[7] which is clearly the meaning here as well. It seems eminently reasonable, therefore, to side with the majority of scholars in taking

---

1998), 15; Richard Horsley, "Submerged Biblical Histories and Imperial Biblical Studies," in *The Postcolonial Bible*, ed. R. S. Sugirtharajah (Sheffield: Sheffield Academic Press, 1998), 152.

The chronology presented below could be controversial, but suffice it to say that the main concern of this essay has to do with the significance and implication of the collection to Paul's ministry and does not depend strictly on my reconstruction.

6. I here agree with the majority of scholars that Gal. 2:1–10 describes the same Jerusalem Council as Acts 15. The polemical overtone of this narrative can be seen in Paul's description of his opponents as "false brothers" (Gal. 2:4).

7. BAGD, 475.

the phrase "to remember the poor" of Gal. 2:10a as a reference to a joint collection effort among gentile churches for the needy in Jerusalem. Since we do not come across any explicit instructions regarding the collection in the extant Galatians, we can safely assume that Paul had given them in some other occasion.

Sound as this answer is, however, it cannot explain the polemical hues with which Paul has painted the collection in Galatians, nor does it explain why Paul would later expend an inordinate amount of his time and energy, not to mention his apostolic prestige, on the project. The nonchalant tone of 1 Corinthians 16 notwithstanding, the collection no doubt occupied central place in his work among gentile churches and became a defining emblem of his apostolate. Just how central the collection was to Paul can be seen in 2 Corinthians, where Paul directly and indirectly mentions the collection no fewer than three more times: in 1:15–16, chapters 8–9, and 12:17–18.[8] That these references are scattered in altogether different letter fragments makes this evidence that much more impressive. Of these the most extensive is chapters 8–9, probably a single letter accompanying a collection party headed by Titus and two unnamed "brothers" (8:6, 16, 18, 22, 23; 9:3). In this letter, Paul extols the Macedonians' generosity for having given to the effort (8:1–5) in spite of their "rock-bottom poverty" (8:2),[9] a comment designed to goad the Corinthians into completing the collection in a timely manner (9:1–5, esp. vv. 2, 4). According to 8:10, the Corinthians had pledged to contribute to the collection a year earlier, an indication that the project had been delayed for at least that long.

We can fairly guess that the Macedonian and Corinthian involvement in the collection effort was long and deep, a suspicion confirmed by Rom. 15:25–27 (esp. v. 26). Still in Corinth, Paul reports that both Macedonia and Achaia, presumably including Corinth, have completed their parts in the collection, and that he will personally convey the funds to Jerusalem.[10] The context for this report is his appeal to the Romans for support in his

---

8. In 1:15–16, with the enigmatic expression "double grace" (*deutera charis*), Paul makes mention of a proposed double visit to the Corinthian congregation. This seems to be the most natural interpretation of the phrase; see Dieter Georgi, *Remembering the Poor: The History of Paul's Collection for Jerusalem* (Nashville: Abingdon Press, 1992), 110; Victor P. Furnish, *II Corinthians*, AB (Garden City, N.Y.: Doubleday, 1984), 133. This proposed visit in all likelihood is related to the collection. Evidently Paul had proposed to visit Corinth on his way to Macedonia and return to Ephesus through the city again — all in an effort to coordinate the collection effort. Paul's subsequent change of mind incurred no small criticism from the Corinthians (2:1–4).

In 12:17–18, Paul defends himself and his associates against the charge of fraud. Referring back to the mission of Titus — which no doubt must have failed to reach its goal of completing the collection — Paul sardonically charges, "I haven't defrauded you through anyone of those I sent you, have I? I urged Titus to go and sent with him our brother: Titus hasn't defrauded you, has he? Didn't we behave by the same Spirit, in the same footsteps?" (12:17–18). Titus's mission must have gone awry for some reason, and Paul is now exercising damage control.

9. Jerome Murphy-O'Connor's apt phrase for *hē kata bathous ptōcheia* (2 Cor. 8:2).

10. This represents a change of plan from what is indicated in 1 Cor. 16:4. In fact, Paul

planned-for Spanish mission. He is about to depart for Jerusalem with the collection; if it is accepted (there is doubt according to v. 31), he will go to Spain via Rome (vv. 22–24, 28–29). In other words, Paul takes the collection to be so central to his own mission that he uses it as a point of departure, literally and figuratively, for his future endeavors.

Just how determined he was to complete the project can be seen already in his parenthetical remark of Gal. 2:10: "[They only asked] that *we* remember the poor, which very same thing *I* was eager to do." The switch from *we* to *I* was made necessary by Paul's split with Barnabas and his subsequent departure from Antioch (Gal. 2:11–13).[11] It is probable that the original Jerusalem Council had been a meeting between the influential churches in Jerusalem and Antioch, and that the resolutions reached therein would have been agreements between these two cities. If that is the case, Paul's departure from Antioch should by right have absolved him from all responsibilities. Yet Paul took it upon himself personally to carry out this task, at tremendous cost.[12] Besides the obvious effort spent on the project, he and his colleagues were suspected of embezzlement (2 Cor. 12:17–18), and the collection even put his life in danger (Rom. 15:31). All this serves only to sharpen our question: What was it about the collection that made Paul willing to sacrifice even his own life?[13]

One answer recognized by the majority of scholars is that Paul was intent on promoting ecumenical unity between gentile and Jewish churches.[14] This is surely right. The collection was a symbol of his mission and a concrete

---

most likely had changed his mind already when he wrote 2 Cor. 1:16b, where he says he had hoped "to be sent on to Judea" by the Corinthians after his double visit.

11. This reconstruction of the events in Antioch can be readily defended and may in fact represent a growing consensus about Gal. 2:11–14.

12. Jerome Murphy-O'Connor, *Paul: A Critical Life* (Oxford: Clarendon Press, 1996), 145; A. J. M. Wedderburn, *The Reasons for Romans* (Edinburgh: T. & T. Clark, 1988), 37–41.

13. Murphy-O'Connor, in *Paul*, 145, thinks it was Paul's conscience that prompted him to continue the collection. But such speculation could hardly account for the comprehensive scope of Paul's efforts.

14. Claimed by, e.g., V. P. Furnish, *II Corinthians*, AB (Garden City, N.Y.: Doubleday, 1984). This is not the place to review the history of scholarship on the collection. Suffice it to say, for now, that the collection could not be merely charity to relieve the economic hardship of the Jerusalem church. The Jerusalem request for funds might well have been prompted by economic hardship, though the length of time it took Paul to complete the collection (at least a year and a half) would indicate that it was not any one particular emergency as such but the general need of the Jerusalem church that was at issue. "Poor" in Gal. 2:10 is notoriously difficult to pin down, which could mean either *economically* poor or *eschatologically* poor. The reference in 2 Cor. 8:14 ("your abundance now might supply their deficiency, so that their abundance might supply your deficiency") might be a bit general, for after all the symmetry of abundance and neediness in this verse might well be just an illustration of equality or equity (*isotēs*). With 2 Cor. 9:12 and Rom. 15:26 ("poor among the saints in Jerusalem"), however, we seem to have incontrovertible evidence that at least some part of the Jerusalem church was genuinely poor in the economic sense. But the exceedingly rich vocabulary that Paul uses in 2 Corinthians 8–9 could not be totally accounted for by a mere concern for the economic plight of the Christians in Judea. Even though there were undoubtedly genuine needs in the Jerusalem church, therefore, some other factors must have motivated the request as well.

expression of his conviction that the church ought to cut across ethnic lines. This is a crucial baseline consensus with which any theory on the collection must reckon. But, sound as it is, this theory does not go far enough. It only pushes the question one step further: Why was the unity between gentile and Jewish congregations so important to Paul that he was willing to risk his life to accomplish it? It might be sobering to recall that Paul was not always the model ecumenist; this is the same Paul, after all, who was ready to consign his fellow Torah-abiding missionaries to the devil![15]

My hypothesis is that Paul consciously pursued the collection as an ethnic Jew, a member of a minority group, a subaltern community under Roman rule. In Christ, the Jewish Messiah who had triumphed over all earthly and secular powers and potentates, he constructed a universalism along Jewish lines which in effect brought all Gentiles into the metanarrative of Israel. This new narrative stood in opposition to and criticism of all Roman imperial political, social, and cultural hegemonic forces, expressions, and institutions, including the patronage system. In bringing Jewish and gentile congregations together, the collection symbolized an emerging universalizing society that came with its own economic principles and bases for structuring life in that society. At the same time, while constructing a universalizing canopy of meanings[16] along Jewish lines, Paul also resisted forces of cultural chauvinism. He severely criticized those who would close the door on Gentiles or insist that Gentiles adapt to Jewish norms before they would be included. Through his effort to bring the collection to a completion, Paul issued a statement against Jewish ethnic exclusiveness. The collection was indeed integral to Paul's mission. It was to him a symbol of resistance and subversion, and it was at heart an anti-imperial and anti-hegemonic protest. At the same time, it was also a daring proposal to reorder economic life together along unabashedly transcendent, universalizing principles.

## Paul's Ethnicity as a Methodological Starting Point

All interpretations and all constructions of reality are ethnocentric. "Ethnocentricity" in this regard does not carry any pejorative sense but is the ineluctable hermeneutical condition from which no interpreter can escape and under which all interpretations are constructed — insofar as no interpreter could escape his or her own ethnicity. The interpretation of an ancient text is always a cross-cultural exercise. The interpreter must bring the cultural background of the text into comparison with his or her own and is thus

---

15. For example, he is ready to lower curses on other missionaries in Gal. 1:8–9; he calls probably the same group of missionaries "false apostles," "deceitful workers," even "ministers of Satan" (2 Cor. 11:13–15).

16. Borrowing the term and concept from Peter Berger. See Peter Berger, *The Sacred Canopy* (Garden City, N.Y.: Doubleday, 1969); and Peter Berger and Thomas Luckmann, *The Social Construction of Reality* (London: Penguin, 1971).

destined to taint the interpretation, wittingly or unwittingly, with some form of ethnocentrism. The interpreter could attempt an emic description of ancient text by describing it from the pure perspective of the original authors, going "native" as it were (using Clifford Geertz's term).[17] In that case there is no cross-cultural understanding, but neither is there true understanding (in the sense of Hans-Georg Gadamer's *Verständnis*) since the interpreter's own horizons are left out of this exercise. Alternatively, the interpreter is left with making an etic attempt to describe the text as "Other," that is, imposing analytic categories in order to describe it in terms intelligible to his or her own cultural and ethnic settings. But in so doing, the interpreter unavoidably inscribes, to however small a degree, his or her modern experience.[18]

Ethnocentricity may be a given in all interpretations, but it does not have to lead to an inexorable ethnocentric politic of identity. As Etienne Balibar has demonstrated, the anthropological theory of Lévi-Strauss, according to which all cultures are equally valid and are therefore above criticism by any other culture, has unintentionally led to the xenophobic rhetorics of ultra-rightist groups in Europe and especially his home country, France. If all cultural groupings have equal right to insular, separate existence, so goes the argument, immigrants and minority groups deemed different from the dominant culture should also keep their distance.[19] What was originally an anti-imperialistic strategy to protect minority rights by sealing them off from intercultural and cross-cultural exchanges has now ironically given fuel to political chauvinism. Ethnocentric hermeneutics, even with all its affirmation of identity and group solidarity, all too easily gives way to cultural and ethnic self-aggrandizement and destructive essentialism. In the felicitous phrase of Homi Bhabha, without cross-cultural and interethnic critique, we are in danger of being seduced by "the celebratory romance of the past" or by the attempt at "homogenizing the history of the present."[20]

There are two approaches to interpreting ethnicity in social anthropology. The primordialist position suggests that ethnicity is a function of "deeply rooted and durable affiliation based on kinship, shared territory and tra-

---

17. Clifford Geertz, *The Interpretation of Cultures: Selected Essays* (New York: Basic Books, 1973).

18. So Brett, "Interpreting Ethnicity," 6–7; see also Howard Eilberg-Schwartz, *The Savage in Judaism: An Anthropology of Israelite Religion and Ancient Judaism* (Bloomington: Indiana University Press, 1990), passim; Pieter F. Craffert, "On New Testament Interpretation and Ethnocentrism," in *Ethnicity and the Bible*, ed. Brett, 155–75; Charles Taylor, "Understanding and Ethnocentricity," in *Philosophy and the Human Sciences* (Cambridge: Cambridge University Press, 1985), 116–33; Khiok-khng Yeo, *Rhetorical Interaction in 1 Corinthians 8 and 10: A Formal Analysis with Preliminary Suggestions for a Chinese, Cross-Cultural Hermeneutic* (Leiden: Brill, 1995), 42 and passim.

19. See Etienne Balibar, "Is There a Neo-Racism?" in *Race, Nation, Class: Ambiguous Identities* (London: Verso, 1991), 17–28; summarized in Brett, "Interpreting Ethnicity," 15–16. See also Homi Bhabha, *The Location of Culture* (London: Routledge, 1994), 37–67.

20. Bhabha, *Location of Culture*, 9.

dition."[21] The constructivist position, on the other hand, sees ethnicity as amorphous and malleable, constantly adapting to changing climates and circumstances, not limited to a particular race, genealogy, or ecology. It credits actors for maintaining the stability of an ethnic group by setting boundaries that divide members from outsiders.[22] Accordingly, while the primordialist approach places its focus on the cultural essence of an ethnic group, the constructivist approach sees ethnic unity as a function not of cultural values and institutional structures that inevitably change but of the maintenance of group boundaries. It is when members of an ethnic group are aware of the existence of boundaries that new cultural values and norms can be adopted, new members be recruited, and structured interactions with outsiders be pursued with confidence. Consequently, the constructivist approach treats an ethnic group not so much as a culture as a social phenomenon. In the words of Fredrik Barth, whose influential 1969 introduction to *Theories of Ethnicity* has done much to conceptualize this position:

> The critical focus of investigation from this point of view becomes the ethnic *boundary* that defines the group, not the cultural stuff that it encloses. The boundaries to which we must give our attention are of course social boundaries, though they may have territorial counterparts. If a group maintains its identity when members interact with others, this entails criteria for determining membership and ways of signalling membership and exclusion. Ethnic groups are not merely or necessarily based on the occupation of exclusive territories; and the different ways in which they are maintained, not only by a once-and-for-all recruitment but by continual expression and validation, need to be analysed.[23]

These "criteria for determining membership and ways of signalling membership and exclusion" can be and often are cultural features, but they should not be confused with a supposedly theoretical set of unchanging, inalienable essence of that particular culture.[24] For example, circumcision might be a

---

21. Brett, in "Interpreting Ethnicity," 12, attributes this position to Edward Shils and, to a lesser extent, Clifford Geertz.

22. The position of Brett (ibid., 12–13) is dependent on Fredrik Barth. On Barth, see below.

23. Fredrik Barth, "Ethnic Groups and Boundaries," in *Theories of Ethnicity: A Classical Reader*, ed. W. Sollors (New York: New York University Press, 1996), 300.

24. Barth starkly decouples culture from ethnicity, even though cultural values can be and are used for the maintenance of ethnic boundaries: "Ethnic boundaries are maintained ... by a limited set of cultural features. The persistence of the unit then depends on the persistence of these cultural differentiae, while continuity can also be specified through the changes of the unit brought about by changes in the boundary-defining cultural differentiae. However, most of the cultural matter that at any time is associated with a human population is *not* constrained by this boundary; it can vary, be learnt, and change without any critical relation to the boundary maintenance of the ethnic group. So when one traces the history of an ethnic group through time, one is *not* simultaneously, in the same sense, tracing the history of 'a culture': the elements of the present culture of that ethnic group have not sprung from the particular set that consti-

criterion for membership in any Jewish group, but one should not take it to be the cultural essence of Judaism. In general, one can distinguish two complementary sets of cultural features used as criteria for marking membership. There are overt signals or signs, "the diacritical features that people look for and exhibit to show identity, often such features as dress, language, house-form, or general style of life." And there are basic value orientations, "the standards of morality and excellence by which performance is judged."[25]

One can readily see that the constructivist approach to ethnicity is especially well suited to the study of Jewish-Gentile relationship in the Pauline churches. The contested issue between Paul and the itinerant teachers in the Galatian church, for example, was precisely one of boundary. When Paul's detractors insisted that gentile converts adopt the overt identity marker, namely circumcision, they were in effect drawing the boundary to coincide with the prevailing Jewish *ethnos*. Paul, for his part, taking the constructivist approach, modeled an entirely and radically new *ethnos* in which "there is no Jew or Greek, no free or slave, no male and female" (Gal. 3:28). The overt identity marker in this new *ethnos* is faith in Christ, made ritually concrete by the public act of baptism, while the basic value orientation governing the internal working of the new group is love (Gal. 5:6, 14). Paul clearly saw no problem redrawing the boundary in the way he did, for he insisted that this was the original intent of the Abrahamic covenant, the true extent of which could now be realized in the inclusion of Gentiles in this new *ethnos*.[26]

Aside from methodological considerations, there are also exegetical reasons to begin with Paul's Jewishness. First of all, ethnicity clearly figured prominently in the Jerusalem Council, which was most likely convened to resolve the problematic relationship between Jewish and gentile Christians over circumcision.[27] If so, the division of labor reached at the conclusion of the council might well have represented a victory for the missionaries to Gentiles. The latter, nevertheless, had to make a concession in the form of a contribution to the church in Jerusalem. Paul's report of it in Gal. 2:10a as

---

tuted the group's culture at a previous time, whereas the group has a continual organizational existence with boundaries (criteria of membership) that despite modifications have marked off a continuing unit"; Barth, "Ethnic Groups and Boundaries," 323.

25. Ibid., 299.

26. Philip F. Esler, "Group Boundaries and Intergroup Conflict in Galatians: A New Reading of Galatians 5:13–6:10," in *Ethnicity and the Bible*, ed. Brett, has already used Barth's constructivist approach for the analysis of intergroup conflicts in Galatians. See Brett, "Interpreting Ethnicity," 14, for using this model for the understanding of shifting cultural values in the peoplehood of Israel down through the ages despite absorbing values and forms from a wide range of cultures, such as Egyptian, Canaanite, Assyrian, Babylonian, Persian, and Hellenistic. Brett also makes a suggestive proposal of using this same model of ethnicity to interpret how dominated groups, once their boundaries are firmly fixed, might willingly and productively use colonial cultural values for the purpose of resisting their colonizers (14–15).

27. These are admittedly shadowy events of which we have a clearer picture in Acts 15. But Paul's insistence that the gentile Titus was not compelled to be circumcised (Gal. 2:3) might well be supporting evidence confirming the report of Acts.

an exception (*monon*) to the general resolution would seem to support this observation.[28] The agreement over the collection was hammered out in the context of an intense wrangling over ethnicity.[29]

Second, an emphasis on ethnicity would help place the collection in the general climate of first-century Jewish-Gentile relationship, in particular as it was manifested in the controversies surrounding the temple tax. Every male over twenty years old was obligated to pay a temple tax of half a shekel for the maintenance of the sacrifice and the cult (Exod. 30:14; Philo, *Spec.* 1.77). This tax would apply to every Levite, Israelite, proselyte, and freed slave (*Shekalim* 1.4), including the so-called God-fearers, according to Josephus (*Ant.* 14.7.2). Women, slaves, and minors were not required to make a contribution, though they could choose to do so (*Shekalim* 1.4). The tax was to be collected from both within Judea and in the diaspora. If the latter, the money would be collected in designated cities to be taken to Jerusalem at appointed days, normally during the Passover (Philo, *Spec.* 1.78; *Prob.* 86). As could be imagined, it must have been a logistically complicated operation of conveying such a large sum of money across great distances. According to Philo, men of high repute, selected from major cities on the basis of their merits, would be appointed "sacred conveyors" (*hieropompoi*) to guide the gift to Jerusalem (*Spec.* 1.77).[30]

Given the obvious similarities between the temple tax and Paul's collection, many have attempted to interpret the latter in light of the former. None is as insistent as Karl Holl, who suggested that the collection was a tax imposed on gentile Christians patterned after the temple tax levied from diaspora Jews and proselytes.[31] It seems difficult to uphold Holl's thesis in its present form, especially since this is clearly not Paul's understanding of it.[32] In none of the passages where Paul mentions the collection does he even hint at a sense of obligation. On the contrary, the opposite is true: Paul repeatedly stresses the voluntary nature of the collection, leaving it to his readers' decision (2 Cor. 8:10–12, 9:7; Rom. 15:26–27). It is possible that the Jerusalem church and Paul had different understandings of the agreement: while the Jerusalem church thought of the collection as a form of tax, Paul and his gentile churches might have taken it to be an entirely voluntary affair.[33] But ultimately, since there is no direct report of the collection except

---

28. Heinrich Schlier, *Der Brief an die Galater*, 10th ed. (Göttingen: Vandenhoeck and Ruprecht, 1949), 46; H. D. Betz, *Galatians: A Commentary on Paul's Letter to the Churches in Galatia*, Hermeneia (Philadelphia: Fortress Press, 1979), 101.

29. Contra Georgi, *Remembering the Poor*, 33–42.

30. For a more detailed discussion, see Keith F. Nickle, *The Collection: A Study in Paul's Strategy*, Studies in Biblical Theology 48 (Naperville, Ill.: Allenson, 1966), 74–86.

31. Karl Holl, "Der Kirchenbegriff des Paulus in seinem Verhältnis zu dem der Urgemeinde," in *Gesammelte Aufsätze zur Kirchengeschichte* (Tübingen: J. C. B. Mohr [Siebert], 1928), 44–67.

32. See the persuasive arguments by Leander Keck, "The Poor among the Saints in the New Testament," *ZNW* 56 (1965): 125–27.

33. This possibility has more recently been raised by Bengt Holmberg, *Paul and Power: The*

those of Paul, it seems abstractly speculative at best to try to differentiate between the two.

Nevertheless, Holl's thesis does point us in the right direction. The temple tax and the special privileges granted to the Jews for the collection of the tax had fostered a general distrust between Jews and Gentiles, and this remains the most useful background against which we interpret the collection. The temple tax levied from the diaspora Jewish communities was a source of friction between the Jews and the Roman authorities. The latter objected that gold was being channeled out of their provinces and funneled into the Jerusalem temple. Cicero's defense of Flaccus, the Roman governor in Asia Minor who seized a sum of money collected for the temple in 62 B.C.E., affords us a glimpse of the authorities' resentment (*Pro Flacco* 28.67):

> When every year it was customary to send gold to Jerusalem on the order of the Jews from Italy and from all our provinces, Flaccus forbade by an edict its exportation from Asia. Who is there, gentlemen, who could not honestly praise this action? The senate often earlier and also in my consulship most urgently forbade the export of gold. But to resist this barbaric superstition was an act of firmness.[34]

Even though the situation was supposedly rectified by the edict of Augustus, under which, *inter alia*, the rights of the Jews to collect temple tax from the diaspora were protected,[35] periodic disputes over this issue were not uncommon. The friction evidently also boiled over to the general public, resulting in great resentment among the populace toward the supposed wealth of the Jews and especially the wealth of the temple. Under these circumstances, the temple tax must have appeared to Gentiles like a grand Jewish scheme for financial extortion or control. Titus, addressing the Jewish tyrants who had surrendered to him, recounts, not without a note of sarcasm, the benevolent acts the Romans have bestowed upon the Jews:

> No, assuredly you were incited against the Romans by Roman humanity. To begin with, we allowed you to occupy this land and set over you kings of your own blood; then we maintained the laws of your forefathers and permitted you, not only among yourselves but also in your dealings with others, to live as you willed; above all (*to de megiston*), we permitted you to exact tributes for God and to collect offerings, without either admonishing or hindering those who brought them — only that you might grow richer at our expense and make preparations

---

*Structure of Authority in the Primitive Church as Reflected in the Pauline Epistles* (Philadelphia: Fortress Press, 1978), 41: "It is not improbable that they interpreted [the collection] differently. The church of Jerusalem understood it as 'a duty' that documented its spiritual supremacy, while Paul gave it a more theological interpretation as an acknowledgment of Jerusalem's actual importance in God's election."

34. Trans. Louis Lord, Cicero, LCL 10.

35. So according to Josephus, *Ant.* 16.160–65; on other Roman authorities see 16.167–70.

with our money to attack us! And then, enjoying such privileges, you turned your superabundance against the donors, and like untameable reptiles spat your venom upon those who caressed you. (Jos. *Bell.*, 6.335–36 LCL)[36]

All this could not but have played an important background in the thinking of Paul the diaspora Jew.

Finally, to take ethnicity as the context in which to understand the collection sensitizes us to Jewish insurrectionary fervor brewing in Jerusalem. According to Josephus, two events in 66 C.E. precipitated the outbreak of the Great Revolt: the Jewish insurgents' capture of Masada and the priests' refusal to accept gifts and sacrifices for the temple from Gentiles (*Bell.* 2.408–9). Temple sacrifices by and for Gentiles were mainly performed on behalf of the emperor (Jos., *Bell.* 2.197); in lieu of taking part in the imperial cult, it was the only Jewish expression of loyalty to the Roman Empire. Cessation of that sacrifice, therefore, could only mean open revolt. It seems reasonable to assume that these anti-Roman feelings had already been brewing at the time of Paul's visit to Jerusalem, a mere ten years before the open revolt.

Paul himself might well be alluding to this explosive situation in Rom. 15:31: "[Offer prayers for me] that (*hina*) I might be *rescued* (*rhyesthai*) from the *unbelievers* in Judea and my ministry to Jerusalem may be acceptable to the saints." Paul always uses "unbelievers" (*hoi apeithountes*) in Romans to refer to Jews who do not acknowledge the messiahship of Jesus (see 2:8; 10:21; 11:30, 31; cf. the use of *apeitheia* in 11:30, 32), and he uses "rescue" (*rhyesthai*) in his letters to refer to deliverance from death or worse (Rom. 7:24, 11:26; 1 Cor. 1:10 3x; 1 Thess 1:10). In this passage, then, Paul is anticipating impending danger about to be brought on by Jerusalemites who are outside the Christian circles. Walter Schmithals has argued on the basis of a single *hina* that the two threats mentioned here — that "unbelievers" might bring harm to Paul and that the collection might be refused — are in fact only one: "the menace from the Jews is connected with the pos-

---

36. See also Tacitus, *History* 5.5: "[The Jewish] worship, however introduced, is upheld by its antiquity; all their other customs, which are at once perverse and disgusting, owe their strength to their very badness. *The most degraded out of other races*, scorning their national beliefs, brought to them their contributions and presents. This augmented the wealth of the Jews.... Those who come over to their religion adopt the practice, and have this lesson first instilled into them, to despise all gods, to disown their country, and set at nought parents, children, and brethren" (*Complete Works of Tacitus*, ed. Moses Hadas, trans. Alfred J. Church and William J. Brodribb [New York: Modern Library, 1942], 659–60; emphasis added). Though proselytes to Judaism were generally derided during Roman times, even to the point of occasional legal proscriptions against conversion (see, e.g., Modestinus, *The Rules*, Book 6; Julius Paulus, *Opinion*, 5.22.3–4), Tacitus's statement raises the distinct possibility that proselytes, who would be required to pay the temple tax, were ridiculed especially for the reason of contributing to Jewish wealth. Many of the Jewish and non-Jewish sources on conversion to Judaism are now collected in Louis J. Feldman and Meyer Reinhold, eds., *Jewish Life and Thought among Greeks and Romans: Primary Readings* (Minneapolis: Fortress Press, 1996), 123–45.

sible rejection of the contributions: 'Pray that the Jews do not harm me and (therefore) my contributions are welcome to the Christians.' "[37]

The acceptance of gifts and sacrifice from Gentiles in the temple has always been ambiguously treated. On the one hand, there seems to be a tradition that contributions to the temple made by Samaritans and Gentiles would be rejected (*Shekalim* 1.5).[38] On the other hand, there is good evidence that Gentiles were always allowed to make sacrifices in the temple; the refusal of gentile sacrifices had such grave implications for the revolt precisely because they had been presupposed all along.[39] Given the heightened anti-Roman fervor, it is not without reason to assume that advocates of independence would exert pressure on the Christian groups in Jerusalem to demonstrate solidarity with their cause. Paul's bringing a substantial gift from abroad would place him squarely in the midst of this mounting tension.[40] If Acts 20:4 indeed describes the gentile entourage accompanying Paul to Jerusalem for the delivery of the gift, as I will argue below to be the case,[41] that would certainly give Paul good reason to fear for his safety.

## The Collection in Light of Jewish Universalism: Romans 15

If Paul conceived of the collection as a means of promoting unity between Jewish and gentile congregations, and there appears little doubt that this was the case, it is only to be expected that it would embroil Paul in a dispute over two competing sets of boundary markers. On the one side were traditional Jewish ethnic boundaries that were based on such overt signs as circumcision and dietary restrictions and on such basic value orientation as the fulfillment of the Torah. On the other were his own expanded boundaries based on a faith-centered reading of the Abrahamic covenant. In Paul's new *ethnos*, the overt sign was faith in Christ which, unlike circumcision, would decouple group identity from genealogical lineage but stress spiritual continuity with the founding event of this new social reality. Basic value orientation that

---

37. Walter Schmithals, *Paul and James* (London: SCM, 1965), 82; cited in James D. G. Dunn, *Romans*, Word Biblical Commentary 38AB (Dallas: Word Books, 1988), 2:879.

38. Text cited in Nickle, *The Collection*, 79 n. 38: "If a heathen or a Cuthean paid the shekel it is not accepted of them."

39. See also *War* 2.412–13; and other texts found in Emil Schürer, *The History of the Jewish People in the Age of Jesus Christ*, vol. 2, A New English Edition, rev. and ed. by G. Vermes, F. Millar, M. Black, and P. Vermes (Edinburgh: T. & T. Clark, 1979), 309–13. There is, of course, the possibility that sacrifices made on behalf of the emperor were sharply distinguished from gentile sacrifices by commoners.

40. See Dunn, *Romans*, 2.880.

41. So Johannes Munck, *Paul and the Salvation of Mankind* (Richmond, Va.: John Knox, 1959), 293–97, 303–4, followed by many others.

permeated the ethos of the group was the new law of Christ — to love each other — replacing the centrality of the Torah.[42]

In Galatians, his strategy has been one of confrontation. There he sets up a binarism that leaves no room for compromise: the new *ethnos* replaces the old, and gentile converts are given no choice but to be incorporated into the new community. In Romans, however, his strategy appears to be much more nuanced. In using the ubiquitous phrase "Jews and Greeks" in the letter, Paul simultaneously appeals to two ethnic myths to make his points. In dividing humanity into Jews and non-Jews, he subscribes to a *myth of otherness* to reinscribe the us-versus-them mentality prevalent among some of his compatriots. In calling all Gentiles "Greeks," he is at the same time subscribing to a *myth of sameness*, in order to reinforce the Jewish-gentile distinction. What Paul adopts here is the language of insiders — that is, insiders as defined by the old boundaries based on genealogy, one that he explicitly rejects in Galatians! Only a Jew would find it acceptable to divide humanity into "Jews and Greeks" (1:16; 2:9–10; 3:9, 29; 9:24; 10:12; and so on),[43] just as only a Chinese would divide the world into "Chinese and Barbarians." Both statements are self-evidently ethnocentric in that they privilege one ethnic group by using them as the standard by which all others are evaluated. Outsiders are made doubly "other" in that their own ethnic distinctiveness is flattened out of existence — as "Greeks" and "Barbarians" regardless of their own ethnicity — for no other reason than that they are different from the insiders. Paul uses this rhetorical strategy of the old distinction between "Jews and Greeks" in order to argue that they are now bound by the same membership requirement, namely faith. The world is indeed divided into Jews and Greeks, but at the end they are equally culpable (chaps. 1–3), just as they are equally in need of grace given through the Last Adam (chap. 5).[44]

As Paul prepares to conclude his letter (15:15–33), reiterating his desire to be supported by the Romans in his Spanish mission (vv. 22–24, 28–29) and reporting on the collection (vv. 25–27, 31), he does so from a Jewish vantage point. He explains that even though he has been appointed an apostle to the Gentiles, he is "a priest of Christ Jesus" bringing "the offering of the Gentiles" which has been "sanctified by the Holy Spirit" (v. 16) and leading them to obedience (v. 18). To quote 15:15–16 in full:

---

42. This is the basic conclusion of Esler, "Group Boundaries and Intergroup Conflict in Galatians," 215–40. Esler's thesis is based on his reading of Galatians, but it is fair to say that it can be generalized as Paul's *modus operandus* in his dealing with gentile churches.

43. To be sure, similar emphasis can be found in 1 Cor. 1:22–24, 12:13; Gal. 3:28. But nowhere else does Paul pursue the relationship between Jews and Gentiles in quite so insistent and systematic manner as he does in Romans.

44. The recent work of Mark D. Nanos, *The Mystery of Romans* (Minneapolis: Fortress Press, 1996), also pursues the same reading of Romans from the perspective of Paul's Jewishness.

I wrote you quite boldly on some points, as if to remind you, because of the grace given to me by God to be a priest [*leitourgos*] of Christ Jesus to the Gentiles, while I perform a priestly [*hierourgōn*] function with regard to the gospel of God, in order that the offering of the Gentiles [*hē prosphora tōn ethnōn*], sanctified by the Holy Spirit, might be acceptable [*euprosdektos*].

The high concentration of cultic language is no accident but is probably a deliberate effort to portray his missionary work among Gentiles as conforming to the requirements of Jewish religiosity. But is it possible that the cultic language used here is also influenced by the collection to be described in verses 25–27, and that the collection is in turn compared with the temple tax?

The evidence is all allusive, but it is not impossible that this is the case. The vast majority of commentators take *tōn ethnōn* in "offering of the Gentiles"[45] as an objective genitive or genitive of apposition and the phrase to mean "the evangelized Gentiles who are consecrated and offered to God as an acceptable sacrifice through Paul's evangelization of them."[46] But if so, this would be the only incident in which Paul expresses such an understanding of his relationship to his gentile converts; elsewhere he talks of presenting his converts as a bride to Christ (2 Cor. 11:2). When he does use sacrificial language, he uses it as a metaphor for the believers' own bodies (e.g., Rom. 12:1) or applies it to himself (Phil. 2:17).[47]

There are several arguments that support taking the "offering" of verse 16 as the object of "the Gentiles." First of all, he describes the Philippians' gift to him as "a fragrant offering, an acceptable sacrifice (*thysia dektē*), well-pleasing (*euarestos*) to God" (Phil. 4:18).[48] Second, the use of *euprosdektos* in Rom. 15:16 possibly anticipates the same use of the word in 15:31, where Paul hopes that the collection will be accepted. In 2 Cor. 8:12, *euprosdektos* is used in relation to the collection. The only other use of the word, in 2 Cor. 6:2, is an exegetical comment motivated by *dektos* in the citation of Isa. 49:8. Paul's usual word to express a well-pleasing sacrifice is

45. *Prosphora* is a *hapax* in the New Testament.

46. Joseph A. Fitzmyer, *Romans: A New Translation with Introduction and Commentary,* AB (New York: Doubleday, 1992), 712. Fitzmyer states, "Because the *finis* of all sacrifice is to bring about in some way the return of sinful human beings to God, Paul looks on his work among the Gentiles as a form of sacrifice, for their conversion has achieved that very purpose. The Apostle of the Gentiles offers to God not slaughtered animals, but repentant human beings, and this is the *prosphora* acceptable to God." Cf. Munck, *Paul and the Salvation of Mankind,* 50–51 (esp. 50 n. 3), 202.

47. Johannes Behm, "*thyō, etc.,*" *TDNT* 3 (1965): 185. Peter T. O'Brien, *The Epistle to the Philippians: A Commentary on the Greek Text,* The New International Greek Testament Commentary (Grand Rapids, Mich.: Eerdmans, 1991), 304–10, disagrees, however, and thinks that Phil. 2:7 speaks of Paul presenting the converts as sacrifice; but O'Brien explicitly rejects any connection between Phil. 2:7 and Rom. 15:16. The evidence of 2 Cor. 2:14–15 is too ambiguous to be of help here; if it does use cultic language, it describes Paul himself as the sacrifice.

48. Georgi, *Remembering the Poor,* 62–67.

*euarestos* (Rom. 12:1–2, Phil. 4:18). Third, if Paul's trip to Jerusalem that is recounted in Acts 20:1–21:6 is the same one anticipated in Romans, Paul's entourage would have included a sizable contingent of Gentiles (Acts 20:4), leaders from the various Macedonian and Achaian cities (though not Corinth) that would have contributed to the collection. It is therefore not out of the question that *tōn ethnōn* can be taken as a subjective genitive and that *hē prosphora tōn ethnōn* contains a double reference: While it speaks of the Gentiles as Paul's offering, it also alludes to the Gentiles' contribution, namely the collection, as an offering.

The use of cultic language in the context of an impending trip to Jerusalem naturally conjures up the image of temple sacrifice. In this respect, it is possible that Paul might be borrowing terms from those associated with the temple tax to describe the collection.[49] As mentioned before, there is no evidence that Paul understood the collection to be a tax imposed on the Gentiles. But that would not prevent him from deliberately drawing parallels between the collection and the temple tax. Paul, first of all, knew he could transport money out of Macedonia and Achaia into Judea. This could only mean that he assumed that he was operating under the same imperial protection, the exemption given to Judaism as a *collegium licitum* for the regular temple tax.[50] Second, there are possible verbal similarities between standard vocabulary established in association with the temple tax and Paul's language in Rom. 15:16. Convoys appointed to bring the taxes to Jerusalem were called *hieropompoi* and Paul thinks of himself as *hierourgounta to euangelion ton theou*. The use of the *hiero*-compound here is striking. The term *hierourgein* is a *hapax legomenon* in the New Testament; the closest parallel is found in a *varia lectio* in 4 Macc. 7:8, where the dying martyr is said to have served as a priest to the law (*hierourgein ton nomon*). Third, while the tax itself was sometimes called *phoros*, a term Paul himself uses in Rom. 13:6, his ministry is a *prosphora*. And while tax collectors working for the Roman authorities are called *leitourgoi tou theou* in Rom. 13:6, Paul calls himself a *leitourgos Christou Iēsou* (on *leitourgos*, see also my discussion of 15:27 below). All these are at best rough echoes, admittedly, not exact parallels or even references, which is evidence that Paul never perceived the collection as a temple tax. But it may be enough to suggest that he saw the collection as in some way functioning in parallel fashion to the temple tax, a well-known institution with which he no doubt would have been familiar.

---

49. Since the temple tax was levied precisely for the purpose of maintaining the cultic functions in the temple. On the cultic function of the collection, see Nickle, *The Collection*, 74–76, 78–80.

50. E. Mary Smallwood, *Philonis Alexandrini Legatio ad Gaium: Edited with an Introduction, Translation, and Commentary* (Leiden: E. J. Brill, 1970), 3–14; E. Mary Smallwood, *The Jews under Roman Rule* (Leiden: E. J. Brill, 1976), 133–34. I owe this point to an unpublished manuscript by Robin Scroggs, "The Political Dimension of Anti-Judaism in the New Testament."

If the foregoing is correct, the composite picture in Rom. 15:16 is that of Paul bringing with him to Jerusalem a group of Gentiles bearing gifts, an event that he describes in cultic terms and that he might have compared with the official temple levy whose main function was cultic. The background of Paul's thinking at this point would seem to point to the eschatological fulfillment prophesied in, among other places, Isa. 2:2–3, 60:4–7, 61:6, and Micah 4:1–2, where the end time is heralded by the wealth of the nations flowing into Jerusalem.[51] In the end time, Zion will become the center of the new world:

> Lift up your eyes and look around; they all gather together, they come to you; your sons shall come from far away, and your daughters shall be carried on their nurses' arms. Then you shall see and be radiant; your heart shall thrill and rejoice, because the abundance of the sea shall be brought to you, *the wealth of the nations shall come to you.* A multitude of camels shall cover you, the young camels of Midian and Ephah; all those from Sheba shall come. They shall bring gold and frankincense — and shall proclaim the praise of the Lord. All the flocks of Kedar shall be gathered to you, the rams of Nebaioth shall minister to you; *they shall be acceptable on my altar*, and I will glorify my glorious house. (Isa. 60:4–7, NRSV, emphasis added)

Such a vision is, of course, political through and through, for it proclaims an all-encompassing sovereignty, to which all empires, including the Roman Empire, must pay obeisance. And Zion is the new capital to which all nations will have to make tributes. This Jewish universalism would serve as a form of resistance as well: the world-governing scope of the colonizers is thoroughly relativized and crippled by this eschatological fulfillment. According to this schema, the gentile converts play a role, albeit a subordinate role, in the climactic drama unfolding in Jerusalem. Their arrival in Jerusalem signals this eschatological age, the gift they bring is an offering acceptable to God, and, if the temple tax indeed stands in the background, they also conform with the general institutional and cultic patterns of the Jerusalem temple.

Many of these points can be corroborated in Paul's explicit description of the collection in Rom. 15:25–28:

> Now I am going to Jerusalem ministering to the saints. For Macedonia and Achaia were pleased to share their resources with the poor among the saints [*hoi ptōchoi tōn hagiōn*] in Jerusalem. They were pleased to do so — and they are their debtors [*opheileta autōn*] — for if the Gentiles shared in their spiritual things [*tois pneumatikois*], they are also obligated to provide a service [*opheilousi . . . leitourgēsai*] for them

---

51. This is the famous thesis of Munck, *Paul and the Salvation of Mankind*, 282–305, but especially 303–4. Fuller references can be found in Dunn, *Romans*, 2.874.

in material things [*tois sarkikois*]. When, therefore, I have completed this and sealed this fruit for them, I will go to Spain through you.

This passage is full of language of subordination, with the result that while Gentiles are fully incorporated into a Jewish milieu, they are nevertheless placed in a subordinate position. Paul does envision the collection to be primarily a voluntary venture (see *eudokein* [*bis*] in vv. 26–27), but he also reiterates twice that Gentiles are indebted to the Jews. The antecedent of "their" in "*their* debtors" (v. 27) is usually taken to be "*the poor* among the saints in Jerusalem" of verse 26.[52] But the general sense of verse 27 would seem to require it to refer to "the saints" of verses 25–26 instead, since it is clear that Paul wants to say the Gentiles have received the divine blessings, that is, the gospel through the Jews in general, Jewish Christians in particular, and not just through "the poor." Accordingly, because it was through the Jews that Gentiles have come to receive the spiritual things, the latter are now "obligated to provide a service" for the former. This they do by means of imparting to Jerusalem "material (literally, fleshly) things" (v. 27). In this manner Paul stresses the subordination of Gentiles in his Jewish vision of eschatological universalism.[53]

The verb *leitourgein* is used only here in the Pauline corpus, and it is unclear whether it has a cultic sense ("to serve as a priest") or a secular sense ("to serve the need") in the present context. Elsewhere in the New Testament it carries the cultic sense of rendering worship to God (so Acts 13:2, Heb. 10:11). The noun *leitourgia* ("cultic service" or simply "service" in the secular sense), on the other hand, is used six times (Luke 1:23; 2 Cor. 9:12; Phil. 2:17, 30; Heb 8:6, 9:21). Among these, the references in Hebrews are probably motivated by its peculiar Christology, and the one in Luke portrays high-priestly work. Of the three uses by Paul, Phil. 2:17 refers to the pouring out of his life as a libation and sacrifice to God; the cultic allusion of this saying is unmistakable. In Phil. 2:30, however, the word appears to refer to a sum of money, which Epaphroditus, "a *leitourgos* of [Paul's] need" (see 2:25), risks his life to bring to Paul. Likewise, in 2 Cor. 9:12, which in language is very similar to Phil. 2:30, the word is used to refer to the collection itself.[54] The evidence thus far is ambiguous. In favor of seeing *leitourgein* in Rom. 15:27 in the cultic sense is the parallel with *leitourgos* (15:16), which has a cultic sense of being a priest (see above). In favor of the secular usage is Phil. 2:25, 30, where *leitourgos* and *leitourgein* have only the secular sense.

---

52. Most commentators, rightly, take *tōn ethnōn* of v. 26 as a partitive genitive: so Murphy-O'Connor, *Paul*, 144; and Dunn, *Romans*, 2.875.

53. H. D. Betz, *2 Corinthians 8 and 9: A Commentary on Two Administrative Letters of the Apostle Paul*, Hermeneia (Philadelphia: Fortress Press, 1985), 124 and n. 284, thinks that the Gentiles owe to the Jerusalem churches in Rom. 15:27.

54. H. Strathmann, *"leitourgeō, etc.,"* TDNT 4 (1967): 227.

On balance, especially in view of the close analogy to 2 Cor. 9:12 and Phil. 2:30, it seems best to take the verb in the secular sense of "providing service to another person." In Rom. 15:16 Paul calls himself "a priest of Christ Jesus," "performing a priestly function the gospel of God." But there is no such parallel in verse 27. Given Paul's emphasis on Jewish identity in Romans 15 in general, it would make little sense to read in 15:27 of Gentiles serving as priests to the Jews.[55] If so, Paul in 15:27 again subtly places Gentiles in a relatively subordinate position. This subordination is further reinforced by the contrast between *pneumatikos* and *sarkikos*. In light of the prevalence of the spirit-flesh contrast in Romans, we ought not weaken the contrast but to understand the terms in the full sense of "spiritual" and "fleshly." In short, since the Gentiles have shared in the "spiritual things" with the saints in Jerusalem, the least they can do is to supply their material needs by supplying them with "fleshly things."

An examination of Paul's ethnocentric vocabulary in Romans 15 yields expected as well as surprising results. Paul consciously constructs a new *ethnos* by using an old insider-outsider distinction (Jews versus Gentiles), but in so doing he also asserts that they are dependent on each other in a complementary way. They have both benefited from each other, albeit to different extents. In Barth's language, mutuality between gentile and Jewish congregations is a part of the "basic value orientations" that define the group boundaries of the new Christ-centered *ethnos*. Paul has constructed a new symbolic universe based on mutual obligation. All this meets our initial expectations. But surprisingly, while Paul insists that the collection for the saints is entirely voluntary in nature, and while he affirms the universal ecumenicity between Jews and Gentiles in the worldwide community, he also makes it quite clear to his readers that it is an essentially Jewish vision in which the Gentiles participate and that it is a Jewish institution (the temple?) into which Gentiles have been incorporated. It would be a gross exaggeration to say that Paul subordinates Gentiles to the Jews, but it would do injustice to Paul if we do not see that, through the collection, he asserts his Jewish identity and at least hints at gentile subordination in the economic structure of the new group.[56]

While espousing a Jewish universalism, Paul also expresses his dismay at ethnocentric chauvinism. He sensed himself to be in mortal danger because of his impending delivery of the collection, apparently from conservative ethnocentric fellow Jews (Rom. 15:31). The cause, as I have shown above, is most likely his insistence on including Gentiles in this universalism. It is the tension between ethnocentricity and inclusiveness that finally imbues the Pauline universalism with paradoxical vitality.

The result of Paul's efforts is a statement that is subtly anti-imperial in that

---

55. Contra Dunn, *Romans*, 2.876.
56. This conclusion contradicts to a large extent that of Dunn, *Romans*, 874.

it constructs a reality outside, beyond, but also encompassing all earthly empires, especially the Roman Empire. This is a cosmic vision into which even non-Jews are ushered. Rather than eschew universal claims, a move postcolonial readers would have liked him to make, he unabashedly constructs a metanarrative based on his own ethnicity, an eschatological universalism. In this, Paul's own ethnic aspirations and integrity are affirmed in a most dramatic way: it subsumes all imperial claims under this overall vision and it subjects all Gentiles under its sphere of influence.

Apart from a broad critique of the Roman Empire, Paul also found fault with the prevailing patronage system that formed the economic backbone of the Roman city. Paul accomplished this, again with delicate subtlety, by distancing the benefactors from the recipients so as not to create a direct obligatory relationship between the two. An examination of Paul's rhetoric in his solicitation letter for the Jerusalem church will underscore this point.

## An Anti-Patronal Appeal: 2 Corinthians 8–9

These two chapters, in my judgment, form a literary unity, amounting to a single letter of recommendation for Titus (8:6, 16–17, 23) and two unnamed "brothers" (8:18–19, 22) appointed to lead an advance delegation to Corinth for the purpose of the collection.[57] In the course of the letter, Paul adds an urgent appeal to the Corinthians to complete the collection, a project to which they had initially pledged their support the year before but which they had yet to bring to satisfactory conclusion (9:2).

Reading this letter through the lens of Romans 15, one is immediately struck by how little the supposedly dire situation of the poor in Jerusalem is used in the appeal. One could speculate that the plight of the Jerusalem church was already so well known to the recipients that Paul could omit mentioning it from this letter, but it seems unthinkable that Paul would not use that crucial piece of information to try to garner sympathy from the Corinthians at all, especially since Paul views the issue as a matter of urgency. In view of all the other rhetorical arguments Paul uses in this letter to the end of completing the collection (e.g., the use of rivalry between the Macedonians and Achaians, 8:1–5, 9:2–4; the sending of an advance party, 9:3, 5; the pressure of his personal visit, 9:4), the omission could not be accidental. The answer may have to do with Paul's desire to decouple the

---

57. For arguments that chapters 8–9 constitute a single letter, see Sze-kar Wan, *Power in Weakness: Conflict and Rhetoric in Paul's Second Letter to the Corinthians*, The New Testament in Context (Harrisburg, Pa.: Trinity Press International, 2000), 112–14. See also Furnish, *II Corinthians*, 429–33; I do not, however, subscribe to Furnish's theory that the whole of chapters 1–9 form one single letter (35–44). Contra Betz, *2 Corinthians 8 and 9*, 3–36; and Georgi, *Remembering the Poor*, 75–79. It should be noted, however, that my remarks below do not depend on a particular theory about the literary composition of these two chapters.

Corinthians' contribution from their patronal expectation that the Jerusalem church could become obligated to them as a result of the gift.

Paul does use the term "lack" or "want" (*hysterēma*) in two passages in this letter (8:14 *bis;* 9:12), but in both cases, Paul chooses his language carefully so as to minimize any connection between the bestowal of gift and its reception by the Jerusalem church. In the first instance Paul speaks of "their want" as a part of a longer note on equality or equity (*isotēs*) in 8:13–14:

> For it is not a matter of relief to others and affliction to you, but it is a matter of equality [*isotēs*]: in the present time, your abundance is to supply *their want* [*hysterēma*], so that *their abundance* may supply *your want* [*hysterēma*], in order that there be equality [*isotēs*].

The most common interpretation of "their want" is that it refers to the material needs of the Jerusalem Christians.[58] This is possible, but that would not be consistent with the clearly metaphorical uses of "their abundance" and "your want" in verse 14b. The latter are unambiguous references to the Jerusalem Christians' abundance and the Corinthians' want. But in what sense are the Corinthians said to be "lacking"? Paul does not mean it in the material sense, for that is the very reason for the writing of this letter. Nor can it be meant in the spiritual sense, since they have just been made rich as a result of Christ's poverty in verse 9 ("For you know the generous act of our Lord Jesus Christ, that though he was rich, yet for your sakes he became poor, so that by his poverty you might become rich"). An appeal to Rom. 15:27 ("since the Gentiles shared in their spiritual things, they are also obligated to provide a service for them in material things") is no help, for it does not in fact speak of the Gentiles' want, only their having shared in the spiritual richness of the Jews.[59] Neither can we solve the problem by taking verse 14b as a reference to a future messianic kingdom,[60] since all this is supposed to take place "in the present time" (*en tō nyn kairō* in v. 14).

It seems most sensible to take verses 13–14 simply as a general illustration of the notion of equity. Paul begins by saying that he intends to appeal to the Corinthians' surplus of funds ("For if the desire is present, it is acceptable for what one has, not what does not have"; v. 12). He then amplifies it by adducing an absurd proposition, that others would be relieved while the Corinthians suffer (v. 13a), a proposition that should be rejected out of hand for it does not take into consideration equity (v. 13b). Clearly the economic situation in Jerusalem inspires the proposition, but only as a support for the notion of equity; the statement is not meant to highlight the plight of the church. Likewise, verse 14 should be read the same way:

---

58. So Betz, *2 Corinthians 8 and 9*, 68; Ralph P. Martin, *2 Corinthians*, Word Biblical Commentary (Waco, Tex.: Word, 1986), 267, among many others.

59. Betz, *2 Corinthians 8 and 9*, 68, evidently realizes this problem.

60. So Georgi, *Remembering the Poor*, 89–90; and Martin, *2 Corinthians*, 267.

the symmetry of aid, which corresponds to a symmetry of want, is again a general illustration of equity. The economic plight of the Jerusalem church probably stands behind "their want" as well, but it remains but a corroborative example of the more general principle of equity. The formula thus begins with equity and ends with equity.[61] If this is correct, the identity of the Jerusalem church, while present throughout Paul's appeal, remains unexpressed and hidden in the background. Paul chooses instead to appeal to the Corinthians' understanding of equity as motivation for contributing to the collection.

In a second passage, "the wants" are explicitly associated with "the saints" (9:12), but here the reference is embedded in such a web of obligations that it would be difficult to deduce from it a direct patronal obligation owed by the Jerusalem church to the Corinthians.

> In everything, you are being made rich [*ploutizomenoi*] for the purpose of every generosity, which produces thanksgiving to God through us, because the ministry of this service [*hē diakonia tēs leitourgias tautēs*] not only supplies the wants of the saints [*ta hysterēmata tōn hagiōn*] but also abounds in many thanksgiving to God. (9:11–12)

The collection, first of all, is termed "the ministry of this service" (*hē diakonia tēs leitourgias tautēs*) in verse 12. The word *leitourgia*, as we saw earlier in light of Rom. 15:27 and Phil. 2:30, could mean the secular sense of "service," and that seems to be the sense here as well.

The "ministry of this service," furthermore, produces "thanksgiving to God," making it formally and functionally parallel to the "generosity" of verse 11, which also produces the same. But generosity comes as a result of the Corinthians' "having been made rich" (*ploutizomenoi*). The participle of verse 11 has no syntactical antecedent, though the context (esp. vv. 6–10) requires that *the Corinthians* be made rich; it is therefore dependent on *hymōn* of verse 10, and God the supplier of seeds is the source of the richness. If all this is correct, a similar kind of circularity as we have seen before governs the logic here as well. Just as it is out of the principle of equality that there be a mutuality of succor and consequently equity (8:13–14), so also in 9:11–12 it is God who makes the Corinthians rich, so that through a service to the saints' needs they could render thanksgiving back to God.[62] Paul makes sure that the Corinthians understand that the giving

---

61. The meaning of equity is probably not that of Hellenistic-Jewish wisdom tradition, to which Philo devoted a sizable treatise (*Her.* 141–206); so Georgi, *Remembering the Poor*, 84–89, 138–40. It could simply be the more general sense of equality or equity being a defining character of nature or the political arena.

62. Betz, *2 Corinthians 8 and 9*, 122–25, suggests that *homologia* in v. 13 means a contractual document binding the giver of the money (the Corinthians) to its recipient (the Jerusalem church). In effect, according to Betz, Paul is making the gentile churches (as represented by the Corinthians) submit to the authority of the Jerusalem church. Betz's thesis, if correct, would greatly strengthen my point here, but I remain skeptical, not the least because that seems to

of money can only be issued out of a sense of equity, an equity that is safeguarded by noting the ultimate source and end of giving. The Corinthian church is in a position to give because God the supplier has provided them with wealth in the first place; accordingly, the ultimately purpose of giving is to render thanksgiving to God. In 9:11–12, just as in 8:13–14, by putting the economic hardship of the Jerusalem church in the background, Paul consciously disengages the Jerusalem church from the gentile churches, so that the former would not be placed in a direct obligatory relationship to the latter.

Paul accomplishes this theologically as well. In chapter 8 he uses Christ's death as a theological foundation upon which he appeals to the Corinthians. He reminds his readers that it is the "poverty" of Christ that makes them rich (v. 9). Whatever else this Christological formula means, one of its points is no doubt the self-sacrificial example of Christ, which the Corinthians ought to emulate. But that does not exhaust the meaning, for the second half of the citation says, "in order that you yourselves [*hymeis*] be rich because of his [*ekeinou*] poverty." Here *hymeis* is emphatic and the use of *ekeinou* instead of *autou*[63] is deliberate: the Corinthians have become rich because of *someone else's* sacrificial giving. This is to say, their wealth is ultimately not their own. Its real source is somewhere else, and it is at best derivative. To reinforce this point, Paul reminds his readers of the story of manna with a citation of Exod. 16:18 in v. 15. Just as God was the real source that stood behind the Israelites' sufficiency, so now God supplies the same sufficiency to the Corinthians.

Likewise in chapter 9, Paul argues that the ultimate source of the Corinthians' wealth is God. Verse 9 is a citation of Ps. 112:9, originally a psalm in praise of the righteous person: "He scattered abroad, / he gave to the needy, / his righteousness abides forever." But Paul changes the subject of the sentence from the righteous man to God in verse 10: "He who supplies seed to the sower and bread for food will supply and multiply your seed and increase the yield of your righteousness." In other words, it is God who is the prime actor: the righteous person acts only insofar as God acts through the person. The result is an ethical truism: one does good work in order to increase one's capacity to do more good work.

---

go directly against what Paul has argued elsewhere (especially Gal. 2:1–10). Betz (124) recognizes the problem, but he thinks that the language here is purposely ambiguous, so as to allow the Corinthians to interpret it one way (that is, in a nonobligatory way) and the Jerusalem to interpret it in another (in a contractual sense). The trouble with this supposition is that 2 Corinthians 9 is not itself the contract but a solicitation letter intended in the main for the Corinthians or, at the very most, a circular letter to Achaia. It is difficult to imagine that it is capable of sustaining the kind of ambiguity required by Betz's theory. Furthermore, as I argue below, in the Roman patronage system, it is usually the moneygiver who played the role of patron and the recipient the role of client, not the other way around.

63. Note also the parallel between *ekeinou* here and *ekeinōn* in *to hymōn perisseuma eis to ekeinōn hysterēma* (8.13). This is further indication that *to ekeinōn hysterēma* has a broader meaning of "others' want."

One could construe a critique of private property in Paul's formulation here, but I propose that his main intention for pointing to God as the ultimate source of wealth is to decouple the Corinthians' monetary contribution from their customary inclination to use that payment to advance patronal power. Decades of research have shown that Roman patronage was a highly influential factor in the Corinthian congregation.[64] Paul refused to accept money from the Corinthian congregation, most likely because he did not want to be bound by the patronage system. From his personal apologia in 1 Corinthians 9, it seems that some itinerant preachers were willing to accept money, and therefore patronage, from the Corinthians, but Paul himself steadfastly refused it (v. 12).[65]

Given his ethnocentric insistence on the ethnic integrity and priority of the Jewish people, which we saw in Romans, it simply would not do for him even to hint at the Jerusalem church's submission to the gentile churches. Yet, a reception of the collection would automatically make the former into client congregations of the latter,[66] since it was the custom for the inferior party, in need of the aid of the powerful and the wealthy, to receive benefits or service.[67] The theological arguments in 2 Corinthians 8–9, I submit, are his solution to this dilemma. While suggesting to the Corinthians that they contribute generously, Paul reiterates the assertion that all generosity and all wealth ultimately come from God, and that the final aim and goal of the collection is likewise the glorification and thanksgiving to God. Accordingly, the Corinthians are no more than middlemen who must be faithful stewards of what has been entrusted to them.

But Paul uses more than theological arguments; he also made certain that the collection was to be solicited from multiple congregations. The basis of the patronage system was power and authority, so that a patron might stand to gain power and position in a vertical hierarchy from having expended on a client. The result was that the client became bonded to the patron out of a sense of gratitude, and the patron maintained that relationship through further giving. When there was a multiplicity of patrons, however, in competition with each other giving to the same client, the vertical structure

---

64. The literature on this is enormous; see, e.g., Stephen C. Mott, "The Power of Giving and Receiving: Reciprocity in Hellenistic Benevolence," in G. Hawthorne, ed., *Current Issues in Biblical and Patristic Interpretation: Studies in Honor of Merrill C. Tenny* (Grand Rapids, Mich.: Eerdmans, 1975), 60–72; Peter Marshall, *Enmity in Corinth: Social Conventions in Paul's Relations with the Corinthians*, WUNT II/23 (Tübingen: J. C. B. Mohr [Siebeck], 1987), 143–47; and the more recent discussion by John Chow, *Patronage and Power: A Study of Social Networks in Corinth*, JSNTSup 75 (Sheffield: JSOT Press, 1992), 38–82.

65. Ronald Hock, "Paul's Tentmaking and the Problem of His Social Class," *JBL* 97 (1978): 562.

66. Furnish, *II Corinthians*, 413, suggests that according to the patronage system, it would place the Jerusalem church in a subordinate position to the gentile churches if the former were to receive money from the gentile churches.

67. Marshall, *Enmity in Corinth*, 143. In return, then, the client would be obligated to show gratitude, or render service or support as requested by the patron.

became destabilized, resulting in a relativization of patronal power. It is this latter strategy, I propose, that Paul has adopted in these two chapters. The consistent reminder of the Corinthians of the Macedonian presence (8:1–4, 9:2–4) is to lower the patronal value of their gift, even as it might also serve to increase the gift itself. If this reading is right, then the solicitation letter in 2 Corinthians 8–9 is, among other things, also an anti-patronal statement.

## Conclusion

In formulating his own understanding of the collection for the saints in Jerusalem, two competing tendencies are discernible in Paul's thinking. On the one hand is the eschatological vision, which Paul the apocalyptic Jew would find amenable and fulfilling. Such a universal claim would satisfy his ethnic longing for restoration of his nation and, even more, fulfill the destiny of his people as the unifier of all peoples on a universal scale. The anti-imperial, anti-colonial implications of such a vision could not be clearer, even if Paul does not — indeed could not in a letter to Rome — fully draw them out. On the other hand, this vision is disclosed in the inclusion of Gentiles who constitute the very sign of its eschatological fulfillment. But the inclusion of Gentiles also entails a fundamental critique of prevailing values and expectations. The first of these values and expectations under review is narrow ethnocentrism. If the entrance of Gentiles is a defining characteristic of this new political and social reality, they can no longer be excluded from fully participating in institutions that have been confined to the *ethnos*. A second is the Roman vertical patronal structure that assumes and assigns superior and inferior statuses to all participants in that structure. Paul insists that only one based on a horizontal solidarity between Jewish and gentile congregations could do justice to the new vision in Christ.

# — 13 —

# PAUL, *EKKLĒSIA*, AND EMANCIPATION IN CORINTH

## A CODA ON LIBERATION THEOLOGY

### Allen Dwight Callahan

ᒣᒣᒣᒣᒣᒣᒣᒣᒣᒣ

It took only a glance at the New Testament to realize that Paul was the author whose situation was more like ours. So even though it was not easy to approach the thought of Paul, we found ourselves drawn closer to it *from politics*.[1]

Paul's *ekklēsia* in 1 Corinthians was an emancipatory project. In 1 Corinthians Paul directs the community of addressees in emancipatory theory and practice. Emancipation is the means and root metaphor of Paul's eschatological politics. It is the politics of the oppressed. We do not have to do here with the classic definition of politics as the concerted action of autonomous individuals guided by rational self-interest. Such a definition of politics is useless in our understanding of what Paul is doing because it is irrelevant for oppressed people. The notion of autonomy begs the question; freedom is not the necessary condition of a politics of the oppressed, but the desired effect. The atomistic Kantian self presupposed in our common notions of politics is free to be political. The oppressed are political to be free. And in Roman Corinth in the first century of the common era, emancipation is the politics of freedom.

Emancipation is the realization of freedom of, by, and for freed people in different areas and dimensions of life. Throughout 1 Corinthians Paul seeks to realize the freedom of his addressees in the face of limits that constitute life in the present, imperfect age. Even in his eschatological fervor Paul did not try to force the end, to bring the age to a close by direct action. The cataclysmic close of this evil aeon was God's responsibility. Its

---

1. Juan Luis Segundo, *The Humanist Christology of Paul* (Maryknoll, N.Y.: Orbis, 1986), 174.

close had been signaled in the death and resurrection of Jesus the Messiah, but the eschatological community of Corinth lived between the already of Jesus' resurrection and the not-yet of their own with the limits of Christian existence.

Liberation holds out the possibility of the complete overthrow of oppressive structures, the possibility of revolution. Emancipation, however, seeks to find freedom in the limit situations that are the life world of those structures. The freedom sought is not life without limits, a conceit of relatively recent vintage. Emancipation does not seek life without limits, but life in which emancipated people can honor their own limits: the limits of time, nature, and history, in short, the hand that destiny has dealt. These are limits, but freedom is constituted by the limits that free people accept for themselves, the contingencies they have acknowledged and embraced. Because these contingencies are above and beyond them, they acknowledge and embrace them as transcendent limits. Freedom is, among other things, always an exercise in transcendence, and emancipation is the realization of freedom in spaces and places circumscribed by transcendent limits.

At times the unfree may realize freedom through strategic cooperation with or accommodation to the forces of hegemony. No hegemony is absolutely comprehensive in its domination. Even in our own time, when satellite surveillance penetrates stratospheric space and subliminal advertising penetrates psychic space, total domination is happily a human impossibility. It is in the era introduced by space satellites and mass media that colonialism was defeated all over the black and brown world. Apartheid regimes in both USAs — that is, the United States of America and the Union of South Africa — were disestablished, and the Berlin Wall was taken apart by those who had been separated by it for three decades. In every historical moment, hegemony allows, overlooks, loses, forsakes, or concedes some free space which emancipatory strategies may exploit.

Emancipation is a species of liberation. We may frame it within the paradigm of liberation theology, but with qualification. In the project of liberation, revolution is the premier praxis. Revolution is a frontal assault on systemic oppression that is seldom practicable for the "wretched of the earth," and then only with the complicity of those who identify with them yet have access to some privilege in that system. Both the great modern analysts of hegemony — such as Karl Marx, Antonio Gramsci, Frantz Fanon — and its outstanding opponents — Toussaint L'Ouverture, Leon Trotsky, Fidel Castro, and so on — hail from this group. Revolution is the road not taken unless and until all other avenues for the pursuit of dignity have been exhausted and no alternative is available. At some point in the spatial and temporal coordinates of the system, the Wretched of the Earth have the advantage of numbers and the devices to apply that advantage; they wage guerrilla warfare, they "fill up the jails," they march great distances in great multitudes.

But revolution, in historical perspective, is seldom possible. It requires congenial conditions that are as rare as they are spectacular. Emancipation, however, is always at least in principle practicable for those who would be free and those who would remain so. Whereas revolution is peculiarly possible, emancipation is perennially so. When the conditions for revolution are not propitious, responsible strategists will opt for other forms of resistance. They seek to exploit the weak links in the chains that Rousseau saw everywhere binding men born free, to find spaces between the bars of the iron cage of Max Weber and places beyond the gaze of the Panopticon of Michel Foucault. They will opt for strategies of emancipation. The project of emancipation suggests that we understand Paul as a strategist negotiating the limit situation of Roman hegemony in the eastern Mediterranean. Latin American liberation theologian Juan Luis Segundo has observed that "Paul is faced with the problem of efficacy, a concrete, limited option, an energy calculus."[2] This qualification of emancipation within the liberation paradigm is important for liberationist readings of Paul.

The hermeneutical paradigm of liberation also posits that the kingdom of God revealed and realized in the words and deeds of Jesus of Nazareth was in conflict with the ruling powers and authorities, and this conflict was necessarily political. We may observe these elements of the liberation paradigm in the pastoral intervention we now call 1 Corinthians. In 1 Corinthians Paul offers theory and practice of his eschatological politics. His emancipatory theory goes beyond the paradigm of the Exodus as the archetypal event of liberation, and he advances manumission, mutualism, and morality as three practices to sustain the project of emancipation in the Corinthian *ekklēsia*. I will review these features briefly as a prolegomenon for an emancipatory reading of Paul's letters.

## A Theory of Emancipation: The Exhaustion of Exodus

The hermeneutical paradigm of liberation posits that God is revealed as a liberator of the people of God in the Exodus. The Exodus is the signal event of God's intervention in history and dramatically demonstrates God's solidarity with the oppressed. Paul harkens back to this mighty act of God when he identifies Christ as the spiritual rock that accompanies the children of Israel in the Exodus (1 Cor. 10:1–4). Paul thus discerns the presence of Jesus in Israel's early struggle to distance itself fully from its previous condition of servitude.

But his reference to the Exodus only begins with the baptism in the vacated Sea. He delineates the historical lessons to be learned from Israel's collective experience after the revolution, so to speak, during the long march

---

2. Ibid., 164.

through the wilderness. We see here the limits of liberation narrowly construed as a revolutionary project. Paul rehearses the biblical narrative of the exhaustion of the Exodus. He thus resists the triumphalism of some of his addressees, who live as though already in full possession of the freedom promised on the far shore of baptism.

For the Corinthians, as for the author of the Wisdom of Solomon and the Jewish philosopher Philo, the events of the wilderness wanderings spiritually signify the salvific Sophia of God that nourish those who are "wise" and the "mature."[3] Paul summons this allusion as a warning to those who think they already arrived, and continues his polemic against the triumphal Corinthian claims to wisdom and dominion. This triumphalist reading of the events of the wilderness as "exclusively positive soteriological symbols"[4] has no language for talking about the protracted struggle for freedom with its complexity, contingency, and danger. Segundo has identified this triumphalism as the premier problem of contemporary liberation theology.[5]

In Black Theology, which shares a strong family resemblance with Latin American Liberation Theology, Charles Shelby Rooks has argued that the theme of exodus, paradigmatic for traditional Black Theology, has become "pragmatically difficult to apply — to the current American situation."

> The biblical image which has been at the heart of the Black man's faith in the eventual appropriation of the American myth must be replaced because it is no longer believable — the idea that America is the Promised Land is compromised almost beyond repair. Injustice, war, ecological devastation, runaway technology, etc., have served to tarnish the dream, perhaps forever.[6]

Rooks proposes as an alternative the image of the Babylonian exile and the Jewish diaspora. In view of similar dystopian disappointments, Segundo notes that the prevalence of political repression in Latin America has led some Latin American theologians to propose a "theology of captivity" as

---

3. Richard Horsley, *1 Corinthians,* New Testament Commentaries (Nashville: Abingdon Press, 1998), 135–37.

4. Ibid., 135.

5. Some Latin American theologians talk about liberation in triumphalist terms, as if it were already within our grasp, when the overall situation in Latin America indicates the need for a bridge between reality and theologizing. Consider the ever-increasing misery of the poor, their obvious lack of orientation, and the growing evidence and signs of further oppression and repression. I must confess that I detect such triumphalism in Gustavo Gutiérrez's more recent work. Despite his many critical-minded specifications, the very title of the work strikes me as off-base: *The Power of the Poor in History.* What power is he talking about? Where has this power been hiding for the past four centuries, since the days of European colonialism? Where has it been hiding for the past century and a half, since the days of political independence? Why doesn't he analyze the how, why, and wherefore of the *powerlessness* of the poor in history instead? Segundo, *Humanist Christology,* 224 n. 254.

6. Charles Shelby Rooks, "Toward the Promised Land: An Analysis of the Religious Experience of Black America," *The Black Church* 2, no. 1 (September 1973): 8.

an alternative to liberation. "As an alternative to a theology of liberation, such a proposed theology must certainly be rejected. No one wants to canonize captivity merely because liberation seems to be moving farther away."[7] Paul's paradigm of emancipation extends beyond the Exodus and so offers a *tertium quid* between the triumphalism of a theology of liberation and the resignation of a theology of captivity.

## Manumission, Morality, and Mutualism as Emancipatory Practices

Orlando Patterson reminds us,

> Corinth, the area of Paul's greatest success, had a level of large-scale slavery which rivaled and possibly surpassed Rome's — its refounding was entirely the work of freedmen, the only such instance of ex-slaves' founding a colony in antiquity. Thus from its very inception Roman Corinth was infused with the ethos and values of the freedman population of antiquity, a social monument to their aspirations and industry.[8]

Paul's treatment of bondage and freedom in chapter 7 is thus emblematic; there we touch the taproot of Paul's root metaphor of slavery in the concrete experience of the Corinthians.

I have argued elsewhere that here Paul speaks of ecclesial manumission, the practice of churches collectively purchasing the freedom of their enslaved members.[9] Paul implies that the Corinthians have bought some of their brethren out of bondage through collective economic exercise of mutualism, "the implicit or explicit belief that *individual and collective well-being is attainable above all by mutual interdependence*."[10] Manumission is not an aberration of slave regimes, but a routinized part of servile domination. Thus, in buying back their enslaved members, the Corinthians, and presumably Paul with them, are in this peculiar way accommodating the peculiar institution of slavery. Yet they do so to exploit a space of freedom left in the Roman system of servile domination. Manumission is not, properly speaking, a liberationist practice. It did not destroy or disestablish the institution of slavery. Manumission is, however, an emancipatory practice, in that it

---

7. Segundo, *Humanist Christology*, 224 n. 254.

8. Orlando Patterson, *Freedom*, vol. 1, *Freedom in the Making of Western Culture* (New York: Basic Books, 1991), 320.

9. "A Note on 1 Corinthians 7:21," *Journal of the Interdenominational Theological Center* 17, no. 2 (1989–90): 110–14.

10. Justin J. Meggitt, *Paul, Poverty, and Survival* (Edinburgh: T. &T. Clark, 1998), 158. Meggitt argues that 2 Thess. 3:6–12 provides evidence that mutualism was a guiding assumption of economic relations, not only *between* but *within* the communities (Meggitt's emphasis.)

finds a space and place for freedom in the limits of Roman slavery. Some Corinthians were made free by the collective economic efforts of sisters and brothers in their eschatological community. Some Corinthians have become free thereby, and Paul would have them stay that way.

The hermeneutical paradigm of liberation posits that God's categorical imperative is to do justice. The rationale for God's intervention in history is to effect just relations in the world: "for Paul, the assemblies at Corinth and elsewhere, as the eschatological people of God, were set over against 'the world' which stood under God's judgment. Indeed, as paralleled in Judean apocalyptic writings — at the judgment the 'saints will judge the world' (6:2)."[11]

Paul insists that justice, precisely forensic justice, is an imperative of the Kingdom of God. This imperative, with kingdom language, is his concluding argument against members of the community bringing suit against each other in the civil court (1 Cor. 6:1–9). Paul understands the crucifixion of Jesus precisely as a confrontation between the revelation of the God's hidden wisdom and the masters and rulers of the world (1 Cor. 2:7–8). In Christ God has already instituted a new regime; this is the eschatological rationale for Paul's insistence on juridical autonomy in 1 Corinthians 6. Paul insists on the imperative of justice, but in a parenetic key; his addressees are the subjects of justice, not its objects. Paul glosses the justification, cleansing, and sanctification in 1 Cor. 6:11 as the justice that is practiced in the community.[12] The saints are not merely the recipients of justice; they are its agents. They must do justice by, for, and among themselves. Paul's interdiction was certainly aimed at the litigation rife between social equals among the lower registers.[13]

The eschatological autonomy for which Paul argues so insistently is also imperative, finally, in the movement's economic life. Paul presses an emancipatory practice in the form of the collection for the saints in Jerusalem (1 Cor. 16:1–4). This international economic reciprocity was an innovation "perhaps unique in the Roman empire or in any ancient empire. By contrast with the vertical and centripetal movement of resources in the tributary political economy of the empire, Paul organized a horizontal movement of resources from one subject people to another."[14] The collection as an inter-assembly practice of mutualism is thus in effect a first fledgling step toward an "international" economic emancipation.

---

11. Horsley, *1 Corinthians*, 246.

12. Elsa Tamez, *Contra toda condena: La justificación por la fe desde los excluidos* (San José, Costa Rica: Editorial Departmento Ecuménico de Investigaciones, 1991), 86.

13. See Meggitt, *Paul, Poverty, and Survival*, 122–25.

14. Richard A. Horsley, "1 Corinthians: A Case Study of Paul's Assembly as an Alternative Society," in *Paul and Empire: Religion and Power in Roman Imperial Society* (Harrisburg, Pa.: Trinity Press International, 1997), 251. Meggitt, *Paul, Poverty, and Survival*, 158, argues that "2 Thess. 3:6–12 provides evidence that mutualism was a guiding assumption of economic relations, not only between but within the communities."

## Conclusion

The Muratorian Fragment, perhaps our oldest canonical list, says the following of Paul's letters.

> He wrote at some length first of all to the Corinthians, next to the Galatians — then he wrote to the Romans at greater length — For the blessed apostle Paul himself, following the rule of his predecessor John, writes only by name to seven churches in the following order — to the Corinthians a first, to the Ephesians a second, to the Philippians a third, to the Colossians a fourth, to the Galatians a fifth, to the Thessalonians a sixth, to the Romans a seventh; although for the sake of admonition there is a second to the Corinthians and to the Thessalonians.[15]

It is only fitting that I propose this thought experiment here, in a collection honoring Krister Stendahl. Stendahl pointed out that the gospel cannot be summarized by any single Pauline slogan. In rejecting the dogmatic formula of "justification of the ungodly" as the theological resume of Pauline thought, Stendahl showed that Paul's argument for justification is not to be found everywhere in his epistles, and thus must not be regarded as the common, let alone, signal element of Paul's thinking. Stendahl effectively de-centered Romans as the focus of Pauline studies. He has argued, and argued persuasively, that we have no warrant to grant Romans pride of place in the Corpus Paulinum. The Muratorian Fragment suggests an alternative: Paul "wrote at some length first of all to the Corinthians." Following this canonical counsel, I have read "to the Corinthians a first" to understand Paul's emancipatory theory and practice, which Paul articulates and argues "at some length first of all to the Corinthians."

Elements of the liberation paradigm are present in 1 Corinthians. In this way Paul points the way for a fruitful, emancipatory future for the theology of liberation. Instead of reading Paul through the liberationist lens, we must read liberation theology and emend the liberation paradigm through the lens of Paul's pastoral interventions. Many theologians and others have heard the death rattle of liberation theology in the din of recent turns of history. The triumph of global capitalism, the demise of the Eastern bloc communist regimes, and the repudiation of liberation theology in the Catholic Church have been cause for observers left, right, and center to begin writing obituaries for classic liberation theology. But the crisis is of older vintage than the fading flower of Marxism. The problem is not that the revolution in Nicaragua may not have accomplished its objectives, and that the church hierarchy has effectively muzzled Catholic liberation theologians. It is a problem profoundly inherent in Christology itself. The problem is not the failure of modern revolutions, but the failure of an ancient revolution,

---

15. James Stevenson, revised W. H. C. Frend, *A New Eusebius: Documents Illustrating the History of the Church to* A.D. *337* (London: SPCK, 1987), 123–25.

the revolution of Jesus, that itself challenges the Christian claim to triumph over the powers. The problem of reactionary powers in Latin America and around the world has been anticipated in the ambiguity of the cross.

It is precisely the embrace of this ambiguity that is Paul's genius, a genius which liberation theology desperately needs as revolution is being crushed beneath the wheel of globalization and reaction in our historical moment. Paul's pastoral intervention in 1 Corinthians is informed by a politics of emancipation, a project inherently political because manumission, morality, and mutualism are by definition communal practices, collective concerted action.

Orlando Patterson reflects a consensus of opinion that Paul's understanding of divine redemption, the purchase with a price of which he speaks so concretely in 1 Corinthians 6 and 7, "is a wholly individual act. All traces of the Judaic conception of collective deliverance are absent,"[16] and that "Paul... has no conception of participative freedom. The idea of the church as a civic community would come much later, under Greek influence."[17] But the emancipatory strategies of 1 Corinthians afford no room for privatized religion. What Paul is doing is politics:[18] "as becomes clear in chapter 12, 'body' was also a well-established political metaphor for the 'body politic,' the citizen body of a city-state (polis)." He is waging resistance to Roman hegemony after the fashion of those without power, privilege, or prestige in the world, slaves, former slaves, and their descendants. He does so in correspondence with communities in the only Roman province reinvented by freedmen and their issue.

And Paul writes to such people as one of them. Jerome (*De viris illustribus* 5) tells us that Paul's family had been taken as prisoners of war from Galilee to Tarsus, and that his father had acquired Roman citizenship after being manumitted from slavery by his Roman master.[19] This ancient legend about Paul's background may be truly apocryphal but is doubtless apocryphally true. Paul identified with the community of freedmen at Corinth because he shared the deracinated, servile ancestry of his addressees. He knew that one who had once been a slave was free only insofar as he had been freed. The slave set free is never *eleutheros* and ever *apeleutheros*. Liberation in Christ is emancipation, "lived as a permanent victory, always contested and always reaffirmed."[20] Though Paul's failure to bring a revolutionary sensibility to Christian existence indeed may remain a problem for classic liberation theology, an emancipatory reading may render him one of liberation theology's greatest hopes in the postrevolutionary present.

---

16. Patterson, *Freedom*, 1:332.
17. Ibid., 342–43.
18. Horsley, "1 Corinthians: A Case Study," 248.
19. Patterson cites the legend (*Freedom*, 1:454 n. 20), understanding its real significance.
20. José Comblin, "Paulo e a mensagem de liberdade," *Estudos Biblicos* 14 (1987): 68.

# — 14 —

# RESPONSE

## PAUL AND THOSE OUTSIDE POWER

## Antoinette Clark Wire

᥆᥆᥆᥆᥆᥆᥆᥆᥆

I VERY MUCH APPRECIATE that Sze-kar Wan approaches Paul's collection as an act of social power with theological meaning rather than as an ethical or theological act divorced from power realities. He makes us see that Paul understands the Gentiles bringing gifts to Jerusalem as the sign of God's ultimate victory in the universal worship of Israel's God. If Corinthian prosperity comes from God and by gentile generosity toward Jerusalem redounds to God's glory through their thanks to God, this trumps even the imperial patronage system. It counters the imperial rhetoric in inscriptions and decrees that declare Corinthian prosperity to be the result of Roman rule, redounding in praise to Roma and the emperor — as the temple tax, in fact, does "redound" to the temple of Jupiter Capitolinus in Rome after the destruction of the temple in Jerusalem.

But is Paul's primary intent in making the collection to exalt God's universal glory over Rome's? The collection seems to me to have at least another more immediate purpose, namely to vindicate one Judaism in the eyes of another. Is Paul not working, first and foremost, to vindicate his messianic mission to the Gentiles in the eyes of, as he puts it, "the saints in Judea" (messianic Jews) and "unbelievers" (nonmessianic Jews), who serve despite Paul as the measure of Jewish identity (Rom. 15:30–32)?

In this light I read Gal. 2:10, "only we should remember the poor," to mean that only this and no other stipulations were added to the Jerusalem Council agreement, especially none about eating practices required of converts as they appear later in Acts 15, vv. 20 and 29. Paul's word "only" shows that other stipulations were being assumed, if not explicitly stated, as shown in the conduct of Peter and Barnabas when James's delegation came to Antioch. Paul, in contrast, claims that the sufficient gauge of Jewish identity for this gentile mission would be in its almsgiving, arguably a more important mitzvah than kashrut. The collection proves that these are legitimate gentile converts. Parallel Gentiles might be the converts Izates and his mother, Helene of Adiabene, who bring gifts to Jerusalem in the famine and thereby demonstrate their full conversion to Judaism.[1] Yet I have not yet been convinced that Paul's collection is anti-imperial except in the broadest sense that Jewish hopes and claims ultimately conflict with imperial claims.

At the same time I can see Professor Wan's point that Palestinian nationalist Jews might resent these Gentiles who bring gifts, as if making the Jews their clients. Here I wonder if we can draw on the letter of James. Though many scholars date it later than the time of Paul, the writer's resentment against the fine reception the rich receive who travel and make money (James 2:1–7, 4:13–5:6) could reflect the resentment in more conservative Jewish-Christian circles against people such as Paul who come bearing gifts. But Paul, nonetheless, is a Hellenistic Jew and apparently expects the collection to help him in Jerusalem.

If Paul is working in Galatians to claim legitimacy for his gentile mission as an almsgiving mission, why does this perception not appear in 2 Corinthians? The Gentiles Paul is addressing in Corinth may not be interested in the competition between one messianic mission and another, but Paul thinks they can be interested in a competition between Greek cities and Roman provinces within Paul's mission as to who is giving more generously, or more willingly, or sooner (2 Corinthians 8–9). Paul wouldn't let the Corinthians compete with Macedonia in supporting him personally, but he incites the competition here. He even assures them a representative in the entourage to Jerusalem (1 Cor. 16:1–4). In other words, the finger movements that get the baby to suck the bottle in Jerusalem are not the same as those that milk the cow in Corinth. But Paul has one goal, to integrate his gentile mission into "the Israel of God," represented for him in the Jerusalem church. And Wan shows why this finally matters, because in this way his work contributes to God's ultimate triumph over empire and death.

Allen Callahan proposes that Paul's project in 1 Corinthians is an emancipatory if not a liberation project, emancipatory in the sense of the best option possible at that time, namely in that free people accept limits. His primary example is the ecclesial manumission of the enslaved that he finds in 1 Cor. 7:17–24. Such manumission does not offer abolition. It offers an improvement for some people in a situation where the promise of manumission continues to make slavery workable for the society at large. This reading of Paul's argument in context is a valuable contribution.

But I cannot follow Callahan in his reading of 1 Corinthians as a whole as a letter characterized by "elements of a liberation paradigm." When manumission is offered as a concession, where available, in an argument for people to remain in the station they held when called, it simply tightens the restrictions on those without this opportunity. This includes, one presumes,

---

1. Josephus, *Ant.* 20.49–53.

the large majority of enslaved people, as well as those under marriage or betrothal agreements, whom Paul in this chapter is trying to persuade to return to marriage. Similarly, Paul's appeal to Exodus traditions in 1 Cor. 10:1–13 is not made to affirm Israel's escape from slavery, but as Paul says, "now this took place as a warning for us" (10:6), that is, a warning not to exercise our freedoms and fall in the wilderness as they did. I do not hear forensic justice, Jesus' words and deeds as the Kingdom of God, and freedom in Christ as major themes of Paul in 1 Corinthians. This is the letter in which Paul's "pastoral interventions," as Callahan speaks of, fall most explicitly on women, to the point of calling for their remarriage where Paul thinks men have been immoral, their head-covering when they are leading worship, and ultimately their silence when speaking in the churches.

In this context I would not use Schweitzer's model of Christ broken on the cross as a cautionary warning "to check any liberationist triumphalism" and bring people into subservience. Even Paul does not argue from Jesus' death at this point. Better to take Christ's cross as a model of faithfulness to the death against all interventions, violent and pastoral, that restrict people's experience of life. I suggest that Paul's genius should be characterized not by his "embrace of ambiguity" in this letter but by his willingness in Galatians and elsewhere to take the risks necessary to liberate Gentiles, including women and slaves, from their role as the contrasting foil for God's people.

# RESPONSE

## HOW ANTI-IMPERIAL WAS THE COLLECTION
## AND HOW EMANCIPATORY WAS PAUL'S PROJECT?

### *Calvin J. Roetzel*

ᘒᘒᘒᘒᘒᘒᘒᘒᘒ

S ZE-KAR WAN'S ESSAY on the anti-colonial rhetoric in Paul's promotion
of the offering for the "poor among the saints" in Jerusalem is fascinating. His contribution will help sensitize Pauline scholars to political
nuances in Paul's rhetoric, and his focus on the collection invites discussion
of Jewish "ethnocentrism" and the patronage system of the Greco-Roman
world. In Paul's discussion of the offering in 2 Corinthians 8–9, Wan finds a
metanarrative that includes Gentiles as well as Jews and, therefore, subverts
Jewish ethnic exclusivism. In Paul's discussion of the mutual indebtedness
of gentile congregations and the Jerusalem church in Romans 15 Wan sees
a frontal assault on the vertical patronage system of the Roman Empire.

This novel and interesting thesis is no easy rehash of the older positions
of Bousset and Wrede, who in separate ways also argued that Paul's "universalism" was a frontal assault on Jewish particularism. Nowhere, however,
does Wan even hint, as they did, that Paul's universalism required a rejection of his Jewish legacy. Wan quite correctly has Paul affirm his status as
an ethnic Jew, albeit a Jew with an "expanded sense of Israel's narrative."
By alerting us to the perplexing issue of how Paul incorporated pagans in
the eschatological community on the basis of faith without renouncing the
Jewish lineage, Wan has addressed one of the most perplexing issues of contemporary Pauline studies. While his coupling of ethnicity and the offering
is persuasive, what is less so is the link he draws between this coupling and
his flat assertion that this ethnic construction of Paul consciously "subsumes
all imperial claims under this overall vision."

Aside from his uncritical use of the term *Christian* to refer to believers in
Jerusalem in Paul's day, Wan's thesis is a highly suggestive way to view the
offering.

Wan's view that this universalistic narrative of Israel was deliberately constructed to subvert the Roman political hegemony poses more of a challenge. After his citation of the NRSV translation of the Masoretic text of Isa. 60:4–7, Wan concludes that the reference to the "wealth of the nations" being brought up to Jerusalem is thoroughly political. Within this context Wan places Paul's description of the collection in Rom. 15:25–28 and underscores the importance of Paul's reference to the Gentiles as "debtors" to the saints in Jerusalem. In doing so Wan claims that Paul reveals his Jewish identity and by implication suggests a gentile subordination. Wan views this move by Paul as "subtly anti-imperial in that it construes a reality outside . . . the Roman Empire." The problem is that the anti-colonial polemic of the text may be a bit too subtle. If that passage is seen as anti-colonial, then any affirmation that acknowledges the power and existence of the God of Israel could be read as anti-imperial as well.

To carry conviction, Wan's argument cries out for a reconciliation of these "anti-imperialistic" statements with Romans 13. Paul there admonishes his addressees to "be subject to the governing authorities" (13:1). He reasons "there is no authority except from God," and that "whoever resists authority resists what God has appointed" (13:2). He concludes that "rulers are not a terror to good conduct, but to bad," and exhorts his hearers to "pay taxes for the authorities are God's servants" (13:6). Any first-century reader who caught the anti-imperial undertone of Paul's remarks would have been very confused by these remarks. Paul's remarks suggest that however provisional the political structure might be, it nevertheless served a useful purpose. Wan recognizes, correctly in my view, the apocalyptic character of Paul's gospel, but he does not explore the tension created by the overlap of the two orders — one provisional and the other eschatological.

Given the eschatological character of Paul's offering, and given Paul's imminent expectation of the end (Rom. 13:11–12), what incentive would there be for Paul to develop an anti-imperialistic program? The kingdom of God would soon replace the Roman hegemony. One might argue that such intense apocalyptic expectation is by implication anti-imperialistic for it anticipates its imminent demise. To some extent, one might argue that this is the nature of apocalypticism. Wan's thesis works if it is not pushed beyond the *implied* meaning of Paul's gospel and the offering associated with it, but it falters if it is pushed to the level of intentionality. But if one makes this move, then another problem arises, namely, that this intentional subversion of Roman hegemony is so general as to be practically useless. But if the subversion is an implied one, then all orders are brought into question or at the very least are relativized by the divine order Paul envisions and the gospel he preaches. At the end of the day one might ask what difference does it make if Paul's subversive remarks were subtly intentional or simply implied? The frank answer might be "very little."

Allen Callahan's concise critique of liberation theology, with a few implications for the interpretation of 1 Corinthians, is an important contribution. It locates the liberal emphasis on the collaborative activity of autonomous individuals totally outside of Paul's theological strategy. It invokes Paul to reject out of hand the "liberal conceit" that seeks a freedom without limits. It underscores Paul's sensitivity to the complexity and contingency the human enterprise imposes on any ideology, and it modifies the Exodus paradigm to capture Paul's emphasis on an intermediate locus between captivity and triumphalism. In all of these emphases, Callahan is true to Paul. In a tour de force he uses Paul as the lens through which he would view liberation theology rather than the reverse. With this agenda on the table Callahan sees manumission, morality, and mutualism as forms of "emancipatory practice." *In nuce*, Callahan believes Paul calls on the Corinthians to buy freedom for enslaved believers (1 Cor. 7:21–23), thereby exploiting the opportunity left open in the Roman institutionalization of slavery. Callahan likewise sees Paul's urging the Corinthians to eschew litigation in the public courts in favor of the ecclesial administration of divine justice as evidence of submission not only to the forensic justice of God's new rule but as agents of that rule (1 Cor. 6:1–9). Finally, Callahan holds that Paul's promotion of the offering for the "poor among the saints" in Jerusalem is meant to promote an "international" mutuality that may have been unique in the Roman Empire (1 Cor. 16:1–4).

Though briefly treated, each instance is enormously suggestive and will offer fruitful ground for further discussion, some of it likely to be heated. Having read this short paper, I shall never read these passages in quite the same way again. While I would like to believe Callahan is entirely correct in his expansion of the thesis sketched here, I would welcome help with some problems I am facing. In Paul's discussion of calling in 1 Cor. 7:25–31, he appears acutely aware of the future's short horizon. He reflects out loud that the "appointed time has grown very short" (7:29) and that "the form of this world is passing away" (7:31). In this circumstance Callahan rightly notes that revolution as the strategy of last resort is unnecessary since Jesus' imminent arrival makes such a desperate measure unnecessary. Nevertheless, in the bright light of the imminent denouement, Paul commands his brothers and sisters to "remain" (*menetō*) in the state in which each was called" (7:24). On the face of it this admonition seems to suggest something like "hold tight, deliverance is at hand." If Paul wanted the believers in Corinth to "hold tight," there would seem to be no imperative to manumit slave brothers and sisters. Moreover, if the purchase of freedom for brothers and sisters in Christ was so important, why was Paul not more explicit about it?

While the great majority of Corinthians had firsthand experience of slavery, and the ethos was suffused with this consciousness, the congregations Paul addresses were hardly exclusively slave or former slave. I need help understanding the interplay between this underclass and those in more advantaged positions (1:26–27) and even in leadership positions in the church.

Callahan's treatment of the offering as an eschatological act of mutuality is highly suggestive. Of special importance is his emphasis on the offering as an "international" [sic] act of "material solidarity" — "a radical, emancipatory innovation" that might have been unique in the Roman Empire. While we are acutely sensitive, and rightly so, to the power inherent in hierarchical relationships, and the need to find mutuality outside of them, I am less certain that Paul was. At many points he seems quite conflicted. He repeatedly addresses his audience as siblings, "brothers and sisters," a form of address that does suggest mutuality, but he also threatens them with a rod like an angry parent about to "beat the living daylights" out of them. That is no act of mutuality (4:14–21). Elsewhere he insists on his own apostolic status (Rom. 1:1) that seems to give him an advantageous position and, at the same time, acknowledge a mutual interest in nurture (Rom. 1:12). This might suggest that unqualified "mutuality" is hardly endemic to Paul's character. Moreover, given the presence of the Septuagint of Isaiah in Paul's blood, and given its emphasis on the gathering of the Gentiles with offerings before the God of Israel in Jerusalem in the last days, I need help in understanding this offering as a "*horizontal* movement of resources from one subject people to another" (emphasis added). This artful statement makes a beautiful point, but I need help squaring it with other experiences and statements that pull in another direction. Even in the face of his denials, the importance of Jerusalem and the Jerusalem church to Paul is obvious (Gal. 1:18–24). He readily acknowledges the priority of Israel to salvation, and the symbolic center of Israel was Jerusalem. He reminds the Gentiles in the Roman church of their derivative nature. They were wild shoots grafted into the domestic trunk (Israel). Israel is the root; they are mere branches (Rom. 11:17–24). From Israel comes Christ according to the flesh; the gentile churches are "debtors" (Rom. 15:27). And then there is the existence of the Corinthians' religious puffery. Given this setting I need help understanding how the offering could be a practicum in mutuality rather than a qualification of the spiritual arrogance of the Corinthians. I have questions, but my response to this paper cannot and must not end with these questions that doubtless will be answered in the coming longer treatment. The final word I wish to say is that this is a brilliant paper — provocative, courageous, insightful, and balanced.

# Contributors

SHEILA BRIGGS is Professor of Religion at the University of Southern California and author of the influential articles "Can an Enslaved God Liberate? Hermeneutical Reflections on Philippians 2:6-11," and " 'Buried with Christ': The Politics of Identity and the Poverty of Interpretation."

ALLEN DWIGHT CALLAHAN is Associate Professor of New Testament and Horace B. Lentz lecturer at Harvard Divinity School and author of *Embassy of Onesimus* (Trinity Press) and *Reading the Talking Book: African Americans and the Bible* (forthcoming).

PAMELA EISENBAUM is Associate Professor of Biblical Studies and Christian Origins at Iliff School of Theology and author of *The Jewish Heroes of Christian History: Hebrews 11 in Literary Context* and "Sirach" in *Women's Bible Commentary.*

NEIL ELLIOTT, PH.D., is Development Director of the Lambi Fund and author of *The Rhetoric of Romans* and *Liberating Paul: The Justice of God and the Politics of the Apostle.*

RICHARD A. HORSLEY is Distinguished Professor of Liberal Arts and the Study of Religion at the University of Massachusetts Boston. Among his many books are *1 Corinthians* in the Abingdon New Testament Commentaries and *Paul and Empire: Religion and Power in Roman Imperial Society* (Trinity Press).

ROBERT JEWETT is Henry R. Kendall Professor Emeritus at Garrett-Evangelical Theological Seminary and Visiting Professor at the University of Heidelberg. Among his many books are *Paul the Apostle to America* and the forthcoming commentary on Romans in the Hermeneia series.

CYNTHIA BRIGGS KITTREDGE is Assistant Professor at Episcopal Seminary of the Southwest and author of *Community and Authority: The Rhetoric of Obedience in the Pauline Tradition* (Trinity Press) and the article on Hebrews in *Searching the Scriptures.*

MARK D. NANOS is author of *The Mystery of Romans: The Jewish Context of Paul's Letter* and a forthcoming book on Galatians.

231

CALVIN J. ROETZEL is the Arnold Lowe of Professor Religious Studies at Macalester College. His books include *The Letters of Paul: Conversations in Context* and *Paul: the Man and the Myth*.

ELISABETH SCHÜSSLER FIORENZA is Krister Stendahl Professor of Divinity at Harvard Divinity School and author of many books, including *Rhetoric and Ethic: The Politics of Biblical Studies; Sharing Her Word;* and *Searching the Scriptures: A Feminist Commentary*.

ALAN SEGAL is Professor of Religion and Ingeborg Rennert Professor of Jewish Studies at Barnard College and Columbia University. Among his books are *Rebecca's Children* and *Paul the Convert*.

SZE-KAR WAN is Associate Professor of New Testament at Andover-Newton Theological School and author of *Power in Weakness: The Second Letter of Paul to the Corinthians* (Trinity Press) and co-editor of *Bible in Modern China: The Literary and Intellectual Impact*.

ANTOINETTE CLARK WIRE is Professor of New Testament at San Francisco Theological Seminary and the Graduate Theological Union. Among her numerous publications are *Corinthian Women Prophets: A Reconstruction through Paul's Rhetoric* and the article on 1 Corinthians in *Searching the Scriptures*.

N. T. WRIGHT is Canon Theologian at Westminster Abbey. Among his many books are *The Climax of the Covenant: Christ and the Law in Pauline Theology* and *What St. Paul Really Said*.

# Index of Ancient Sources

## HEBREW BIBLE

**Genesis**

| | |
|---|---|
| 1:26–27 | 87, 88 |
| 2:7 | 87, 88 |
| 12 | 133 |
| 12:1–3 | 132, 133 |
| 12:3 | 138 |
| 15:6 | 137 |
| 17:2–6 | 133 |
| 17:5 | 138 |
| 20:7 | 186 |

**Exodus**

| | |
|---|---|
| 16:18 | 213 |
| 30:14 | 200 |

**Deuteronomy**

| | |
|---|---|
| 32:43 | 69 |

**Joshua**

| | |
|---|---|
| 24:2–3 | 134 |

**2 Samuel**

| | |
|---|---|
| 7:14 | 167 |

**Psalms**

| | |
|---|---|
| 2:7 | 167 |
| 8 | 168 |
| 8:7 | 168 |
| 9:17 | 187 |
| 110:1 | 168 |
| 112:9 | 213 |
| 117:1 | 69 |

**Isaiah**

| | |
|---|---|
| 2:2–3 | 207 |
| 10 (LXX) | 69 |
| 11 | 69 |
| 11:10 | 70 |
| 11:11 | 71 |
| 26:19 | 96 |
| 49:1–6 | 132 |
| 49:8 | 205 |
| 60:4–7 | 207 |
| 61:6 | 207 |

**Jeremiah**

| | |
|---|---|
| 1:4–5 | 132 |

**Daniel**

| | |
|---|---|
| 2 | 96, 98 |
| 7 | 94, 96 |
| 8 | 94 |
| 8–10 | 96 |
| 9 | 94 |
| 10–12 | 94, 96 |
| 12:2 | 96 |
| 12:3 | 96 |

**Micah**

| | |
|---|---|
| 4:1–2 | 207 |

## NEW TESTAMENT

**Mark**

| | |
|---|---|
| 10:42 | 70 |

**Acts**

| | |
|---|---|
| 13:2 | 208 |
| 15:1 | 188 |
| 15:5 | 188 |
| 15:20 | 188, 224 |
| 15:29 | 188 |
| 17:7 | 165 |
| 18:24 | 85, 88 |
| 20:1–21:6 | 206 |
| 20:4 | 203, 206 |
| 21:25 | 188 |

**Romans**

| | |
|---|---|
| 1 | 36, 66 |
| 1–3 | 204 |
| 1–4 | 20 |
| 1–8 | 66 |
| 1:1 | 230 |
| 1:3 | 70 |
| 1:3–4 | 167, 168 |
| 1:4 | 70 |
| 1:8–32 | 39 |
| 1:9 | 39 |
| 1:12 | 63, 68, 230 |
| 1:14 | 62, 65 |
| 1:16 | 36, 59, 204 |
| 1:16–17 | 35, 170 |
| 1:17 | 36 |
| 1:18–32 | 36, 37, 58, 65, 137 |
| 1:24–27 | 37 |

**Romans (continued)**

| | |
|---|---|
| 2:5 | 70 |
| 2:8 | 202 |
| 2:9–10 | 204 |
| 2:29 | 180 |
| 3:9 | 204 |
| 3:20 | 36 |
| 3:21–4:25 | 172 |
| 3:29 | 204 |
| 4 | 135, 141 |
| 4:5 | 137 |
| 4:9 | 140 |
| 4:16 | 139 |
| 4:16–22 | 139 |
| 4:17 | 144 |
| 4:17–22 | 144 |
| 5–8 | 172 |
| 5:11 | 204 |
| 6 | 118 |
| 6:6 | 118 |
| 6:12–20 | 39 |
| 6:15–19 | 38 |
| 6:18 | 118 |
| 6:19 | 39 |
| 6:20–23 | 37 |
| 6:22 | 118 |
| 7 | 2 |
| 7:24 | 202 |
| 8 | 52 |
| 8–15 | 53 |
| 8:4–17 | 38 |
| 8:18–27 | 172 |
| 8:28 | 52 |
| 8:29 | 174 |
| 9–11 | 3, 172, 190 |
| 9:5 | 166 |
| 9:6–9 | 141 |
| 9:14–33 | 67 |
| 9:24 | 204 |
| 10:4 | 67 |
| 10:12 | 204 |
| 10:21 | 202 |
| 11 | 35, 71 |
| 11:13–32 | 38 |
| 11:16–18 | 70 |
| 11:17–24 | 230 |
| 11:17–32 | 67 |
| 11:25–27 | 96 |
| 11:26 | 33, 202 |
| 11:30 | 202 |
| 11:31 | 202 |
| 11:32 | 202 |
| 12 | 178 |
| 12–13 | 172 |
| 12–15 | 38 |
| 12–16 | 167 |
| 12:1 | 39, 205 |
| 12:1–2 | 38, 206 |

| | |
|---|---|
| 12:1–7 | 35 |
| 12:2 | 21 |
| 12:3 | 38 |
| 12:5 | 68 |
| 12:10 | 68 |
| 12:16 | 68 |
| 13 | 52, 53, 65, 66 |
| 13:1 | 228 |
| 13:1–7 | 20, 21, 38, 39, 52, 59, 67, 172 |
| 13:1b–c | 66 |
| 13:2 | 39, 228 |
| 13:3 | 39 |
| 13:4 | 38, 39, 52 |
| 13:6 | 38, 52, 206, 228 |
| 13:7 | 67 |
| 13:8 | 67 |
| 13:8a | 68 |
| 13:10 | 68 |
| 13:11–12 | 228 |
| 13:11–14 | 37 |
| 13:12 | 70 |
| 14 | 62 |
| 14–15 | 172 |
| 14–16 | 68, 71 |
| 14:1–15:7 | 61 |
| 14:3 | 61 |
| 14:13 | 68 |
| 14:19 | 68 |
| 15 | 62, 209, 210 |
| 15:5 | 68 |
| 15:7 | 61, 68, 69 |
| 15:7–13 | 182 |
| 15:8 | 70 |
| 15:9–13 | 69 |
| 15:11b | 69 |
| 15:12 | 167 |
| 15:14–16 | 39 |
| 15:15–16 | 204 |
| 15:15–33 | 204 |
| 15:16 | 65, 204, 205, 206, 207, 209 |
| 15:18 | 204 |
| 15:22–24 | 195, 204 |
| 15:24 | 71 |
| 15:25–26 | 208 |
| 15:25–27 | 194, 204, 205 |
| 15:25–28 | 192, 207, 228 |
| 15:26 | 208 |
| 15:26–27 | 200, 208 |
| 15:27 | 208, 209, 211, 212, 230 |
| 15:28–29 | 195, 204 |
| 15:30–32 | 224 |
| 15:31 | 192, 195, 202, 204, 205, 209 |
| 16 | 61 |
| 16:3–5 | 62 |
| 16:3–16 | 62 |

| | |
|---|---|
| 16:6 | 68 |
| 16:10–11 | 65 |
| 16:10b | 62 |
| 16:11b | 62 |
| 16:16 | 59 |
| 16:17–20a | 59 |
| 16:23 | 121 |
| 28 | 71 |

**1 Corinthians**

| | |
|---|---|
| 1–4 | 90, 98 |
| 1:10 | 202 |
| 1:10–12 | 73, 88 |
| 1:12 | 60 |
| 1:17 | 98 |
| 1:17–20 | 87, 90 |
| 1:17–25 | 125 |
| 1:18–21 | 98 |
| 1:18–24 | 87 |
| 1:18–2:5 | 98 |
| 1:20 | 96, 98 |
| 1:21 | 98 |
| 1:26 | 87 |
| 1:26–27 | 229 |
| 1:26–31 | 98 |
| 2:1 | 90, 98 |
| 2:1–4 | 90 |
| 2:1–5 | 87 |
| 2:4 | 90 |
| 2:6 | 87, 99 |
| 2:6–8 | 92, 96 |
| 2:6–10 | 99 |
| 2:6–3:4 | 87, 125 |
| 2:7 | 98 |
| 2:7–8 | 221 |
| 2:8 | 92, 105, 106, 125 |
| 3:5–15 | 88 |
| 3:5–23 | 99 |
| 3:5–4:21 | 125 |
| 3:9–17 | 73 |
| 3:10–15 | 85 |
| 3:10–17 | 99 |
| 3:21–23 | 88 |
| 3:22 | 107 |
| 3:23 | 106 |
| 4:1–21 | 99 |
| 4:2–5 | 99 |
| 4:7 | 127 |
| 4:8 | 106 |
| 4:8–10 | 87 |
| 4:8–13 | 73, 90 |
| 4:9–13 | 26 |
| 4:10 | 127 |
| 4:14 | 106, 107 |
| 4:14–15 | 144 |
| 4:14–21 | 230 |
| 4:16 | 106 |
| 4:19 | 90 |

| | |
|---|---|
| 4:20 | 99 |
| 5 | 91, 100, 116 |
| 5:1–13 | 100 |
| 5:2 | 116 |
| 5:6–8 | 73 |
| 5:7 | 100 |
| 6 | 100, 115, 118, 221, 223 |
| 6–7 | 223 |
| 6:1–9 | 221, 229 |
| 6:1–11 | 74, 91, 100 |
| 6:2 | 221 |
| 6:9 | 73 |
| 6:11 | 221 |
| 6:12 | 73, 87 |
| 6:13 | 87 |
| 6:13–14 | 100 |
| 6:16–17 | 73, 114 |
| 6:19–20 | 114 |
| 6:20 | 100, 118 |
| 7 | 16, 100, 113, 114, 115, 116, 118, 120, 220, 223 |
| 7:1 | 87 |
| 7:2 | 115 |
| 7:4 | 115 |
| 7:5 | 87 |
| 7:9 | 116 |
| 7:11 | 127 |
| 7:12 | 100 |
| 7:17 | 111 |
| 7:17–24 | 127, 225 |
| 7:21 | 12, 127 |
| 7:21–22 | 7 |
| 7:21–23 | 229 |
| 7:21–24 | 111, 113, 114, 123 |
| 7:21c | 111 |
| 7:21d | 111 |
| 7:22 | 100, 113, 114, 128 |
| 7:23 | 113, 114, 118 |
| 7:24 | 111, 229 |
| 7:25 | 87 |
| 7:25–31 | 229 |
| 7:29 | 229 |
| 7:29–31 | 74, 91 |
| 7:31 | 113, 229 |
| 7:32–35 | 113 |
| 7:35 | 73 |
| 7:36–38 | 87 |
| 8 | 61 |
| 8–10 | 90, 100 |
| 8:1 | 73, 88 |
| 8:4 | 88 |
| 8:6 | 87 |
| 8:7 | 88 |
| 8:9 | 88 |
| 8:10 | 73, 88 |
| 8:11 | 100 |
| 8:13 | 73 |
| 9 | 67, 73, 122, 214 |

1 Corinthians (continued)

| | |
|---|---|
| 9:1 | 100 |
| 9:1–18 | 122 |
| 9:3–7 | 122 |
| 9:8–10 | 73 |
| 9:12 | 100, 122, 214 |
| 9:12a | 85 |
| 9:13 | 73 |
| 9:13–14 | 122 |
| 9:15 | 122 |
| 9:15–19 | 90 |
| 9:18 | 122 |
| 9:25 | 116 |
| 10 | 61 |
| 10:1–3 | 73 |
| 10:1–4 | 88, 218 |
| 10:1–13 | 100, 226 |
| 10:1–22 | 74 |
| 10:3–4 | 87 |
| 10:6 | 226 |
| 10:14–22 | 91, 100 |
| 10:18 | 73 |
| 10:23 | 73, 87 |
| 10:33 | 73 |
| 11:2–16 | 8 |
| 11:3 | 107 |
| 11:3–16 | 88 |
| 11:13 | 106 |
| 11:17–34 | 61, 100, 101 |
| 11:23–26 | 100 |
| 11:26 | 101 |
| 12 | 223 |
| 12–14 | 90, 100 |
| 12:1 | 87 |
| 12:3 | 100 |
| 12:7 | 73 |
| 12:8 | 87 |
| 13 | 73 |
| 14:2 | 87 |
| 14:3–5 | 73 |
| 14:7–9 | 87 |
| 14:12 | 73 |
| 14:14 | 87 |
| 14:17 | 73 |
| 14:21 | 73 |
| 14:23 | 87 |
| 14:26 | 73 |
| 14:26–40 | 126 |
| 14:27–28 | 87 |
| 14:32 | 106 |
| 14:33 | 106 |
| 14:33–35 | 26 |
| 14:33b–36 | 59 |
| 14:34 | 106 |
| 14:34–35 | 8, 105, 108 |
| 15 | 96, 99, 186 |
| 15:1–19 | 99 |
| 15:3–4 | 92 |
| 15:7 | 98, 127 |
| 15:9–10 | 186 |
| 15:12 | 87 |
| 15:12–34 | 96 |
| 15:20 | 98 |
| 15:20–24 | 99 |
| 15:23–28 | 105, 106, 108, 179 |
| 15:24 | 125 |
| 15:24–28 | 92 |
| 15:25–28 | 168, 174 |
| 15:27–28 | 106 |
| 15:28 | 106, 107 |
| 15:35–49 | 96 |
| 15:35–57 | 99 |
| 15:42 | 87, 100 |
| 15:43–53 | 174 |
| 15:44–49 | 87 |
| 15:51–52 | 96, 100 |
| 15:52–54 | 87 |
| 15:53–54 | 100 |
| 16:1–4 | 192, 193, 221, 225, 229 |
| 16:16 | 106 |

2 Corinthians

| | |
|---|---|
| 2:14–16 | 25 |
| 3:18 | 174 |
| 4:10 | 26 |
| 6:2 | 205 |
| 6:4–10 | 26 |
| 8 | 139, 213 |
| 8–9 | 192, 194, 214, 215, 225, 227 |
| 8:1–4 | 215 |
| 8:1–5 | 194, 210 |
| 8:2 | 194 |
| 8:6 | 194, 210 |
| 8:9 | 211 |
| 8:10 | 194, 211 |
| 8:10–12 | 200 |
| 8:12 | 205, 211 |
| 8:13–14 | 211, 212, 213 |
| 8:13a | 211 |
| 8:13b | 211 |
| 8:14 | 211 |
| 8:14b | 211 |
| 8:15 | 213 |
| 8:16 | 194 |
| 8:16–17 | 210 |
| 8:18 | 194 |
| 8:18–19 | 210 |
| 8:22 | 194, 210 |
| 8:23 | 194, 210 |
| 9 | 213 |
| 9:1–5 | 194 |
| 9:2 | 210 |
| 9:2–4 | 210, 215 |
| 9:3 | 194, 210 |

| | |
|---|---|
| 9:4 | 210 |
| 9:5 | 210 |
| 9:7 | 200 |
| 9:9 | 213 |
| 9:10 | 212, 213 |
| 9:11 | 212 |
| 9:11–12 | 212, 213 |
| 9:12 | 208, 209, 212 |
| 10–13 | 14, 85 |
| 10:5 | 164 |
| 10:5–6 | 61 |
| 11:2 | 205 |
| 11:2–3 | 47 |
| 11:4 | 61 |
| 11:20–21 | 61 |
| 11:22 | 191 |
| 12:1 | 189 |
| 12:17–18 | 194, 195 |

**Galatians**

| | |
|---|---|
| 1 | 189 |
| 1:1 | 150 |
| 1:1–10 | 153 |
| 1:2 | 157 |
| 1:4 | 96 |
| 1:6 | 152 |
| 1:6–7 | 149, 150, 155 |
| 1:6–9 | 155 |
| 1:7 | 152 |
| 1:8–9 | 150 |
| 1:9 | 150, 155 |
| 1:11–13 | 153 |
| 1:11–17 | 132, 133, 135 |
| 1:11–24 | 131 |
| 1:11–2:21 | 153 |
| 1:13 | 135, 155 |
| 1:13–14 | 191 |
| 1:13–16 | 150, 154 |
| 1:13–18 | 97 |
| 1:15 | 132, 133, 153, 185 |
| 1:15–16 | 97, 154, 194 |
| 1:17 | 154 |
| 1:18 | 153 |
| 1:18–24 | 230 |
| 1:18–32 | 154 |
| 1:23–24 | 136 |
| 2 | 34 |
| 2:1 | 193 |
| 2:1–2 | 153, 193 |
| 2:1–10 | 154, 193 |
| 2:2 | 154 |
| 2:3 | 154, 193 |
| 2:4 | 152, 193 |
| 2:5 | 152, 153, 154 |
| 2:5–7 | 153 |
| 2:7–9 | 154, 193 |
| 2:10 | 195, 224 |

| | |
|---|---|
| 2:10–11 | 192 |
| 2:10a | 193, 194 |
| 2:11–13 | 195 |
| 2:11–21 | 154 |
| 2:12 | 152 |
| 2:12–14 | 154 |
| 2:14 | 154, 156 |
| 2:14–21 | 157 |
| 2:15 | 131 |
| 3:1 | 157, 158, 159 |
| 3:1–5 | 152, 153, 155 |
| 3:2–3 | 152 |
| 3:3 | 34 |
| 3:5 | 145 |
| 3:6–9 | 138 |
| 3:6–24(–4:7) | 153 |
| 3:14 | 145 |
| 3:26–4:7 | 136 |
| 3:28 | 8, 127, 199 |
| 3:29 | 140, 141 |
| 4 | 141 |
| 4:1–11 | 176 |
| 4:3 | 137 |
| 4:8 | 34 |
| 4:8–10 | 146 |
| 4:8–21 | 153, 155 |
| 4:9 | 137 |
| 4:11 | 155 |
| 4:17 | 152, 157 |
| 4:19 | 144 |
| 4:19–21 | 155 |
| 4:22–30 | 153 |
| 4:29 | 152 |
| 5:1–4 | 152, 158 |
| 5:1–12 | 152 |
| 5:2 | 34 |
| 5:2–18 | 155 |
| 5:2–6:18 | 153 |
| 5:3 | 34, 150 |
| 5:5 | 158 |
| 5:6 | 199 |
| 5:7 | 152 |
| 5:7–12 | 155, 156, 158 |
| 5:10 | 152, 155 |
| 5:10–13 | 152 |
| 5:11 | 34, 149, 155, 159 |
| 5:11–15 | 158 |
| 5:13 | 68 |
| 5:13–15 | 158 |
| 5:14 | 199 |
| 5:15–26 | 158 |
| 5:24–26 | 158 |
| 5:25 | 186 |
| 6:1 | 158 |
| 6:1–10 | 158 |
| 6:2 | 158 |
| 6:4 | 158 |

Galatians (continued)
6:9–10                                                    159
6:12                                              34, 158
6:12–13                              152, 155, 156
6:12–15                                      158, 187
6:13                                                       34
6:17                                                     159

Ephesians
1:19–22                                               174

Philippians
1:27                                                       55
2                                              117, 174
2:3–8                                                   158
2:5–8                                                   181
2:5–11                        174, 176, 177, 181
2:6–11                                                 92
2:10–11                                               179
2:17                                              205, 208
2:25                                                     208
2:30                                              208, 212
3                                                          174
3:1                                              173, 175
3:2–6                                                   176
3:2–7                                                   173
3:2–11                        175, 178, 179, 181
3:2–16                                                 175
3:4–6                                              175, 191
3:4–7                                                   135
3:4–11                                        173, 178
3:6                                                       185
3:7–8                                                   131
3:7–9                                                   185
3:7–11                                        177, 180
3:8                                                       181
3:9                                                       180
3:10                                                     181
3:10–11                              175, 177, 181
3:11                                                     181
3:12–16                                               175
3:15–16                                               178
3:17                                              173, 175
3:17–19                                               175
3:17–21                                               178
3:18–19                                               178
3:20                                              55, 173
3:20–21              168, 173, 174, 175, 181
3:21                                      174, 175, 179
4                                                          67
4:1                                              173, 179
4:18                                              205, 206

Colossians
2                                                          176

1 Thessalonians
1:9                                                       91
1:10                                                     202
2:19                                                       25

3:12                                                       68
3:13                                                       25
4:11                                                       91
5:3                                                         25

2 Thessalonians
1:3                                                       68
4                                                          186
4:9                                                       68

Titus
3:3                                                       64

Hebrews
8:6                                                       208
9:21                                                     208

James
2:1–7                                                   225
4:13–5:6                                               225

1 Peter                                                   55

## APOCRYPHA AND PSEUDEPIGRAPHA

Wisdom of Solomon
6–10                                              85, 88, 89

*1 Enoch*
51:1–2                                                 96
71:15                                                   96
91:11–17                                               94
91:85–91                                               94
93:1–10                                                94

*2 Baruch*
14:13                                                   96
15:8                                                     97
44:8–15                                                 97
83:4–9                                                  97

*4 Ezra*
7:12–13                                                96
7:50                                                     96
7:112–13                                               96
7:119                                                   96
8:1                                                       96
8:2                                                       96

*Jubilees*
11.16–17                                               134

4 Maccabees
7:8                                                       206

Pseudo-Philo
L.A.B. 23.5                                           134

*Testament of Moses*
10:8–10                                                96

## PHILO

| | |
|---|---|
| Contempl. | 126 |
| Flacc. 84–85 | 158 |
| Her. 141–206 | 212 |
| Legat. 8–13 | 32 |
| Migr. 92 | 154 |
| Mos. 2:49–51 | 38 |
| Prob. 86b | 200 |
| Somn. | |
| 2 | 33 |
| 2.181 | 64 |
| Spec. | |
| 1.51–53 | 157 |
| 1.77 | 200 |
| 1.78 | 200 |
| 1.308–10 | 157 |
| Virt. | |
| 212–17 | 134 |
| 212–27 | 157 |

## JOSEPHUS

| | |
|---|---|
| **Against Apion** | |
| 2.137, 140–42 | 134 |
| 2.164–67, 186–87, 218–19 | 38 |
| **Antiquities** | |
| 1.7 | 134 |
| 1.154–57 | 134 |
| 1.167–68 | 135 |
| 1.192 | 154 |
| 2.159–60 | 134 |
| 12.226 | 140 |
| 13.318–19 | 154 |
| 14.7.2 | 200 |
| 14.185–267 | 148 |
| 16.160–65, 167–70 | 201 |
| 18.34–48 | 154 |
| 20.49–53 | 225 |
| **Jewish War** | |
| 2.197 | 202 |
| 2.345–404 | 32 |
| 2.348 | 33 |
| 2.357 | 32 |
| 2.408–9 | 202 |
| 2.412–13 | 203 |
| 3.336–408 | 23 |
| 5.363–68 | 32 |
| 6.312–13 | 23 |
| 6.335–36 | 202 |

## MISHNA, TALMUD, AND OTHER JEWISH LITERATURE

| | |
|---|---|
| Avot 3:2 | 31 |
| Baba Mezia 59b | 150 |
| Baba Qamma 38a | 187 |
| Sanhedrin | |
| 10–12 | 187 |
| 105a | 187 |
| t. Sanhedrin 13.2 | 187 |
| b. Shabbat 33b | 32 |
| Shekalim | |
| 1.4 | 200 |
| 1.5 | 203 |
| Sifra 86b | 187 |

## CLASSICAL AUTHORS

| | |
|---|---|
| **Anonymous** | |
| Ad Herennium 2:6:10 | 28 |
| Einsiedeln Eclogues | 37 |
| **Apuleius** | |
| Golden Ass 9.12.12 | 119 |
| **Aristotle** | |
| Politics | |
| 5.1.6 1301b27 | 81 |
| 1254a 22–24 | 29 |
| Rhetoric | |
| 1.10.4/1368b | 155 |
| 1.1376 | 28 |
| 2.10 | 158 |
| **Calpurnius Siculus** | |
| Bucolica | 37 |
| **Cicero** | |
| De finibus 2.15 | 62 |
| De officiis | |
| 1.47 | 65 |
| 2.16 | 121 |
| De provinciis consularibus | |
| 10 | 30, 38 |
| De re publica | |
| 3 | 30, 38 |
| 3:41 | 28 |
| 3:45 | 28, 38 |
| 5:6 | 28, 77 |
| Pro Flacco | |
| 14–16 | 28, 38 |
| 28.67 | 201 |
| Pro Murena 21ff. | 77 |

**Diodorus Siculus**
  *World History* 1.55                    *154*

**Dionysius of Halicarnassus**
  *On the Ancient Orators*
    Pref. 1–3                           *78, 79*

**Eusebius**
  *Prep. Ev.* 9.17.3–4, 9.18.1           *135*

**Horace**
  *Satires* 1.9.60–72                     *154*

**Jerome**
  *De viris illustribus* 5               *223*

**Julius Paulus**
  *Opinion* 5.22.3–4                      *202*

**Juvenal**
  *Satires* 14.96–106                     *154*

**Lucian**
  *Vit. Auct.* 43                         *138*

**Marcus Aurelius**
  *Meditations* 1.17.2, 1.17.6            *116*

**Martial**
  *Epigrams* 7.35.3-4, 82; 11.94          *154*

**Modestinus**
  *The Rules* Book 6                      *202*

**Ovid**
  *Epistulae ex Ponto* 3.6.25            *171*

**Pausanias** 1.20.5                      *79*

**Persius**
  *Satires* 5.179–84                      *154*

**Petronius**
  *Satyricon* 68.8; 102.13–14             *154*

**Plato**
  *Apology*
    24A                                  *36*
    29D                                  *36*
    35A                                  *36*
    38D                                  *36*
  *Laws* 4.417B                          *64*

**Plautus**
  *Captivi*
    690                                  *120*
    998–1000                             *119*

**Plutarch**
  *The Fortune of the Romans* 318    *28*
  *Moralia*
    8.5.7                                *158*
    814F                                 *31*
  *Quomodo adolescens poetas*        *67*

**Pseudo-Quintilian**
  *Declamations* 274                     *158*

**Quintilian**
  *Institutio Oratoria*
    2.13.15–17                           *83*
    8.6.54                               *149*

**Seneca**
  *De clementia* 49                      *77*

**Strabo**
  *Geographics*
    1.4.9                                *63*
    16.2.37                              *154*

**Suetonius**
  *Domitian* 12                          *154*
  *Nero* 15, 16                          *123*

**Tacitus**
  *Annals*                               *37*
  *Histories*
    4:17:2                               *37*
    5.5                                  *202*
    5.5.2, 8–9                           *154*

**Terence**
  *Phormio* 248–50                       *120*

**Velleius Paterculus**
  *History of Rome*
    2.126                             *28, 77*
    2.99                                 *37*

**Vergil**
  *Aeneid* 6.847–53                       *75*

**Xenophon**
  *Memorabilia* 1:2:40–46                 *28*

# General Index

ᘛᘛᘛᘛᘛᘛᘛᘛᘛᘛ

Abraham
  faith of, 139–41
  Gentile believers and, 136–45
  as model for Paul, 132–36, 145
  monotheism and, 134
  promises and blessings of God, 133, 139
Adams, Edward, 135, 137
African American criticism of Paul, 7–8
agape, 67–68
Alcock, Susan E., 19, 79
antifactionalist rhetoric, 125
anti-Jew sentiment. See also Jews and Judaism
  climate in Rome, 53
  Galatians and, 152
  interpretation of Paul, 44, 164, 178
anti-Judaism, 2, 3, 9–10, 20, 39, 41, 175–76,
  182. See also Jews and Judaism
apocalyptic language and literature, 94–96,
  101, 105
apocalypticism, Judean, 93, 96–102, 105–7,
  188
Apollos, 61, 84–88, 101, 106, 126
apostles, Jerusalem, 153–54
assembly (of saints), 49–50, 82, 100,
  124–28. See also ekklēsia
Aune, David E., 74, 83

Balibar, Etienne, 197
baptism, 104, 108, 118, 199
barbarians, 63–65
Barclay, John M. G., 21–22, 24, 32, 33, 34,
  132, 192
Bartchy, S. Scott, 26, 111–12, 114
Barth, Fredrik, 198, 199
Bartky, Sandra Lee, 45, 46
Baur, Ferdinand Christian, 19, 20, 34
beneficial ideology, 31
benevolence, 30–31, 37
Berger, Peter, 84, 196
Betz, Hans Dieter, 27, 90, 200, 208, 210–13
Bhabha, Homi, 197
biblical studies
  colonialism and, 9–10, 12–13
  context analysis, 14
  empire in, 17
  ethics of interpretation, 40–45, 50–52
  hermeneutics of suspicion, 56

historical-critical method, 13
inquiry, rhetoric of, 40–45
interpreter's context, 14
liberationist voices, 42
public health model, 40–42, 47–53
claim to universalism, 11
Western cultural approaches, 11–12
Black theology, 6–7, 219
Bornkamm, Günther, 34
Botha, Jan, 66, 103
Bowie, E. L., 78, 80, 81, 82
Boyarin, Daniel, 9, 10, 20, 22, 34, 140, 144,
  188, 191
Bradley, K. R., 110, 112–13
Brett, Mark G., 192, 197, 198, 199
Briggs, Sheila, 7, 110–23, 128–29
Brunt, P. A., 28, 30
Bultmann, Rudolf, 97

Caesar, cult of, 76–77, 161, 202–3
Callahan, Allen Dwight, 7, 117, 216–23,
  225–26, 229–30
Campbell, William S., 35
captivity, theology of, 219–20
Carr, Wesley, 92
Castelli, Elizabeth, 26, 48, 82, 103
Cavanaugh, William, 39
ceremonial (epideictic) rhetoric, 28–29, 80,
  81
chauvinism, 41, 197, 209
Chomsky, Noam, 29, 38
Chow, John K., 24, 77, 107, 127, 214
Christ. See Jesus Christ
Christians and Christianity
  baptism and, 108, 199
  circumcision and, 177
  enslavement to sin, freedom through
    Christ, 113–14, 118, 119
  identity and, 180–81, 186–90
  pagan practices, 146
  procreation through religious instruction,
    143–44
  sectarian identity, 152
  as slaveowners, 121
  social status relative to slaves, 115, 123
  suffering and, 159
Christos, Paul's use of, 166

circumcision
  conversion and, 186–88
  as identity marker, 34, 155–57, 176–77, 199
  proselytes and self-identity, 157
  and salvation, 187–88
Clark, Donald L., 80
Clarke, M. L., 80
Cleage, Jr., Albert B., 6.
Cohen, Shaye, 143, 151, 157
collection for the Saints, 196, 213, 214, 224–25, 227–29
  as anti-imperial and anti-hegemonic protest, 196, 209
  chronology, 193–96
  as emancipatory practice, 221
  equity principle, 211–14, 221
  ethnicity in, 200, 202
  Paul's mission, 195, 225
  resistance and subversion, a symbol, 196
  temple tax and, 200–201, 204–7
  unity, ecumenical promotion of, 195–96, 203
  universalizing society, a symbol, 196
  voluntary nature of, 200, 206, 208–9
Collins, John J., 95, 97, 154
colonialism, 9–10, 21, 34, 45, 217
Colson, Frank H., 33
Comblin, José, 223
Cone, James H., 6
conformity motives, 77
conservatism, social, 26–27
conversion
  and circumcision, 186–88
  of Gentiles, 69–71
  of Paul, 184–86, 190
  Paul's politics, 22–24
  as prophecy, 70
Corinthians
  community described, 100–101, 106, 125–26
  empire, power and patronage, understanding, 24
  spiritual status, transcendent, 87–90
Corinthians, First, letter to. *See also* Index of Ancient Sources
  authorship questioned (14:33b–36), 59
  emancipation in, 216
  God's anti-imperial fulfillment, 99
  liberation paradigm, 222
  Paul's rhetoric in, 49–50
  political content, 73–74
  relationships, hierarchical, 106–7
  rhetorical analysis, 73–74, 82–87
  spiritual transcendence, 87–90, 101–2
  structure underlying, 98–101
Corinthians, Second, letter to, 210–15. *See also* Index of Ancient Sources

Cotter, Wendy, 148
Craffert, Pieter F., 197
Cranfield, C. E. B., 63, 69
Crawford, M. H., 31
Cranford, Michael, 137, 141
Crossan, John Dominic, 18, 93
crucifixion, 99, 118
cultural imperialism, Roman, 21–22

Dahl, Niels, 149, 153, 190
Daly, Mary, 8
Danker, Frederick, 24
Dauge, Yves Albert, 63
Davies, Philip R., 94
Davies, W. D., 136
de Lange, N. R. M., 32–33
de Ste. Croix, G. E. M., 18, 19, 24, 28–31, 79
deliberative rhetoric, 28
democracy, emergence of and politics of otherness, 46
detrimental and dangerous effects, 4, 6, 9, 41
Diaspora as result of imperialism, 93–94
*dikaiosynē*, 170–73
documentary evidence, authentication of, 59
domination, slavery and salvation, 118–19
Donfried, Karl P., 25
"double standard," 20–21
Downing, Gerald, 35, 163
dualism, 46–47, 55–56
DuBois, Page, 28, 46
Dunn, James D. G., 20, 22, 35, 69, 70, 137, 160, 161, 176, 203, 207, 208, 209

egalitarian theology (of the cross), Paul's advocacy of, 61
Eilberg-Schwartz, Howard, 142–44, 197
Eisenbaum, Pamela, 130–45, 186
*ekklēsia*, 50, 73–74, 80, 85–86, 91, 106–8, 216. *See also* assembly
  imperialistic voices, 60–62
  politics and, 53–57, 59, 60
Elliott, Neil, 10, 17–39, 51–53, 58–62, 65–66, 71, 77, 91, 92, 104–5, 161, 171–74
emancipation, 114, 128, 216–23, 225–26, 228–30
emperor, Christ as, 92–93
emperor cult, role in social control, 76–77, 161, 202–3
empire 17, 24, 34, 37, 58–61
  *ekklēsia* in relation to, 90–93, 108
  God's overcoming of, 97
  of inclusion replacing empire (imperial), 68
  Paul on, 18, 59–62, 90–93, 173–83
  resistance to, 37
  rhetoric and, 26–27, 75, 77, 80–81, 90–93

Romans (letter) as challenge to, 39
slavery in, 110–11
true, of Messiah, 179
epideictic rhetoric, 28–29, 80, 81
equity principle, 211–14
Esler, Philip F., 34, 156, 157, 192, 199, 204
ethics, 43, 56, 65
of interpretation, 40–45, 50–52
personal, 87–88
ethnicity, 191–92, 197–200, 202
ethnocentrism, 20, 196–97, 204, 209
*ethnos,* new, Christ-centered, 199, 203–4, 209
*euangelion,* in political subversion, 92–93, 168, 172
evasion, discourse of, 110, 117, 119–20
exodus, the, 218–20, 226

Fanon, Frantz, 217
faith, 139–41, 144–45
faithfulness, covenant of, 170–72, 180
fear as motive for conformity, 77
Fee, Gordon D., 106, 175
feminist criticism, 7–8, 44, 226
feminist theology, 6
Finley, M. I., 112
Finn, Thomas M., 152
Fitzgerald, William, 119
Fitzmyer, Joseph A., 205
Fortes, Meyer, 142
Foucault, Michel, 48, 62, 218
Fredriksen, Paula, 18, 23, 24, 34
freedom, 112, 217
Furnish, Victor P., 38, 90, 194, 195, 210, 214

Gabba, Emilio, 79
Gager, John G., 39
Galatians, letter to. *See also* Index of Ancient Sources
anti-Jewish criticism in, 152–53
autobiographical narrative, 153
basis of, 146–49
call to remain in Christ, 156–59
controversy explained, 34–35
Genesis 12 similarities, 133
influencers identity, 151–58
inter-Jewish perspective, 157–59
as rebuke, 149–50, 156–57
rhetorical approach, 149–50, 156
Galinsky, Karl, 18, 79
Garlan, Yvon, 112
Garnsey, P. D. A., 18, 19, 77, 80
Gaston, Lloyd, 34, 35
Geertz, Clifford, 197, 198
gender dualism, 47
gender language, 41, 105
Gentile-Christian ideology, 35–36

Gentiles
Abraham and, 136–45
conversion and, 69–71, 146–48, 192
hope of, 69–71
identity, social dimensions of, 156
inclusion of, 1, 69, 146–49, 153, 155–57, 192, 199
inheritance claim, 140–41
Jewish-Gentile distinction, 204
kinship relationships, 140–42, 145
mutuality obligation, 209
righteous, 147–49
salvation of, 188
subordinate to Jews, 207–9
temple sacrifices, 203
Georgi, Dieter, 10, 24, 25, 35, 36, 54, 61, 66, 91, 171, 172, 174, 194, 200, 205, 210, 211, 212
Glenn, Cheryl, 78
God
anti-imperial fulfillment of history, 99
empire, overcoming, 97
Gentiles as people of, 137, 153, 155
glorification and thanksgiving, collection for the Saints, 214
imperialism result of approval, 30, 32, 66, 71
justice and, 36–39, 170–73, 221
slavery to, 113–14, 118–19
"golden age" (Roman), 36–38
Goodenough, E. R., 32–33
Goodman, Martin, 31, 75
Gordon, Richard, 18, 76
gospel and Paul, 164–67
gospel of the crucified, 92
Grabbe, Lester, 94
Gramsci, Antonio, 217
Greco-Roman rhetoric, 90
Gutiérrez, Gustavo, 219

Hansen, G. Walter, 149
Harrill, J. Albert, 112–14
Hays, Richard B., 69, 139, 141
Hendrix, Holland, 24
Hengel, Martin, 166
hierarchy in relationships, 106–7
historical-critical method, 13, 59
Hock, Ronald, 214
Hoff, M., 79
Hoffman, L., 143
Holl, Karl, 200
Holmberg, Bengt, 200
Holmstrand, Jonas, 153
honor and shame language, 20–21, 37
Horsley, Richard, 1–16, 18, 22, 23, 27, 48–50, 72–102, 104, 105, 107, 108, 124–27, 161–63, 173, 193, 219, 221, 223

Howard, George, 151
Hultgren, A. J., 131
Hutcheon, Linda, 150
*hypotassesthai*, 106–7

identification, politics of, 47–49
identity, establishment of
  by baptism, 199
  Christian converts, 186–90
  Christian, Messiah-centered, 180–81
  by circumcision, 157, 177, 186–88, 199
  ethnocentric politic of, 197
  by faith in Christ, 203–4
  Gentile converts, 192
  groups, defined by, 191–92
  Jewish identity, 140–44, 192, 224
  politics of, 46–49. *See also* politics of
    othering
  rhetoric and politics, 47–49
  social dimensions of, 156
imperial rhetoric, 124–27
imperial society, 74–82, 87–90, 105–7
imperialism, 58–59, 71, 105, 107. *See also*
    empire
  collection for the Saints as protest of, 196
  culture of, 17, 21–22
  defeat of through execution of Jesus,
    98–99
  Diaspora as result of, 93–94
  fear, consent, and conformity, 77
  God's approval resulting in, 30–32, 66
  identity with as prestige, 34
  imperialistic voices and *ekklēsia*, 60–62
  Jesus' opposition to, 18
  Jewish-Roman political accommodation
    of, 31–33
  Judean aristocracy in, 31
  Judean history and, 93–94
  language as replication of, interpreting,
    108–9
  patronage system in, 76–77
  Paul's opposition to, 61, 91–96, 161–62,
    209–10
  rhetoric and, 30, 74–82, 90–93, 96–102,
    101
  Romans, Paul's letter to, 35–36
  social control in, 76–77
inclusive praise, theme of, 69
interpretation
  ethics and politics of, 41, 44, 53–57
  interpreter's role, 14, 47, 196–97
Israel's destiny under imperialism, 33–34,
    190

Jacob, W. M., 183
Jaeger, Werner, 64, 91
Jay, Nancy, 142

Jenkins, Richard, 156
Jerusalem apostles, 34, 152–54
Jerusalem Council, 193, 195, 199
Jesus Christ, 70, 102, 222–23
  and Caesar, contrast, 173–74
  Christians enslaved to, 113–14, 122
  Davidic messiahship of, 166–70
  as emperor, 92–93
  empire in interpretation of, 17–18
  enslavement of, 118
  faith in and identity, 203–4
  as *kyrios*, 25, 168–69, 174
  resurrection of, political implications, 23,
    97–98
Jewett, Robert, 22, 33–34, 58–71, 151
Jews and Judaism. *See also* anti-Jew
    sentiment; anti-Judaism
  ethnocentrism, 19–20
  Gentile inclusion, 147–49, 154–55, 192
  Gentile subordination, 207–9
  and Greeks, 204
  identity of, 33–34, 140–44, 192, 224
  kinship relationships, 140–42
  mutuality obligation, 209
  as pagans, 176–77
  Paul and, 22, 34
  Roman political accommodation, 31–32
  salvation and, 34, 88–89, 190
  temple tax, 200–201
  universalism and, 207, 209
  wealth of, 201
Jones, A. H. M., 28, 79, 80
Jones, Jr., Amos, 7
Jones, Kathleen, 45
Judean churches, Paul's (Saul's) persecution
    of, 23
Judge, E. A., 74
judicial rhetoric, 27–28, 80
justice, 170–71, 172, 221
justification, 38, 146, 170–73, 180–81

Kallas, James, 38
Käsemann, Ernst, 2, 38, 66, 97
Kautsky, John, 18, 28, 29, 30
Keck, Leander E., 38, 200
Keienburg, Fritz Hermann, 66
Kern, Philip, 153
Khiok-Khng, Yeo, 9, 197
kinship relationships, 137–42
Kirchhoff, R., 114
Kittredge, Cynthia Briggs, 27, 54, 103–9,
    127–28
Koester, Helmut, 25, 91, 92, 168, 174
Koptak, Paul E., 153
Kraemer, Ross Shepard, 108
Kugel, James, 133, 134
Kühl, Ernst, 64

Kuss, Otto, 64
Kwok, Pui-lan, 9
kyriarchy, 46

*leitourgia* (service), 208
Lenski, Gerhard, 18
liberation, 217–20
liberation theology, 5, 7, 36, 42, 217–19, 222, 223, 225–26, 228–30
Lloyd, Genevieve, 46
Longenecker, Bruce, 170
Longenecker, Richard N., 25, 164
love, mutual (the love), 67–68
Luckmann, Thomas, 84, 196
Luttwak, Edward A., 75
Lyons, George, 151

Mack, Burton, 78, 80, 83, 85, 96
MacMullen, Ramsay, 74, 75
Malherbe, Abraham, 149, 163
Malina, Bruce, 148
manumission, 111–14, 120–21, 220–21, 225, 229. *See also* slavery
marriage, 105–6, 115, 117
Marrou, H. I., 74
Marshall, Peter, 24, 90, 214
Martin, Dale B., 31, 114, 122
Martin, Ralph P., 211
Martin, Troy, 147
Martyn, J. Louis, 132, 137, 151
Marx, Karl, 217
Matlock, R. Barry, 97
Matthews, Shelly, 103
Maurer, Christian, 70
Mearns, C., 175
Meeks, Wayne, 19, 43, 91, 163, 164
Meggitt, Justin J., 19, 122, 220, 221
messianic redemption and Roman rule, 32
*metanoia,* applied to Paul, 184–87
Michel, Otto, 62
Minear, Paul S., 64, 65
Miranda, José Porfirio, 36
Mitchell, Margaret M., 31, 73, 91, 125
monogamy, social and prostitution, 115
morality, 43
Mott, Stephen C., 214
Moxnes, Halvor, 20–21, 38
Mullins, Terence Y., 61, 62, 149
Munck, Johannes, 34, 203, 205, 207
Muratorian Fragment, 222
Murphy-O'Connor, Jerome, 194, 195, 208
mutualism and emancipation, 220–21, 230
myths of otherness and sameness, 204

Nanos, Mark, 20, 22, 39, 131, 146–59, 186, 204
new perspective, 2, 13, 19–22, 130
Newman, Barclay, 62

Neyrey, Jerome H., 158
Nickelsburg, George W. E., 95, 151
Nickle, Keith F., 200, 203, 205
Nida, Eugene A., 62
Nolland, John, 154
Nutton, V., 31, 81

Oakes, Peter, 173, 178
obedience, rhetoric of, 54, 67
obligation, 200
    as ethics, 64–65
    indebtedness and, 65, 67–68
    Paul's calling and, 62, 64
    social context of, 65, 68
O'Brien, Peter T., 205
Okin, Susan Moller, 46
Olbrechts-Tyteca, L., 28, 29, 38, 78, 80
O'Neill, J. C., 38
Osiek, Carolyn, 55, 140
othering, politics and rhetoric, 45–49, 59, 62–65
outsiders, inclusion of, 68, 69–70

paganism and pagans, 176–77
Pagels, Elaine, 20, 26
particularism vs. universalism, 19–20
Parvey, Constance F., 8
paternity, genealogical and religious, 142–44
patriarchy, social formation of politics of othering, 46
patronage system, 107–8, 127–28, 210
    and collection for the Saints, 214–15
    social control, role in, 76–77
Patterson, Orlando, 57, 110, 118, 120, 220, 223
Paul, 47, 199, 218, 223
    Abraham and, 132–37, 141–45, 186
    anti-Jewish interpretation, 44, 164, 176–78, 182
    anti-Semitism, 182
    apocalyptic perspective of, 21, 93–101
    Apollos and, 61, 84–88, 101, 106, 126
    apostolic praxis, 25–26
    call or conversion, 21–24, 62–64, 130–36, 146, 184, 186
    Christology, 166–70
    as *convert*, 184–87, 190
    egalitarian theology, 35, 61
    empire and, 59–62, 90–93, 160–64, 173–83, 189–90
    Gentiles and, 141–45
    and gospel, 71, 91–92, 164–67
    imperialism, opposition to, 61, 91–92, 96, 161–62, 209–10
    as Jew, 33–34, 74, 91, 131, 175, 191–92
    Jews and Judaism, 22, 34, 35, 176–77
    manumission of slaves, 120–21

Paul (continued)
  mission of, 69–71, 192–96, 225. *See also*
    collection for the Saints
  non-Christian Judaism, view of, 163
  on obligation, 67–68
  paganism, opposition to, 164, 174–75,
    182
  patronage system and, 107–8, 210, 214–15
  politics of othering, resistance to, 62, 65
  scholarly criticism and interpretation, 1–10
  self-description, 39, 162, 191
  on sexual behavior and moral standards,
    115–17
  as social conservative, 26–27
  uniting of Jews and Gentiles, 141–42, 195
  on universalism, 20, 186, 188–90
  Western understanding of, 2–3
Paul, letters of, 26, 131, 222. *See also* Index
    of Ancient Sources
  exegetical and interpretive readings,
    alternative, 53–57
  political analysis of, 47–53
  rhetorical criticism and apocalypticism,
    96–99
Paul, theology of, 3, 33, 35
  eschatological vision, 25–26
  imperial context of, 25, 161–64
  Israel's destiny, 34–34
  Jesus as Messiah, 166–70
  political context, 24–26, 168
  of the state, 38–39
  of Torah and Israel, 33–35
Paul and Politics Group, 11, 15, 42, 162
Pauline legacy of social conservatism, 26–27
Pauline studies, 22, 54, 56, 131
  ethics of interpretation, 50–52
  paradigm shift to political, 19, 43–44, 51,
    55
  politics and rhetoric of othering, 45–47
  politics of, 12–13
  politics of meaning, 47–53, 57
  scholarly criticism of interpretations, 5–10
  Stendahl's initiatives, 1–5
  struggle for political awareness in, 13–14
  subordination, politics and rhetoric of,
    54–55
  traditional versus contemporary, 43–44
Pearson, Birger A., 85, 88
Pedersen, Sigfred, 62
Perelman, Chaim, 28, 29, 38, 77, 80
Perelman, Chaim, 28
persuasion, coercive force and, 29–31,
    77–78. *See also* rhetoric
Peterson, Norman, 26
Philippians 3, 173–79, 181. *See also* Index of
    Ancient Sources
Philo of Alexandria, 85
Pickett, Raymond, 25

Pitt-Rivers, Julian, 148
Pogoloff, Stephen M., 80, 84
Pohle, Lutz, 66
political rhetoric, 74–82, 90–93, 106
politics
  of interpretation, 44, 47–57
  of othering, 45–49, 59, 62–65
poor, remembering the, 193–95, 210–11,
    224
Porter, Stanley, 27
Porton, Gary G., 155, 157
postcolonial criticism in biblical studies,
    9–10
power
  benevolence and, 30–31
  evasion discourse and, 110
  rhetoric and, 28–30, 75, 81
Price, Simon R. F., 18, 25, 34, 76, 82, 147,
    163
prostitution, 114–16
public health model of biblical interpretation,
    40–43, 47–53

racism, politics of othering, and
    rationalization, 45–47
Ramsaran, Rollin, 83
Reasoner, Mark, 35, 65
reciprocity, ethic of, and obligation, 65
Reed, Jeffrey, 27
relationships, hierarchical order, 106–8
revolution and liberation, 217–18
rhetoric, 28–29, 31, 53, 54, 56, 74, 77–80,
    81, 82, 101–2, 125, 197
  as culture, 74–75
  deliberative, 28
  empire and, 26–27, 74–82
  epideictic, 28–29, 80, 81
  of evasion, 120, 128–29
  in Greek cities of Roman empire, 78–79,
    82
  of identification, 47–49
  imperialism and, 29–30, 78, 96–102, 124,
    124–27
  of inquiry and ethics of interpretation,
    40–45
  judicial, 27–28, 80
  politics and, 27–33, 50–52, 56, 74–82,
    90–93
  power and, 30, 75, 77, 81
  in social control and cohesion, 75, 77–79
  study of in Roman empire, 80–81
  xenophobic (example, France), 197
rhetorical analysis, principles of, 82–83
"rhetorical city" of Greek empire, 81–82
Richardson, Peter, 31
Riekkinen, Vilho, 66
Robbins, Vernon K., 83, 85, 96

Roberts, Jennifer Tolbert, 78
Roetzel, Calvin, 20, 25, 34, 227–30
Roman law, Christ as fulfillment of, 67
Romans, letter to, 35, 37–39, 52, 53, 59, 62, 66, 67, 171. *See also* Index of Ancient Sources
  context interpretations, 35–39
  double standard in, 20–21
  Gentile-Christian ideology, 35–36
  God's justice, 36, 170–73
  and Jewish ethnocentrism, 35–36
  justice (concept of) addressed in, 36–39, 170–73
Rooks, Charles Shelby, 219
Rousselle, Aline, 117
Ruether, Rosemary Radford, 19

Said, Edward, 17, 29, 30
saints, assembly of, 49–50
Saldarini, Anthony, 24
Saller, Richard, 18, 19, 77
salvation, 3, 9, 44, 91, 118, 137, 172, 187, 188
  doctrine of justification, 181–82
  Jewish role in, 34, 88–89, 190
  as process of domination, slavery before God, 118–19
  and wisdom, 88–89
Sanders, E. P., 19, 20, 163, 191
Sandmel, S., 162
Sansone, David, 68
Scharffenorth, G., 66
Schlier, Heinrich, 70, 200
Schmithals, Walter, 202, 203
Schottroff, Luise, 36
Schürer, Emil, 203
Schüssler Fiorenza, Elisabeth, 7–8, 10, 11, 26, 40–57, 58–62, 65, 71, 72, 78, 85, 103
Scott, James C., 27, 32
scripture vs. revelation, authority, 150
Scroggs, Robin, 26, 206
Second Temple Judaism, 93–94, 176–78, 180, 182
Segal, Alan, 9, 23, 130–31, 135, 138, 152, 155, 184–90, 191
Segovia, Fernando F., 11
Segundo, Juan Luis, 36, 216, 218, 219, 220
sexual behavior
  asceticism, 87
  monogamy, 115
  *porneia*, 116–17
  prostitution, 114–16
  slavery, 115–17
  women and, 37, 87
Siker, J. S., 132
Silberman, Neil, 23

slaves and slavery, 110–23. *See also* manumission
  brutality as theology, 117–20
  evasion discourse, 110, 117, 119–20
  as metaphor, 114, 117–19, 123, 220
  misconceptions of, 112–13
  prostitution and, 114–16
  sanction of, 110–11, 119
  sexual exploitation of, 115–17
  social status and, 121–23
  support of in Pauline texts, 6
Sleeper, C. Freeman, 7
Smallwood, E. Mary, 206
Smith, Christopher C., 152
Smith, Dorothy E., 45, 46
social conservatism, Pauline legacy, 26–27
social control and cohesion
  rhetoric's role in, 75, 77–78
  slavery and manumission, 111–14
*Sophia,* wisdom, 87–89, 219
Spelman, Elizabeth V., 46
spiritual transcendence, 87–90, 101–2
Stark, Rodney, 162
Stendahl, Krister, 1–5, 9–10, 19, 40–44, 72, 103, 130–32, 146–47, 160, 184, 190–92
Stevenson, James, 222
Stowers, Stanley K., 35–37, 83, 91, 136, 138, 139, 149
Strathmann, H., 208
Strobel, Adolf, 67
submission rhetoric, 56, 78
subordination, 52
  Gentiles to Jews, 207–9
  language of, 26, 108, 208
  as proper hierarchical order, 106–9
  rhetoric, 54, 56
Sugirtharajah, R. S., 9, 192
supersession, ideology of, 35–36
Swain, Simon, 75, 78, 80, 81, 82, 84

Tamez, Elsa, 221
Taubes, Jacob, 56
Taylor, Charles, 197
temple sacrifices, 202–3
temple tax, 200, 201, 204–7
Theissen, Gerd, 24, 40, 42
Thiemann, Ronald F., 55
Thompson, L., 151
Thurman, Howard, 6
transcendence, spiritual, 87–90, 101–2

universalism, 11, 19–20, 186, 188–90, 207, 209, 227–29
  and collection for the Saints, 196, 203–10
  ecumenical, 141–42, 195, 207, 209
  eschatological, 209–10
  Judaism and, 19–20

Vermes, Geza, 37
Vogt, Joseph, 63, 112

Walker-Ramisch, Sandra, 148
Wallace-Hadrill, Andrew, 77
Wan, Sze-kar, 191–215, 224–25, 227–29
Watson, Francis, 137
Weber, Max, 218
Wedderburn, A. J. M., 195
Weems, Renita J., 6, 9
Welborn, Lawrence L., 73, 74, 81
West, Gerald O., 27
White, John L., 25, 149
Wilckens, Ulrich, 67, 69

Wilder, Amos, 95, 100
Wimbush, Vincent L., 55
Wire, Antoinette Clark, 8, 24, 73, 85, 89, 103–6, 107, 108, 224–26
wisdom and salvation, 87–89
Woolf, Greg, 19
women prophets, 106–8
"wretched of the earth," 217
Wright, N. T., 25, 33–34, 141, 160–83, 189–90

Young, Iris Marion, 45

Zahn, Theodor, 63
Zanker, Paul, 18, 76